BY APPOINTMENT TO
H.R.H. THE DUKE OF EDINBURGH
MARINE PHOTOGRAPHERS

BEKEN OF COWES

OCEAN LINERS

BY APPOINTMENT TO
H.R.H. THE DUKE OF EDINBURGH
MARINE PHOTOGRAPHERS

BEKEN OF COWES

OCEAN LINERS

Philip J. Fricker, C. Eng., M.I. Mech. E.

Photographs by
The late Frank William Beken, F.R.P.S.
Alfred Keith Beken, F.R.P.S.
Kenneth John Beken, F.R.P.S.

Reed's Nautical Books

London   Hamburg   Boston

First published in Great Britain 1992 by
THOMAS REED PUBLICATIONS LIMITED
Hazelbury Manor
Wadswick
CORSHAM
Wiltshire
SN14 9HX
UK

ISBN 0 947637 42 7

Production consultant:
PAPERWEIGHT, 379 Lewisham High Street, London

Typeset by Falcon Graphic Art Ltd
Wallington, Surrey

Printed and bound in Hong Kong by
Imago Publishing

FRONTISPIECE
In April 1992 the latest ship of the Royal Caribbean Cruise
Line, the *Majesty of the Seas*, sails to join her twin sister
Monarch of the Seas at present cruising in the Caribbean.
Anchored off Cowes the previous night, with every light
aboard glowing, and floodlit decks, she gave the appearance
of a small city afloat.

Here seen passing us at 22 knots, she made not a sound,
nor emitted a puff of smoke, and this from a ship of 74,000
tons. Built at the 'Chantier de l'Atlantique in St Nazaire in
France, this fine modern cruise liner contrasts vividly with the
others seen in this volume over a period of the last hundred
years, and is perhaps a foretaste of what we shall see afloat in
the twenty-first century, a credit to the designers and builders
of today.

Contents

Abbreviations

AA	anti-aircraft
AMC	armed merchant cruiser
B & W	Burmeister & Wain
b.h.p.	brake horse power
BI	British India
CGT	Compagnie Générale Trans-Atlantique
CMB	Compagnie Maritime Belge
CPR	Canadian Pacific Railway or simply CP-Canadian Pacific
CTC	Charter Travel Company (name by which Russian State owned passenger ships are operated)
DOAL	Deutsche Ost Afrika Linie (German East Africa Line)
E & A	Eastern & Australian Steamship Company
HAPAG	Hamburg American
HSAL	Hamburg South America Line
HP	high pressure
HMAS	Her/His Majesty's Australian Ship
HMCS	Her/His Majesty's Canadian Ship
i.h.p.	indicated horse power
IMM	International Mercantile Marine Co.
KNSM	Koninklijke Nederlandsche Stoomboot Maatschappij (Royal Netherlands Steamship Co.)
LCI	landing craft infantry
LP	low pressure
LSI (L)	landing ship, infantry (large)
MAN	Maschinenfabrik Augsberg-Nurnberg (German diesel engine type)
MORFLOT	(Ministervo Morskoi Flot) 'Ministry of Seagoing Fleet'
NCL	Norwegian Cruise Line
NDL	Norddeutscher Lloyd
NZSC	New Zealand Shipping Company
P & O	Peninsular & Oriental
p.s.i.	pounds per square inch (pressure)
PSNC	Pacific Steam Navigation Company
RNVR	Royal Naval Volunteer Reserve
SGTM	Société Générale de Transports Maritimes à Vapeur
s.h.p.	shaft horse power
SOVTORGFLOT	(Sovietsky Torgovaya Flot) 'Soviet Merchant Fleet' replaced in 1960s by 'Morflot'
UAL	United American Line
UC	Union Castle
USS	United States Ship
VNSM	Vereenigde Nederlandsche Sheepvart Maatschappij (Netherlands Steamship Company)
2SCSA	Two stroke cycle single acting
2SCDA	Two stroke cycle double acting
4SCSA	Four stroke cycle single acting
4SCDA	Four stroke cycle double acting

Applies to diesel engines

A note on the tabular information

Dimensions
Overall length is given, and beam. The gross tonnage was often altered during the vessel's career, after refits. Where considerable variation occurred additional figures are given.

Power and Speed
The horsepowers given for the main engines are those attained in normal operation. Often higher powers could be achieved when necessary, especially from steam machinery. Service speeds are the ones usually quoted, and could usually be exceeded by a knot or two when desired.

Passengers
Often passenger numbers in each class varied during the ship's career, due to alteration to accommodation etc. Figures quoted, however, give a good indication of the vessel's capacity.

Acknowledgements

I should like to acknowledge the considerable assistance I have received during the preparation of the text for this book.

Mrs Kathleen Harrison and the staff of Cowes Library and Maritime Museum have always been most helpful in obtaining the publications I requested. These were often bound volumes of technical journals, dating back many years. All staff remained cheerful in spite of my requests sometimes being made at busy times. Likewise librarians at Newport, Southampton and Portsmouth were always very helpful in obtaining information.

My wife Mariane deserves a special vote of thanks for typing the original manuscript from my rather illegible writing, a real feat.

I am of course greatly indebted to the various authors of books, magazine articles, technical papers etc. listed in the bibliography. Much use has been made of the material featured here. Readers wishing for more information on particular ships will find this very useful for reference. I have tried to make the text as accurate as possible, but sometimes different sources give different information. Membership of the World Ship Society and the Paddle Steamer Preservation Society has added much to my knowledge of shipping over many years.

Preface

This book features a unique selection of passenger liner photographs from the famous archives of the Beken family of Cowes. The earlier ones were taken by the late Frank Beken and the later ones by Keith and Kenneth, the present owners of the family business. This is the first time that such a large number of their liner photographs has appeared in a single volume.

The pictures cover a period of over a hundred years and they provide an interesting pictorial record of how passenger ships have changed during that time. Each photograph is accompanied by a short text providing details of the vessel and her seagoing career. Some ships had long lives of 40 years or more, while others had very brief lives. Some of the photographs are of historic interest too, such as the last photograph of the ill-fated Titanic which was taken by Frank Beken as she sailed through Cowes Roads on her maiden voyage.

The photo of the ill-fated Britannic is perhaps not up to Beken's usual high standard. I recall the late Frank Beken telling me many years ago that it was very poor weather when he took this. It was wartime and he felt he just had to go out and photograph this ship as he somehow sensed he may not get another chance. Sadly he was proved right; she was sunk soon afterwards.

Most of the vessels featured have now gone — been broken up or become the victims of marine disaster. Some, however, are still in service. A number of present-day cruise ships are included. Readers will be able to decide which they prefer, the modern profile or the perhaps more elegant look of some of the older vessels.

The day of the ocean liner, i.e. those ships on regular services to distant places carrying passengers and some cargo, is virtually at an end. The jet aircraft has superseded them. Most large passenger ships afloat today are engaged in the cruising business. These of course fulfil a useful role, being purpose-built for the leisure industry.

The vessels featured are mainly the ones which used the port of Southampton, either on a regular basis or as occasional visitors. As a consequence, some well-remembered ships are not included. However, for many years Southampton was Britain's premier passenger port and the vessels that came here formed a good cross-section of the world's ocean liners. Troopships also sailed from here and some of these are included — they carried some very important passengers.

We hope that readers will enjoy looking at these splendid pictures and reading about the ships themselves. No other volume contains such a fascinating and nostalgic record of a bygone era.

Philip J Fricker

From the late 1880s to the early 1900s photography of shipping was fraught with difficulties. The use of slides containing glass negatives in our cameras did not allow us time to take a second picture quickly, for during the time taken to reset the shutter and change the slide, the liner, perhaps travelling at 15 knots, had travelled some distance from our 'best viewing' angle. Couple this with the angle of the sun, the weather conditions prevailing, and the possibility of the liner not coming into the area for some months, it is remarkable that we have these records.

The larger ships such as the *Leviathan, Majestic* and *Olympic*, after a stormy crossing of the Atlantic and then the English Channel were seen to have a long slow roll from side to side as they entered Spithead. This continued up Southampton Water and often presented difficulties on docking. With the advent of stabilisers this is not now seen.

As we enter a new decade shipping also enters a new era. Just as the old Imperial Airways aircraft lumbering its way to India gave way to Concorde reaching faraway places in hours, so have the liners of yesteryear given way to the modern luxury liners. Thus we have included the very latest liner to be launched at the time of going to press, the aptly named *Majesty of the Seas*.

Keith & Kenneth Beken

A – Z of Liners

Albert Ballin

Name: **Albert Ballin** (1923); **Hansa** (1935); **Sovietsky Soyuz** (1955)

Line: HAPAG

Builders: Blohm & Voss, Hamburg; launched December 1922, completed June 1923

Dimensions: Gross tonnage 20,815/ Length 627 ft/Beam 72.8 ft

Machinery

Engines: 2 sets steam turbine single reduction geared to twin screws, 13,500 s.h.p.

Boilers: 4 single-ended, 4 double-ended cylindrical steam, 225 p.s.i.

Service speed: 16 knots

Major Refits

1930: Blohm & Voss, higher-powered turbines, 29,000 s.h.p. 4 watertube boilers, 400 p.s.i., superheated with forced and induced draught. Cargo capacity reduced, additional bunkers added for extra fuel-oil requirements, 19 knots
1934: Blohm & Voss, lengthening, 677 × 72.8 ft, 21,131 tons, 21.5 knots
1949-54: rebuilding, 23,009 tons

Regular Routes

Hamburg – New York

Passenger Capacity

1923: 1st 274, 2nd 340, 3rd 960
1934: 1st 204, Tourist 361, 3rd 400

Sister-ships and near sisters

Deutschland (1923), **Hamburg** (1926), **New York** (1927)

Photograph 1931

THE HAPAG fleet had been decimated by the 1914–18 war, and reconstruction took many years. However, by operating a joint service with United American Lines they made a remarkable recovery on the North Atlantic route. Early in 1922 HAPAG made plans for four new vessels for their intermediate service; these were to be of about 20,000 tons each, of fairly modest speed, but capable of carrying a large number of passengers and considerable cargo. The *Albert Ballin*, named after the great German shipowner, was the first to enter service in 1923, followed by three near-sisters the *Deutschland, Hamburg* and *New York* in 1924, 1926 and 1927 respectively.

The superstructure of the *Albert Ballin* was comparatively short and squat. She had a straight stem, cruiser stern and four masts. The two funnels (one of which was a dummy) were initially fairly short, but were lengthened, shortened and finally heightened again during her career. Unusual features were the blisters on either side of the hull, which gave stability. (The ship was also fitted with Frahm anti-rolling tanks.) Passenger accommodation ranged from the comfort of first-class cabins to third-class dormitories.

After a successful maiden voyage in July 1923 the vessel soon became popular with the large numbers of emigrants travelling to America. The voyage from Hamburg to New York usually took about ten days, calling at Southampton and from 1924, Cherbourg. Towards the end of the decade, however, when the US government imposed restrictions on immigration, the *Albert Ballin* and her sisters became uneconomic for the company. Accordingly a re-engining programme was begun. This had the effect of increasing her speed to 19·5 knots, a considerable improvement. The rejuvenated ship started her faster crossings in 1930; when all four vessels had received similar treatment the service was a good one.

In 1934 she again returned to the shipyard for a substantial facelift, this lengthened her by nearly 40 feet and adding a bulbous forefoot, and increasing her speed by a further two knots. In this year an unfortunate accident occurred in which she ran into and sank a tug, the *Merkur*, in Bremerhaven, causing seven fatalities.

In 1935 the Nazi government decided that, since Albert Ballin had been a Jew, the ship could no longer bear his name. Renamed *Hansa*, she continued the transatlantic service until the outbreak of war. During the war she was used as an accommodation and training ship for the German navy, based in Hamburg. She was also employed as a transport, and it was on a voyage from Gdynia

with evacuees in March 1945 that she struck a mine off the port of Warnemünde. Refugees took to the boats, and attempts were made to take the stricken vessel in low. However, she sank, in fairly shallow water.

In 1949 a Russian salvage concern succeeded in raising the ship and towed her away. Several years of rebuilding and refitting followed at Antwerp and Warnemünde. She was renamed *Sovietsky Soyuz*. In 1954, while still incomplete, she was badly damaged by explosion and fire. The following year, however, after restoration, she was delivered to the Sovtorgflot and became one of the biggest ships in the Russian merchant fleet. With a single funnel of modern design and two masts only, she was placed on the service from Vladivostok to Kamchatka.

The ship continued to serve in Far Eastern waters, and in 1971 was given an extensive refit at Hong Kong. She was then 48 years old. In 1980 her name was shortened to *Soyuz*. A year later she was broken up, after a remarkable life of nearly sixty years.

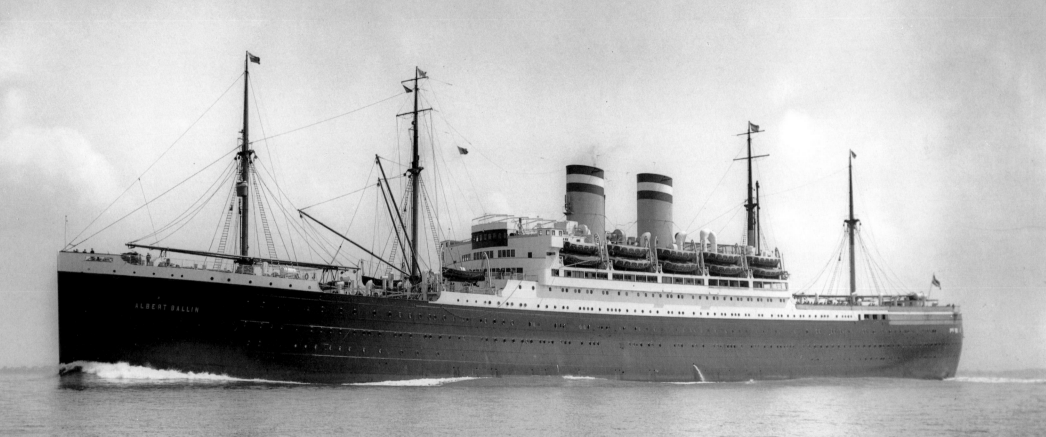

Alcantara

IN THE 1920s competition on the South American route prompted the Royal Mail company to order two new ships of 20,000 tons, the *Asturias* and *Alcantara*. The latter's namesake had been lost after an encounter with a German raider in 1916.

The *Alcantara* had a large cargo capacity, as was normal on this route, and catered especially for first-class passengers. The hull had a straight stem and cruiser stern; her superstructure was well proportioned, with two squat funnels.

In 1934 the decision was taken to convert the two sister-ships to steam. Although they had become popular with the public, their speed of 16 knots could not compete with the vessels owned by the Blue Star Line, the Hamburg–South America Line and various Italian companies, which were capable of 20 knots. The reconditioning resulted in a new profile – the forepart of the hull was lengthened, and the funnels heightened by about 15 feet. The average speed was improved to 19 knots, and earlier problems with vibration were almost eliminated.

In September 1939 the *Alcantara* was taken over by the Admiralty for conversion to an armed merchant cruiser. She sailed in convoy to Malta for fitting out, carrying a large number of Royal Navy personnel as relief crews for other ships. She reached Malta safely despite attacks from U-boats and a collision with the Cunard liner *Franconia*. After necessary hull repairs in Alexandria, the *Alcantara* returned to Malta to be fitted with eight 6-inch guns; her forward funnel (a dummy one) was removed, and at its base a mounting for two 3-inch AA guns was substituted. These were useful for close-range defence against low-flying aircraft.

She was now assigned to patrol duties in the South Atlantic, a dangerous area frequented by German commerce raiders. In early 1940 she was patrolling a stretch of the South American coast from Rio de Janeiro to the river Plate in company with the *Queen of Bermuda* and *Dunnottar Castle*. These liners were not really suitable as armed merchant cruisers, being too large and ill equipped in comparison with the German commerce raiders, which were smaller and armed with modern guns, torpedoes and spotter aircraft. However, they had the advantage in terms of speed and were the only vessels available.

On 28 July 1940 the *Alcantara* had an encounter with the German raider *Thor*, which had been flying the Swedish flag to avoid detection. She was struck on the starboard side by the waterline, and started to take in water. The wireless cabin was wrecked, and there were a number of casualties. However, the German ship eventually decided to break off the action, fearing the arrival of other British warships. The *Alcantara* made for Rio de Janeiro, where the damage was repaired, but soon returned to further long patrol periods. In 1940, while in Southampton, she was hit by incendiaries during an air raid; these were quickly dealt with by her crew. A refit in Newport News in December 1941 led to the removal of her mainmast, the replacement of her original guns with more modern ones and the installation of radar, an aircraft catapult and a Fairey Seafox float plane.

By 1943 there was no longer a need for armed merchant cruisers. Their casualties had been high. Accordingly the *Alcantara* was converted at Birkenhead into a troopship. Over the next few years her voyages in this capacity took her to the Mediterranean, Singapore, India, Ceylon, the East Indies and across the Atlantic.

Upon being returned to the Royal Mail, she was given a complete refit by Harland and Wolff, regaining her mainmast, but now with only one funnel. In October 1948 she left on her first post-war voyage to the river Plate. The *Andes* was also on this route. For the next ten years she maintained a regular and largely uneventful service on this route. The exception was an occasion in May 1954 when she lost her starboard propeller in Buenos Aires harbour, and was forced to return to Southampton on only one screw. In June 1958 the *Alcantara* was finally taken out of service and, under her last name of *Kaisha Maru*, sailed for the breakers' yard at Osaka in Japan.

Name: Alcantara

Line: Royal Mail

Builders: Harland & Wolff, Belfast; launched 23 September 1926, completed February 1927

Dimensions: Gross tonnage 22,181/ Length 656 ft/Beam 78.4 ft

Machinery

Engines: 2 sets Harland/B&W 8-cylinder 4 stroke double acting air injection diesel, twin screw 15,000 b.h.p.

Service speed: 16 knots

Major Refits

1934-5 Harland & Wolff, conversion from diesel to steam: 2 sets of Parsons triple expansions single reduction geared turbines, s.h.p. 20,000; speed 19 knots

Boilers: 3 Johnson watertube, 425 p.s.i. superheated to 750°F, forced and induced draughting.
22,209 tons, 666 × 78.4 ft

Regular Routes

Southampton – River Plate

Passenger Capacity

1927: 1st 432, 2nd 223, 3rd 322 (cabins), 453 (open berths)
1935: 1st 331, 2nd 223, 3rd 768
1948: 1st 221, 2nd 185, 3rd 470

Sister-ships

Asturias (1926)

Photograph 1948

Almanzora

Name: *Almanzora*

Line: Royal Mail

Builders: Harland & Wolff, Belfast;
launched 19 November 1914, completed
September 1915

Dimensions: Gross tonnage 15,551/
Length 589 ft/Beam 67.3 ft

Machinery

Engines: 2 four-cylinder triple expansion
for wing propellers. Exhause steam
turbine for central screw. Triple screw

Boilers: coal-fired, 180 p.s.i.

Service speed: 17 knots

Major Refits

1923 conversion to oil fuel

Regular Routes

Southampton – River Plate

Passenger Capacity

1st 400, 2nd 230, 3rd 760

Sister-ships

'A' class: *Aragon* (1905), *Amazon* (1906),
Araguaya (1906), **Avon** (1907), *Asturias*
(1907), **Arlanza** (1912), **Andes** (1913),
Alcantara (1914)

Photograph 1925

BETWEEN 1905 and 1915 the Royal Mail Company built nine ships to serve on their South American route. The *Almanzora* was the last to be completed. In her third-class accommodation she carried many workers from Spain and Portugal to South American ports; her five holds were insulated for carrying frozen meat.

However, before the ship could be completed she was taken over by the Admiralty, and converted for use as an armed merchant cruiser. Her armament consisted of eight 6-inch guns, two 6-pounder anti-aircraft guns and a Maxim gun. She also carried a large number of depth charges which could be laid over the stern. Her size of 15–16,000 tons made her more suitable as an AMC than the larger liners.

The *Almanzora* was commissioned at Belfast on 29 September 1915, and in October left to join the Tenth Cruiser Squadron, which operated between Scotland and Iceland, and also in the Denmark Strait. Their job was to intercept and investigate all merchant ships in the area and to engage enemy raiders. The *Almanzora*'s base port was Liverpool, where she returned at the end of each month of patrolling.

In December 1916 she sailed to Sierra Leone on a wild-goose chase after the German raider *Moewe* ('Seagull'). On the return trip she escorted a convoy back to Britain. After returning to the Northern Patrol until July 1917, the ship spent the rest of the war on escort duty, the U-boat menace having become acute. The route was usually from Halifax, Nova Scotia, to Plymouth or Liverpool, occasionally from Rio de Janeiro, Dakar or Sierra Leone. In December 1917 a working party from the ship took part in a cleaning-up operation after the terrible ammunition-ship explosion in Halifax harbour.

The Armistice found the *Almanzora* at Sierra Leone awaiting a convoy. She soon sailed for Liverpool, and was finally decommissioned at Belfast on 14 January 1919. Her war service had taken her 191, 949 miles.

Her maiden voyage as a passenger liner began on 14 January 1920. For the next 19 years, the *Almanzora* ran a regular service on the South American route. She was converted to burn oil fuel in 1923. Her running-mates at first on the service were the *Andes*, *Arlanza*, *Avon* and *Araguaya*. The full voyage from Southampton to the river Plate took 18 days, calling at Cherbourg, Corunna, Vigo, Lisbon, Cape Verde, Rio and Buenos Aires. (It had taken 22 days before omitting some ports of call)

The company had intended to replace the old ship with the new *Andes*, but on the outbreak of war in 1939 she was pressed into service as a troopship. Her first voyage was to Halifax, followed by a series of voyages round the Cape. In May 1941 she sailed in a large convoy from Gourock to the Western Desert, unfortunately colliding with the *Orduna* en route, but suffering no serious damage. While at Suez, the *Almanzora* and *Georgic* were both attacked by enemy aircraft. The *Georgic* was set on fire and the *Almanzora* helped with rescue operations, before returning to the UK with her complement of 1,000 Italian prisoners of war.

In July 1943 she was one of the transports for the attack on Sicily. In September of that year, while she was on a Mediterranean convoy, an enemy aircraft crashed into the side of the ship causing a violent explosion, but little long-term damage. On a Red Sea passage she rescued stranded passengers, mostly West African troops, from the *Orbita*, which had been grounded, and landed them at Aden.

In 1945 the ship carried members of the Czech government to Constanza and 2,000 Russians to Odessa. On her return trip she carried 200 internees from concentration camps, landing them at Marseilles. In August 1945 the *Almanzora* was in Madras, in preparation for the reoccupation of Malaya. However, the Japanese surrender resulted in the ship being sent to Singapore, where she embarked about 1,600 civilians and Service personnel who had been liberated from Japanese POW camps. She was in fact an open ship, prepared to take anyone who wanted to go back to the UK.

A tumultuous reception greeted her in January 1946 when she took Dutch repatriates to Amsterdam. In November of that year she was sold to the British government, although still under Royal Mail management. She continued to be used for repatriation of troops, and transport of ex-prisoners and garrisons. Finally sold for breaking up, she was towed to Blyth in September 1948. The ship's bell, however, was removed and preserved in the Royal Mail War Memorial in the company's head office in London.

America

THE *America* was planned by US Lines as a replacement for the *Leviathan*, which had proved too expensive to run on the North Atlantic route. Designed by Gibbs and Cox, and built at Newport News, she was larger than her predecessors, the *Washington* and *Manhattan*. She had a graceful curved stem and spoon-type stern. The two funnels, the forward one of which was a dummy used for ventilation purposes, gave her an elegant profile, but were found to be too short to keep smoke from the decks, and were lengthened at an early stage.

On completion in July 1940 the *America* was sent cruising to the West Indies, as hostilities made it impossible to operate on the transatlantic run. However, after a year she was taken over by the US navy for use as a troopship and renamed *West Point* after the military academy of that name. She was America's largest troop-ship, her speed of 22–24 knots serving her in good stead; her armament consisted of four 5-inch guns. She sailed in the Pacific, Indian and Atlantic oceans transporting thousands of troops and other personnel who included prisoners of war, Red Cross staff and war brides. From 1944 she was on the 'home run' across the North Atlantic. Her wartime service took her half a million miles, which she accomplished without a major overhaul.

In July 1946 the *America* was finally released from the navy and went back to her builders for a complete overhaul. On 14 November she commenced her first voyage with paying passengers from New York to Le Havre via Cobh and Southampton. She continued on this route for some years, sometimes destined for Cherbourg or, from 1951, Bremerhaven. In 1952 she was joined by the *United States*, which eclipsed her in both size and speed. In the early sixties she sometimes went winter cruising to Bermuda, San Juan and Nassau.

A dispute by the ship's crew in 1963 resulted in the cancelling of a sailing from New York in September, and she was in fact laid up until early the following year, incurring heavy losses. She recommenced sailing in February, but in November US Lines sold her to the Greek Chandris Group. The popularity of air travel had begun to take its toll, and she proved costly to operate.

Her new owners gave her a complete reconditioning at Piraeus, which included making her fully air-conditioned, and removing her main mast. She now had a grey hull with blue funnel and white crosses, and was renamed the *Australis*. She spent some years doing round the world voyages, usually commencing and finishing at Southampton, and going to Australia via Suez on the way out and Panama on the return trip. When the Suez Canal was closed between 1968 and 1975 the ship proceeded via the Cape.

In 1977, however, the ship was laid up at the port of Timaru in New Zealand pending a decision on her future. In April 1978 she was sold to an American travel firm called Venture Cruises. She sailed for New York, and was refitted and was, once again given the name *America*. Unfortunately, her passenger accommodation was in a poor state and the few short cruises she ran led to many complaints, forcing the company to sell her back to the Chandris Group in August 1978. In 1979 she was once more renamed, as *Italis*, when her forward dummy funnel was removed. For a few months she commenced a Mediterranean cruise service, sailing from Barcelona. In 1980 she received the rather unusual name of *Noga*. In 1984 she was yet again renamed, as *Alferdoss*, and is now owned by Silver Moon Ferries of Panama. In 1988 following repairs after engineroom flooding, she was removed to Eleusis Bay, Piraeus where (1991) she remains.

Name: *America* (1940); ***West Point*** (1941); ***America*** (1946); ***Australis*** (1964); ***America*** (1978); ***Italis*** (1979); **'*Noga*'** (1980), ***Alferdoss*** (1984)

Line: US Lines (1940-64); Chandris Group (1964-78); Venture Cruises Ltd. (1978); Chandris Group (1978-84); Silver Moon Ferries (1984-)

Builders: Newport News Shipbuilding and Dry Dock Co.; launched 31 August 1939, completed 1940

Dimensions: Gross tonnage 33,532/ Length 723 ft/Beam 93.2 ft

Machinery

Engines: 2 sets triple expansion reduction geared turbines driving twin screws, 37,400 s.h.p.

Boilers: 6 Babcock and Wilcox oil fired watertube, with forced draught, 425 p.s.i., superheated to 725°F

Service speed: 22 knots

Major Refits

1964 reconditioning at Piraeus — installation of air-conditioning, removal of mainmast, signal mast incorporated into after funnel

Regular Routes

New York — Le Havre — Bremerhaven (1946-64)
Southampton — Suez — Australia — Panama — Southampton (1964-78)

Passenger Capacity

1940: Cabin 543, Tourist 418, 3rd 241
1946: Cabin 516, Tourist 371, 3rd 159
1964: 2300 one class

Sister-ships

None

Photograph 1947

Andania

Name: **Andania**

Line: Cunard

Builders: Hawthorn Leslie & Co., Hebburn on Tyne, launched 1 November 1921, completed 1922

Dimensions: Gross tonnage 13,950/ Length 538 ft/Beam 65.3 ft

Machinery

Engines: 2 Parsons compound turbines double-reduction geared to twin screw shafts, 8,500 s.h.p.

Boilers: 2 double-ended and 2 single-ended cylindrical 220 p.s.i.

Service speed: 15 knots

Regular Routes

Liverpool — Montreal/New York

Passenger Capacity

Cabin 484, 3rd 1,222

Sister-ships

Ausonia (1921), Antonia (1922), Aurania (1924), Alaunia (1925), **Ascania** (1925)

Photograph 1926

THIS ship was one of the Cunard 'A' class, two others of which, the *Ascania* and *Ausonia*, also feature in this book. She was built by Hawthorn Leslie & Co at Hebburn on Tyne. Launched on 1 November 1921, she was completed by May the next year and set off on her maiden voyage from London and Southampton to Montreal on 1 June. In most respects she was very similar to the *Ascania*, except that, like the *Ausonia* and *Antonia*, she had a separate 'island' bridge which was not integrated into the superstructure.

The *Andania* settled down on the Canandian route and over the years, like her sisters, became very popular with passengers. The ships were only 15-knot vessels, but were very comfortable and steady to travel on. In 1924 the vessel made her first voyage from Hamburg and Southampton to Halifax and New York. In 1927 she switched to the Liverpool route, making her first voyage from there to Montreal via Greenock and Belfast.

In 1928 accommodation, which had been cabin and third class, was altered to cabin, tourist, and third class.

The ship continued on the route for the next few years, but in the early thirties the Depression caused passenger trade to Canada to a fall off. The *Andania* was laid up in 1932 for a couple of years. After Cunard had merged with White Star she came back into service again, sailing now from Liverpool to New York. The ship became well known on both Canadian and US services.

On 14 December 1937 the *Andania* was involved in a collision in the Thames. She collided in thick fog with the tanker *British Statesman* moored at a jetty. Both ships were damaged, but there were no casualties. The *Andania* was soon repaired, and set off on her next voyage to Halifax only a couple of days late.

When war came the ship was on the Liverpool to New York route. She was quickly taken over for fitting as an armed merchant cruiser at Cammell Laird's Birkenhead yard. She received the standard armament for AMC's of eight six-inch guns and a couple of three-inch anti-aircraft weapons. Like many others, HMS *Andania* was sent on the Northern Patrol, where she did most useful work.

On the evening of 15 June 1940, however, when well south of Iceland, she was struck by a torpedo on her starboard side aft and was soon flooded and listing. Her gunners were in action firing at a periscope which was visible, while the engineers reduced the list by transferring fuel oil. Several other torpedoes were fired from the U-boat but no other hits were made. For a while it seemed possible to save the vessel, but the pumps were unable to cope with the inflow of water. The *Andania* had to be abandoned, and eventually sank at about 7 o'clock the following morning. Most of the crew were picked up by an Icelandic trawler. (The U-boat concerned was 'UA', which had been originally intended for the Turkish navy.) The *Andania* was the only one of the 'A' class to be sunk during the war.

The *Antonia* of 1922 was also earmarked for conversion to an AMC but was first used for trooping. She was later bought by the Admiralty and converted to a heavy repair ship. Commissioned in August 1942 as HMS *Wayland* she had a defensive armament of four 4-inch eight two-pounders and eight 20-mm AA weapons. The ship saw service in the Mediterranean and Indian Ocean, and was finally broken up in 1948 at Troon.

The *Alaunia* of 1925 became an armed merchant cruiser, and did much useful patrol work in the Atlantic and later in the Indian Ocean. In the later part of the war she was converted to a heavy repair ship, and was commissioned as such without change of name in August 1945. She ended her days as a training-ship for engine-room personnel, and was eventually sold for scrap in 1957 and broken up at Blyth.

The *Aurania* of 1924 also became an AMC. In this role she survived a rather dramatic collision with an iceberg while on convoy duty in July 1941. In October that year she was torpedoed, but again survived, managing to reach the Clyde safely.

She too was later reconstructed as a heavy repair ship, and blossomed forth in May 1944 as such, now named HMS *Artifex*. She did good service in the Far East before joining the reserve fleet after the war, and finally being sold to Italian breakers in 1961.

Andes

Name: ***Andes*** (1913); ***Atlantis*** (1930)

Line: Royal Mail

Builders: Harland & Wolff, Belfast; launched 8 May 1913, completed September 1913

Dimensions: Gross tonnage 15,620/ Length 589 ft/Beam 67.3 ft

Machinery

Engines: 2 4-cylinder triple expansion engines for wing propellers, L.P. turbine for central screw

Boilers: 4 cylindrical coal-fired, 180 p.s.i.

Service speed: 17 knots

Major Refits

1930 Liverpool, boilers converted to oil

Regular Routes

Southampton – River Plate

Passenger Capacity

1913: 1st 380, 2nd 250, 3rd 700
1930: 1st 450
1948: 3rd 900

Near Sister-ships

For complete list of 'A' class ships see *Almanzora* specification

Photograph 1913

THIS elegant ship was one of the 'A' class vessels built for the South American service. Constructed by Harland & Wolff at Belfast, she was launched on 8 May 1913 and completed by September that year. She sailed on her maiden voyage from Liverpool to Chile on the 26th of that month.

The ship had originally been laid down for the Pacific Steam Navigation Co (PSNC), but transferred to Royal Mail on the stocks. Her first voyage was in fact over the PSNC route, but she then switched to the Southampton – river Plate service, and became very popular. However, war broke out and she was taken over in March 1915 for conversion to an armed merchant cruiser. (Several of the 'A's were in fact put to this use.) The *Andes* was armed with eight 6-inch guns and a couple of six-pounders; she could also carry depth charges. She joined the celebrated Tenth Cruiser Squadron which operated the Northern Patrol. The *Arlanza* and *Alcantara* also joined this squadron, as did the *Almanzora* in September 1915.

On 28 February 1916 the *Andes* was on her way to relieve the *Alcantara* in the area between the Shetlands and the Norwegian coast. On the morning of 29 February a signal was received from the C.-in-C., Grand Fleet. An enemy raider was believed to be coming out! That morning HMS *Alcantara* stopped a vessel purporting to be the Norwegian *Rena*. While the British crew were preparing to board her, the other ship suddenly lowered her bulwarks and opened fire at short range on the AMC. The *Alcantara* quickly responded, and the two ships shelled each other with great intensity. The *Alcantara* eventually sank, but had inflicted severe damage on the enemy vessel, which was in fact the armed commerce raider *Greif*. The German crew abandoned their sinking ship, which was finally sent to the bottom when the cruiser HMS *Comus* and the destroyer *Munster* arrived on the scene. The *Andes* also fired on the enemy from a distance, probably causing damage.

The *Andes* continued her Northern Patrol duties, later switching to Atlantic convoy work when this system was introduced in 1917.

The *Andes* was refitted at Belfast before resuming the Southampton – river Plate service. Now followed a steady ten-year service on the route commencing in November 1919. She sailed with the *Arlanza*, *Almanzora* and others of the 'A' group. Although rather eclipsed when the 22,000-tonners *Asturias* and *Alcantara* joined in 1926 and 1927, the *Andes* and her sisters still remained popular.

However, by 1930 the world slump was being felt, and passenger requirements on the route had fallen off. The *Andes* was withdrawn and converted to a cruise liner at Liverpool. Accommodation was improved, and, painted white and renamed *Atlantis*, she looked resplendent. The ships cruising itinerary took her world-wide. She cruised to the Baltic, Norwegian fjords, Mediterranean, West Indies, South America, South Africa and the Pacific Ocean. The *Atlantis* was present at the Silver Jubilee Fleet Review in 1935 and the Coronation Review in 1937, both held at Spithead.

In August 1939 the ship was at Danzig; her cruise was cut short and she returned to London, later proceeding to Southampton. She was now converted to a hospital ship with some 400 beds. As HM Hospital Ship No.33 her war service was outstanding. At first stationed at Alexandria, she returned to the UK for the ill-fated Norwegian campaign. (The ship had been bought by the Ministry of War Transport but was still managed by Royal Mail.) She was bombed off Norway on 1 and 5 May 1940, fortunately without damage, and brought back 430 wounded to Liverpool. She returned again and on 8 June, brought back more wounded. The British withdrawal was now proceeding.

In September 1940 she again went to the Eastern Mediterranean via the Cape, and for the next two years ran between Alexandria, Suez, and Durban, occasionally to Bombay, carrying wounded from the desert campaign. In May 1942 she spent some time at Diego Suarez during the Madagascar invasion, and later that year took wounded from Alexandria back to the UK after El Alamein. A voyage to New York with American wounded from North Africa was followed by a trip to Durban and back with wounded.

In the autumn of 1943 the *Atlantis* was involved with exchanging sick and wounded POW's. She voyaged to Lisbon and Algiers with Italians, and from Glasgow to Gothenburg to exchange British and German POW's. During 1944 she made some fourteen voyages from the UK to the Mediterranean, followed later by some cross-Channel trips from Southampton to Cherbourg. After a short refit at Liverpool, the ship continued her mercy work with voyages between the Mediterranean and the USA.

During her fine war service the *Atlantis* had steamed about 280,000 miles, carrying 35,000 wounded. In 1948 the ship was chartered for four years as an emigrant carrier to Australia and New Zealand.

In 1952 this splendid old ship went to the breakers at Faslane.

Andes

IN THE late 1930s the Royal Mail Company decided to build a ship of about 25,000 tons for the South American route which could also be used for cruising. She was larger than her predecessors on the route, the *Asturias* and *Alcantara*, and had a good cargo capacity with five holds, much space being insulated for the transport of meat, fruit and other refrigerated products.

The *Andes* was completed in September 1939, and sea trials were waived due to the outbreak of war. She was laid up for a short time at Holy Loch in Scotland, but in November of that year was taken over as a troop transport. Some of her fittings were removed at Liverpool and she set off for Halifax, Nova Scotia, returning with Canadian troops.

The wartime career of the *Andes* was a remarkable one. With her large fuel capacity she could undertake long voyages without the need to replenish, and her good speed was useful in an emergency. Initially she could carry 3,000 troops, but this number was gradually increased to 4,500. Her defensive armament consisted at first of one ancient Hotchkiss gun; during the course of the war she acquired two big guns, a six-inch and a four point five-inch, four twin and four single Bofors, 14 Oerlikons and two twelve-pounders, an impressive battery for a troop-ship.

The second voyage of the *Andes* was to Colombo, Singapore and Hong Kong, to land troops. She then proceeded to New Zealand to embark men of the New Zealand Expeditionary Force in readiness for the expected invasion of Britain after Dunkirk, returning as part of a large convoy. Trooping voyages continued, to the Middle East and Canada. From December 1941 to May 1942 the ship made a tremendous circumnavigation of the world, sailing some 38,000 miles and carrying over 14,000 men; she visited Freetown, Durban, Bombay, Suez, Colombo, Australian ports, Panama, Halifax and Boston before returning to the UK.

The *Andes* now made some South African and transatlantic voyages before taking part in the North African landings. At the height of the campaign she ran a shuttle service between New York, Halifax and Casablanca.

In 1943 the *Andes* was refitted. The propeller-shaft brackets were stiffened to solve vibration problems caused by the damage from severe weather conditions. The following year she was also fitted with radar. She spent that year mostly on the transatlantic run with occasional voyages to Cape Town, and was in fact en route from South Africa to the UK when the war in Europe ended. Soon afterwards she carried the Norwegian government back to their native land and was given a great reception in Oslo.

From June to September 1945 the *Andes* sailed around the world via Panama, Wellington, Sydney, Fremantle, Karachi and Suez. During this voyage news was received of the Japanese surrender. Her arrival at Southampton in September was her first appearance at that port for many years. Her government service, however, was not yet over. Her next duty was to return Australian and New Zealand servicemen to their home countries, and 1946 found her making voyages to Singapore and Saigon, followed by others to Bombay and the Mediterranean. When she was at last handed back to the Royal Mail Company she had steamed 520,000 miles and carried 350,000 troops.

After refitting at Belfast which involved overhauling the machinery and altering the passenger accommodation to reduce the numbers in first class the *Andes* left Southampton on her first Royal Mail voyage to South America on 22 January 1948. For the next ten years she maintained a regular service to Buenos Aires, along with the *Alcantara*, stopping at Cherbourg, Lisbon, Las Palmas, Rio de Janeiro, Santos and Montevideo.

In 1950 two minor mishaps befell the *Andes*. She collided with a Swedish vessel, the *Colombia*, in thick fog off Santos in Brazil, and was slightly damaged. A few months later she grounded in the river Plate, incurring minor damage to her propellers. In 1952 slight turbine problems forced her to reduce her speed to 18 knots, to which she kept for the rest of her career.

From 1955 the ship was often taken off the South American route and sent cruising to the Mediterranean, northern capitals, West Indies and South Africa, occasionally visiting Cuba. She was in fact most suitable as a cruise ship, and in 1959 the decision was taken to convert her permanently to that role. She was considerably altered externally, the superstructure being extended fore and aft and two 44-ft motor launches being installed for ferrying passengers ashore. Cargo-handling gear was removed and air-conditioning fitted in passenger accommodation, which was spacious. For the next ten years the *Andes* cruised continuously and was extremely popular.

In 1970 her age began to tell and she became uneconomic to run. She arrived at Southampton for the last time on 4 May 1971, and immediately sailed to Ghent for breaking up.

Angelina Lauro

THIS ship was built for the Nederland Lines service to the Dutch East Indies. In the late 1930s the company decided on a fast ship which could carry some 700 passengers and complete the round voyage in about nine weeks. The *Oranje* was built with this in mind. She was an elegant ship. The hull had a curved stem and modern cruiser stern. Superstructure was substantial but well proportioned, with a pear-shaped funnel. She had a single mast, and carried 10 deck cranes. A notable feature was the pronounced tumble home of the midships part of the ship. There was a total of eight decks for passengers. The ship's trials were satisfactory and she achieved 26 knots, giving her plenty in reserve. This in fact made her one of the fastest motorships in the world at that time.

After a couple of cruises to Madeira, the *Oranje* set off on her maiden voyage. She went via the Cape due to the onset of war. Her return voyage was terminated at Lisbon and she returned to Surabaja, where she was laid up for a considerable time. Early in 1941 the ship was offered to the Australian government as a hospital ship. After dry-docking at Singapore she sailed for Sydney, where conversion took place at the Cockatoo dockyard; she could then accommodate some 650 casualties. Still under the Dutch flag, HMAS *Oranje* proceeded to Suez via Batavia and brought casualties back to Australia and New Zealand. She was kept busy in her humane role for the next few years, Sydney being her home port for most of the time. She went to and from the Middle East and visited East and South African ports as well. Docking at Singapore now being impossible, she had to use the facilities at Simonstown in 1942. In January 1944 the ship came back to the UK, arriving at Avonmouth on 14 March. She then made a series of Mediterranean voyages. The following year 1945 found her out in Australia and New Zealand again, from where she made more Far Eastern voyages before returning to the UK in early 1946. She had voyaged 382,600 miles, transporting over 32,000 casualties.

Some more voyaging to the Far East now followed, bringing back ex-POWs. On 18 July 1946 the *Oranje* arrived back at her home port of Amsterdam for the first time in nearly seven years. She was given a great welcome.

The ship now resumed the Amsterdam – Batavia service and was gradually refitted during the next three years. Her running-mates were the *Johan van Oldenbarnevelt* and *Johan de Witt*. The changing political situation, however, soon made the route no longer viable. The *Oranje* then switched to a round-the-world service, out via Panama to Auckland and Sydney, returning via Singapore and Suez. This she combined with cruising.

In the late 1950s an agreement with Rotterdam Lloyd resulted in a joint round-the-world service with three ships, the *Johan, van Oldenbarnevelt, Willem Ruys* and *Oranje*. The route followed was from Amsterdam and Southampton to Sydney and back, the *Oranje* alternating with the *Willem Ruys*. The *Johan* usually went out via Suez and back via Panama. The service was barely viable due to competition from other lines and aircraft. Cruising still played an important role.

In 1964 the *Oranje* was sold to the Italian company Achille Lauro of Naples. Renamed *Angelina Lauro*, she had a major reconstruction at Genoa lasting seventeen months. She had required a new flared bow, and the superstructure was entirely reshaped. A new lido deck was incorporated, and internal accommodation and public rooms were all revamped. The most striking alteration was in the fitting of a new winged funnel of modern design. During this work a fire broke out on board, claiming six lives. The ship's route was now from Europe to Australia, not an unfamiliar one for her. Taking emigrants was still an important business. The route was usually from Bremerhaven and Southampton to Sydney and Wellington via Suez. She was joined by her old friend *Willem Ruys*, now renamed *Achille Lauro*. When the Suez Canal closed she went via Capetown. The route sometimes varied and Southampton later became the terminal.

In 1970 the Australian immigrant contract went to the Greek Chandris Company, and the *Angelina*'s profitability decreased. She made her last line voyage in 1972, then became a permanent cruise vessel. She cruised from Florida to the Caribbean, and later in the Mediterranean.

The year 1978 found her doing seven-day cruises from San Juan (Puerto Rico). On 30 March 1979 the ship was swept by a disastrous fire while she was at St Thomas in the Virgin Islands. It rapidly engulfed the whole ship, and so much water was pumped on board that the *Angelina Lauro* sank at her berth. Sadly, she was now only fit for scrapping, and after she had been refloated, a tug arrived to tow her to Taiwan shipbreakers. She never reached there; In the Pacific a list developed, and the tow had to be parted. The ex-*Oranje* sank to the depths on 24 September 1979.

Antilles

Name: Antilles

Line: Compagnie Generale Transtlantique

Builders: Arsenal de Brest, completed 1952

Dimensions: Gross tonnage 19,828/ Length 600 ft/Beam 80.4 ft

Machinery

Engines: 2 Rateau-type turbines geared to twin screw-shafts, 44,000 s.h.p.

Service speed: 22 knots

Boilers: 4 oil-fired watertube steam pressure 909 p.s.i., superheated to 905°F

Regular Routes

Le Havre – W. Indies

Passenger Capacity

1st 404, Cabin class 285, Tourist 89, Crew 360

Sister-ship

Flandre (1952)

Photograph 1960

THIS ship was built for the CGT's service to the Caribbean. She was constructed by the naval dockyard at Brest. Launched on 26 April 1951, the vessel was completed by the end of 1952. Delivered on January 1953, she made a couple of cruises before sailing on her maiden voyage from Le Havre to the West Indies in May.

As can be seen, the ship was of rather striking appearance. The hull had a cruiser stern and a very modern curved and flared bow with a bulbous forefoot. It contained four decks, and superstructure above was nicely proportioned with a rather massive funnel on top. Much light alloy was used in the ship's upperworks. Accommodation and amenities on board were very good. Three classes of passengers were carried, and public rooms and cabins were claimed to be equal to those on the best of the ships on the North Atlantic service. The *Antilles*, like most ships on this route, had considerable cargo capacity, with electric cranes for working it.

Propelling machinery consisted of two turbines geared to twin screw shafts. Service speed was a very respectable 22 knots, steam being supplied by four watertube boilers. The ship made a couple of cruises, to Portugal and North Africa and to the Mediterranean, before starting the West Indies service.

The *Antilles* and her sister *Flandre*, built at a Dunkirk yard, were both intended for the Caribbean route but in the event the latter sailed to New York for much of the time. She did, however, join the *Antilles* on the Caribbean service during the winter months until 1958. A typical route for our subject was Le Havre-Southampton-Vigo-San Juan-Pointe à Pitre-Fort de France-La Guaira-Trinidad and Barbados. This varied from time to time. Sometimes the ship called at ports such as New Orleans, Galveston, Bermuda, Nassau, Kingston etc. The *Colombie*, a fine old-timer, was also her running-mate for a while, but was sold to the Greeks in 1964.

And so the *Antilles* steamed steadily on the West Indies route. Together with the *Flandre* she was used also for winter cruising out of San Juan or Guadeloupe to other nearby Caribbean islands. The ships were fairly successful in this role, but had not really been designed for cruising, and lacked a lido deck. The *Flandre* had in fact returned to the West Indies route in 1962, but was sold to the Italians in 1968. The *Antilles* continued on the service, but in 1971 she met with a tragic end. While homeward-bound from San Juan to Le Havre on the evening of 8 January that year she struck an uncharted rock off the small island of Mustique. A fuel tank was ruptured, causing oil to spill out into the boiler-room, where it immediately burst into flames. The ship's fire-fighters made valiant efforts, but the conflagration was too much for them. The passengers took to the boats. Fortunately, the *Antilles*' distress calls were quickly answered, and soon several vessels were on the scene. These included the French ships *Point Allegre* and *Suffren*. The *Queen Elizabeth 2* happened to be cruising nearby, and soon appeared to help with the rescue. Due to the fine work of all concerned, no lives were lost. The *Antilles*, however, capsized, broke in two, and became a total loss with no hope of salvage. A sad ending indeed for a very fine ship.

Her sister *Flandre* enjoyed better fortune. Renamed *Carla C*, after extensive refitting expressly for cruising, she has had a long and successful career.

Aquitania

THE *Aquitania* was built as a running-mate for the *Mauretania* and *Lusitania* on the Cunard transatlantic service. She had a greater capacity than her predecessors on the route, the *Lucania* and *Campania*, and was fast enough to maintain a weekly service from Liverpool.

After trials the *Aquitania* became the first ship to enter the new Gladstone dry dock at Liverpool to have her hull cleaned. On her maiden voyage to New York she averaged over 23 knots, and on the return carried more passengers (2,649) than had ever travelled in a British ship from that port. However, only three round voyages had been made before she was taken over by the Admiralty for use as an armed merchant cruiser. She was quickly fitted with six-inch guns and dispatched on patrol on 8 August 1914. Later that month, however, she collided with the Leyland liner *Canadian*; both ships sustained some damage, and the *Aquitania* was forced to return to Liverpool. By this time the Admiralty had decided that her size made her too vulnerable to be used as an AMC, and consequently her guns were removed and she was laid up, together with the *Mauretania*.

In May 1915 the *Aquitania* was used as a troop transport during the Gallipoli campaign. In four months she transported about 30,000 troops, her capacity and speed making her suitable for the purpose. In August, as the campaign had gone badly, she became a hospital ship, her large public rooms on the upper decks being transformed into wards. After a short refit in mid-1916 she continued in this role until the end of the year. For almost the whole of 1917 she was laid up, but, in 1918 she again became a transport bringing American troops to Europe. During this time she was 'dazzle-painted' and had a rather bizarre appearance. On 9 October 1918 she had the misfortune to collide with one of her escorting US destroyers in rough weather off the coast of Ireland. Twelve lives were lost on the USS *Shaw*, but the *Aquitania*, with 8,000 troops on board, reached Southampton safely.

After the Armistice the Aquitania was used to repatriate American and Canadian troops. By mid-1919 she had returned to commercial service, making her first voyage from Southampton on 14 June. After extensive refitting on Tyneside, she resumed regular service on the North Atlantic route. With the *Berengaria* and *Mauretania* she was part of the Cunard express service which, together with the trio of the White Star line, offered a twice-weekly service from Southampton. In winter there was an occasional cruise.

The ship's accommodation was progressively altered to account for the fact that there were fewer passengers in the third class owing to restrictions on immigration to the US.

The Depression badly affected passenger traffic, so that the *Mauretania* and *Aquitania* were both forced to run cruises to the Mediterranean and South America. In 1934 the merger with White Star gave the *Majestic* and *Olympic* as new running-mates. During this time little befell the *Aquitania* except that she twice went aground in the Solent, on one occasion for 26 hours, but without suffering any serious damage.

By 1936 the *Olympic* and *Majestic* had been withdrawn, but the *Queen Mary* had joined the service. In 1938 the *Aquitania* made an extensive cruise of 11,400 miles to South America. Cunard had intended to replace her with the *Queen Elizabeth*, but the war intervened and she was again taken over for trooping. Her first duties involved bringing Canadian troops to the UK. In March 1940 she was dispatched to Sydney to take Australian troops to the Middle East. Over the next few years her trooping work involved visits to ports worldwide such as Rio, Cape Town, Fremantle, Suez, Aden and Wellingtôn. An extensive refit in New York in 1940 gave her two 6-inch guns and several smaller ones.

In 1942 the *Aquitania* was used to carry American evacuees from Hawaii to the USA after Pearl Harbour, and the following year saw her bringing American and Canadian troops to Britain. Once hostilities were concluded, the ship was employed on repatriation work, taking a large complement of Australians and New Zealanders home, and Canadians and their brides across the Atlantic. In 1946 she acted as conference ship for a meeting of British, French, American and Russian foreign ministers in New York. In May 1948 she began a regular immigrant service to Canada, after an overhaul which adapted the ship to take over 1,700 people in 'austerity class'. The eastward runs brought tourists to Europe. Old age now brought the *Aquitania*'s career to a close; after reaching Southampton in December 1949 she was sold for breaking up. On Feb 19 1950 the old ship sailed from Southampton to Faslane.

Name: **Aquitania**

Line: Cunard

Builders: John Brown, Clydebank; launched 21 April 1913, completed 10 May 1914

Dimensions: Gross tonnage 45,647/ Length 901 ft/Beam 97.1 ft

Machinery

Engines: Triple-expansion direct drive steam turbines, 4 screws, 62,000 s.h.p.

Boilers: 21 double-ended Scotch type, coal-fired, forced draught, 195 p.s.i.

Service speed: 23 knots

Major Refits

1919 Tyneside, conversion of boilers to oil fuel
1936 new propellers fitted

Regular Routes

Southampton/Liverpool – New York

Passenger Capacity

1914: 1st 618, 2nd 614, 3rd 1998
1926: 1st 610, 2nd 950, Tourist 640

Sister-ships

None

Photograph 1922

Arandora Star

Name: **Arandora Star** (originally *Arandora*)

Line: Blue Star

Builders: Cammell Laird, Birkenhead, completed May 1927

Dimensions: Gross tonnage 12,857/ Length 535 ft/Beam 68.2 ft

Machinery

Engines: Geared steam turbines, twin screw

Boilers: 5, 3 double-ended, 2 single-ended, designed to burn oil or coal, 200 p.s.i.

Service speed: 16 knots

Major Refits

1936 removal of mainmast, 15,501 tons

Regular Routes

London – river Plate

Passenger Capacity

1st class only: 164, later 420

Sister-ships

Almeda (1926); Andalucia (1927); Avelona (1927); Avila (1927)

Photograph 1936

THIS ship was one of five built for the Blue Star Line's passenger and cargo service to South America. They were intended to provide a fortnightly service from London to the river Plate. The *Arandora*, as she was originally known, was completed in 1927. She had two funnels, the after one being a dummy which served as a ventilator for the engine-room, and a total of eight decks. She did not spend long on the river Plate route, as competition from other companies, notably the Royal Mail Line, was strong. In 1929 she was fitted out as a cruising ship; her superstructure was extended, cargo space filled in and passenger accommodation greatly increased. In 1936 her mainmast was removed, altering her appearance further.

After adding the suffix 'star' to her name, she began cruising, to Norway and the Northern capitals in summer, and the Caribbean and South America in winter. Spring and autumn cruises were usually to the Mediterranean and the North African Atlantic coast. In 1935 she took part in the Silver Jubilee Review of the Fleet, and in 1937 in the Coronation Review.

In August 1939 her cruising programme had to be curtailed. She sailed in September for New York with Americans anxious to get home, before being taken over for war duties. Although she was of the right size for an armed merchant cruiser, her top weight would have caused stability problems when fitted with 6-inch guns. Therefore she undertook instead anti-torpedo net trials in the Channel. Although these proved successful, the nets never came into widespread use. Grey-painted, she proceeded to Liverpool, and then sailed to Norway for the evacuation of British, French and Polish troops. The return journey to Glasgow was made in convoy, and safely despite several bombing attacks.

The *Arandora Star* next undertook several journeys to France to take on board Allied personnel who had not managed to escape from Dunkirk. From Bayonne and St Jean de Luz she succeeded in taking on board 3,000 men, with enemy aircraft overhead, and bringing them back safely to Liverpool. Her next duty was to take several hundred German and Italian internees, together with some German prisoners of war, to Canada. She was to sail alone relying on her speed and zig-zagging for safety. She had also been armed with two guns with which to defend herself if necesary, a 4.7 inch and 12-pounder. The ship left Liverpool on 1 July 1940, with 712 Italian 478 Germans, an armed guard of 200 soldiers and a crew of 174 on board. She safely rounded Malin Head, the northern-most point of Ireland, that night, and set a course for St John's, Newfoundland. However, the next morning she was spotted by a German U-boat, the U-47, whose commander, Gunther Prien, had been responsible for sinking the battleship *Royal Oak* the year before. Having identified the *Arandora Star* as an enemy ship, the captain fired his last remaining torpedo. It hit the liner in the after engine-room on the starboard side, flooding the compartment and killing those inside. The explosion wrecked the ship's turbines and both generators, and as a result no emergency order could be issued, since the communications system was no longer functioning. The ship took thirty minutes to sink, during which time ten lifeboats and a number of rafts were launched, although some of the passengers were elderly and at first reluctant to leave the ship. The captain, and the German captain of the liner *Adolf Woermann*, who was a prisoner of war on board, both went down with the ship. The survivors were spotted by an RAF flying-boat and a few hours later picked up by the Canadian destroyer *St Laurent*. The final death toll was 805, of whom 486 were Italians and 175 Germans. The U-47 was sunk in the Atlantic in March 1941 and the entire crew was lost.

(Note: Some sources give slightly different numbers of casualties etc. from those stated above.)

Arcadia

P & O had to rebuild their fleet after the war, and a number of fine passenger liners followed in fairly quick succession. The 28,000-ton *Himalaya* was the first in 1949 followed by the *Chusan*, 24,000 tons, in 1950. *Arcadia* was the next followed by the *Iberia*.

The *Arcadia* was built for the Australian service. This route was a most important one for the P & O, until aircraft took over some years later. She was an attractive looking ship. The hull had a curved raked stem, good sheer and modern cruiser-type stern. Upperworks were nicely proportioned, with a funnel of pleasing design. She had a total of nine decks, and was well provided with the usual type of public rooms. There were no less than sixteen of them. She catered for first class and tourist passengers; the former were mainly amidships, and the latter farther aft.

A few of the public rooms may be mentioned. The fine first-class observation lounge was forward on the boat deck, offering splendid sea views. Most of the first-class rooms were on the promenade deck, and included writing-rooms, library, main lounge, ballroom and cinema and veranda café. The lounge was a large, high, room with large windows and concealed lighting. A mural within featured an 'Arcadian' scene, appropriately. At the forward end of this deck was a children's nursery with balcony above. Tourist rooms were also well appointed. These were mostly lower down on 'A', 'B' and 'C' decks. Both dining saloons were on 'D'. There were two swimming-pools, one for each class. These were situated at the aft end of the promenade deck.

Trials being satisfactory, the ship set off on her maiden voyage. She was given a great welcome in Australia and ports en route, including Bombay and Colombo. On returning to Tilbury she set forth on a Mediterranean cruise which terminated at Southampton. Further cruising from the Hampshire port followed. When she was returning to Tilbury in September to prepare for an Australian voyage she had the misfortune to sink a small tug which was assisting her and sadly five crewmen on the little vessel were lost.

By the time the *Arcadia* made her second Australian voyage her sister *Iberia* was also on the route. The ship became a popular member of the service as she steamed steadily to and fro, for the first few years of her career combining line voyages to Australia with cruising from British ports. In April 1959 she went to Harland and Wolff, Belfast, for an extensive refit. Air-conditioning was now extended throughout the accommodation, and this was all upgraded to keep her in line with modern requirements. During this refit an outbreak of fire occurred in one of the after holds, but was dealt with before much damage resulted.

The mixture of cruising and line passages continued. On 22 November 1959 she made her first cruise from an Australian port, sailing from Sydney round the South Pacific islands. In December she made her first voyage across the Pacific to San Francisco and back.

More cruising from Southampton and Sydney followed; she was being much used in this role. In January 1961 the *Arcadia* ran aground on a coral reef outside Honolulu, but was refloated with only superficial damage. In general the ship enjoyed a more or less trouble-free career, although she did get delayed for a couple of days at Bombay in February 1963 with engine problems, which were soon rectified.

Air travel was now robbing P & O of many passengers. There was also competition from State-subsidized Russian liners. The need for a large fleet was decreasing, through the *Arcadia* was still kept busily employed in her dual role. Her operations during the 1970s were pretty varied: she sometimes proceeded to Sydney via Panama, and in 1973 made a world cruise, ending at Southampton. She also became very popular for her cruises from San Francisco to Alaska, and was in fact based for a while on the American west coast, cruising also to Mexico.

In the meantime she had been altered to a one-class vessel, taking a large number of tourist class only. The ship's west coast cruising era ended in March 1975, when she returned to Southampton for a refit at Thornycroft's. A few cruises from here followed, then the *Arcadia* sailed to Sydney via the Cape. She now replaced the *Himalaya* on the Australian station. Returning to make some cruises from Southampton in early 1976, she spent the rest of her career Down Under. At length the P & O purchased the Swedish *Kungsholm* in 1978 and renamed her *Sea Princess* with the intention of using her to replace the *Arcadia* in Australia. On 29 January 1979 the veteran left Sydney for the last time and was given a tremendous send-off. On arrival at Singapore her passengers transferred to the *Sea Princess* for the return voyage to Australia. The *Arcadia* was sold to shipbreakers in Taiwan, and sailed from Singapore to Kaohsiung, arriving on 28 February 1979.

Name: **Arcadia**

Line: P & O

Builders: John Brown & Co., Clydebank; launched 14 May 1953, completed February 1954

Dimensions: Gross tonnage 29,734/ Length 721 ft/Beam 90.2 ft

Machinery

Engines: 2 sets triple expansion geared turbines, twin screws 42,500 s.h.p.

Boilers: 3 Foster-Wheeler oil-fired watertube, controlled superheat, 620 p.s.i.

Service speed: 22 knots

Regular Routes

Southampton – Sydney

Passenger Capacity

1954: 1st 675, Tourist 735
1970: Tourist 1350

Sister-ships

Iberia (1954)

Photograph 1956

Arkadia

THIS vessel started life as the *Monarch of Bermuda*, a graceful 22,000 ton three-funnelled liner. She was built for Furness Withy and Company for the luxury service from New York to Bermuda. As built, the vessel looked very different from the photo shown here, which depicts her later in her career. Originally the hull had a rather straight stem with a slight flare, and the ship sported three well-spaced funnels (the third being a dummy) and two masts. Superstructure was of a similar proportion to that in the photo. Since this was a luxury service, most of the ship was devoted to passenger-carrying. There was little cargo capacity, Propelling machinery was turbo-electric, the *Monarch* being one of the largest vessels to have this type of installation at the time. After a successful maiden voyage in November 1931 the ship remained on the Bermuda route until the outbreak of war. When the *Morro Castle* was burnt off the New Jersey coast, on 8 September 1934, the *Monarch* rescued 71 passengers from the blazing ship.

In September 1939 she was taken off the route, and sent across the Atlantic with a contingent of Canadian troops. At Liverpool she was converted for use as a troopship. Initially was fitted to carry only about 1,400, but as the war progressed the capacity was increased to 4,000. After a short spell of transatlantic trooping she became involved in the ill-fated Norwegian campaign, transporting troops there and later evacuating them. While on a return voyage, laden with 2,000 troops, she narrowly escaped enemy air attack by entering a dense fog bank. The *Monarch* then made a number of voyages to the Middle East, and took part in the North Africa campaign, transporting troops for the assault on Oran. She was hit by a heavy shell during this operation, but suffered little damage. She was later employed carrying troops for the invasion of Italy, and bringing Americans to Europe for the final campaign. She continued trooping until the end of the war, having steamed 400,000 miles and carried 160,000 people.

While she was undergoing work at Tyneside to reconvert her to a passenger liner, a devastating fire swept through her, and she was completely gutted. The hulk was towed to Granton on the Firth of Forth and lay there while a decision was made about her future. Eventually, as tonnage was in short supply, the major job of restoration was put in hand. Much damaged steelwork had to be burned away and completely replaced, using 3,000 tons of new steel. In addition to her internal reconstruction, the after dummy funnel was removed and the forward one replaced by an ingenious

'dipod' which did duty as a mast as well. Her mainmast had been taken out also, and the foremast reduced in height.

She was now owned by the Ministry of Transport, which renamed her *New Australia*, and managed by Shaw Savill. Her colours were black hull, white upperworks and buff funnel with black top. She was to be used for taking emigrants to Australia, and consequently had only one class of accommodation. Her first voyage in this new role was from Southampton to Sydney via Suez, leaving on 15 August 1950. She kept up the service, interspersed with a spell of trooping during the Korean war, until 1957, when her charter to the Australian government expired.

In January 1958 she was sold to the Greek line and registered under the Arcadia Steamship Company of Andros. Substantial modernization took place at the Blohm and Voss yard in Hamburg. Her foremast was removed and replaced by a couple of derrick posts; a more modern funnel was fitted. Further modifications took place in 1961. With the new name of *Arkadia*, she was employed on transatlantic voyaging and cruising. She set off on her first voyage from Bremerhaven to Montreal on 2 May 1958. The usual route was Bremerhaven-Amsterdam-Tilbury-Le Havre-Cobh-Quebec-Montreal. In winter she cruised from New York and Boston to Bermuda, the Bahamas and the Caribbean. This operation later transferred to Southampton for cruises to Portugal, the Canaries and West Africa. In her later years her cruising activity increased as the Atlantic voyaging declined due to competition from air travel.

In November 1966 the *Arkadia* was withdrawn, and sold to breakers in Spain, arriving at Valencia in December.

Name: *Monarch of Bermuda* (1931); ***New Australia*** (1949); ***Arkadia*** (1958)

Line: Furness Withy (1931-47); Ministry of Transport (1947-58); Greek Line (1958-66)

Builders: Vickers-Armstrongs, Newcastle-on-Tyne; launched 17 March 1931, completed November 1931

Dimensions: Gross tonnage 22,424/ Length 579 ft, 589 ft (1958)/Beam 76.4 ft

Machinery

Engines: Turbo-electric: Turbines by Fraser & Chalmers. Generators and 4 propulsion motors from General Electric Company, quadruple screw

Boilers: 8 Babcock & Wilcox watertube, 400 p.s.i., superheated to 650°F

Service speed: 19.5 knots

Major Refits

1947-50 Thornycroft, Southampton, restoration, 20,256 tons
1958 Blohm & Voss, Hamburg, modernisation

Regular Routes

New York – Bermuda
Southampton – Sydney
Bremerhaven – Montreal

Passenger Capacity

1931: 1st 830
1947: 1600 one class
1958: 1st 150, Tourist 1150 (transatlantic voyaging), 650 one class (cruising)

Sister-ships

Queen of Bermuda (1933)

Photograph 1960

Arlanza

Name: Arlanza

Line: Royal Mail

Builders: Harland & Wolff, Belfast; launched 23 November 1911, completed June 1912

Dimensions: Gross tonnage 15,044/ Length 589 ft/Beam 65.3 ft

Machinery

Engines: 2 four-cylinder triple expansion engines driving wing propellers, low pressure turbine driving central screw, triple screw, 14,000 i.h.p.

Boilers: 4 cylindrical coal-fired, 180 p.s.i.

Service speed: 17 knots

Major Refits

1929 conversion to oil fuel

Regular Routes

Southampton – river Plate

Passenger Capacity

1st 400, 2nd 230, 3rd 760

Sister-ships

For complete list of 'A' class ships, see *Almanzora* specification

Photograph 1913

THIS vessel was one of the A class ships for Royal Mail's service to South America. She was built by Harland and Wolff at Belfast, launched on 23 November 1911 and completed by June the following year. The *Arlanza* set off on her maiden voyage from Southampton to the river Plate in September 1912.

She was practically identical to the *Almanzora* of 1915, which is described in this book. She was two feet less in beam than the later vessel, but otherwise very similar. These ships represented the final development of the A class.

The *Arlanza* attracted considerable attention when she entered the service, since she was the biggest ship to be used on it up to that time. An elegant, sturdy ship, she soon become very popular on the route, as in fact were all the A class vessels.

The ship left Buenos Aires on 31 July 1914 as war clouds gathered in Europe. She steamed steadily across the South Atlantic until 16 August, when she was about 200 miles south of the Canaries. Here she was overhauled by a fast four-funnelled vessel and received the order 'Stop or I will sink you'! The newcomer proved to be the German commerce raider *Kaiser Wilhelm der Grosse* and the *Arlanza* had no option but to obey instructions. She was ordered to dismantle her wireless aerials and throw them overboard. The enemy raider then inquired how many women and children were on board. When informed '335 women and 97 children', the German captain replied, 'You may proceed, I have no further orders for you.' Chivalry at sea still prevailed in those early days of the war. The *Arlanza* then proceeded to Las Palmas, where her captain informed the appropriate authorities including the Admiralty of the incident.

Like her sisters *Alcantara*, *Andes* and later the *Almanzora*, the *Arlanza* was fitted out as an armed merchant cruiser and became a member of the Tenth Cruiser Squadron patrolling the lonely northern waters. This work mainly involved stopping and examining merchant vessels passing through the area. She was armed with eight 6-inch guns, a couple of six-pounder anti-aircraft weapons and one or two machine guns. Depth charges were also carried. The AMCs kept ceaseless vigil on this vast sea area, maintaining the blockade of Germany.

In October 1915 HMS *Arlanza* had a rather different duty. She was sent to Archangel to bring some Russian high officials to the UK for an important conference. She left Archangel on 21 October with the delegates on board, and some valuable platinum as well. Several other ships accompanied her, including some minesweeping trawlers. The Germans had mined the approaches to the White Sea early in the war, and in spite of all precautions the *Arlanza* struck a mine on 22 October when off Sazonova, on the Kola Peninsula. The stoutly built vessel did not sink, and was eventually towed ashore and beached. Here she remained until she was eventually repaired and reached the UK safely. She was then able to continue her hazardous work. Her important passengers in the meantime had been taken on board HMS *Orotava* and brought safely to their destination.

In December 1916 the ship, in company with HMS *Almanzora* and several others, made a sweep of the Atlantic in search of the enemy raider *Moewe* which was making a nuisance of herself. They didn't find her. The *Arlanza* continued her useful patrol and escort work for the remainder of the war and was then reconverted back for Royal Mail service.

She set off on her first post-war voyage from Southampton to the river Plate on 27 July 1920, and for the next eighteen years was to give steady, reliable service with few incidents befalling her. She had been a coal-burner all through her early career, but was converted to oil fuel in the late twenties. In December 1929 the *Arlanza* and a German vessel rescued the crew of the sinking Italian freighter *Casmona* in severe weather. In 1931 she conveyed the Prince of Wales and Prince George from South America to Lisbon.

Although newer ships such as the *Asturias* and *Alcantara* joined the fleet, the *Arlanza* still remained popular and continued in service until 1938. In August that year a farewell party was held on the old ship at Montevideo. On arrival at Southampton on 6 September she was withdrawn, and went for scrapping at Blyth.

Arosa Kulm

Name: **Cantigny** (1919); **American Banker** (1924); **Ville d'Anvers** (1940); **City of Athens** (1946); **Protea** (1947); **Arosa Kulm** (1952)

Line: American Merchant Lines 1924-31; United States Lines 1931-40; Société Maritime Anversoise SA 1940; various owners 1940-7; Panamanian Lines etc 1947-51; Compania Internacional Transportadora (later Arosa Line Inc) 1951-9

Builders: American International Shipbuilding Corp., Hog Island, Pa.; launched 27 October 1919, completed 1920

Dimensions: Gross tonnage 7,430, 8,929 (as Arosa Kulm)/Length 450 ft/Beam 58 ft

Machinery

Engines: 2 steam turbines double reduction geared to single-screw 6,000 s.h.p.

Boilers: 6 oil-fired watertube

Service speed: 15 knots

Regular Routes

North Atlantic route

Passenger Capacity

1926: 80 Tourist
1946: 200 Tourist
1948: 965 Tourist

Sister-ships

Vessels of 'standard class' built in this period

Photograph 1955

THIS vessel was one of the standard 7,500-ton type built by the American International Shipbuilding Co. of Hog Island, Pennsylvania. She was launched on 27 October 1919 as the US Army transport *Cantigny*, and completed the following year. The series of ships built here were known as Hog Island B type. Originally some seventy were to be built, but the cessation of hostilities meant that only twelve were completed. They were the smallest of the 'standard' wartime transports, the *President Harding* (which features in this book), being an example of the larger type. Their appearance was rather unusual – they seemed to 'hog', or 'droop' at each end.

The *Cantigny* was one of many that were converted to commercial use. She became a member of the American Merchant Lines operated for the US Shipping Board by J.H. Winchester & Co. Now named *American Banker*, she commenced her commercial career in 1924 with a sailing from New York to London on 24 April.

The ship had a rather different appearance then from that depicted in our photograph, which shows her much later in her career. The hull had a straight stem and rather similar type of stern. It had three decks, and the superstructure above was quite short amidships with a vertical funnel on top. There were wells forward and aft, and four sets of derricks ('goalposts') for cargo working. Cargo was of great importance, and the ship had seven holds.

Originally the *American Banker* carried twelve passengers only, being principally a cargo ship. Numbers were progressively increased during her career.

In 1929 the USSB sold American Merchant Lines and the US Lines to P.W. Chapman & Co. Ltd. In 1931, however, both became members of the newly formed United States Lines of Nevada.

The *American Banker* and her sisters continued on the Atlantic route. There were seven of them in total. The others were the *American Merchant*, *American Farmer*, *American Shipper*, *American Trader*, *American Importer* and *American Traveler*. They continued steaming steadily to and fro during the thirties. Sometimes calls were made at Plymouth. Along with the *President Harding*, the ships were transferred to Belgian registry in 1940, becoming members of the specially formed Société Maritime Anversoise SA of Antwerp. This was to enable them to continue trading. The Neutrality Act of November 1939 had forced US Lines to suspend sailings of their ships to most European ports.

This had a most unfortunate result. Six of the seven ships were sunk by U-boats during 1940–1. The one survivor was our subject. She had been renamed *Ville d'Anvers* in 1940, and after the war had a rather varied career for some years.

She was reacquired by the US Lines but soon transferred to the Isbrandtsen Line, who disposed of her to a Honduran concern. Renamed *City of Athens*, her passenger capacity was increased. During this time she was associated with several companies, but there were financial difficulties and she was sold to Panamanian Lines in August 1947, renamed *Protea* and had an extensive refit at Genoa. Her appearance was greatly altered, and passenger capacity again increased to over 900, most being accommodated in dormitories. During the next few years she was variously employed by Panamanian Lines and an Italian company making voyages to Australia, Central America and South America.

In August 1951 the *Protea* was acquired by the Compania Internacional Transportadora and made voyages to Indo-China and Canada for them, and on charter. The company become known as the Arosa Line and the ship got her final name-change to *Arosa Kulm*. She now sailed on the Canadian route, typically Bremerhaven-Zeebrugge-Southampton-Halifax. Summer-season voyages were to Quebec and Montreal.

The itinerary varied, and sometimes London, Le Havre, and Plymouth were ports of call.

By 1954 the company became known as Arosa Line Inc., with a new house-flag. Although sailing under the Panamanian flag, ownership was really Swiss, with headquarters at Geneva. The ship now appeared as in our photograph, looking very much a passenger liner. The 'goalposts' had long gone. Sometimes she voyaged to New York and elsewhere instead of Canada.

The company had four ships in operation. In addition to the *Arosa Kulm* it had the 9,000-ton *Arosa Star*, the 17,300-ton *Arosa Sky* and the 20,000-ton *Arosa Sun*. Passengers, however, were on the decline. Some of the ships went cruising to gain extra revenue, but financial difficulties occurred. The *Arosa Sky* was sold in 1958, but finances did not improve. When the *Arosa Kulm* arrived at Plymouth on 6 December 1958, en route from Jamaica to Bremen, she had a writ nailed to her mast by Customs officials. In April 1959 the company was declared bankrupt. The *Arosa Kulm* was soon sold for scrapping at Bruges, when she arrived there in May 1959.

Arundel Castle

THE Union Castle Line was taken over by the Royal Mail Group in 1912. Plans for modernizing the fleet included the building of two vessels of over 19,000 tons considerably larger than any of the existing ships. They were to be named the *Windsor Castle* and the *Arundel Castle*. The keel of the *Arundel Castle* was laid on 6 November 1915, but wartime work took priority, and she was not in fact completed until 1921. She had four funnels, unusually for a ship of her size, and was the first of the Union Castle mailships to have a cruiser stern.

As her accommodation and facilities were much superior to those found on earlier mailships, the *Arundel Castle* soon became very popular. Although she was bigger than any previous vessel on the route, her speed was a modest 17 knots adequate for the service at that time. For her return journey to the UK after her maiden voyage she was crowded to capacity, and passengers included General Smuts and members of his cabinet on their way to the Imperial Conference. In March 1922 she was joined by her sister-ship the *Windsor Castle*, which had been built on the Clyde. These two were in fact the last steamships to be constructed for the mail service until the *Edinburgh Castle* and *Pretoria Castle* of 1948. Both ships continued reliably in service without any serious mishaps. The *Arundel Castle* was involved in a collision with the steamer *Maud Llewellyn* in Southampton Water, in November 1926 but no major damage was caused to either.

Competition on the South African route was strong. In 1933 an Italian company signed an agreement with the South African government for a subsidized service between South and East Africa and Mediterranean ports. The ships to be used were larger and faster than those of the Union Castle. The latter, once more an independent company, signed a new Freight Agreement in 1934 which required additional refrigeration capacity, and a new mail contract of 1936 in which it agreed to reduce the passage time from 16 to 14 days. This meant a major reconstruction of most of the mail ships to bring them up to the required speed. The *Arundel Castle* was the first to return to the shipyard for lengthening of the hull, and the fitting of new engines twice as powerful as the old. Her four funnels were replaced by two larger ones, and accommodation was improved.

The new faster mail service began in 1938, but was soon interrupted by the war. The *Arundel Castle* became a valuable troop-ship, often voyaging around the Cape to land soldiers in Suez, Bombay or Singapore. On one convoy in September 1940 she was joined by five of the Union Castle's other ships: *Athlone Castle, Winchester Castle, Capetown Castle, Windsor Castle* and *Durban Castle*. She also carried troops for the North African campaign and the Sicilian landings. In 1944, under diplomatic immunity, she brought Allied prisoners of war back from Germany to Britain. She came through the war unscathed, but at the end did not immediately return to commercial service. In 1947 she became an emigrant ship transporting settlers out to South Africa. Along with the *Winchester Castle* and *Carnarvon Castle*, she continued this work until April 1949. After some trooping service in the Mediterranean, she went to Belfast for reconversion to a passenger liner.

Returning to the mail run in 1950, by far the oldest ship on the route, she now catered for two classes only, first and tourist. She continued on the service for another eight years, until the new *Pendennis Castle* appeared to replace her. Sold for demolition in Hong Kong, the *Arundel Castle* left Southampton for the Far East on 30 December 1958.

Name: *Arundel Castle*

Line: Union Castle

Builders: Harland & Wolff, Belfast; launched 11 September 1919, completed April 1921

Dimensions: Gross tonnage 18,980/ Length 661 ft/Beam 72.5 ft

Machinery

Engines: Compound single-reduction geared turbines, twin screws, 15,000 s.h.p.

Boilers: 9 double-ended, 2 single-ended Scotch type, 220 p.s.i.

Service speed: 17 knots

Major Refits

1937: Harland & Wolff, triple-expansion Parsons single reduction geared turbines

Boilers: 4 Babcock-Johnson watertube, 425 p.s.i., speed 20 knots, 19,118 tons, 686 × 72.5 ft

Regular Routes

Southampton – Cape Town and South African ports

Passenger Capacity

1921: 1st 234, 2nd 362, 3rd 274, Steerage 300
1937: 1st 219, 2nd 167, Tourist 194
1949: 1st 164, Tourist 371

Sister-ships
Windsor Castle (1922)

Photograph 1958

Ascania

THIS ship was one of Cunard's celebrated 'A' class of 14,000 tons, built in the 1920s for North Atlantic service. She was to be mostly used on the Canadian route, and sailed on her maiden voyage from London to Montreal on the 22 May 1925.

The *Ascania* was an attractive-looking vessel. The hull had a straight stem and elegant counter stern. The superstructure above was well proportioned, with a slim, nicely raked funnel amidships. She was one of a group of six vessels built as replacement tonnage for vessels lost during the war. The *Ausonia*, *Antonia* and *Andania* were the first trio, the *Ascania*, *Alaunia* and *Aurania* the second. All six were generally very similar, a small difference being that the first three each had a separate 'island' bridge, while in the latter three it was integral with the main superstructure. The route followed was usually from London and Southampton via Cherbourg to Quebec and Montreal in the summer and to Halifax in winter. She made the occasional voyage from Liverpool or Glasgow, and sometimes also went to New York.

In December 1934 the *Ascania* was involved in a dramatic rescue in the Atlantic. The 3,500-ton freighter *Usworth*, owned by the Dagleish Company of Newcastle, got into difficulties in mountainous seas when her steering gear failed. She eventually made temporary repairs to her gear and was able to proceed, only to be hit by tremendous seas which caused her grain cargo to shift. She listed about twenty-five degrees to port, and seas were entering through damaged hatches. The situation was desperate when the *Ascania* arrived in answer to an SOS. Oil was pumped out to help calm down the raging seas. The *Jean Jadot*, a Belgian vessel, sent a boat across pulled by 10 volunteer crew. They succeeded in taking off 14 of the *Usworth*'s crew of 26, but tragically the boat capsized on the return journey and 12 men were lost, including two of the gallant boat's crew. A volunteer crew from the *Ascania* was quickly mustered, and they pulled across in the heavy seas to the stricken freighter. Three of the *Usworth*'s crew jumped overboard and attempted to swim to the boat, but this was impossible in the oily water and, despite attempts to pick them up, they were lost. The remaining nine, however, were taken off and with great difficulty were brought safely back to the Cunarder.

On 16 October 1935, when peacefully alongside the loading dock at Montreal, the *Ascania* was struck by the 6,000-ton freighter *Norwegian* of Liverpool while the latter was manoeuvring. Fortunately,

little damage ensued to either vessel.

In July 1938 the *Ascania* ran aground near Bic in the St Lawrence. Some flooding occurred, and she lost her port propeller. She was refloated without much difficulty, but had to go back to Quebec for repair, her passengers making other arrangements for travelling.

On the outbreak of war the ship was converted at Birkenhead to an armed merchant cruiser. She was given an armament of eight 6-inch guns and a couple of 3-inch A A weapons. For the first part of the war HMS *Ascania* was engaged on patrol and escort duties in the Atlantic, very vital work. In October 1941, however, she departed from the Clyde with a Middle East convoy. The ship left the others at Port Elizabeth and proceeded to Australia and New Zealand. She then spent some months patrolling the Pacific with the New Zealand navy's AMC *Monowai*.

In August 1942 the *Ascania* returned to the UK via Panama. She was to spend the rest of the war as a troop-ship and as an LSI(L) (landing ship, infantry, large). In the latter role she was much involved with putting troops ashore with her assault craft (carried in special davits) during the Sicilian and Italian campaigns. The *Ascania* finished the last war years as a troop-ship, and continued in this role until returned to Cunard in September 1947. She then had a partial refit before reopening the Liverpool to Halifax service on 20 December.

In 1949 the ship was given an extensive reconditioning at Alexander Stephen's yard at Linthouse, and on 21 April 1950 resumed the Canadian service. She was in fact the only one of the 'A' class left to Cunard. The *Andania* had been sunk during the war, and the other four bought by the Admiralty for conversion to repair ships.

The *Ascania* remained based at Liverpool. Others on the route included the 20,000-tonners *Franconia* and *Scythia*. Sometimes the ships ran to New York in addition to the Canadian route. The new 22,000-tonners *Saxonia*, *Ivernia*, *Carinthia* and *Sylvania* appeared from 1954 onward. They had been specially designed for the route. In September 1955 the *Ascania* was transferred to Southampton, still on the Canadian run.

On 16 November 1956 the old ship was withdrawn. She had a final fling, taking troops out to the Mediterranean, before sailing on 30 December from Southampton to the breakers at Newport, Monmonthshire.

Name: *Ascania*

Line: Cunard

Builders: Armstrong Whitworth, Newcastle-on-Tyne; launched 20 December 1923, completed May 1925

Dimensions: Gross tonnage 14,013/ Length 538 ft/Beam 65.3 ft

Machinery

Engines: 2 Parsons compound turbines, double reduction geared to twin screw shafts, 8,500 s.h.p.

Boilers: 2 double-ended, 2 single-ended cylindrical, 220 p.s.i.

Service speed: 15 knots

Major Refits

1949 Linthouse, reconditioning, 14,440 tons

Regular Routes

London – Southampton – Cherbourg – Quebec – Montreal
London – Southampton – Cherbourg – Halifax
Liverpool – Quebec – Montreal

Passenger Capacity

1925: Cabin 500, 3rd 1,200
1950: 1st 198, Tourist 498

Sister-ships

Ausonia (1921), **Andania** (1922), **Antonia** (1922), **Aurania** (1924), **Alaunia** (1925)

Photograph 1927

Asturias

Name: Asturias

Line: Royal Mail

Builders: Harland & Wolff, Belfast, completed January 1926

Dimensions: Gross tonnage 22,071/ Length 656 ft/Beam 78.4 ft

Machinery

Engines: 2 sets Harland 8 cylinder 4 stroke double acting air injection diesel engines, twin screws, 15,000 total b.h.p.

Service speed: 16 knots

Major Refits

1934 Harland & Wolff, conversion from diesel to steam: 2 sets Parsons triple expansion single reduction geared turbines, 20,000 s.h.p.; speed 19 knots

Boilers: 3 Johnson watertube, 425 p.s.i., superheated to 750°F, forced and induced draughting 666 × 78.4 ft, 22,048 tons

Regular Routes

Southampton – river Plate

Passenger Capacity

1926: 1st 410, 2nd 232, 3rd 768
1934: 1st 330, 2nd 220, 3rd 768

Sister-ships

Alcantara (1927)

Photograph 1935

THE *Asturias*, almost identical to her sister *Alcantara*, was built by the Royal Mail Company for use on the highly competitive South American route of the 1920s. A successful maiden voyage from Southampton to the river Plate was followed by steady voyaging. Like her sister, she was converted to steam turbine machinery in 1934 to improve her speed and decrease vibration. She sometimes did cruising as well, in addition to her South American voyaging. She arrived back in Southampton from a Mediterranean cruise on 26 August 1939, and this was to be her last peacetime voyage for many years.

The *Asturias* then sailed for Belfast to be fitted out as an AMC, or Armed Merchant Cruiser. This involved a good deal of work. Her dummy fore-funnel was removed; eight 6-inch guns and some smaller anti-aircraft weapons were fitted. Searchlights and other necessary equipment were added, and towards the end of September 1939 HMS *Asturias* sailed for Scapa Flow.

She was to spend some time now on the Northern Patrol. In mid-1940 the *Asturias* was ordered down to the South Atlantic, where she patrolled the Rio de Janeiro-Santos area. For a while she replaced her sister AMC HMS *Alcantara*, which had been in action with the German armed raider *Thor*.

In July 1941 the ship had a lengthy refit at Newport News dockyard, Virginia. Here her elderly 6-inch guns were replaced by more up-to-date ones, and she was given a fairly modern fire-control system. She now sported an aircraft catapult and a Fairey 'Seafox' float plane, very useful for spotting purposes. An early-pattern radar system was also fitted. The ship's mainmast was removed, and destined never to be replaced. After all this work the *Asturias* returned to the South American Station early in 1942, and patrolling and escort work continued. At one time she was made flagship of the division.

The *Asturias* was used in rather unusual roles as well, escorting floating docks being towed across the South Atlantic. On the first occasion the dock didn't complete the voyage. It sprung a leak in mid-ocean, and had to be scuttled. In July 1943 the *Asturias* was again on a similar escort duty accompanied by five anti-submarine vessels. The tow started from Bahia Blanca, and the dock eventually reached its destination but, sadly, the *Asturias* did not. With the advantage of hindsight the advisability of sending such a large vessel to accompany a very slow-moving convoy may be questioned. However, the tow had reached a position between St Pauls Rocks and Freetown when the *Asturias* was torpedoed. The Italian submarine *Ammiraglio Cagni* was patrolling in this region, and sighted the slow-moving convoy on 25 July. Manoeuvring into position, she fired two torpedoes. The track of the first one was seen on board the AMC and by a swift helm movement it was avoided, but the big ship was unable to avoid the second one.

Soon there was 30 feet of water in the engine and boiler rooms. Desperate efforts were made by the crew to plug apertures and prevent further flooding. A powerful tug, the *Zwarte Zee*, arrived on the scene to tow the stricken vessel. Meanwhile the floating dock continued on its way to its destination, Dakar, accompanied by part of the escort. The remainder stayed with the *Asturias* and tug while they attempted to reach Freetown.

On 1 August the African port was reached safely. The ship lay anchored in the river for a lengthy period. For some eighteen months she lay idle, but early in 1945 it was decided to attempt to tow her to Gibraltar for dry docking. This was a voyage of some 2,000 miles, a rather hazardous one too. The ship had been crudely patched up in the meantime, and was fairly watertight. Two tugs, the *Thames* and again the *Zwarte Zee*, arrived on the scene, and on 8 February the long tow commenced accompanied by seven corvettes as escort. The *Asturias* arrived safely on 27 February and spent about three months in dry-dock undergoing further patching up and internal cleaning. The war in Europe was now over, and on 30 May she was again towed away, this time back to her builders Harland & Wolff at Belfast. The torpedo had done much damage, but although considered a constructive total loss, the ship was repaired and converted to a troopship, since tonnage was at a premium.

The *Asturias* had by this time been bought by the Ministry of Transport and was to be managed by Royal Mail. She never returned to the South American service but spent her remaining years taking emigrants to Australia and trooping.

The ship remained on the Southampton to Sydney route until 1953. She then went on to trooping work, bringing back British troops from Korea. Further refurbishment took place the next year and she continued to be usefully employed until sold to the breakers at Faslane in 1957. Just before scrapping commenced she had yet one more part to play – that of the ill-fated *Titanic* in the film *A Night to Remember*.

Athlone Castle

THIS ship, like her sister the *Stirling Castle*, was built by Harland and Wolff at Belfast, as part of Union Castle's rebuilding programme of the 1930s. She was launched on 28 November 1935 by the Countess of Athlone, and completed by May 1936. She set off on her maiden voyage from Southampton to Cape Town on the 22nd of the month. The Earl of Athlone, brother of Queen Mary, had been a very popular Governor General of South Africa from 1923 to 1931, and the ship was the first Union Castle liner to bear this name.

In design and appearance she was identical to her sister, having a cruiser stern with well-raked and curved stem, and a pear-shaped funnel. She served for a long time on the South African route, and officially inaugurated the new faster mail service in 1938 when she sailed from Southampton on 22 December. The voyage now took 14 days, instead of 16 days 15 hours. The harbour at East London, South Africa, had posed berthing problems, especially in adverse weather conditions. A scheme was put in hand to construct a large basin to facilitate big vessels turning. It was completed in 1937, and some comparatively small ships tried it out successfully. *The Athlone Castle*, however, provided the real test of the basin when she arrived there on 3 November. The senior pilot took the big ship in and berthed her satisfactorily, to everyone's delight. Later that day the basin was officially opened and a celebratory banquet held on board the ship as she lay alongside the new Buffalo harbour.

During the war years the *Athlone Castle* was taken over as a troopship and was also for a time converted to an LSI(L), for carrying assault craft. She made numerous trooping voyages to South Africa and the Middle East. In 1940 she acted as commodore ship on one of these large convoys, the ships assembling off Belfast for the long voyage round the Cape. Vice Admiral Sir R. Hill, on board the *Athlone Castle*, was Commodore of this great fleet, which included no less than five other Union Castle ships, the *Winchester, Capetown, Windsor, Arundel* and *Durban* Castles.

The two sister-ships were very suitable for long voyaging, since refuelling was not a problem. They were able to carry up to 5,000 troops, a very useful capacity, and also carried valuable cargo. Both were often used to bring American troops to Europe. The *Athlone Castle* came through the war unscathed, having sailed about half a million miles and carried 150,000 personnel. Afterwards she made some journeys to Australia and elsewhere, repatriating troops.

After release from government service in 1946, she was sent to Belfast for refitting. She soon returned to the South Africa run, making her first post-war commercial voyage in 1947. She remained on this route for many years. From January 1957 it was decided that mail ships operating from Southampton should have their masts painted white. The *Athlone Castle* was the first to use this new colouring. In 1960 the ship made a voyage from Cape Town to Southampton for Max Wilson, the cut-price travel entrepreneur. Fares were substantially reduced for this trip and the vessel was fully booked.

By the mid-1960s, however, the mail service was due for a further acceleration. The *Athlone Castle* would not have been able to make the required speed, and consequently was withdrawn from service. Her final voyage from South Africa ended on her arrival in Southampton on 6 August 1965. She then went to breakers at Taiwan, arriving at Kaohsiung on 13 September of that year.

Name: Athlone Castle

Line: Union Castle

Builders: Harland & Wolff, Belfast; launched 28 November 1935, completed May 1936

Dimensions: Gross tonnage 25,564/ Length 725 ft/Beam 82 ft

Machinery

Engines: 2 Harland Burmeister & Wain 10-cylinder diesel engines driving twin screws, 24,000 b.h.p.

Service speed: 20 knots

Major Refits

1939 conversion to troopship
1946 Belfast, reconversion to passenger liner

Regular Routes

Southampton – Cape Town and South African ports

Passenger Capacity

1936: 1st 242, Cabin 487
1947: 1st 245, Tourist 538

Sister-ships
Stirling Castle (1936)

Photograph 1958

Atlantic

THE Matson Navigation Company of America dated from 1882. It was formed for trading in the Pacific. The *Malolo* – as the *Atlantic* was first named – was laid down at William Cramp's yard at Philadelphia on 4 May 1925, and launched on 26 June the next year. Completed by May 1927, the ship sailed on her maiden voyage from San Francisco to Honolulu on 16 November.

The hull had a cruiser stern and slightly raked stem. It contained four decks, three being continuous. Above, the superstructure was well proportioned with the two funnels nicely spaced. Subdivision was complete, with twelve watertight bulkheads. The *Malolo* had in fact been built under US navy supervision, with a view to being used in wartime as an armed merchant cruiser or armed troop-ship.

The ship's career started rather dramatically. She set off for trials on 24 May 1927, but in dense fog off Nantucket was in collision with the Norwegian cargo ship *Jacob Christensen*. The *Malolo* was struck on the port side near the bridge, damage extending below the waterline and causing extensive flooding. Both boiler-rooms were flooded, but due to her excellent subdivision she remained afloat and was towed into New York, where repairs took several months to complete. On 22 October that year she again set out on trials which were satisfactory and passed off without incident. The vessel then sailed on her positioning voyage through the Panama Canal to San Francisco.

The *Malolo's* maiden voyage to Honolulu was an instant success. She was the first large passenger liner built for the Californian-Hawaiian tourist trade, and at once became very popular. With her high speed she reduced the voyage time from San Francisco to Hawaii from about 7 days to 4½. In addition to her regular run the ship also undertook Pacific cruising, sometimes visiting Australia and New Zealand. Rather curiously, it was apparently decided in 1937 that the name *Malolo* was an unlucky one in Hawaiian folklore, and so the ship was renamed *Matsonia*.

In late 1941 the ship was called for duty by the US navy and converted for trooping. The *Matsonia's* duties took her to many major theatres of war in the Pacific, transporting troops and supplies. Often she sailed in convoy, but her high speed enabled her also to sail unescorted. In addition to the war areas such as Guadalcanal and the Solomon Islands she also went to Australia. The *Matsonia* was the first big troop-ship to visit the Solomons, which were of course under Japanese air attack at the time. Her wartime service record was 385,549 miles steamed, 176,319 per-

sonnel carried. She was decommissioned in April 1946, and soon recommenced her peacetime service to Honolulu. After a short while she went for a refit at San Francisco.

Until 1948 the ship continued on the route, although not fully restored to her pre-war splendour. In the immediate post-war years passengers tended to be fewer, and after completion of her last voyage to Hawaii that year she was withdrawn from the route. The original intention was to give the ship an extensive refit to bring her in line with modern requirements. Shipyard costs had, however, risen dramatically and so the Matson company put her on the sales list.

She was bought in October 1948 by Mediterranean Lines Inc. of Panama, a holding subsidiary of the newly formed Home Lines. An extensive refit followed at the Ansaldo Shipyard, Genoa, and the ship was renamed *Atlantic*. She now catered for three classes of passengers, and in May 1949 made her first Home Line voyage from Genoa and Naples to New York. The service prospered, and the ship was still a popular vessel to travel on. In early 1952 she switched to a service from Southampton to New York via Le Havre, and later to Quebec, or Halifax in winter.

On 23 December 1954 the ship was renamed *Queen Frederica*, after the Queen of Greece. (She was actually registered in Piraeus as the *Vasilissa Freideriki* but was invariably known by the English version of the name.)

On 29 January 1955 the ship commenced a service from Piraeus to New York, and for the next few years she was on transatlantic service, sometimes sailing also to Canada, starting from Cuxhaven or Le Havre.

In November 1965 the *Queen Frederica* was sold to the Chandris Group. Her winter service now was on the Southampton to Australia and New Zealand route via the Cape. During the summer months she voyaged between New York and the Mediterranean; interspersed with some cruising to Bermuda and the Caribbean. Later she served more or less continuously on the Australia and New Zealand run, and also did occasional round-the-world voyaging. The late 1960s and early 1970s found her doing charter cruising, mostly in the Mediterranean, with short periods of lay-up.

In late 1973 this fine vessel, now 46 years old, was laid up for the last time at Perama near Piraeus. Various schemes for further employment came to nought, and scrapping eventually commenced. In February 1978 a fire on board hastened her final demise.

Name: *Malolo* (1927); *Matsonia* (1937); *Atlantic* (1949); *Queen Frederica* (1954)

Line: Matson (1927-48); Home Lines (1948-65); Chandris (1965-73)

Builders: William Cramp & Sons, Philadelphia; launched 26 June 1926, completed May 1927

Dimensions: Gross tonnage 17,232/ Length 582 ft/Beam 83.3 ft

Machinery

Engines: 2 sets steam turbines, single reduction geared, twin screw, 25,000 s.h.p.

Boilers: 12 oil-fired watertube, 280 p.s.i.

Service speed: 20 knots

Major Refits

1948 Ansaldo, Genoa, alteration to accommodation, 20,553 tons
1961 Genoa, improvement to accommodation, 21,329 tons

Regular Routes

San Francisco – Honolulu
Southampton – New York/Quebec
Piraeus – New York
Southampton – Australia, New Zealand

Passenger Capacity

1927: 1st 693
1948: 1st 349, Cabin 203, Tourist 626
1954: 1st 132, Cabin 116, Tourist 931
1961: 1st 174, Tourist 1,005

Sister-ships and near-sisters

Mariposa (1932), *Monterey* (1932), *Lurline* (1933)

Photograph 1952

Ausonia

THIS ship was one of the celebrated Cunard 'A' class built during the 1920s to replace some earlier 'A's lost during the war. The Canadian service was an important one, especially during this time. (see *Ascania*)

The *Ausonia* was launched from Armstrong Whitworth's yard at Newcastle on 22 March 1921, completed by June and sailed on her maiden voyage from Liverpool to Montreal on 31 August. The ship was a very attractive one, as can be seen from the photograph. In general she was very similar to the *Ascania* except for having a separate 'island' bridge. Like all the 'A's, she catered for cabin-class and third-class passengers and had the economical cruising speed of 15 knots.

The ship soon moved to the normal London-Canada route, joining with her sisters *Andania* and *Antonia* sailing from the King George V dock. The route was usually London-Southampton-Quebec-Montreal. Sometimes the ships called at Hamburg, while in winter, when the St Lawrence was frozen, the Canadian terminal was Halifax. The other three 'A's, *Aurania, Ascania,* and *Alaunia,* joined the Cunard fleet in 1924, 1925, and 1925 respectively, and the company now had six excellent ships in service.

In 1927 accommodation became cabin, tourist and third class. At that time *Alaunia, Ascania* and *Andania,* were maintaining a weekly service from London to Quebec and Montreal via Southampton and Cherbourg. That year the *Andania* switched to a Liverpool sailing, and in 1928 the *Aurania* came to London. All six of them could be switched around as desired. The *Ausonia* continued steadily in service without any major mishaps or incidents befalling her during the twenties and thirties. When war came, she was taken over for conversion to an armed merchant cruiser. The 'A's were considered about the right size for this type of duty.

The *Ausonia* was converted for this role on the Tyne, at the yard which was now Vickers-Armstrong's. Here she was given an armament of eight 6-inch guns and a couple of 3-inch AA weapons. As HMS *Ausonia,* she left, after satisfactory trials, for Portsmouth and then Halifax, Nova Scotia. Here she took up her new role as escort for North Atlantic convoys. The ship carried out this dangerous service for the next couple of years. The usual procedure was to escort eastbound convoys to a position south of Iceland. The ship would then refuel at Hvalfjord near Reykjavik before escorting a westbound convoy to Halifax.

She had refits in 1941–2, and also did some patrol work farther south in the Atlantic. The need for AMC's was now diminishing and in June 1942 the Admiralty bought the *Ausonia* from Cunard and converted her at Portsmouth into a repair ship. This took a long time. She was fitted out with engineering workshops which included facilities for machining, fabrication, platework, pipework and electrical repairs. She became a most useful vessel for carrying out most types of repair work. Her big guns were of course removed and she had the defensive armament of twenty 20 mm cannons fitted.

The ship recommissioned in May 1944, and soon sailed east of Suez. She was based for a while at Kilindini near Mombasa, Kenya, and later at Aden and Trincomalee. Her crew were involved in carrying out repairs to various ships and landing craft which had been damaged. She remained in Eastern waters until 1946, when she returned to the UK, arriving back in Greenock on 2 August that year.

For a time HMS *Ausonia* was with the reserve fleet at the Gareloch, then came south to Chatham and Sheerness, and up to Rosyth. She had a refit at Chatham in 1951 lasting until 1954, which included replacing her boilers. The ship was then laid up at Millwall until June 1957, when it was decided that she should replace HMS *Ranpura* as fleet repair ship at Malta. After refurbishment at Devonport, the ship proceeded out to the Mediterranean, arriving in October 1958. She remained here for the rest of her naval service. From June 1962 she was the flagship of the Flag Officer, Mediterranean Flotillas. She also acted as accommodation and repair ship for the 5th Submarine Division.

British forces in Malta were being gradually run down. On 7 August 1964 HMS *Ausonia* left the island for Portsmouth, and in September 1965 she was sold to Spanish breakers and left under tow for Castellon, where she was broken up.

The ship had thus had rather a remarkable career spanning some 43 years. As a repair ship she looked very different from the Cunard passenger liner of pre-war days. She had a vertical funnel and masts with deck cranes and other equipment fitted. Her hull, however, still retained its elegance.

Name: Ausonia

Line: Cunard

Builders: Armstrong Whitworth, Newcastle; launched 22 March 1921, completed June 1921

Dimensions: Gross tonnage 13,912/ Length 538 ft/Beam 65.3 ft

Machinery

Engines: 2 Parsons compound turbines double reduction geared to twin screw shafts, 8,500 s.h.p.

Boilers: 2 double-ended, 2 single-ended cylindrical, 220 p.s.i.

Service speed: 15 knots

Major Refits

1942-44 Portsmouth, conversion to naval repair ship
1951-4 Chatham, replacement of boilers

Regular Routes

London – Southampton – Quebec – Montreal
London – Southampton – Halifax (winter)

Passenger Capacity

Cabin 510, 3rd 1,178

Sister-ships

Andania (1922), *Antonia* (1922), *Aurania* (1924), *Alaunia* (1925), **Ascania** (1925)

Photograph 1933

Avon

Name: Avon; HMS **Avoca** 1916-19

Line: Royal Mail

Builders: Harland & Wolff, Belfast; launched 2 March 1907, completed June 1907

Dimensions: Gross tonnage 11,073/ Length 535 ft/Beam 62.3 ft

Machinery

Engines: 2 quadruple expansion engines, twin screw, 7,000 i.h.p.

Boilers: 3 double-ended, 3 single-ended Scotch-type, 210 p.s.i.

Service speed: 15 knots

Major Refits

1916: conversion to AMC
1919: reconversion to passenger service

Regular Routes

Southampton – river Plate

Passenger Capacity

1st 300, 2nd 140, 3rd 1200

Near-Sister-ships

('A' class) *Aragon* (1905), *Amazon* (1906), *Araguaya* (1906), *Asturias* (1907), **Arlanza** (1912), **Andes** (1913), *Alcantara* (1918), **Almanzora** (1915)

Photograph 1912

DURING the period 1905–1915 nine vessels were built for the Royal Mail's South American Service. These were all known as the 'A' class, and were basically of similar design, although tonnages varied. The *Avon* was the fourth ship of the series, and was in fact the only one of the nine to have an English name. The ship was built at Harland and Wolff's yard at Belfast, and launched on 2 March 1907. Completed in June, she commenced her maiden voyage from Southampton to the river Plate on the 28th of that month.

The ship had an elegant appearance. The hull had good sheer, a straight stem and counter stern. It contained three overall decks, and the superstructure was well proportioned.

She catered for first class, second class and steerage, and accommodation, (especially first class) was good. She had numerous single-berth cabins and suites de luxe; the ornate tastes of the South American clientele were well provided for. The ship also catered for the more modest tastes of seasonal workers and emigrants who travelled from Spain and Portugal to South America. The *Avon* had a large cargo capacity, there being five hatchways. Much of the hold space was refrigerated for the carriage of frozen meat from the Argentine. Hydraulic cranes were used for cargo working. The normal route taken by the service to South America included the following ports: Corunna, Vigo, Oporto, Lisbon, Madeira, St Vincent, Pernambuco, Bahia, Rio de Janeiro, Santos, Montevideo and Buenos Aires. The *Avon* soon become a popular member on the run. There were now five 'A' class on the route, the others being the *Amazon, Araguaya, Aragon* and *Asturias*. It was found, however, that during slack periods they were not all necessary. The *Avon* accordingly went cruising on occasion. Sometimes she sailed from New York to the West Indies, and sometimes she cruised from the UK The Norwegian fjords became a popular venue.

The outbreak of war found the *Avon* homeward bound and she was diverted to Liverpool. Later in August 1914 she found herself taking troops across the Channel to France. The ship kept on this service until early 1915, when it was found that the normal ferry steamers and other small ships could perform this task quite adequately. In early 1916, therefore, she was taken over by the Royal Navy and converted into an Armed Merchant Cruiser. It so happened that there was already a destroyer of the same name, so our subject became HMS *Avoca* for the duration. She was armed with eight 6-inch and two six-pounder anti-aircraft guns. Most of the AMCs were attached to the Tenth Cruiser Squadron, but the *Avoca* was sent out to the Pacific to join the 15th Squadron. She was based at Esquimault, Vancouver Island. The patrol area for this unit was the west coast of the USA and South America as far as Cape Horn. This was a vast area for patrolling, but an important one. German ships were to be found in South American ports, and there was plenty of pro-German feeling.

In mid-1916 while coaling in the Falklands she received orders to go to the Squadron's South American base in Segura Bay, Peru. Here she received orders to proceed at once to Santa Cruz, Mexico, where the Governor had seized all British property and confiscated goods from British-owned shops. The ship proceeded to the Mexican port, arriving on 4 July. An armed party was sent ashore to investigate.

The Governor, who blamed his subordinates for the confiscation, was informed that if the property was not restored to its rightful owners by nine the next morning it would be necessary for HMS *Avoca* to turn her eight-inch guns on the town! The property was quickly restored. A further visit by the ship's party was made and the Governor was thanked for his prompt action. He was informed that in the event of further trouble the British ship would return.

The ship later transferred to escort duty across the Atlantic, which she did successfully without any incidents. She came through the war unscathed, and was released from naval service early in 1919. Guns were removed and, refitted and given her old name *Avon* again, she resumed the river Plate service. The ship sailed on her first post-war voyage on 14 November. Often she was taken off the South American run to go on cruises to the Norwegian fjords and to the Mediterranean. In 1927 she engaged for a short period in a luxury cruise service between New York and Bermuda.

The *Avon* was now more or less a permanent cruise liner and her hull was painted white in 1927, adding further to her elegant appearance. She made some round-Britain cruises in 1928, and again visited the fjords during 1929. This, however, was to be her last year. The world depression was hitting the shipping market, and the *Avon* was laid up at Southampton in September. Sold in early 1930, she went to the breaker, T.W. Ward at Briton Ferry.

Balmoral Castle

THIS elegant vessel was built for the Union Castle's mail service to South Africa. She was constructed at the Fairfield Yard at Glasgow. Launched on 13 November 1909, the ship was completed by February 1910 and soon afterwards sailed on her maiden voyage.

She was a very fine-looking ship. The hull had a straight stem and elegant counter stern. It contained four decks, and the superstructure above was quite low and nicely proportioned. The bridge (promenade) deck and poop deck were combined, unlike those of earlier vessels in the fleet which were separate. Two well-spaced slim funnels on top added to her attraction.

The ship catered for three classes of passengers, first, second and third, accommodation and public rooms being of a good standard. A good cargo capacity was provided by four holds.

The mail ships had developed steadily over the years. The *Balmoral Castle* and her sister *Edinburgh Castle*, built by Harland and Wolff at Belfast, were the latest pair in a successful line which began many years earlier. They exceeded in size the *Walmer Castle*, *Armadale Castle* and *Kenilworth Castle* of 1902–4, but by a comparatively small margin.

The *Balmoral Castle* had the rather special distinction of being the first of the UC mail liners to be fitted with the new-fangled wireless telegraphy equipment. After completing two voyages to South Africa, the ship made three cruises round the Isle of Wight with special guests to demonstrate this: Marconi himself was on board for one of them. Later on during that year it was decided that the Prince and Princess of Wales should go to South Africa to open the first Union Parliament, for the inauguration of the Union of South Africa. However, King Edward VII died and the Prince succeeded to the throne as King George V. The Duke and Duchess of Connaught, together with Princess Patricia, were therefore chosen to go out instead, and the *Balmoral Castle* was selected as their Royal Yacht for the voyage. Special accommodation was arranged on board for the royal guests, and she was given a naval crew, although some of the Union Castle personnel (mostly engineers and stewards) remained. The ship's funnels were painted yellow for the occasion.

HMS *Balmoral Castle* was commanded by Commodore R.E. Wemyss, later to become Admiral of the Fleet Lord Wester Wemyss. She left Portsmouth on 11 October 1910. A fine painting by Norman Wilkinson depicts her leaving the port, sailing past HMS *Victory*, which was then moored in the harbour.

The ship visited the island of St Helena en route, where the Duke invested the Governor with the KCMG

The final stages of the voyage were not without incident. Thick fog enveloped the coast in the vicinity of Cape Town, and apparently a boat was sent ashore to find out where they were! This incident was later denied by the Navy, but the diary of the Commodore makes it clear that the ship had to anchor for a while so that their position could be accurately determined. Fortunately, the fog cleared somewhat and the *Balmoral Castle*, arrived safely at Cape Town on 31 October, receiving a great welcome. The opening of Parliament took place on 6 November, and in due course the ship brought the royal party back to England. The *Balmoral Castle* then reverted to being a Union Castle mailship and resumed her regular voyaging early in 1911.

In August 1914 the *Balmoral Castle* was one of several Union Castle ships assigned to bring troops back from South Africa to the UK Many British soldiers who occupied garrisons there were needed in England and in France. The other ships involved were the *Briton*, *Goorkha*, *Dunluce Castle*, *Kenilworth Castle* and *Guildford Castle*, and altogether they took on board about 4,000 troops with some guns and other equipment. The ships left Cape Town on 27 August in a convoy escorted by the cruisers *Hyacinth* and *Astraea*. Later, South African troops were to be brought over as well, the first batch on board the *Balmoral Castle* in September 1915.

The ship continued, however, on the mail route until 1917, when she was taken up for trooping. She was now mostly engaged in bringing American troops across the Atlantic to the UK, and for this work she was placed under the management of the Cunard Line. In February 1919 the ship made a voyage to Australia with returning troops. Soon afterwards she was back on the normal mail route again. She had come through the war unscathed, although Union Castle had lost no less than eight ships during the conflict.

The *Balmoral Castle* sailed steadily on the mail run throughout the twenties and for most of the thirties. She was a reliable vessel, and retained her popularity even when much bigger and more modern vessels joined the fleet. The *Balmoral Castle* survived until 1938, when she was withdrawn. She would not have been able to manage the extra speed necessary for the 'accelerated' schedules, and she was scrapped in 1939.

Name: Balmoral Castle

Line: Union Castle

Builders: Fairfield Shipbuilding & Engineering Co., Glasgow; launched 13 November 1909, completed February 1910

Dimensions: Gross tonnage 13,361/ Length 590 ft/Beam 64.5 ft

Machinery

Engines: 2 quadruple expansion reciprocating engines, twin screws

Boilers: 6 double-ended, 4 single-ended cylindrical, coal-fired 220 p.s.i.

Service speed: 17 knots

Regular Routes

Southampton – Cape Town

Passenger Capacity

1910: 1st 320, 2nd 220, 3rd 270
1930: 1st 120, 2nd 68, 3rd 200

Sister-ships

Edinburgh Castle (1910)

Photograph 1913

Batory

THE Gdynia-America Line dates from 1930, when three elderly vessels were purchased from the Baltic America Line, for a service to New York via Copenhagen and Halifax. Replacements would be required before many years, and the new company decided to have a couple of much bigger ships built, which would offer markedly better facilities and could be used for cruising as well. This resulted in the *Batory* and her sister *Pilsudski*, each of over 14,000 tons, being ordered.

The *Batory* (named after Stefan Batory, a sixteenth-century Polish King) was launched on 3 July 1935, completed in April 1936 and sailed on her maiden voyage from Gdynia to New York on 18 May. She normally took about 8½ days to complete the voyage from her home port to New York, calling at Copenhagen and often Cherbourg and Halifax, a pleasant, leisurely crossing. In the off season she cruised to the Caribbean, Bermuda etc. The ship was at sea when the Nazis invaded her homeland and reached New York, where she lay for a while. The Polish government in exile decided the ship should be used by Britain and she was put under the control of the Ministry of War Transport and managed by Lamport and Holt.

Having been converted at Halifax for trooping, the *Batory* brought Canadian troops to the UK. After a Mediterranean voyage further conversion work took place on the Clyde. The ship was then involved in the ill-fated Norwegian campaign of May 1940. Other Polish ships taking part in this unfortunate affair included the new 11,000-ton motorships *Chrobry* and *Sobieski*. Unfortunately, the former was sunk by air attack on 15 May with considerable loss of life. However, the *Batory* survived and, together with the *Sobieski* and a number of British ships, succeeded later in evacuating some 15,000 troops from Norway after the campaign had disastrously failed.

After the evacuation from Dunkirk, on 16 June the *Batory*, together with the *Sobieski*, *Georgic*, *Duchess of York* and a few smaller ships, succeeded in bringing home 13,000 troops from the St Nazaire region. On 19 June the two Polish ships, together with the *Ettrick* and *Arandora Star*, once again crossed the Channel. This time many troops were brought back from the Bayonne area, including many Poles. During 1941 she was employed bringing troops across from Canada.

In mid-1942 the ship was fitted out as an LSI(L) She now carried some twenty-two landing craft slung in davits, and could put troops ashore quickly. She played a most useful role in the North African campaign in November, putting troops ashore for the assault on Oran, and was also much involved in the Sicilian landings in July 1943. Hostilities over, the Polish ship spent more time repatriating troops; then in March 1946 she was handed back to her owners.

A complete refit in Antwerp was prolonged owing to a fire on board, but in April 1947 the *Batory* returned to peacetime transatlantic service once more. She sailed on the route Gdynia – Copenhagen – Southampton – New York. In the cold war climate of the time various incidents took place which made it difficult for her to continue in service. Some crew members asked for political asylum from time to time; a convicted spy, Gerhard Eisler, made his escape on the ship, and she lost her popularity with the US authorities. The outcome was that stevedores and shipyard workers refused to handle the vessel. Harbour authorities insisted that she arrived in daylight and be escorted in. The situation became impossible, and in January 1951 the Poles withdrew her from the service.

Under the banner of Polish Ocean Lines she commenced a Far Eastern service to Karachi and Bombay via the Mediterranean and Suez. The ship had to be given a refit to make her suitable for tropical voyaging, and her hull was painted grey. She alternated this with cruising, often from Southampton or Copenhagen, to the Mediterranean, Canary Islands, Norwegian fjords etc.

When the Suez Canal was closed in 1956 the long route round the Cape was not viable for the ship. She commenced voyaging to Canada, since she was not yet welcome in New York. After a big refit at Bremerhaven she became primarily a tourist class ship. Her hull was painted black again, and the service became very popular. The ship sailed mainly on the route Gdynia – Copenhagen – Southampton (and sometimes Tilbury) – Montreal. United States restrictions were later relaxed, and the Polish ship was able to visit such American ports as New Orleans and Boston.

The *Batory* continued to be very usefully employed throughout the fifties and sixties until the spring of 1969 when, now 33 years old, she was retired. The old ship was for a time used as a museum ship/hotel and restaurant at Gdynia. She was sold for breaking up in Hong Kong in 1971.

Name: Batory

Line: Gdynia-America (1936-51); Polish Ocean Lines (1951-71)

Builders: Cantieri Riuniti dell Adriatico, Monfalcone; launched 3 July 1935, completed April 1936

Dimensions: Gross tonnage 14,287/ Length 526 ft/Beam 70 ft

Machinery

Engines: 2 Sulzer 2-stroke 9-cylinder diesel engines, twin screws, 12,000 s.h.p.

Service speed: 18 knots

Major Refits

1939 Halifax and Clyde, conversion for trooping
1942 conversion to LSI(L)
1947 Antwerp, reconversion to passenger liner

Regular Routes

Gdynia – New York
Gdynia – Karachi – Bombay

Passenger Capacity

1936: Tourist 370, 3rd 400
1947: 1st 412, Tourist 420
1957: 1st 76, Tourist 740

Sister-ships

Pilsudski (1935)

Photograph 1948

Begoña

THIS ship started life as a wartime-built 'Victory' ship of a type known as a VC2-S-AP2. Many of these vessels were constructed in US yards. They were faster than the well-known 'Liberty' type, and were very useful ships. Built mainly as cargo-carriers, some were purchased by shipping companies after the war and converted to passenger-carrying. Our subject was one such.

The *Vassar Victory* was built by the Bethlehem-Fairfield shipyard at Baltimore. Launched on 3 May 1945, she was completed by the end of the month. (Construction was very rapid on these wartime-built vessels.) By the time of her completion the war in Europe had ended. The *Vassar Victory* was bought in 1947 by the Sitmar Line of Italy.

As built the hull had a raked stem and cruiser stern. It contained two decks and seven watertight bulkheads. Superstructure above was rather short, and comprised boat, cabin, and bridge decks. These contained the rather austere accommodation.

On taking the ship over the Sitmar company made some improvements to the passenger accommodation. She was renamed *Castelbianco*, and was to be employed transporting displaced persons from the various camps in Europe, and other emigrants, out to start new lives in Australia, Canada and South America. The ship at this stage could take about 480 passengers.

The *Castelbianco* set off on her first voyage from Genoa to Australia with refugees in March 1948. She was under contract to the International Refugee Organisation (IRO) in company with other Sitmar vessels. She voyaged sometimes elsewhere, to Central America, for instance.

In October 1952 she was sent to the shipyard of Cantieri Riuniti dell' Adriatico at Monfalcone for rebuilding. A complete, much larger superstructure was fitted with greatly enhanced passenger accommodation. Now with a more modern funnel, she looked rather as our photograph shows her, though with a white hull. Her name was amended to *Castel Bianco*, as two separate words.

Commencing in the spring of 1953, the ship made regular voyages from Genoa to Central and South America, with occasional visits to Australia. Her running-mate was the *Castel Verde*, also a former Victory ship whose original name was *Wooster Victory*.

In 1957 the *Castel Bianco* was sold to the Compania Transatlantica Española, usually known as the Spanish Line. The ship was given a fairly major refit internally, all her dormitory accommodation being replaced and general improvements made. Her amenities included a swimming-pool. Externally the vessel remained much the same, apart from being repainted with a black hull and funnel, as she appears in our photograph. She was renamed *Begoña*. The *Castel Verde* was also bought by the Spanish company and renamed *Montserrat*.

The *Begoña* ran at first on a service from Italy and Spain to the Canaries, Central America and Cuba. Soon she was put on a Southampton – Spain – Central America route. The *Montserrat* was also on this. A typical itinerary was: Southampton-Corunna-Vigo-Las Palmas-Tenerife-La Guaira-Cartagena-Kingston (Jamaica)-Curaçao-La Guaira-Trinidad-Vigo-with plenty of ports, which varied a little from time to time.

Both the *Begoña* and *Montserrat* were popular vessels and steamed steadily on the route for many years. In 1962 our subject was fitted with air-conditioning.

On 27 September 1974 the *Begoña* sailed from Southampton on her usual voyage, but had to put into Tenerife with engine problems. She was able to continue after repairs but later broke down again and had to be towed into Bridgetown, Barbados. It was soon found that the trouble was too serious for repairs to be a viable proposition. There was no alternative but to sell the ship for scrapping. She went to the breakers at Castellon, Spain, in December that year.

The *Begoña* in fact was the last passenger liner to sail for the once great and well-remembered Spanish company. High fuel costs and air competition had put paid to their operations.

Name: **Vassar Victory** (1945); **Castel Bianco** (1947); **Begoña** (1957)

Line: US Maritime Commission (1945-7); Sitmar (1947-57); Compania Transatlantica Española (1957-74)

Builders: Bethlehem-Fairfield Shipyard, Baltimore; launched 3 May 1945, completed May 1945

Dimensions: Gross tonnage 7,604/Length 455 ft/Beam 62 ft

Machinery

Engines: 1 Westinghouse cross-compound turbine, double reaction geared, single screw, 6,000 s.h.p.

Boilers: 2 oil-fired watertube, 525 p.s.i.

Service speed: 15 knots

Major Refits

1952 Cantieri Riuniti, Monfalcone, larger superstructure, modernized funnel
1957 internal renovation, 10,139 tons

Regular Routes

Genoa – Central and South America
Southampton – Spain – Central America

Passenger Capacity

1947: 480
1952: 1,200
1957: 830

Sister-ships

Wooster Victory (1945) – later *'Montserrat'*

Photograph 1969

Belgenland

THE Red Star Line (officially the Société Anonyme de Navigation Belge-Americaine) was founded in Antwerp in 1873. The original purpose was to transport freight and passengers to Philadelphia, but very soon the Antwerp – New York route became of more importance. Red Star became closely associated with the American Line of 1893, and later was absorbed into the giant International Mercantile Marine Company. The ships were manned on a truly international basis. American, Belgian, British, Scandinavian and German personnel were to be found among the crews. Early Red Star ships were of quite moderate size, but bigger ones began to appear. The *Kroonland* and *Finland* of 1902 were of about 12,000 tons, and the later *Lapland* of 1909 was some 18,000. This latter ship proved so successful on the 'immigrant run' that plans were put in hand for a much larger vessel. Harland and Wolff of Belfast were given the job of building this 27,000 ton ship which forms our subject.

She was launched in December 1914, and bore the inscription *Belgenland, Antwerpen* on her stern. This was a valiant conviction by her owners that she would eventually sail from the great Belgian port, although by this time it was in the hands of the advancing German forces. In fact nine years were to pass before this big ship eventually did sail from Antwerp.

Urgent naval work claimed first attention at Harland & Wolff's yard, and work on the new Red Star ship was slow. However, it was realized that she could be partially completed and sent to sea as a cargo ship as every available vessel was needed. Accordingly in 1917 the ship went to sea as a member of the White Star fleet, though still under I.M.M. ownership. She had been renamed *Belgic* to conform with the standard White Star system of naming, and looked very different indeed from the photograph we show here. She had only a very low superstructure, two funnels and three masts. Dazzle-painted, as were many other vessels at that time, she ran principally on the Liverpool to New York route, often with a call at Halifax. Troop accommodation was fitted in 1918 at New York, and the *Belgic* could now transport about 3,000 Servicemen. After the war ended she spent much time taking Americans back home again. In 1921 the ship was temporarily laid up at Liverpool, but in March 1922 she returned to her Belfast builders to be completed to her original design.

By March 1923 she had been completed, and had sailed for Antwerp. She was still under British registry, with 'Liverpool'

on her stern instead of 'Antwerpen', but she had received back her original name *Belgenland*. By 1923 the immigrant trade from Antwerp had declined considerably. In fact when the *Belgenland* completed her 'maiden' voyage to New York in April that year she carried only about 250 passengers. Other work, obviously, had to be found for such a big ship, and cruising played a big part in her activities over the next few years, in addition to her transatlantic duties. These cruises were very lengthy, often round the world, which involved a voyage of some 28,000 miles, calling at many ports en route. The ship carried only a relatively small number of passengers on these exotic trips, about 400–500.

Belgenland's running-mates on her normal service from Antwerp to New York included the *Lapland* already mentioned and the 11,900 ton *Zeeland*, together with several other ships, all considerably smaller than herself and much cheaper to run.

However, the Depression years were soon to come, and shipping services were seriously affected. Prohibition had also come to the United States, and in the 20s and early 30s the ship undertook some short 'cruises to nowhere' from New York. Americans who could not buy liquor in their own country could get as much as they liked on board this elegant vessel.

As the Depression bit deeper the big ship made fewer voyages on the regular Red Star route Antwerp to New York. These ceased entirely in 1932, and employment was restricted to cruising, with periods of idleness. Late in 1934 came the news that she would be transferred to the American flag; she was to be renamed, refurbished and used on short cruises only. With the addition of two outdoor swimming-pools and a lido deck with real sand, she blossomed forth as the *Columbia*. Sadly, however, the venture was not a success in spite of extensive advertising and publicity. She was laid up and then sold to the breakers in 1936, and was broken up at Bo'ness in Scotland.

Name: ***Belgenland*** (1914); ***Belgic*** (1917); ***Belgenland*** (1923); ***Columbia*** (1935)

Line: (White Star [1917-23]); Red Star (1923-34); Atlantic Transport Co. (1935-6)

Builders: Harland & Wolff, Belfast; completed 1917

Dimensions Gross tonnage 27,132/Length 696.5 ft/Beam 78.4 ft

Machinery

Engines: 2 4-cylinder triple expansion engines for wing propellers, each of 6,000 i.h.p.; 1 low pressure Parsons reaction turbine for central screw, direct drive 6,500 s.h.p. 3 screws

Boilers: 10 double-ended Scotch type boilers, oil fired, 215 p.s.i.

Service speed: 17 knots

Major Refits

1922 Harland & Wolff, completion to original design

Regular Routes

Antwerp – New York

Passenger Capacity

1st 500, 2nd 600, 3rd 1500

Sister-ships

None

Photograph 1928

Berengaria

THE *Berengaria* began life as the *Imperator*, the first of the HAPAG giant liners to be brought on to the transatlantic route of the great German company. The other two were the *Vaterland* and *Bismarck*. Each vessel was a little larger than her earlier sister. Only the *Imperator* and the *Vaterland* actually made voyages under the HAPAG flag.

The *Imperator* was built by the Vulcan Yard at Hamburg. She was launched on 23 May 1912 and completed in April the following year. In May 1913 she took passage down the Elbe to Cuxhaven. She grounded briefly during the journey – not surprisingly, as such a large vessel had never passed down the river before. During her North Sea trials a rather alarming discovery was made. The ship lacked initial stability – or, more bluntly, was top-heavy. She heeled over at the slightest provocation and was slow to return to the upright condition.

The maiden voyage was due to take place soon, but further bad luck occurred. A 'flash fire' was accidentally started by a workman on board, and although damage was not too serious, there were five fatalities. Repair work necessitated a delay, but the big ship set off from Cuxhaven to New York on 10 June 1913 and was cordially greeted at Southampton, Cherbourg and New York as befitted the largest liner in the world. She exceeded the ill-fated *Titanic* and the *Olympic* by about 6,000 tons.

More misfortune struck the ship in September that year while she was docked at Hoboken. Another outbreak of fire occurred; it was quite quickly extinguished, but not before the large amount of water pumped aboard caused the ship to list ominously. Her departure was only delayed about two days, but something had to be done about her stability problems. These were dealt with soon after her return to Germany, during repairs to fire damage. Weighty panelling was replaced by lighter coverings. Canework furniture took the place of much heavier equipment. Much of the marble furnishings went also. Some permanent ballast was added to the ship. The most noticeable effect, however, was the removal of some 9 feet from the tops of each funnel. All these alterations seem to have put the ship right, and from now on she was a steady vessel.

The *Imperator* made her last sailing to New York under HAPAG ownership on 8 July 1914. On her return to Germany she was laid up in Hamburg for the duration of the war.

However, after the Armistice the *Imperator* was once more made ready for sea. She was at first allocated to the United States, and spent the period May to August 1919 as a US Army transport repatriating American servicemen. Placed next under Cunard management, the ship made her first voyage under the company's flag from Liverpool to New York in February 1920. In June that year the British terminal was moved to Southampton. In February 1921 Cunard became the owners of the *Imperator* – or, more correctly, joint owners with White Star of the ship and her sister *Bismarck*. The latter became the *Majestic*, while our subject became very well known as the Cunard *Berengaria*.

The ship left Southampton under this name for the first time on 16 April 1921. She badly needed a refit, but had to wait for this till later in the year. She then had a thorough overhaul by Armstrong Whitworth on the Tyne, which lasted about six months. Much reconditioning and alteration was carried out to her accommodation, and her boilers were converted to burn oil fuel. The refurbished ship left the Tyne and returned in May 1922 to join the *Aquitania* and *Mauretania* on the express service from Southampton to New York. This she carried out for the next 16 years with great regularity, during which time she became a most popular vessel.

During the early 1930s, as passenger volume decreased due to the Depression, the *Berengaria* like other members of the fleet did her share of cruising. This included what were known as 'booze cruises' from New York during the Prohibition era. They were carried out during late autumn, winter and spring, and later in summer as well. Cunard and White Star had combined in 1934, and withdrawals soon took place. By 1935 only the *Majestic*, *Aquitania* and *Berengaria* remained on the service. In May 1936 the splendid *Queen Mary* appeared on the scene.

The *Berengaria* had been troubled by some fairly small outbreaks of fire on board from time to time. One occurred in October 1936 at Southampton, affecting several cabins, and in March 1938 she had a rather more serious one in New York. The US authorities were not satisfied with her as a fire risk and she returned to Southampton without passengers. Cunard had originally intended her to remain in service until the new *Queen Elizabeth* was ready, but it was felt that the expense of putting her to rights for perhaps only a couple of years could not be justified. She was sold for scrapping in November 1938 and went to Jarrow for breaking up, to help relieve unemployment there. Final demolition took place at Rosyth in 1946.

Name: *Imperator* (1919); *Berengaria* (1921)

Line: HAPAG (1913-19); Cunard (1921-38)

Builders: Vulcan, Hamburg; launched 23 May 1912, completed April 1913

Dimensions: Gross tonnage 52,117/ Length 909 ft/Beam 98.1 ft

Machinery

Engines: 4 direct drive AEG-Vulcan turbines, Parsons type. Quadruple screws, 74,000 s.h.p.

Boilers: 46 watertube, 235 p.s.i.

Service speed: 23 knots

Major Refits

1921: Armstrong Whitworth, conversion of boilers to oil fuel
1933 Southampton. Improvement to public rooms and accommodation

Regular Routes

Cuxhaven – New York
Southampton – New York

Passenger Capacity

1913: 1st 908, 2nd 972, 3rd 942, Steerage 1772
1922: 1st 972, 2nd 630, 3rd 606, Tourist 515

Sister-ships

Vaterland (1914), *Bismarck* (1922)

Photograph 1922

Berlin

THE Swedish American Line was a comparative newcomer on the North Atlantic scene. The Company dated from November 1914 and commenced operations a year later, with one ship. Since this happened to be one of the few neutral ships carrying on a transatlantic service in wartime, the Line prospered. It later bought another vessel, secondhand, after the war, and as business was satisfactory, decided to have a brand-new ship built. The 18,000-ton *Gripsholm* took shape at the yard of Armstrong Whitworth and Co Ltd at Walker-on-Tyne.

She was launched on 26 November 1924 and completed the following year. After successful sea trials she proceeded to Gothenburg, receiving a great welcome in the Swedish port – undoubtedly she was the pride of the country's merchant fleet. She sailed on her maiden voyage to New York on 21 November 1925. The *Gripsholm* was to remain on this route for many years, coupled with cruising work, during the 'off' season.

Our photograph shows the ship later in her career, but as built she had a straight stem and two rather slender funnels. The vessel had all the appearance of being a steamship, but was in fact driven by diesel engines. Heating and ventilation on the Thermotank system was provided for all three classes. This was especially important, as the ship operated on a northerly route to New York. Considerable cargo capacity was provided for, with six holds. The forward part of the hull was specially strengthened for working in ice conditions.

The *Gripsholm* soon settled down to regular transatlantic duty, coupled with cruising. She made her first Mediterranean cruise in 1927, and made an annual cruise to South America. The ship was well suited to a cruising role, being economical to run. Her 'running-mates' on the Swedish line's Atlantic service included the 12,000-ton *Stockholm*, the Company's first vessel, and the 11,000-ton *Drottningholm*, which had started life as the Allen liner *Virginian* in 1905. Both of them were steamships. The *Gripsholm* was in fact the first passenger motorship built for transatlantic service. She proved so successful that the company ordered another motorship. The 20,000-ton *Kungsholm*, built in Germany, joined the fleet in 1928.

On the outbreak of war in 1939 the *Gripsholm*, as a neutral ship, still kept up her normal voyaging for a while. However, from 1940 onward she was more and more used on diplomatic and 'mercy' work of various kinds. This included employment by the International Red Cross for exchanging prisoners of war and wounded. She sailed under 'safe passage' arrangements. By this time she had a white hull: a picture depicts her at this time with the words *Diplomat Gripsholm Sverige* painted in large letters amidships, together with the Swedish flag and blue and yellow vertical bands. The ship came through the war unscathed, and was then engaged on repatriation work across the Atlantic, until recommencing her commercial sailings from Gothenburg to New York via Southampton in March 1946.

In 1949–50 the *Gripsholm* had a fairly extensive rebuilding at the Howaldtswerke Company's yard at Kiel. Her external appearance underwent a radical change. She was given a new raked stem, which increased her overall length, and her two slender funnels were replaced by a couple of larger ones. These alterations considerably improved her appearance. Internally considerable improvements were made to passenger and crew accommodation; she was now air-conditioned throughout.

The *Gripsholm* was back on the Gothenburg – New York route in 1950. Later a call at Bremerhaven was added in an attempt to improve tourist traffic. This proved very satisfactory, and became a regular feature. On 18 July 1952 the *Gripsholm* took part in a dramatic sea rescue when she saved 45 men from the burning Norwegian cargo ship *Black Hawk*, some 75 miles from New York.

The next year a new ship, the 22,000-ton *Kungsholm* made her appearance, and the *Gripsholm* was then sold to a new company, the Bremen – America Line, in which both Swedish American and Norddeutscher Lloyd had shares. (Swedish American retained half-ownership of the *Berlin* until 1959.) Initially her name was unchanged on the route Bremerhaven – New York, which she commenced on 1st Feb 1954. She now flew the German flag and was in fact the first passenger ship flying these colours to enter New York for about 14 years. In January 1955 she was renamed *Berlin* and painted in full NDL colours.

The old ship continued on the Bremerhaven – New York route, often via Southampton and/or Halifax. She also continued her cruising role. This went on for a further eleven years, during which time she became the oldest passenger vessel in North Atlantic service. Our photograph, taken in 1960, shows her in the final period of her distinguished career. Remarkably, she still retained her original engines. The *Berlin* made her final Atlantic sailing in September 1966, and in October that year went to the breakers in Italy.

Name: *Gripsholm* (1925), ***Berlin*** (1955)

Line: Swedish American (1925-1954); Bremen-America/NDL (1954-66)

Builders: Armstrong Whitworth, Walker-on-Tyne; launched 26 November 1924, completed 1925

Dimensions: Gross tonnage 17,993/ Length 573 ft/Beam 74.5 ft

Machinery

Engines: 2 Burmeister & Wain 6-cylinder 4-stroke double acting diesel engines, twin screws, 13,500 b.h.p.

Service speed: 16 knots

Major Refits

1950: Howaldtswerke, Kiel, engines overhauled, new generators fitted, new raked stem, funnels enlarged 19,105 tons, 590 × 74.5 ft

Regular Routes

Gothenburg - New York
Bremerhaven – New York

Passenger Capacity

1925: 1st 127, 2nd 482, 3rd 948
1938: Cabin 182, Tourist 494, 3rd 902
1955: 1st 98, Tourist 878

Sister-ships

None

Photograph 1960

Braemar Castle

THIS ship was in fact the last 'intermediate' liner to be built for Donald Currie's Castle Line. Soon afterwards this company and the Union Line amalgamated to form Union Castle. She was constructed by Barclay Curle and Co on the Clyde and completed in 1898, making her maiden voyage that year to South Africa. As can be seen, the ship was an attractive-looking one. The hull had a straight stem and counter stern. It contained two overall decks with a forecastle, bridge and poop above them and a long midships boat deck. She had a nicely raked funnel and four masts. She was, incidentally, the first 'intermediate' steamer to be built without yards on her foremast, it being unlikely that sails would be needed.

The *Braemar Castle* is generally regarded as being the best of the Castle Line's intermediate ships. She became very popular with passengers, and her cargo capacity was useful as well, in particular for carrying bananas from Tenerife and Las Palmas. In 1899 the *Braemar Castle* brought in some 2,000 tons of the fruit to Britain. This was the largest cargo of bananas to arrive on a single ship up to that time.

The merger of Union and Castle Lines in 1900 made little difference to the ship, which continued on the service, although some of the other Castle 'intermediates' were withdrawn. The *Tintagel Castle* and *Avondale Castle* kept running, and the three of them, with the 'G' class vessels, maintained the service from London.

During the Boer War the *Braemar Castle* was involved with a certain amount of trooping work, but, maintained her place on the normal service run. On 7 May 1901 the *Tantallon Castle* ran ashore at Robben Island, north of Cape-Town, in fog. This was in calm weather, and the ship had been going dead slow. The *Braemar Castle*, *Raglan Castle* and *Avondale Castle* were quickly on the scene and made attempts to tow the liner off. They failed to do so, however, and the ship became a total loss. The *Braemar Castle* was also one of those which took some of the *Dunottar Castle's* passengers to the Cape in November 1901. The latter had become disabled when a shaft broke, and had to be eventually towed back to the UK for repair. In January 1902 the *Braemar Castle* herself nearly came to grief when she was stranded on the Isle of Wight. Fortunately, she was refloated after a couple of days.

The ship continued on the service until 1909. By this time she had become a little outclassed by more recent vessels, and now adopted another role, as a troopship. She was given a white hull with blue riband and the yellow funnel of the government's peacetime hired transport service. She was an excellent choice for this duty, and was mainly employed on Far Eastern voyaging, sometimes calling at the Cape. She also made occasional voyages on her former intermediate service as well.

When war came in 1914 the *Braemar Castle* was one of the first transports to take troops to France. She was very actively employed during this year and the next, trooping to France, and also out to the Mediterranean for the ill-fated Gallipoli campaign. In October 1915 she was converted to a hospital ship, and did good work in this humane role, spending most time in the Mediterranean and Near East. Other Union Castle ships serving here included the *Dunluce Castle* and *Gloucester Castle*.

On 23 November 1916, however, she had the misfortune to strike a mine in the Mykoni Channel in the Eastern Mediterranean. Four lives were lost in the explosion, but the ship was successfully beached and temporarily patched. She was then taken to Malta, but the dockyard was so busy with naval work that the vessel had to be repaired at La Spezia, Italy. She then returned to service as a hospital ship and ambulance transport.

She made a trip to Canada in December 1917, and the following year took part in the 'Murmansk Venture'. This was the campaign in North Russia to prevent large quantities of stores and equipment falling into German hands after the Russian surrender. The *Braemar Castle* was the base hospital ship at Murmansk. Her decks were boarded in to provide extra accommodation and to keep out the cold, with the result that she became known as 'Noah's Ark'! Surrounded by ice, the ship lay there for about a year. Each day parties of Russian refugees were set to work breaking up the ice which threatened to 'pinch' the vessel. Some famous people visited the ship, including the great explorer Sir Ernest Shackleton.

As the campaign drew to a close the *Braemar Castle* sailed back to Leith with sick and wounded. The war being over, her career as a hospital ship came to an end, but she continued as a troop-ship, voyaging mostly to India, until June 1920. She made an 'intermediate' sailing to South Africa that year, and then did more trooping to India and China. In 1922 she was involved in carrying troops in connection with the dispute over the new boundaries of Greece and Turkey. In 1924 the *Braemar Castle* completed her last trooping voyage and was sold for scrapping in Italy.

Name: **Braemar Castle**

Line: Castle Line (1898-1900), Union Castle (1900-24)

Builders: Barclay Curle & Co., Glasgow; completed 1898

Dimensions: Gross tonnage 6,266/Length 470 ft/Beam 52.2 ft

Machinery

Engines: quadruple expansion, single screw, 4,400 i.h.p.

Boilers: 4 single-ended cylindrical, coal-fired, 205 p.s.i.

Service speed: 15 knots

Major Refits

1909 conversion to troopship
1916 La Spezia, repair after mine damage

Regular Routes

London – South African ports

Passenger Capacity

1st 60, 2nd 120, Steerage 170

Sister-ships

None

Photograph 1902

Bremen

Name: Bremen

Line: Norddeutscher Lloyd

Builders: A.G. Weser, Bremen; launched August 1928, completed 24 June 1929

Dimensions: Gross tonnage 51,656/ Length 938 ft/Beam 102 ft

Machinery

Engines: 4 sets triple expansion single reduction geared turbines, 4 screws, 130,000 s.h.p.

Boilers: 20 oil-fired water tube boilers, 327 p.s.i.

Service speed: 27 knots

Major Refits

1930 funnels increased in height

Regular Routes

Bremerhaven – New York

Passenger Capacity

1st 800, 2nd 500, Tourist 300, 3rd 600

Sister-ships

Europa (1930)

Photograph 1931

NORDDEUTSCHER LLOYD of Bremen, a company given its charter in 1856, had long been renowned for its fast passenger vessels on the North Atlantic. NDL ships sailed on world-wide services, with the Atlantic Ferry as their premier one. In 1914 the company had no less than 494 ships sailing on 40 routes, but the 1914–18 war virtually obliterated this vast fleet. The rebuilding after the war was a slow process. NDL's one big transatlantic liner of the 1920s was the 32,000-ton *Columbus*, which completed her maiden voyage to New York in 1923. A few years later NDL decided to enter the 'high-speed stakes' once again and to provide two large express liners for the Bremerhaven – New York route. Speeds of 26–27 knots would be necessary for these ships to maintain a six-day schedule and perhaps gain the Blue Riband for Germany. At that time, of course, Cunard and White Star liners virtually dominated the express service, the *Mauretania* being the speed queen. Accordingly plans were put in hand for the *Bremen* and her virtual sister *Europa*. Both names were well known in German shipping history.

The *Bremen* was built at the A.G. Weser Yard in that city. She was launched in August 1928, and completed the following year. As can be seen in the photograph, she was a splendid-looking vessel, giving the impression of immense power. The hull had fine lines with a bulbous forefoot, straight stem moderately raked and fairly pronounced sheer forward. The ship had a modified cruiser-type stern and a Oertz streamlined rudder. Instead of having bilge keels, Frahm anti-rolling tanks were fitted. These were an early attempt to improve passenger comfort, and can be said to have been fairly successful. The topmost, small sports deck contained an interesting innovation – an aircraft catapult complete with a small aircraft.

The *Bremen's* trials took place in the North Sea from 27 June to 6 July 1929, and on 16 July she sailed on her maiden voyage to New York commanded by Captain Leopold Ziegenbein. Things went well, and in spite of a period of reduced speed she beat the westbound record of the *Mauretania* with an average of 27.83 knots. To add to the excitement of those on board, a little float seaplane was catapulted off the ship when she was some 625 miles from New York. About four hours later the plane came down on the Hudson near the NDL pier and landed the mails. A few hours later the big ship arrived to a tumultous reception. Although a novel feature, the catapult installation lacked practical value, being costly to operate. It was removed by 1935.

There were a few teething troubles, however. The original short funnels were not very effective in keeping the smoke clear of the decks, and were increased in height by fifteen feet. Some vibration problems in the after part of the ship were successfully dealt with during a refit in 1933, and in general the *Bremen* continued to run very successfully until the outbreak of war.

During this time NDL had a fine trio of ships on the Atlantic ferry. In addition to the *Bremen* and her sister-ship, the *Columbus* was performing well. Now equipped with turbines, she could manage voyages at 23 knots. This latter ship often went cruising during the winter months, and the *Bremen* sometimes did likewise. In February 1939 she made a cruise right round South America, and in doing so became the largest passenger vessel to pass through the Panama Canal up to that time. She also sailed through the Straits of Magellan.

When the ship sailed from Bremerhaven on 22 August 1939 she carried a large complement of American passengers who wished to return to the United States before hostilities began. On 1 September she slipped out of New York, this time without passengers. Once out in the Atlantic the lights were extinguished and the great ship headed on a north-easterly course to pass near Iceland and round the northern coast of Norway to the Russian port of Murmansk. She arrived there on 6 September and stayed till early December, when she made a dash down the coast, eventually arriving at her home port of Bremerhaven. During this epic voyage she had been sighted on 12 December by the British submarine *Salmon*, which ordered the German liner to stop. She did not do so, and the submarine commander was about to fire a warning shot when he had to dive on the approach of an enemy aircraft. Lieutenant-Commander Beckford then decided he could not torpedo a passenger ship anyway, and so the *Bremen* escaped.

The Germans proposed using both the big express liners for Operation Sealion, the planned invasion of Britain, and both went to Hamburg for this purpose. However, this was never realized, and the *Bremen* returned to Bremerhaven for use as an accommodation ship. On 16–18 March 1941 she was very badly gutted by fire, and partially capsized. The conflagration, which had been deliberately started by a disgruntled crew member, spelt the end of this fine ship. She was damaged beyond repair, and broken up.

Bremen

THE French Company Compagnie de Navigation Sud-Atlantique dated from 1912, and provided a passenger and mail service from Bordeaux to South American ports. In 1936 the Company named a new ship after the famous French scientist Louis Pasteur. Launched in February 1938, she was scheduled for completion by mid-1939. This was not to be, however, as fire broke out on board in March of that year and caused serious damage. The result was that the *Pasteur* was not completed until August, just before the outbreak of war. The new vessel had an impressive, rather powerful-looking appearance. She had nine decks in all, and eleven main bulkheads. The hull had a curved, rounded and flared stem with a cruiser stern. The superstructure was somewhat heaped up forward and topped by an enormous funnel. The ship had considerable cargo capacity, as was usual on the South American route. There were two holds and tween decks forward and rather similar arrangements aft, where there was also garage accommodation for cars. A considerable volume of refrigerated space was available for cargoes of meat and fruit.

War had now broken out, so the *Pasteur*'s maiden voyage was postponed. She was laid up at St Nazaire. However, by June 1940 the fall of France was imminent. The new ship was taken to Brest, and here she loaded French gold reserves and transported the valuable cargo across to Halifax, Nova Scotia. She sailed unescorted, her high speed being a most useful attribute on this occasion.

After the fall of France she was taken over by the British Government as a troop-ship, and was to prove most useful in this role. Now under Cunard White Star management, she was one of the fastest troopers used during the war. About the only ones to exceed her in speed were the two 'Queens'. During the next few years she visited most theatres of war, her speed enabling her to travel in small unescorted convoys.

The ship was much involved in taking troops to the Middle East via the Cape, and was a familiar visitor to ports such as Freetown, Cape Town, Durban, Aden and Suez.

During the latter part of the war the *Pasteur* was almost exclusively on North Atlantic duty, transporting many thousands of troops at high speed. During the entire war she transported about 300,000 personnel and steamed over 370,000 miles. Afterwards, she helped to repatriate American and Canadian troops. Although hostilities in Europe were at an end, the big ship was by no means finished with trooping. The French Government retained the *Pasteur* as a ferry, transporting military and civilian personnel to the French colonies. She was back under Sud Atlantique's management and painted in peacetime colours again, a change from wartime grey. The ship continued on the Far Eastern route for the next ten years, an important if rather mundane task.

By 1956 the Pasteur had become surplus to requirements on the run, and in 1957 she was withdrawn and laid up at Brest. Thoughts now turned to the possibility of using her on the Atlantic ferry, as a running-mate for the *Ile de France*. Nothing came of this, however, and later that year the ship was purchased by the German Norddeutscher Lloyd Company of Bremen.

She received an extensive refit to make her suitable for North Atlantic service, and was now given a famous name *Bremen*. She was a great success from the start, making her first sailing from Bremerhaven to New York via Southampton and Cherbourg in July 1959. She remained on the Atlantic ferry for most of the year, but in the winter months went cruising to warmer climes, usually the Caribbean, becoming very popular in this role.

Air competition was now ousting the large liners from the Atlantic trade. Both Cunard 'Queens' had been retired in the late 1960s and the *Bremen* now spent a great deal of her time cruising, interspersed with some Bremerhaven-New York passages. Machinery problems occured from time to time causing delays. In October 1971 the ship was sold to International Cruises, part of the Chandris (Greek) Group. In 1972 she became the *Regina Magna* after refitting, and was used entirely for cruising.

However, being a large vessel with powerful machinery she was a fuel-hungry ship. With the huge increase in oil fuel prices around this time she soon became uneconomic to run. She was laid up in 1974 at Piraeus and spent the next three years out of work.

In 1977 the once proud liner, now rusting and run down, was again sold, to the Philippine-Singapore Ports Corporation for use in Jeddah, Saudi Arabia as an accommodation ship for workers there. She was renamed *Saudi Phil 1* and later *Saudi Filipinas 1*. The old ship (now in a neglected state) was no longer required by early 1980 and she was sold to breakers in Taiwan. She never reached there, however. While under tow she developed a list in bad weather and finally sank in the Arabian Sea on 9 June 1980, a sad end for what had been a fine ship.

---

*Name: **Pasteur** (1939); **Bremen** (1957); **Regina Magna** (1972); **Saudi Phil I** (1977)*

Line: Compagnie de Navigation Sud-Atlantique (1939-57); Norddeutscher Lloyd (1957-71); International Cruises (Chandris) (1971-7)

Builders: Chantiers et Ateliers de St. Nazaire (Penhoet); launched February 1938, completed 1939

Dimensions: Gross tonnage 29,253/ Length 697 ft/Beam 87.9 ft

Machinery

Engines: 4 sets Parsons triple expansion single reuction geared, quadruple screw, 62,000 s.h.p.

Boilers: 10 Penhoet oil-fired watertube, forced draught, 441 p.s.i., superheated

Service speed: 23 knots

Major Refits

1957 Bremen Vulcan, Vegesack, internal reconstruction, overhaul of machinery, stabilizers fitted, 32,336 tons

Regular Routes

France — Far East
Bremerhaven — New York

Passenger Capacity

1939: 1st 287, 2nd 126, 3rd 338
1959: 1st 216, Tourist 906

Sister-ships

None

Photograph 1959

Bretagne

THIS ship was built for the service of the SGTM (Société Générale de Transports Maritimes à Vapeur) from Mediterranean ports to South America. Constructed by the yard of Chantiers et Ateliers de St Nazaire (Penhoet), she was launched on 20 July 1951 and completed by January 1952. She set off on her maiden voyage from Marseilles to Buenos Aires on 14 February of that year.

As can be seen, the vessel was a good-looking one. The hull had a nicely raked stem, good sheer and a cruiser stern. It contained two overall decks and a shade deck. Upperworks were well proportioned, with an attractive funnel on top. Passenger accommodation was for first, tourist and third class. Public rooms, especially first class, were very elegant, and the ship had all the amenities usually expected, including a swimming-pool. Since there was much emigrant traffic on this route, the third-class numbers were considerable for a 16,000-ton vessel. Some of these were in cabins and some in dormitories. There was good cargo capacity also.

The *Bretagne* made a couple of short cruises before setting off on her maiden voyage. She had a sister ship on the route, the *Provence*, which had been built in 1951 by the Swan Hunter Yard at Newcastle. These two vessels were the largest French liners trading to South America. Ports used included Marseilles, Genoa, Naples, Barcelona, Dakar, Bahia, Rio de Janeiro, Santos, Montevideo and Buenos Aires. Unfortunately, this service initially quite profitable gradually declined. The ships were rather expensive to run, and aircraft were gradually taking most of the passenger traffic.

In November 1960 the *Bretagne* was chartered to D & A Chandris of Piraeus, and had a refit at Genoa. Passenger accommodation was modified to cater for first class and tourist. In May 1961 the ship voyaged on the route from Piraeus to Sydney, and also did some cruising from New York to Nassau and Bermuda for the American-based Caribbean Cruise Lines. This was only for a relatively short time in 1960 and 1961, mostly during the summer period.

In September 1961 Chandris bought the ship outright, and she was now registered at Piraeus for the Europe-Australia Line. On 22 September she sailed from Southampton to Brisbane, and then ran on the Southampton – Sydney service.

In 1962 the ship was renamed *Brittany* but her career was soon to come to an unfortunate end. On 28 March 1963 she went in for engine repairs to the shipyard at Skaramanga. On 8 April there was an outbreak of fire on board which quickly spread. The burning ship was beached next day, but was so badly damaged that scrapping was the only option. She went to the breakers at La Spezia, Italy, in 1964.

Her sister *Provence* was more fortunate. She eventually became the *Enrico C* of the Italian Costa Line, and has had a long and successful career. The SGTM passenger service to South America came to an end in 1962. It had commenced as long ago as 1867.

Name: **Bretagne** (1952); **Brittany** (1962)

Line: SGTM (1952-61); Europe-Australia (1961-64)

Builders: Chantiers et Ateliers de St. Nazaire, Penhoet; launched 20 July 1951, completed January 1952

Dimensions: Gross tonnage 16,335/ Length 581 ft/Beam 73.1 ft

Machinery

Engines: 2 sets Parsons triple expansion turbines, single reduction geared to twin screw shafts, 15,000 s.h.p.

Boilers: 3 Penhoet oil-fired watertube, 570 p.s.i., superheated to 840°F

Service speed: 18 knots

Major Refits

1960 Genoa, modernisation of passenger accommodation

Regular Routes

Marseilles – Buenos Aires
Southampton – Sydney

Passenger Capacity

1952: 1st 149, Tourist 167, 3rd 974
1960: 1st 150, Tourist 1,050

Sister-ships

Provence (1951)

Photograph 1961

Britannic

Name: Britannic

Line: White Star

Builders: Harland & Wolff, Belfast; launched 26 February 1914, completed December 1915

Dimensions: Gross tonnage 48,158/ Length 903 ft/Beam 94 ft

Machinery

Engine: 2 sets 4-cylinder triple expansion, driving wing propellers, steam turbines for central screw, 60,000 total i.h.p.

Boilers: 24 double-ended, 5 single-ended cylindrical, 215 p.s.i.

Service speed: 21 knots

Regular Routes

(never employed in peacetime service)

Passenger Capacity

1st 790, 2nd 830, 3rd 953 (planned)

Near Sister-ships

Olympic (1911), **Titanic** (1912)

Photograph 1916

THIS fine vessel was the third and last of the 'Olympic' class of giant liners. Regrettably, she had a very short life. Like the *Olympic* and *Titanic*, the *Britannic* was built by Harland and Wolff at Belfast. There is some evidence to suggest that originally her name was to have been '*Gigantic*'. The names of the two earlier ships signified 'huge and imposing', and this one was a suitable title for the new giant. However, after the *Titanic* had been tragically lost White Star probably felt a different style of name should be chosen. They selected one which had been used on an earlier ship. The 5,000-ton *Britannic* (1874–1903) had served the company well, holding both westbound and eastbound speed records for a time.

The big vessel was launched on 26 February 1914, and work continued on her when war broke out. In November 1915 the Admiralty decided she would be very suitable for use as a hospital ship, and she was completed as such, being delivered in December that year. She could accommodate about 3,300 casualties.

The *Titanic* disaster had caused much attention to be paid to safety. The double bottom, for example, was extended to some 4 feet above the waterline, and the ship's beam increased by 2 feet. There were sixteen transverse bulkheads, some reaching to 40 feet above the waterline. Like the *Titanic*, her promenade deck was enclosed for part of its length. Externally the most striking difference to that ship was the increased number of lifeboats. The provision of gantry-type davits can be clearly seen, especially around the after funnel. Five sets were fitted to the *Britannic*, three on the starboard side, two on the port. Each set was capable of launching six boats. Also, claimed the patentees, each pair of davits could launch boats from whichever side was preferable, i.e., the port pair could also launch the starboard boats over the port side if the ship was listing to port, and vice-versa. This only applied, of course, if funnels were not in the way! As in the case of the earlier giants, the after funnel was a dummy, serving as an engine-room vent. Due to the various improvements made, the gross tonnage of the *Britannic* was over 48,000, and made her one of the largest vessels afloat at that time.

The new ship carried out brief trials in December 1915, and was commissioned in Liverpool on the 12th of that month. There were many casualties from the ill-fated Gallipoli campaign and from Salonika. The *Britannic*'s first voyage was to Mudros, on the Greek island of Lemnos. She returned from there to Southampton with a full complement of sick and wounded, arriving back on 9 January 1916. Another voyage soon followed, this time to Naples, where wounded were brought out to her from smaller vessels; she returned to Southampton with them in early February. A period of lay-up followed before she was sent out again on mercy work. Temporarily de-requisitioned in May, after a brief refit at Belfast, she was recalled in August. The big ship was proving most useful in this role, and two more voyages to Naples and Mudros followed.

However, when she was passing through the Aegean Sea on her sixth voyage she met disaster. The ship was in the Kea Channel off the Cyclades Islands in the early morning of 21 November 1916 when a great explosion occurred on her starboard side towards the bow. The big ship began to sink. For some reason, probably due to distortion, the watertight door system forward failed to operate and water poured unchecked into five compartments, including the two forward boiler-rooms. The captain altered course in an attempt to beach the ship, but this proved impossible. There were 1,134 persons on board, and lifeboats were swiftly launched. Unfortunately, two were shattered by the ship's propellers, which protruded above the water, still rotating.

Within an hour the great vessel had heeled over to starboard and sunk, going down much more rapidly than the *Titanic* had done. The accepted cause was that she had struck a mine, most probably laid by the submarine minelayer *U-73*. An additional explosion may well have been caused by coal dust igniting, the whole causing great destruction. There was some suggestion that the ship may have been torpedoed, possibly from a shore installation, but no real evidence came to light to support this theory. Twenty-one lives were lost, largely as a result of the smashed lifeboats. (Some sources quote a higher figure, but the British official record of ships lost gives the above.) Lifeboat launching and rescue operations must have been efficient for such a comparatively small loss of life. A distress call had been sent out and soon warships appeared on the scene, including destroyers *Scourge* and *Foxhound* and the armed boarding steamer *Heroic*. One of those rescued, stewardess Violet Jessop, was a survivor from the *Titanic*, and had also been on board the *Olympic* when she was involved in a collision in 1911.

Britannic

AT THE time of entering service the *Britannic* was the largest motorship under the British flag. She was in fact the second largest one in the world, exceeded in size only by the Italian *Augustus*.

The White Star service from Liverpool to New York was maintained in the 1920s by the steamers *Adriatic*, *Baltic*, *Cedric* and *Celtic*, very popular vessels. However, the latter two dated from 1902 and the others were not much younger. Replacements were necessary, and the *Britannic* was ordered as the first of these, followed some two years later by a sister ship, the *Georgic*. Both were to be used for cruising as well. Sea trials were successfully completed and the *Britannic*'s maiden voyage, which included calls at Belfast and Glasgow, passed off satisfactorily. High speed was not required since this was not an 'express' service, but she could comfortably manage 18 knots with a bit in reserve. The ship continued in regular service, with the three steamers *Baltic*, *Cedric* and *Adriatic*. During the slack winter seasons she usually cruised to the West Indies.

In June 1932 her sister *Georgic* joined her on the route. There were now two modern motorships running. The *Cedric* had been sold for scrapping at the end of 1931, after a long and distinguished career. The *Baltic* went the same way in February 1933. The two new ships and the *Adriatic* continued the service and all three went cruising in the winter. In 1934 the White Star Line merged with Cunard to form Cunard-White Star. The *Adriatic* was sold in November 1934 and the two motorships then shared the Liverpool service with the Cunarders.

In 1935 they were transferred to a new London-New York service with calls at Southampton and Le Havre. This meant they were the largest liners to come up the Thames at that time. The ships continued on this route until the outbreak of war. The *Britannic* was requisitioned as a troopship in late August 1939, like many other vessels. At first she was able to carry about 3,000 troops, but this was later increased to 5,000.

In September 1939 the ship sailed to Bombay, returning with various British personnel. Her war service was very considerable, and she was to be found in many theatres. Among other things, she was much involved in bringing American troops across for the invasion of Sicily. Probably her most important work was transatlantic duty, bringing troops across to the UK and Europe. In 1944, for instance, she transported about 20,000 men. By the end of the war she had carried some 180,000 personnel and motored 367,000 miles.

After the war ended the *Britannic* was engaged in repatriation work, and in March 1947 was released from government service. The ship now went back to Harland and Wolff's yard at Liverpool, where she was given a complete refit. The accommodation for passengers and crew was almost completely rebuilt. However, in general the old ship looked very much as she had done when first coming into service. The *Britannic* again sailed from Liverpool on her original route to New York, and went cruising as well. She now catered for first class and tourist and was still painted in the colours of the old White Star line. This was a nice touch, as by 1947 the name of the former great company had virtually disappeared from the shipping scene.

She left Liverpool on her first post-war voyage to New York via Cobh on 22 May 1948. She was to continue this route again for more than ten years, although her winter cruising became an important revenue-earning feature. A mishap befell her on 1 June 1950 when she collided with the 8,000-ton American cargo ship *Pioneer Land* in the Ambrose Channel, fortunately without much damage. In January 1953 and again in 1955 she carried out lengthy Mediterranean cruises each lasting nearly two months.

By the late fifties her machinery began to give trouble. She still had the original air-injection diesel engines which were now very outdated. It speaks well for their design and construction that they had served her so well throughout her long career.

Now thirty years of age, the old ship completed her last voyage when she arrived in Liverpool from New York on 4 December 1960. She was withdrawn, and sold to breakers at Inverkeithing.

Name: Britannic

Line: White Star later Cunard-White Star

Builders: Harland & Wolff, Belfast; launched 6 August 1929, completed May 1930

Dimensions: Gross tonnage 26,943/ Length 712 ft/Beam 82.3 ft

Machinery

Engines: 2 Harland/B & W 10-cylinder 4-stroke double-acting air injection diesel, each 10,000 s.h.p., twin screws

Service speed: 18 knots

Major Refits

1947 Harland & Wolff, rebuilding of accommodation, plating in of well deck, 27,778 tons

Regular Routes

Liverpool – New York
London – New York

Passenger Capacity

1930: Cabin 504, Tourist 551, 3rd 498
1947: 1st 429, Tourist 564
1960: 1st 369, Tourist 608

Sister-ships

Georgic (1932)

Photograph 1935

Canberra

BY THE mid-1950s P & O had decided that larger, faster vessels were needed for their Australian service. The construction of two new ships, the *Canberra* and *Oriana*, would also enable them to provide a Pacific service.

The *Canberra* was launched by Dame Pattie Menzies, the wife of the Australian Prime Minister, on 16 March 1960, and set off on her maiden voyage from Southampton to Australia on 2 June 1961. Her design was quite different from any previous P & O vessel; she was the first passenger ship of her size to have engines aft. Her first voyage was a success. From Sydney she proceeded to Auckland, Honolulu, Vancouver, San Francisco and Los Angeles, before returning to Southampton via Suez. On her fourth voyage, however, problems with boilers forced her to cut short her trip and return home via the Panama Canal, the first time she had done so. A refit at Southampton cured the problem; at this time her funnels were heightened to improve smoke-dissipation, and stability was improved by adding ballast. The *Canberra* then visited New York several times, before resuming her Australia/Pacific sailings.

When outward-bound in the Mediterranean in January 1963, about 150 miles from Malta, there was an explosion and fire on board which severely damaged the main switchboard. It resulted in all power being lost and the main engines put out of action. The ship drifted helplessly for a time, while the company's *Stratheden* which happened to be in the vicinity stood by. Eventually some power was restored and the *Canberra* managed to reach Malta. The passengers were flown to Australia and New Zealand, while the ship sailed back on one engine to Belfast for repairs. The accident was caused by a circuit-breaker switch being thrown by mistake.

Once back in service, the ship continued on the Australian route with interludes of cruising. In 1966 she was stranded in Southampton during the seamen's strike, which caused many cruises to be cancelled. In 1967 the Suez Canal was closed as a result of the Egyptian–Israeli war, and remained so for eight years. The *Canberra* was on a Mediterranean passage at the time, and shortly due to enter the Canal. A message was received ordering her to turn back and proceed via the Cape. She thus narrowly escaped the fate of other vessels which were trapped in the waterway for some years.

The number of line voyages between the UK and Australia now declined considerably, as air travel took over. Pacific services were also affected. The necessity to travel via the Cape had of course added days to the passage-time and contributed to the decline in number of passengers. At the end of 1972 the *Canberra* was withdrawn from the route.

In 1973 both the *Canberra* and her sister the *Oriana* were converted to one-class ships for all-year-round cruising. (One disadvantage of the *Canberra* is her considerable draught of some 35 feet, which precludes her from berthing alongside a quay in some ports.) Based at Southampton, she sailed mainly on two- or three-week cruises. In 1974 she went on a successful world-cruise, which has since become an annual event.

After returning from a world trip in 1982, the vessel was taken over by the British Government for use as a troop-ship in the Falklands campaign. She was quickly fitted out at Southampton to carry a large number of troops. Helicopter pads were built over the swimming-pools, operating theatres and wards were set up on board and numerous other essential alterations were made. She sailed for the Falklands on the evening of Good Friday, with some 2,000 men of the Parachute Regiment and Royal Marine Commandos on board. She reached Ascension Island on 20 April, after a refuelling stop at Freetown. It was decided to sail her to San Carlos Bay in the East Falklands – a big risk for such a large ship, as she had only a few anti-aircraft weapons on board. Anchoring in the bay, she swiftly landed troops who were able to establish a bridgehead. She was soon under air attack. After taking on casualties, she moved to a rendezvous with the *Queen Elizabeth 2* at the island of South Georgia. The *Canberra* embarked troops from the Cunard ship and headed back to the Falklands to land them. After the Argentine surrender on 14 June, she returned thousands of prisoners to the mainland under an escort of Argentine warships. On her return to Southampton she underwent much renovation work, before setting sail once more on a cruise on 11 September 1982.

In January 1987 the *Canberra* rescued a round-the-world yachtsman and his family who had taken to a life-raft after their yacht sank off the coast of Mexico. Her sister ship the *Oriana* was retired in 1986, so she remains the last survivor of the P & O mail fleet.

Name: **Canberra**

Line: P & O

Builders: Harland & Wolff, Belfast; launched 16 March 1960, completed May 1961

Dimensions: Gross tonnage 45,270/ Length 820 ft/Beam 102 ft

Machinery

Engines: 2 1500 KW turbo-alternators supplying current for 2 6,000 volt propulsion motors, 85,000 total s.h.p.

Boilers: 3 Foster-Wheeler watertube fitted with external superheaters, forced draught, 750 p.s.i. superheated to 950°F; 1 auxiliary boiler

Service speed: 25 knots

Major Refits

1962 Southampton, funnels heightened, boilers renovated
1986-7 Bremerhaven, accommodation improvements

Regular Routes

Southampton – Sydney

Passenger Capacity

1961: 1st 596, Tourist 1,616
Cruising: 1,737 one class

Sister-ships

None but **Oriana** (1960) of similar size

Photograph 1960

Capetown Castle

THE Union Castle company had to undertake a considerable rebuilding programme in the mid-1930s to enable the speeding up of the South African mail service to take place. In addition, some of the existing fleet had to be re-engined and in some cases lengthened to achieve the required speed. The *Athlone Castle* and *Stirling Castle* were the first two new ships to be built in anticipation of the new higher speed requirement, and our subject followed a couple of years later. The mail contract signed in 1936 required the voyage to Cape Town to be completed in 14 days. This was to apply from December 1938.

The *Capetown Castle* was built by Harland and Wolff, Belfast. She was launched on 23 September 1937, completed in April the following year, and in fact sailed on her maiden voyage from Southampton to Cape Town on the 29th of that month. On this route the transport of fruit was most important, together with wool, hides, and of course the mail. From Britain a great variety of goods were shipped out; heavy machinery, tractors and suchlike usually figured prominently. The ship's maiden voyage passed off successfully, and she was to become a very useful member of the fleet. The Cape Run sometimes included calls at Ascension Island, St Helena and Walvis Bay. She was now the Union Castle flagship.

The outbreak of war in September 1939 found the *Capetown Castle* en route to Durban. She remained on the mail run for a while, but was soon taken over as a troop-ship, proving invaluable in this role, as were several other Union Castle ships. She often voyaged in convoys on her old route to South Africa and up the east coast. She went to many a port never visited by Union Castle ships before. A lengthy voyage took place in late 1942: the ship was in Bombay when ordered to Suez to pick up some German POWs. She then voyaged down the east coast to Durban and Cape Town. Due to the presence of U-boats, the big ship then proceeded across the South Atlantic and up the west coast of South America to Panama, thence through the Canal, up to New York and across the Atlantic once again to the UK. In company with the *Athlone Castle* and *Stirling Castle*, much of her trooping time was in fact across the Atlantic with American troops. Towards the end of the war she repatriated South African troops from Egypt. During her war service she had steamed around 484,000 miles and transported over 164,000 personnel, in addition to much useful cargo.

The *Capetown Castle* was now released from government duty and went to Harland and Wolff, Belfast, for a much-needed refit. Many of her valuable fittings had been removed when she was converted to a troop-ship, and these were now replaced. Modifications were carried out to passenger accommodation, and machinery given a thorough overhaul.

The ship made her first post-war sailing from Southampton to the Cape on 9 January 1947. Now followed a long period on this run, on which she again became a very popular vessel. The steamers *Pretoria Castle* and *Edinburgh Castle* had joined the fleet in 1948. These were somewhat larger than the *Capetown*, and she lost her title as flagship. The voyage time to the Cape had now been reduced to 13½ days.

The ship's accident-free service was marred on 17 October 1960 when a serious engine-room explosion resulted in seven crew deaths. This occurred in the compressed-air starting system when the ship was near Las Palmas. She was out of service for one voyage while repairs were carried out, her place taken by the intermediate vessel *Braemar Castle*.

The *Capetown Castle* hit the headlines in early 1965 when twenty gold ingots to the value of £100,000 disappeared from a temporary strong-room on board. However, these were recovered at the end of her next voyage when they were found still on the ship, cunningly cemented away in a secret place. Two crew members were convicted of the theft.

The new mail contract, to come into force in 1966, would reduce the voyage time to 11½ days. Seven ships only would be required instead of eight. Two new ships would be ordered, but these would be high-speed cargo vessels. They eventually blossomed forth as the *Southampton Castle* and *Good Hope Castle*.

The *Capetown Castle*'s near-sisters *Athlone Castle* and *Stirling Castle* went to the breakers in 1965 and 1966 after long and honourable careers. The *Capetown Castle* too was nearing the end of her fine service. She would not be speedy enough for the accelerated contract. However, from 1965 she did some one-class extra voyages to the Cape after a short refit. These involved calls at Madeira and the Atlantic Islands if required. This programme lasted for a couple of years, but in 1967 the old ship was withdrawn and sold for breaking up in Italy, where she arrived in September. Throughout her 29 years she remained one of the biggest motor passenger liners afloat.

Name: Capetown Castle

Line: Union Castle

Builders: Harland & Wolff, Belfast; launched 23 September 1937, completed April 1938

Dimensions Gross tonnage 27,002/Length 734 ft/Beam 82.5 ft

Machinery

Engines: 2 Harland/B & W 10-cylinder double acting 2-stroke cycle oil engines, twin screw, 28,000 b.h.p.

Service speed: 20 knots

Major Refits

1946 Harland & Wolff, reconversion to passenger liner

Regular Routes

Southampton – Cape Town, and South African ports

Passenger Capacity

1938: 1st 292, Cabin 500
1947: 1st 250, Tourist 550

Near-Sister-ships

Athlone Castle (1936), *Stirling Castle* (1936)

Photograph 1958

Cap Polonio

Name: Vineta (1915), **Cap Polonio** (1915)

Line: Hamburg-South America (1915-19); Union Castle (1919); P & O (1919); Hamburg-South America (1921-35)

Builders: Blohm & Voss, Hamburg; launched 25 March 1914, completed August 1916

Dimensions: Gross tonnage 20,576/ Length 662 ft/Beam 72.5 ft

Machinery

Engines: 2 sets 4-cylinder triple expansion driving wing propellers, exhaust steam turbines for central screw, 20,000 i.h.p.

Boilers: 14 watertube

Service speed: 18 knots

Major Refits

1921 Hamburg, conversion to oil-firing

Regular Routes

Hamburg – river Plate

Passenger Capacity

1st 356, 2nd 256, 3rd 100, Steerage 850

Sister-ships

None

Photograph 1919 (in P & O colours)

THE trade to South America had built up steadily in the years preceding the First World War. British and European companies vied with each other on this rather lucrative route, and ships steadily increased in size.

The 20,000-ton *Cap Polonio* was ordered for the Hamburg–South America Line from the Blohm and Voss yard at Hamburg. She was launched on 25 March 1914. However, the new ship was not to be completed as a passenger liner for some time. Fitting out was temporarily suspended due to the outbreak of war. In December 1914 work started to convert her to an armed merchant cruiser. It was felt at the time that she would be useful in this role, and in early February 1915 she blossomed forth as the armed raider *Vineta*. She had two funnels only in this guise, being minus the after, dummy one. The ship was armed with four 5.9-inch guns and four of 4.1-inch calibre. She did not prove successful, however. Trials carried out were unsatisfactory, there being problems with the boilers, and speed was not up to naval requirements, being only about 17 knots. She was rejected, and returned to the Hamburg company. Now with her name again *Cap Polonio*, she was completed, but then laid up for the duration of the war at Hamburg. The ship was a fine-looking vessel indeed. The hull with its straight stem, good sheer and elegant counter stern had well-proportioned superstructure and three nicely spaced funnels atop. There were six decks, three of them full-length, and eleven main bulkheads. The hull was given bulges each side to improve stability. Cargo capacity was considerable there being five holds and hatchways.

After the defeat of Germany the ship was one of those surrendered to the Allied Shipping Commission. First she was allocated to the United States, but shortly afterwards passed to the Shipping Controller, London. Union Castle were appointed managers, and the big German ship was dispatched on the Cape Run, after an overhaul. This voyage was something of a disaster; it seems that the Germans had found some means of sabotaging her machinery while she was in Hamburg. The ship sailed on 21 June 1919 from Plymouth for Cape Town and Durban, painted in Union Castle colours with a large complement of passengers and returning South African troops. She eventually reached Cape Town on 18 July having had a number of breakdowns en route and achieved a maximum speed of 12 knots. The continuation to Durban was abandoned, while some attempt was made to make some machinery adjustments.

These do not appear to have been very successful. Despite her sluggishness, she was one of the most luxurious vessels to have visited Cape Town, and plenty of passengers were forthcoming for her return trip to the UK. This proved to be a long, slow voyage, the machinery behaving in much the same manner as on the outward run.

Union Castle lost interest in the ship, and after a refit at Devonport Dockyard the *Cap Polonio* came under P & O management. However, her performance did not improve. She made one return voyage to Bombay, and was beset by similar problems to those which occurred on the Union Castle run. P & O soon discarded her, and she was then laid up at Liverpool. In 1921 the ship was sold back to her original German owners, and in July that year sailed for Hamburg.

Now followed a lengthy refit lasting about seven months. She was thoroughly overhauled, and converted to oil-firing. In February 1922 the *Cap Polonio* at last sailed on the route she had been intended for, from Hamburg to the river Plate. She was now capable of her designed speed of 18–19 knots, and was without doubt the most luxurious vessel on the route. This meant that it was not economical to keep her on the route all the year round, and she was used on cruising work from the Plate during the off-season. These cruises took her to various places, as far south as Tierra del Fuego and as far north as the Baltic.

Meanwhile in 1924 the 13,700-ton *Monte Sarmiento* entered the service, followed next year by her sister *Monte Olivia*. These two were motorships and cheaper to run, though slower. However, a larger vessel was also ordered to provide real luxury on the route. This was the 27,500-ton *Cap Arcona*, which was to be the running-mate for our subject. She entered service in November 1927, and rather eclipsed the *Cap Polonio*. She was turbine-powered, with twin screws, and about a knot faster. Soon after this the economic slump started to take effect. Both ships continued in operation, and in 1931 the *Cap Polonio* was given an extensive overhaul at Hamburg to bring her closer to the standard of the newer ship. Later that year, however, she was laid up. In September 1933 she was adapted for use as an exhibition ship at Hamburg. This was to be her last useful role. Various schemes such as use as a floating hostel failed to materialize, and this fine vessel was sold for scrapping in June 1935 and broken up at Bremerhaven.

Carinthia

THIS ship started life as one of Cunard's quartet built for the Canadian service. She was launched from John Brown's Clydebank yard on 14 December 1955, completed by June 1956 and set off on her maiden voyage from Liverpool to Montreal on the 27 of that month. All four ships, the others being the *Saxonia*, *Sylvania* and *Ivernia*, were very similar in design and appearance. Like the others, she steamed steadily to and fro on the Liverpool–Montreal route, switching to New York in the winter months when the St Lawrence river was frozen.

With her sister *Sylvania*, the *Carinthia* continued to be based at Liverpool when the *Saxonia* and *Ivernia* transferred to Southampton in 1957. The Canadian service, initially quite successful, began to suffer from lack of passengers as more people took to the air. By 1962 the *Carinthia* was the only one of the quartet remaining on the Liverpool–Montreal route, the *Sylvania* being now on the New York service. By 1967, now painted white, she was used for cruising only. The last Cunard passenger sailing to Montreal took place that year, and the *Carinthia* transferred to Southampton. In October Cunard announced that the *Carinthia* and *Sylvania* would be withdrawn, and they were both laid up at Southampton. Unlike their two sisters, they had not had extensive refits to make them more suitable for cruising. They remained laid up, and in February 1968 both were sold to the Italian Sitmar company.

During her Canadian service the *Carinthia*, had been reliable but had had a few fairly minor problems. In April 1959 she suffered propeller damage when striking ice in the St Lawrence, and the following year there were a couple of small fires on board, soon put out. In 1960 the ship was chartered by the Canadian government to make a few trooping voyages. This no doubt provided Cunard with some useful revenue. In August 1961 the ship collided in fog with the Canadian 7,000-ton ship *Tadoussac* in the lower St Lawrence, fortunately without serious damage to either of them. There were also problems from time to time with striking crewmen and shipyard workers. A strike by the latter group in 1961 delayed her annual overhaul. In April 1966 the ship was struck by a freak wave and eighty passengers were injured.

Although Sitmar had purchased the two Cunarders, they still continued to be laid up at Southampton. The *Carinthia* had been renamed *Fairland* and her sister *Fairwind*, both typical Sitmar names.

In January 1970 both ships sailed for Trieste to be converted to cruise liners. This reconstruction changed them beyond recognition. The *Fairland* (ex-*Carinthia*) was once more renamed, and became the *Fairsea*. She commenced service for Sitmar in November 1971. The ship now had a considerably different profile from that of our photograph: the upper decks had been entirely reconstructed, and a modern streamlined funnel replaced the Cunard round-topped one. There were now lido areas and three outdoor swimming pools. Modern cabin accommodation was provided for just over 900 cruise passengers, and facilities included closed-circuit television, a sauna and a gymnasium. The *Fairsea* now proceeded to America's west coast. Initially based at Los Angeles, she cruised to Mexico, and also operated summer cruises to Alaska from San Francisco, a favourite route for Americans.

After operating these cruises for over a decade the *Fairsea* was replaced on the routes by the brand-new 38,000-ton *Fairsky*. She now introduced cruises through the Panama Canal from Los Angeles to Curaçao during the winter months, while still doing some Mexican ones in summer-time. In 1984 the ship was further updated by having her public rooms along the promenade deck rebuilt and cabins refurbished. In July 1986 she again began Alaskan cruises, this time sailing from Seattle.

In October 1988 the *Fairsea* went into the Pacific, cruising from Los Angeles to Tahiti and on to Australia and New Zealand waters. She was at this time undertaking over thirty cruises of various sorts a year.

In 1988 P & O acquired Sitmar Cruises. The purchase included four vessels, the *Fairwind* (ex *Sylvania*), *Fairsky*, *Fairstar* (ex-troopship *Oxfordshire*) and the *Fairsea*. Now renamed *Fair Princess*, she sails under the Princess Cruises banner. In 1990 her cruises usually took her to the Mexican coast, again from Los Angeles. She is now Liberian-registered, is fully air-conditioned and stabilized.

Name: **Carinthia** (1956); **Fairland** (1968); **Fairsea** (1971); **Fair Princess** (1988)

Line: Cunard (1956-68); Sitmar (1968-88); P & O (1988-)

Builders: John Brown & Co., Clydebank; launched 14 December 1955, completed June 1956

Dimensions: Gross tonnage 21,947/ Length 608 ft/Beam 80.4 ft

Machinery

Engines: 4 Parsons turbines double reduction geared, twin screw, 24,500 s.h.p.

Boilers: 4 oil-fired watertube, 550 p.s.i.

Service speed: 20 knots

Major Refits

1970 Trieste, new funnel, reconstruction of superstructure

Regular Routes

Liverpool – Montreal
Liverpool – New York

Passenger Capacity

1956: 1st 154, Tourist 714
1990: 925 one class

Sister-ships

Carmania (1954); **Ivernia** (1955); **Sylvania** (1957)

Photograph 1957

Carisbrook Castle

Name: Carisbrook Castle

Line: Castle (1898-1900); Union Castle (1900-22)

Builders: Fairfield Shipbuilding & Engineering Co., Glasgow; completed 1898

Dimensions: Gross tonnage 7,626/Length 485 ft/Beam 56 ft

Machinery

Engines: 4-cylinder quadruple expansion, 8,500 i.h.p., single screw

Boilers: 3 single-ended, 3 double-ended Scotch boilers, 180 p.s.i.

Service speed: 16 knots

Major Refits

1914 conversion to hospital ship

Regular Routes

Southampton – Cape Town
London – Durban via Suez

Passenger Capacity

1st 250, 2nd 140, (3rd unknown)

Sister-ships

None

Photograph 1919

DURING the latter part of the nineteenth century there was considerable rivalry between two of the major companies operating services to South Africa, the Union Line and Donald Currie's Castle Line. (They eventually combined to form Union Castle, but in the 1890s were still separate concerns.) The Union liner *Scot* of 1891 had decisively proved herself to be faster than any of the 'Castles', but was very costly to operate. The later Union ships *Briton* and *Norman* were slower than the *Scot* but much cheaper to run. Likewise, when the *Carisbrook Castle* appeared on the scene in 1898 she had not been designed for high speed. In retrospect she can best be described as an intermediary between earlier ships and the later, bigger mailships such as the *Edinburgh Castle* and *Balmoral Castle*.

This 7,600-ton vessel was built on the Clyde at the Fairfield Yard. She was undoubtedly a fine-looking ship, as can be seen in the photograph. The hull had a straight stem, elegant counter stern and a nice sheer. The ship had a long forecastle and poop, three masts and a largish, well-proportioned funnel. These were two complete decks, with an extensive sheltered promenade one below the boat deck. Accommodation was of a good standard, although by all accounts rather inferior to that of her Union Line contemporaries.

For the first time in the Castle fleet the first-class passengers, some 250, were housed amidships. About 140 second class were carried aft, whilst the third class were accommodated forward. The ship also had a fair cargo capacity, with four hatches. She was in fact the last single-screw mailship built for the Castle line. Although not as fast as the celebrated *Scot*, she had the very respectable service speed for a 'Cape boat' of 16 knots, with a knot or two in reserve if required.

The ship commenced her career fairly quietly and settled down to give reliable if unspectacular service. Apparently she acquired the reputation of being something of a 'roller' in rough weather, a not unusual characteristic of many ships. In April 1899 she completed a voyage from Cape Town to Southampton in 14 days 17 hours 3 minutes, which put her second only to the *Scot* in speed.

As often happens in the competitive shipping world, the *Carisbrook Castle* was very soon overshadowed by more up-to-date tonnage. Two twin-screw ships came into service in 1899 and others followed, but the *Carisbrook* continued on the long Cape run. The outbreak of the Boer War that year did not seriously affect the mail service, although a number of vessels of both Union and Castle fleets were taken over as troopers and hospital ships. The *Carisbrook Castle* continued on her normal route during this time.

By the time the war ended in 1902 the Union and Castle companies had combined to form Union Castle. The new company became very successful and well respected on the 'Cape Run'. In 1910 the advent of the bigger ships *Balmoral Castle* and *Edinburgh Castle* meant that the *Carisbrook Castle* was removed from the mail run and placed on the East African service between London and Durban via Suez. She remained on this popular route until 1914. In that year two ships specially designed for this run came into operation, the 10,600 ton *Llandovery Castle* and her near-sister *Llanstephan Castle*. The *Carisbrook* was thus redundant, but not for long. The outbreak of war meant she was taken over for use as a hospital ship. She transported sick and wounded men across the Channel and also spent much time in the Mediterranean in 1915 and 1916. Among other duties she transported a Canadian Field Hospital from Alexandra to Salonica. She also took wounded from Mudros to the Egyptian port during the ill-fated Dardanelles campaign. For some time she ran a 'ferry' service between Malta and Salonica. When peace was declared the *Carisbrook Castle* was loading wounded soldiers at Le Havre. She came through unscathed, and was luckier in this respect than several other of the Company's vessels. The *Glenart Castle*, *Dover Castle* and the above-mentioned *Llandovery Castle* were all sunk by German U-boats whilst doing duty as hospital ships. Our photograph shows the *Carisbrook Castle* in her wartime role.

In 1919 she again did duty for a while as an ambulance transport in the Mediterranean, and in August of that year returned to Union Castle. She was of course by now completely outclassed as a mail ship, but still retained her useful turn of speed. The mail fleet was depleted owing to wartime requirements and ship losses, so the old ship ran for a time on her original route. The big ships *Arundel Castle* and *Windsor Castle* appeared on the scene in 1921–2 and the *Carisbrook Castle* left the mail fleet for good. After a further short period on the East African service she was withdrawn, and went for scrap in 1922.

Carmania

Name: *Saxonia* (1954); ***Carmania***
(1962); ***Leonid Sobinov*** (1973)

Line: Cunard (1954-73) Black Sea
Shipping Co (USSR) (1973-90)

Builders: John Brown & Co., Clydebank;
launched 17 February 1954, completed
August 1954

Dimensions: Gross tonnage 21,637/
Length 608.3 ft/Beam 80.3 ft

Machinery

Engines: 4 Parsons turbines double
reduction geared, twin screw, 24,500
s.h.p.

Boilers: 4 watertube, 550 p.s.i.

Service speed: 20 knots

Major Refits

1962-3 John Brown, conversion to cruise
ship, 22,592 tons

Regular Routes

Liverpool – Montreal
Rotterdam – Southampton – Quebec –
Montreal

Passenger Capacity

1954: 1st 125, Tourist 800
1963: 1st 117, Tourist 764

Sister-ships

Ivernia (1955), ***Carinthia*** (1956),
Sylvania (1957)

Photograph 1965

THE passenger/cargo service to Canada from Liverpool had always been important to Cunard. After the Second World War it was maintained by four rather elderly vessels, the *Ascania, Franconia, Samaria,* and *Scythia.* These 20,000-ton ships dated from 1925, 1923, 1922, and 1921 respectively. However, they were now nearing the end of their economic life, and the company decided to build four ships to replace them. These were to be named *Saxonia, Ivernia, Carinthia,* and *Sylvania* and all were built at John Brown's Clydebank yard. They were all in service by 1957.

The *Saxonia* was completed first. Launched on 17 February 1954 by Lady Winston Churchill, wife of the Prime Minister, she entered service later that year. She sailed on her maiden voyage from Liverpool to Montreal on 2 September. The *Saxonia,* as built, was a handsome ship. The hull was given a nicely raked stem, good sheer, and cruiser stern. Superstructure above was fairly low, with an elegant round-topped funnel amidships. The single mast abaft the bridge made for an attractive profile. All four ships were built to the maximum dimension which would enable them to steam up the St Lawrence as far as Montreal. The *Saxonia* was fitted with Denny–Brown fin stabilizers, and was in fact the first Cunard vessel to have them.

The new ship soon became very popular on the Canadian route. The immigrant trade was very important in those days, and she could take 800 in the tourist class. She steamed steadily to and fro, gradually being joined by her three sisters. The four older ships were withdrawn. In 1957 the *Saxonia*'s terminal was moved to Southampton, but the number of passengers requiring sea passage had started to decrease. In 1962 it was decided to refit the ship and her sister *Ivernia,* to make them more suitable for cruising in addition to Atlantic crossings. The *Saxonia* was accordingly dispatched to John Brown's yard at Clydebank. Much work was done on the ship. Air-conditioning was extended throughout, and cabins were given improved facilities. Much refurbishment of public rooms took place. The three after holds and cargo-handling equipment were dispensed with, together with the after docking bridge. A new large lido deck with swimming-pool, cocktail bar and night club was incorporated here. The ship emerged from John Brown's painted overall in Cunard's cruising green, and looking in fact like a smaller version of the *Caronia.* Her name was changed to *Carmania.* Her sister *Ivernia* had been given similar treatment, and was now named *Franconia.*

The *Carmania* now cruised during the winter months, mostly in the Caribbean from Port Everglades. She had in fact done a little cruising before her refit. During the summer her Canadian route was now Rotterdam – Southampton – Quebec – Montreal. Later she was employed on Mediterranean fly – cruises in addition to Caribbean winter cruising, and her hull was painted white. The accent was now on cruising, line voyaging being less important.

On 12 January 1969 she had the misfortune to run aground on a sandbank near San Salvador Island in the Bahamas. She remained fast for five days but was eventually refloated. Her passengers, however, had been transferred to the Italian liner *Flavia.* The *Carmania* had incurred some damage and had to go to Newport News for repairs. Unfortunately, the Admiralty chart for the area was later found to be in error. On 11 May that year the *Carmania* collided with the Russian ship *Frunze* but only minor damage resulted. However, rising costs were reducing the profitability of the vessel. Cunard were acquired by Trafalgar House, who wished to reduce costs by employing a foreign catering crew. Unions opposed this move, and a bitter dispute ensued. It was also realized that further costly improvements would have to be made to the ship. The result was that the *Carmania* and *Franconia* were both laid up in Southampton in late 1971, and in 1972 were taken to the river Fal for further lay-up.

In August 1973 both ships were sold to a Panamanian concern, the Nikreis Maritime Corporation, who were acting on behalf of the Russian state shipping company Morflot. They were overhauled at South Shields by Swan Hunter. The *Carmania* was now renamed *Leonid Sobinov,* and her sister became the *Fedor Shalyapin.* The former now proceeded out to Australia for cruising under her Russian ownership, and also for some Australia-UK voyages. She was managed by CTC Lines. The *Fedor Shalyapin* was similarly employed. The invasion of Afghanistan in 1979 by the USSR resulted in the *Leonid Sobinov* being banned from Australian ports and having to proceed instead to the Russian port of Nakhodka on the Pacific coast. In the service of the Russian Far East Shipping Co she continued her cruising and other work. In 1990 she was refitted in Greece and later reported laid up in Piraeus. In 1990 she was transferred to Transblasco Four Shipping Co. of Malta.

Carnarvon Castle

UNTIL 1926 the mail ships of the Union Castle fleet had all been steamships, but in that year the first of the motorships entered the fleet. The *Carnarvon Castle* was built by Harland and Wolff at Belfast, and was completed in 1926. She had the typical profile of motorships of her day: her hull had a straight stem with cruiser stern, upperworks were well proportioned and she had two rather squat elliptical funnels, the forward one being a dummy.

The ship set off on her maiden voyage from Southampton to Cape Town on 16 July and by all accounts caused something of a sensation on arrival, so different was she from all the other members of the mail service.

In 1936 the company entered on another mail contract with the South African government in which the passage time for the mailships from Southampton to Cape Town was reduced from 16 days 15 hours to not more than 14, to apply from December 1938. Only the latest two members of the fleet were fast enough to meet this requirement. The others would have to be re-engined with more powerful machinery, and in some cases lengthened as well.

The *Carnarvon Castle* returned to Harland and Wolff at Belfast for the necessary alterations. After successful trials the ship returned to the mail run in July 1938. She had been lengthened and now had a single funnel.

During 1939 the war clouds were gathering. When the ship arrived in Table Bay during the second week in September passengers were discharged. The ship then sailed to Simonstown, where she was fitted out as an armed merchant cruiser. She was given a main armament of eight 6-inch guns together with a couple of 3-inch anti-aircraft weapons and six Lewis machine guns. Patrol work in the South Atlantic followed for many long months. On a dull December day in 1940 the ex-mail liner encountered a German surface raider, the *Thor*. She was an ex-fruit ship of 3,144 tons with a main armament of six 5.9-inch guns. In addition she had a number of smaller guns, was equipped with four torpedo tubes, and also carried mines. The Captain had learnt by an intercepted wireless message that the AMC was in the vicinity and hoped to avoid her. However, on 5 December a large vessel loomed up out of the mist when the *Thor* was about 550 miles south of Rio, and signalled the *Thor* to stop. (The latter at the time was disguised as a Yugoslav ship.) The British AMC then fired a warning shot and, realizing he could no longer avoid an engagement, the German

captain hoisted his battle ensign and opened fire at a range of about 14,000 yards. According to the German account the sun broke through spasmodically and the British ship was silhouetted against the misty horizon, making a larger target. An enemy shell damaged her electrical control gear early in the action, and guns had to be fired independently by hand control. Nevertheless, the British ship kept up a good, if slightly irregular, rate of fire. The *Thor* kept up a steady fire and also fired a couple of torpedoes which missed.

By 0844 range had been reduced to about 8,000 yards and the British AMC had been hit a number of times. There were several outbreaks of fire on board, and the internal communication had been badly disabled. Accordingly the ship turned to port and sailed off in a northerly direction to try to control the fires. Having no wish to re-open the engagement, the *Thor* made off to the eastward. She had expended no fewer than 593 rounds of ammunition, about 70 per cent of her supply, and had escaped damage. The British ship had not been so fortunate. Twenty-seven enemy shells had found a mark, and her casualties numbered four killed and 28 wounded. The fires were eventually put out and the ship set a course for Montevideo, where she arrived on 7 December. Some plates salvaged from the wreck of the *Graf Spee* were used to patch her hull. The *Carnarvon Castle* later crossed to Cape Town for full repairs.

Patrol work continued to occupy the AMC until she was converted to a troop-ship at New York in 1944. She continued this important work until she was released in March 1947, but did not return immediately to the mail run. An emigrant service was set up to take settlers to South Africa, and the *Carnarvon Castle* made the inaugural sailing in June 1947. The service lasted until the spring of 1949 and her 'running-mates' included the *Winchester Castle* and *Arundel Castle*. The ship then went for a much-needed refit at Belfast. This was a long task, and she did not resume the mail run until June 1950.

Two new mailships, the *Pretoria Castle* and *Edinburgh Castle*, both powered by steam turbines, had entered service in 1948. Later on the *Pendennis Castle*, *Windsor Castle* and *Transvaal Castle*, all steamships, took their place in the fleet. A new schedule of 11½ days would soon apply, and the *Carnarvon Castle*'s speed was not sufficient for this. After her arrival at Southampton on 1 June 1962 she was withdrawn and sold to Japanese breakers.

91

Name: **Carnarvon Castle**

Line: Union Castle

Builders: Harland & Wolff, Belfast; launched 14 January 1926, completed June 1926

Dimensions Gross tonnage 20,063/Length 655.75 ft/Beam 73.5 ft

Machinery

Engines: 2 8-cylinder 4-stroke double-acting air injection Harland/B & W, 13,000 b.h.p.

Service speed: 16 knots

Major Refits

1938 Harland & Wolff, re-engining; 2 10-cylinder 2-stroke double-acting airless injection Harland/B & W engines, 24,000 b.h.p., service speed: 20 knots, 20,122 tons, 686.25 × 73.5 ft, 2 funnels replaced by 1

Regular Routes

Southampton – Cape Town, and South African ports

Passenger Capacity

1926: 1st 311, 2nd 276, 3rd 266
1950: 1st 216, Tourist 401

Near Sister-ships

Winchester Castle (1930); **Warwick Castle** (1931)

Photograph 1950

Caronia

Name: **Caronia** (1948); **Columbia** (1968); **Caribia** (1968)

Line: Cunard (1948-68); Universal (1968-74)

Builders: John Brown & Co., Clydebank; launched 30 October 1947, completed December 1948

Dimensions: Gross tonnage 34,183/ Length 715 ft/Beam 91.5 ft

Machinery

Engines: 2 sets Parsons triple-expansion geared turbines, twin screw, 35,000 s.h.p.

Boilers: 6 Yarrow watertube, 600 p.s.i., superheated to 800°F

Service speed: 22 knots

Major Refits

1965 Harland & Wolff, alteration to accommodation and superstructure

Regular Routes

Southampton – New York

Passenger Capacity

1st 581, Cabin 351 (Line voyages)
1st 600 (cruising)

Sister-ships

None

Photograph 1949

THIS attractive-looking vessel was Cunard's post-war venture into the cruise line market. She was classed as a dual-purpose ship, to be used also for Atlantic crossings. The hull had a well-raked stem and cruiser stern. The superstructure was nicely proportioned, with a massive funnel. A single tripod mast completed her elegant profile. The huge funnel, incidentally, was claimed to be the largest one ever constructed for a passenger liner. In high winds it acted as a huge sail, but seems to have done its job very efficiently.

The most striking feature of this ship was her colour-scheme: she was painted in four shades of pale green, which was intended to reflect the sun's rays and keep the ship cooler in the tropics.

The *Caronia*'s maiden voyage to New York passed off satisfactorily, and from then onward cruising was to be the mainstay of her career for the next eighteen years. Her first cruises were to the Caribbean, and then on to longer voyaging. The cruise programme varied a little from year to year, but a typical one might be as follows: A world cruise from January to April would be followed by a Mediterranean one. One or two Atlantic crossings would then precede a very popular North Cape and Northern Capitals cruise. This would be around mid-summer, and perhaps a straight Atlantic crossing would be followed by a further Mediterranean cruise, finishing with a couple of Caribbean cruises from New York. The *Caronia* would then return to Southampton in November for her annual overhaul, lasting six weeks or so. Often the Mediterranean cruises were extended to include visits to Black Sea ports as well.

Few incidents seem to have befallen this ship as she carried out her world-wide cruising. She was generally reliable in spite of some steerage and stability problems. In April 1963, when the ship was nearing the end of her world cruise in very stormy conditions off the Newfoundland Banks, she was hit by a huge wave. Such was the force that a mass of water struck the high-up observation lounge, shattering several large windows. Fortunately, no injuries resulted. A mishap also befell the ship in April 1958. She was on her world cruise and at Yokohama in windy conditions had the misfortune to strike a lighthouse on a harbour breakwater, pushing it into the sea. The ship suffered bow damage and had to be repaired at nearby Yokosuka naval yard. In June 1956 she ran aground near Messina, Sicily but was soon refloated with little damage.

In the late 1950s the *Caronia* started to lose money on some cruises. Her running costs were considerable, since she was a luxury vessel, with the crew/passenger ratio being about 1/1 or even greater when not fully booked.

However, Cunard continued to run her, and of course some of her cruises were still profitable, especially the North Cape and Round-the-world ones.

By the mid-1960s the ship's problems increased, and she was sent to Harland & Wolff at Belfast in October 1965 for a substantial 'face-lift'. A good deal of redecorating was done to passenger accommodation, and a large lido deck and new open-air swimming-pool built. Once the doyen of cruise ships, she was now having to compete with a new generation of Dutch, Norwegian, Italian and Swedish vessels. The *Caronia* made her final Cunard cruise on 29 September 1967 from New York to the Mediterranean with only 340 passengers. She arrived back at the US port on 16 November, sailing the next day for Southampton with no passengers. She was laid up there and offered for sale. A proposal from Yugoslavia to use her as a hotel ship on the Dalmatian coast came to naught. The ship lay at Southampton under 'care and maintenance' until, in the summer of 1968, she was sold to a Greek-financed Panamanian concern known as Universal Line, sometimes also called Star Line.

The ship went out to the Mediterranean and was refitted at Piraeus and Naples. She was first renamed *Columbia* and then *Caribia*. She returned to New York early in 1969. Plans were made to send her on a series of Caribbean cruises, but these were never realized as she suffered a bad engine-room explosion on 5 March. She was off Martinique at the time, and one man was killed. Passengers had to be sent ashore, to be later flown home, and the disabled ship was towed back to New York. Here she remained laid up at various berths for the next five years amidst financial arguments, law suits, and trouble with local authorities. All the while the once splendid ship deteriorated. Various reactivation schemes came to naught. An auction sale was held on board in February 1974, when most removable fittings were sold, and then in April the ship, towed by the German tug *Hamburg*, set off on a long, slow voyage to Taiwanese shipbreakers. She never got there. On 12 August, during severe weather, the empty ship was thrown on to a breakwater at Guam. She sank and broke into three parts. As she was a hazard to shipping, her wreck was broken up in situ, a sad ending.

Carthage

Name: Carthage

Line: P & O

Builders: Alexander Stephen & Co.,
Linthouse; launched 18 August 1931,
completed November 1931

Dimensions: Gross tonnage 14,304/
Length 540 ft/Beam 71.2 ft

Machinery

Engines: 2 sets Parsons single reduction
geared turbines, twin screw, 15,000 total
s.h.p.

Boilers: 4 Yarrow oil-fired watertube, 425
p.s.i., superheated to 725°F

Service speed: 18 knots

Major Refits

1944 Norfolk, Virginia, converted to
troopship
1947 Alexander Stephen, reconversion to
passenger liner, funnel heightened

Regular Routes

London – Hong Kong via Suez

Passenger Capacity

1931: 1st 175, 2nd 196
1948: 1st 181, Tourist 213

Sister-ships

Corfu (1931)

Photograph 1932

THIS ship and her sister *Corfu* were built for P & O's Far Eastern service. Both were constructed at the yard of Alexander Stephen and Sons at Linthouse on the Clyde. The *Carthage* was launched on 18 August 1931, completed by November and set off on her maiden voyage early in December. (There had been a previous *Carthage* in the P & O fleet, a 5,000-tonner of 1881.) The hull had nice sheer, with cruiser stern and raked stem. Upperworks were quite low, with a couple of funnels on top, the aft one being a dummy. There were three full-length decks, upper, main and lower, with orlop below. Above the upper deck were a forecastle and bridge deck extending to the stern. The boat deck over the mid-length was fairly short.

The *Carthage* completed her trials successfully in November 1931, during which she achieved speeds of 19½ knots. She arrived in London on 1 December and a week later set off on her maiden voyage to the Far East. She was to keep up this service steadily until the outbreak of war in 1939. The *Corfu* was also on the route, having sailed on her first voyage a little earlier on 16 October. By way of a change she also made occasional voyages to Australia during this time, for instance in April 1932 and June 1936.

The Far Eastern route was from London and Southampton to Hong Kong via such ports as Marseilles, Suez, Aden, Colombo, Penang, Singapore. It was usually extended to Shanghai, Kobe and Yokohama. The ship proved reliable in service, and few incidents befell her. In February 1932, while she was in Shanghai, some Chinese shells fell uncomfortably close fortunately without damaging the ship. The Japanese attack on China was in progress, and the British vessel may have been mistaken for a Japanese one.

When war broke out in 1939 the *Carthage* was in Hong Kong, homeward-bound. She was ordered to Colombo, where her passengers and cargo were discharged, and she then went to Calcutta. Here she was quickly fitted out as an armed merchant cruiser. Her dummy funnel was removed and she was armed with eight 6-inch guns and a couple of 3-inch anti-aircraft ones. HMS *Carthage* was commissioned in January 1940, and set forth on duties in the Indian Ocean. This comprised on the whole patrols and convoy escort work, a job which she carried out very efficiently.

In late 1941 the ship was actively involved in 'Operation Bell-ringer'. A convoy of five Vichy French ships escorted by the sloop *François d'Iberville* left Tamatave in Madagascar in an attempt to reach France. The convoy was intercepted by the British cruisers *Devonshire* and *Colombo* and the AMCs *Carnarvon Castle* and *Carthage* together with six units of the South African defence force from Durban (a mine-clearance flotilla). The French crews tried to sabotage their ships by starting fires on board and attempting to scuttle them, but to no avail. The French sloop was forced to return to Madagascar, and the five merchant ships were escorted into South African ports. One vessel, the *Cap Padaran* having sabotaged her machinery, was towed by the *Carthage* into Port Elizabeth. This all resulted in some valuable tonnage being secured for the Allies at a time of desperate shortage. The *Carthage* had a refit at Southampton in 1942 before returning to the Indian Ocean again.

In late 1943 it was decided to convert her for trooping. This was carried out in the USA at Norfolk, Virginia and completed by January 1945. She was then much engaged in taking troops and other personnel to the East and repatriating civilians and POWs. This was continued after the war was over. The ship was eventually released, and went back to her builders in February 1947. Here she was converted back to a peacetime vessel. Much improvement took place to passenger and crew accommodation. The forward well deck was filled in and the funnel heightened. The dummy funnel was not replaced. With a white hull and buff funnel, the *Carthage* made her first post-war commercial sailing to the Far East in July 1948. She was to continue steadily for the next 12 years. The *Corfu* and *Canton* had both survived the war and were also operating, the service being a monthly one.

The *Carthage* completed her last sailing on the route when she arrived in London on 13 February 1961. She was now almost thirty years old, and had reached the end of her economic life. Shortly afterwards she sailed for the breakers at Osaka in Japan. For this voyage she was named *Carthage Maru*.

Her sister *Corfu* had also served as an AMC and troopship, and she too went to Japanese breakers in 1961. Both were replaced on the Far East route by the ex-Belgian ships *Jadotville* and *Baudouinville*, bought by P & O and renamed *Chitral* and *Cathay* respectively. Air travel, however, was beginning to take over and the service had not many more years to run.

Castel Felice

THERE has always been considerable movement of Indian emigrants and workers to East and South Africa. The British India Company had provided a service between these countries for many years with several 'K' class ships of about 7,000 tons. In the late 1920s the company decided to build a couple of larger ships for the route, and the *Kenya* and her sister *Karanja* were ordered from Alexander Stephen's yard on the Clyde. The ship was launched on 27 August 1930, completed in December that year and sailed out to India that month to take up station.

Having completed trials successfully and sailed out East, the ship commenced her regular route. This was between Bombay and Durban via the Seychelles and East African ports. There was also a service between Rangoon, Madras and East Africa. The *Kenya* steamed back and forth with commendable regularity for some ten years, performing a very useful service. Soon after war broke out, however, she came back in convoy to the UK bringing various military and civilian personnel. She was taken up at first for use as a troop-ship. In July 1941 she had her first change of name to *Hydra*, but did not retain this for long. In October that year she was converted by the Admiralty to a Landing Ship Infantry (LSI). Her name now became HMS *Keren*. She carried her big landing craft overside, and these could be quickly launched to put large numbers of troops ashore. She was now engaged for some time in training exercises in Scottish waters, where the landing techniques were gradually perfected for future use on hostile shores.

In this role she took a big part in the Madagascar invasion in May 1942. She was also very much engaged on the invasion of North Africa. In particular she took part in the assault on Algiers in November 1942.

The invasion of Sicily in July 1943 went under the name of 'Operation Husky'. HMS *Keren* again played a major role in this. She sailed in convoy from Port Said together with some more LSIs and miscellaneous vessels, carrying the 231st Infantry Brigade. When the convoy arrived in their intended position off the island a confused sea made conditions difficult for the landing craft, but they eventually got ashore safely. The *Keren* was involved in various other wartime activities, and was bought outright by the Admiralty after the war, in 1946. During the conflict her armament had consisted of one 6-inch gun, one twelve-pounder AA gun and twelve 20-mm cannons. She could carry a total of 24 landing craft of various types.

The *Keren's* armament and landing craft were now removed in preparation for a return to a peacetime role, but this was not to occur for some years. She was at first laid up in Holy Loch until transferred to the Ministry of Transport for sale in 1948. A slight mishap befell her in February 1949, when she ran ashore after breaking adrift. She was soon repaired, and that year was bought by the Alva Steamship Company, a subsidiary of Sitmar (Societa Italiana Transporti Marittimi). She still remained laid up, however, while a further series of name changes occurred – first back to *Kenya* then *Keren*, then back again to *Kenya*. In 1950 she got yet another name, *Fairstone*, but this was for only a short while, as she soon reverted to *Kenya* and *Keren* yet again.

In 1950–1 the ship was extensively rebuilt and refitted at Antwerp, and later Genoa. Her appearance was completely altered in this process. Among other changes she now had a curved stem, the forward well was decked in, the superstructure enhanced and the promenade deck extended to the stern. Most obvious was her new funnel, much larger than before. Masts were removed and replaced by derrick posts. The ship now received her final name of *Castel Felice* and was to carry on commercial sailing of a world-wide nature for a further eighteen years. The *Castel Felice* at various times flew the Italian, Liberian and Panamanian flags.

She now often did duty as an emigrant ship. Her first voyages in her fresh role were from Genoa to Sydney and from the Italian port to the Caribbean and South America. Later in 1954 she did some North Atlantic sailings, which were to feature quite often in her programme over the years. She sailed from Bremerhaven to Quebec or New York, often calling at Southampton. The Australian run, out via the Cape and returning via Panama, was another regular feature.

Another refit in 1955 resulted in the vessel being air-conditioned throughout and having the addition of a swimming-pool. She now catered for a small number of first class and a large number of tourist class. From 1958, with running-mates *Fairsky* and *Fairsea*, she did many paid passage emigrant runs to Australia. In 1961 she had another refit, becoming now a one-class vessel, and was seen regularly on the Southampton to Sydney service, sometimes proceeding to Auckland. She also did North Atlantic voyaging, and cruised from Australian waters as well.

The ship was still on the Australia run when she was finally withdrawn, and went to breakers in Taiwan in October 1970.

Name: **Kenya** (1930); **HMS Keren** (1941); **Castel Felice** (1952)

Line: British India (1930-46); Sitmar (1949-70)

Builders: Alexander Stephen & Co., Linthouse, launched 27 August 1930, completed December 1930

Dimensions: Gross tonnage 9,890/Length 487 ft/Beam 64.3 ft

Machinery

Engines: 2 single reduction geared turbines, twin screw, 11,000 s.h.p.

Boilers: 7 single-ended oil-fired cylindrical with superheaters, forced draught, 250 p.s.i., 1 auxiliary boiler

Service speed: 16-17 knots

Major Refits

1951 Antwerp/Genoa, new funnel, lengthened, masts removed, 493 × 64.3 ft
1955 12,478 tons

Regular Routes

Bombay – Durban via Seychelles and East Africa

Passenger Capacity

1930: 1st 66, 2nd 120, 3rd 1700
1951: Cabin 596, 3rd 944
1955: 1st 28, Tourist 1173
1961: Tourist 1400

Sister-ships

Karanja (1931)

Photograph 1962

Chignecto

Name: **Greek** (1893); **Segura** (1906); **Pembrokeshire** (1908); **Chignecto** (1913)

Line: Union (1893-1900); Union Castle (1900-06); Royal Mail (1906-27)

Builders: Harland & Wolff, Belfast; launched 17 May 1893, completed August 1893

Dimensions: Gross tonnage 4,747/Length 400.5 ft/Beam 47.2 ft

Machinery

Engines: 2 3-cylinder triple expansion reciprocating engines, twin screw

Boilers: 2 coal-fired double-ended Scotch type, 180 p.s.i.

Service speed: 12 knots

Regular Routes

Southampton – Cape Town – Durban
London – Japan
Halifax – West Indies

Passenger Capacity

1st 52, 2nd 66, 3rd 60 (emigrants in between decks 500)

Sister-ships

Gaul (1893); **Goth** (1893)

Photograph 1913

THIS little vessel was built for the Union Line's intermediate service to South Africa. She had a long, active career under several names and on differing routes. The ship was constructed at Harland and Wolff's yard at Belfast and completed in 1893. She set off on her first voyage to South Africa that year.

Our photograph shows her late in her career. However, she remained practically unaltered in appearance all her life. Her hull had good sheer, with elegant counter stern and straight stem. It contained three decks with five cargo hatchways, forecastle, bridge deck and poop. Two well-raked masts and a slender funnel made for an attractive profile. The ship catered for first, second and third class passengers in fairly modest but comfortable accommodation in the midships superstructure. This is what would be expected in an intermediate vessel of only 4,700 tons.

The *Greek* and her two sisters *Gaul* and *Goth* were the forerunners of a very successful series of intermediate ships known as the G class. A later one of these was the larger *Galician* (later to be renamed *Glenart Castle*). These ships, although on a secondary service, were of great value to the Union Line. In earlier years the intermediate service had been carried out by older, ex-mail steamers which had become outmoded for first-line duties. The idea of building ships specifically for the secondary service began with the Castle Co.'s *Doune Castle* and *Lismore Castle* of 1890.

The *Greek* and her sisters began their successful careers, and by 1900 the G class was well established. The later ones were considerably larger than the first trio, but all the class were generally similar in appearance, although some had three masts. They became very popular with the travelling public, and provided a leisurely voyage out to Cape Town, Port Elizabeth, East London and Durban. On amalgamation with the Castle Line, all passed into the Union Castle fleet. It is generally conceded that the Union ships at the time of the merger were superior to the Castle liners. This applied to both the mail steamers and the intermediate ones.

Larger and faster ships came into service, and by 1906 the original 'G' trio had become a little outdated. In that year the *Greek* and *Gaul* were sold to the Royal Mail Company. The former was renamed *Segura* and the latter *Sabor*. They were put on a service from Mexico to Cuba for a short while. When Royal Mail secured, with Brocklebanks, a half-interest in the Shire Line in 1907, the two ships were put on a service from London to the Far East.

They were now given 'shire' names. The *Segura* (ex-*Greek*) became the *Pembrokeshire*, and her sister the *Carmarthenshire*. They began sailing the long route to Malaya, Hong Kong, Shanghai and Japan in 1909.

Soon after this the *Pembrokeshire* received about the only external alteration of her career. A couple of derrick posts were added to the after end of her forward well deck.

In 1913 Royal Mail took on a service from Canada to the West Indies under a Canadian government subsidy. This was a fortnightly one from Halifax. The *Pembrokeshire* and her sister were sent across the Atlantic to operate this, the service being to Bermuda, the West Indies, Trinidad and Georgetown, British Guiana. More name-changes followed, now for the last time. The *Pembrokeshire* became the *Chignecto*, as she appears in our photograph. Her sister was renamed *Chaleur*. A couple of other Gs, the *Goth* now renamed *Cobequid*, and the *Guelph* now called the *Caraquet*, joined the service. The former was lost by shipwreck in 1914 and the latter was taken over for war service.

The *Chignecto* and *Chaleur* continued on the route during the war. After hostilities ended the original contract eventually ran out, but the ships continued under an extension arrangement. Both steamed steadily on until 1927, when they were sold for scrapping in Holland.

Chitral

Name: *Jadotville* (1956); *Chitral* (1961)

Line: Compagnie Maritime Belge (1956-60); P & O (1961-75)

Builders: Chantiers et Ateliers de St Nazaire (Penhoet), launched 30 November 1955, completed June 1956

Dimensions: Gross tonnage 13,724/ Length 557 ft/Beam 70.2 ft

Machinery

Engines: 2 Parsons steam turbines double reduction geared, single screw, 12,500 s.h.p.

Boilers: 3 oil-fired watertube, 625 p.s.i., superheated to 840°F

Service speed: 16.5 knots

Regular Routes

Antwerp – Matadi
London – Yokohama

Passenger Capacity

1956: 300 one class
1961: 231 one class

Sister-ships

Baudouinville (1957)

Photograph 1969

THIS ship and her sister *Baudouinville* were built for the Belgian Company's service to the Belgian Congo (now Zaire). The Compagnie Maritime Belge (CMB) dated from 1895, and ran a passenger/cargo service. Most ships on the route had been medium-sized and these two 13,000-tonners were bigger and faster than any previous ones.

The *Jadotville* was built in France by the St Nazaire Shipyard, usually known simply as Penhoet. Launched on 30 November 1955, the ship was completed by June the following year and set off on her maiden voyage from Antwerp to Matadi on 23 July.

She was a fine-looking vessel, as can be seen in the photograph which shows her in her later P & O days. A typical passenger/cargo ship of that era, she had an attractive appearance. The hull had a nicely raked stem, and superstructure was well proportioned, with a rather splendid funnel on top. This latter was known as a 'Lascroux' type.

There were seven decks for passengers, which were all one-class, and public rooms and amenities were very good. Plenty of deck space was available for recreation and an open-air swimming-pool was provided. The dining saloon was a very large one and a lounge, cinema, veranda cafe and smoking-room featured on board. The ship had six holds, some space being for refrigerated cargoes. Service speed was 16½ knots, but she could work up to 18 if required.

The *Jadotville*'s trials were satisfactory and she soon settled down on the route, becoming at once very popular. She was joined in 1957 by her sister, and with the two vessels a most useful service was provided.

However, in 1960 the Belgian Congo became independent and an unhappy political upheaval followed. Many of the ship's passengers had been Belgian officials travelling to and fro, who no longer did so. Air travel had also made inroads on business. The net result was that the *Jadotville* and her sister were put up for sale. They were purchased in February 1961 by the P & O company; our subject was renamed *Chitral*, while the other became the *Cathay*. They were now put on P & O's Far Eastern service, where they replaced the *Corfu* and *Carthage*.

The two newcomers were virtually unaltered for their new duties, apart from a slight rearrangement of passenger accommodation. Now painted in P & O colours they fitted in well with Far Eastern voyaging, and they also went cruising. The *Chitral* set off on her first P & O voyage from London and Southampton to Yokohama on 2 March 1961. A Far East round voyage took about three months.

However, the passenger trade declined over the years, and the situation was not helped by the closure for some time of the Suez Canal.

In 1970 the *Chitral* made a number of Mediterranean cruises from Genoa. Earlier that year she had made her final UK – Far East voyage. She was now transferred to the Eastern and Australian Steamship Company, a subsidiary of P & O. From late 1970 she operated a passenger/cargo service between Australia, the Far East and Japan. The *Cathay* had been transferred also, and both ships soon became popular on the route. Both had good cargo capacity as noted, but 'containerization' soon began to take over, and this factor, coupled with increasing air competition, forced E & A to abandon the service.

The *Chitral* was sold to shipbreakers in Taiwan in December 1975, a victim of the advance of technology. Her sister was more fortunate. She was sold to the Chinese, and has had two changes of name to *Kenghsin* and *Shang Hai*. Under the latter name she is still in service in the Far East.

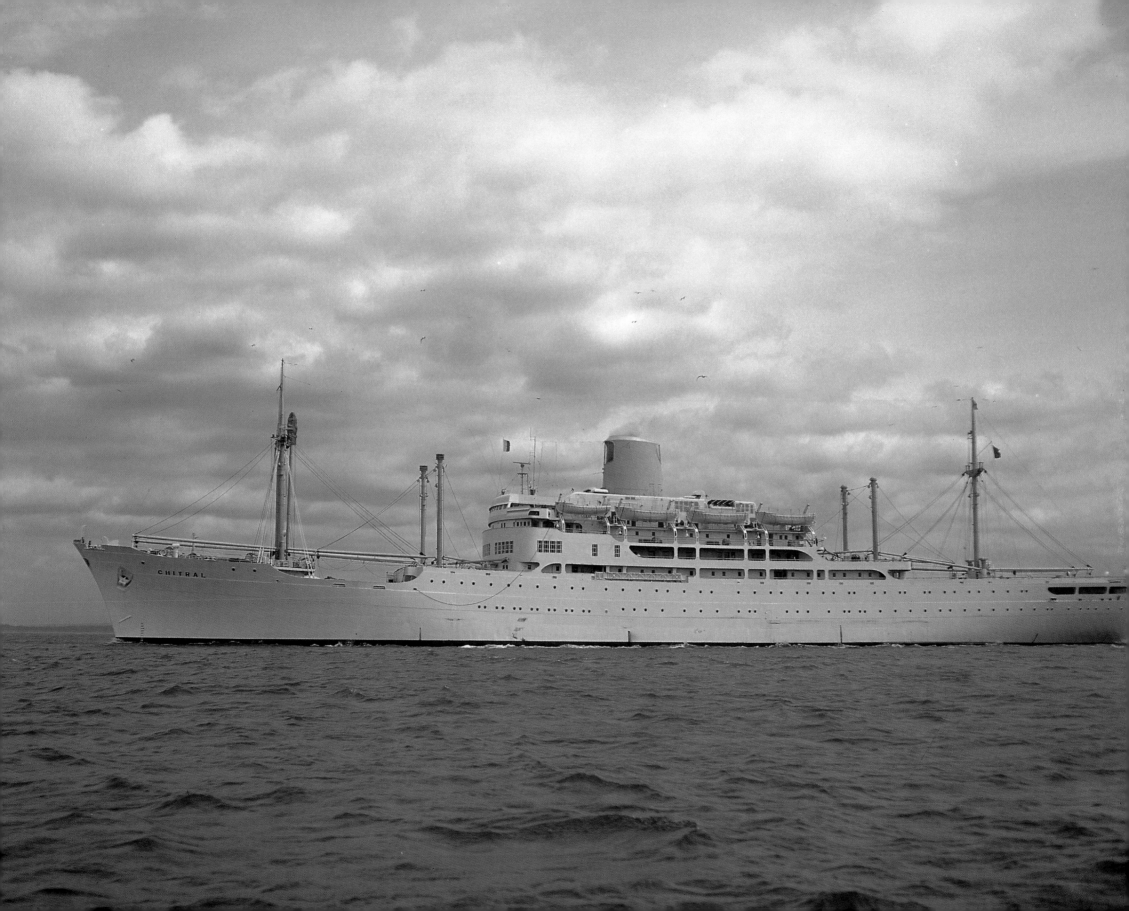

Chusan

Name: Chusan

Line: P & O

Builders: Vickers-Armstrongs, Barrow;
launched 28 June 1949, completed June
1950

Dimensions: Gross tonnage 24,215/
Length 677.5 ft/Beam 85 ft

Machinery

Engines: 2 sets Parsons single and double
reduction geared turbines, twin screw,
34,000 s.h.p. (max. 42,500)

Boilers: 4 Foster Wheeler watertube
controlled superheat 600-850°F, 525 p.s.i.

Service speed: 22 knots

Major Refits

1952: Thornycroft funnel top fitted
1959/60 Belfast, improvements to
accommodation

Regular Routes

London – Hong Kong
London – Sydney via Bombay

Passenger Capacity

1st 475, Tourist 551

Sister-ships

None

Photograph 1950

THIS ship was built for the Far Eastern service of the company. She was in fact the largest vessel P & O ever employed on this route. Constructed by Vickers – Armstrong at Barrow and launched on 28 June 1949, she was completed a year later, setting off on her first line voyage to Bombay on 15 September 1950.

The *Chusan* was fitted with Denny-Brown fin stabilizers, the first large passenger liner to have them. This proved to be a very worthwhile fitment, later to become quite a normal feature of large passenger ships. The *Chusan* can claim, therefore, to be one of the pioneers of this system.

The *Chusan* now proceeded to make four short cruises prior to commencing her Far Eastern voyaging. Cruising was, as noted above, to play a large role in the ship's activities. All was well, and the new vessel set off on 15 September on her first voyage to Bombay and back. This went off satisfactorily, and on 7 November she set off from London on her first full-length Far Eastern run as far as Hong Kong. She soon settled down to regular voyaging, and later Japanese ports were also included. During the summer and autumn months the ship went cruising, and was to gain a very high reputation in this field.

In 1951, for example, her cruises took in such ports as Madeira, Casablanca, Lisbon, Naples and Barcelona for passengers who preferred the sun. Those who liked northern waters could go by *Chusan* to Gothenberg, Oslo, Bergen and Andalnes. The next years cruising followed a similar pattern, but included some Mediterranean ports as well. The ship underwent a slight alteration in appearance in 1952 when she was fitted with a 'Thornycroft' funnel top. This greatly helped in keeping smoke and fumes clear of the upper decks.

The ship continued her voyaging and cruising throughout the decade, building up a fine reputation. On 12 June 1953 she had the misfortune to be in collision with the 6,000-ton cargo ship *Prospector* in fog near the South Goodwin Lightship. She had sailed from Tilbury on a cruise, but had to return to port for repairs. Little damage was caused, and the ship sailed again on the 15th.

On 11 April 1959 the *Chusan* set off on a round-the-world voyage. This was in fact the first time a P & O ship had done so – a unique distinction. The voyage took 92 days and covered about 32,000 miles; some 24 ports were visited, including such places as Port Said, Bombay, Colombo, Singapore, Manila, Yokohama, Vancouver, San Francisco, Los Angeles, Panama, Trinidad, and Las Palmas. During this trip a cruise was made from San Francisco to the Hawaiian Islands and back via Vancouver. The ship had now been in service for over nine years, and a quite extensive refit was undertaken by Harland and Wolff at Belfast. P & O had decided to update the amenities on board several of their large passenger vessels to make them more competitive with foreign companies. The *Chusan's* accommodation was substantially improved, and she was now air-conditioned throughout.

The Company's services were now becoming more extensive, with a network of trans-Pacific routes as a natural extension of the Australian and Far Eastern ones. The P & O and Orient passenger fleets came under joint management in 1960, the new operating subsidiary being known as P & O – Orient Lines. Round-the-world sailings became a feature in both east–about and west–about directions. Until 1963 the *Chusan* had remained mainly on the Far Eastern route, coupling this with her cruising activities. In the summer of that year, however, she transferred to the Australian service sailing from London to Sydney via Bombay, Singapore and Melbourne. She then made the first of many cruises from Australian ports and was to become a very familiar sight in Australian waters in both her cruising and trans-Pacific roles.

The *Chusan* continued reliably in operation through the 1960s and early 1970s. On 8 February 1970 she had the rather sad distinction of making the last scheduled call of a P & O passenger ship at Bombay. In the early seventies the Australian trade had begun to decline. The *Chusan* made a good many cruises from the UK during this time. Her schedule in 1971, for example, included the most popular cruising areas – northward to Copenhagen, Bergen, Narvik, southward to Lisbon, Casablanca, Madeira and also into the Mediterranean. Sadly, in 1972 the P & O announced that a number of passenger ships would be withdrawn, and these included the *Chusan*. Air travel had begun to virtually takeover by now. The Company had realized that the passenger-ship future lay more and more in cruising, and 'custom-built' ships for this purpose were the most suitable.

In the early months of 1973 the *Chusan* did cruising from South Africa, and then set off on the homeward voyage to Southampton, where she arrived on 19 March. The ship was then sold to breakers in Taiwan and left port on her final voyage east on 12 May.

Columbus

BEFORE the 1914–18 war the NDL company had laid down two large vessels for their transatlantic service. They were to be named *Columbus* and *Hindenburg*. However, the war intervened to upset these plans. The former ship war ceded to Britain and became the White Star *Homeric*. Her near – sister's story follows a different pattern.

Before the war German mercantile tonnage was about 11 per cent of the world's total. Afterwards it had decreased very considerably, due to war losses and the enforced surrender of ships. The *Hindenburg*, however, was at a very early stage of construction, and was not required to be handed over to the Allies. She was therefore duly completed for the NDL company, although work proceeded rather slowly owing largely to material shortages. It was decided to rename this ship *Columbus*, since this was not a Germanic name. (There was still considerable bitterness in the shipping world and elsewhere against Germany, due in large part to the wartime U-boat campaign.)

The big ship was due to be launched on 17 June 1922, but unfortunately she stuck on the ways and it was not until 12 August that she eventually took to the water. She was completed in November 1923, and commenced her maiden voyage from Bremerhaven to New York on 22 April 1924. The ship as built resembled the above-mentioned *Homeric* in a general way, although her superstructure was a little less 'piled up'. Like the earlier vessel, she had originally two tall, rather slender funnels. With her straight stem and elegant counter stern, she was quite an attractive-looking vessel. The hull had five overall decks, and was subdivided by 14 watertight bulkheads. There were five holds, three forward and two aft, served by five hatchways. Passenger accommodation and amenities were of the high standard associated with German passenger ships, and she catered for three classes. The usual pattern of public rooms were to be found on board – dining saloons, smoking-rooms, library, verandah, gymnasium – all very well appointed. The huge Social Hall was an especially fine feature.

The NDL company were very proud of their fine new vessel, by far the largest post-war German liner at that time. The ship's 'running-mates' on the North Atlantic included the recently completed 13,000-ton vessels *Munchen* and *Stuttgart*. These two were 15-knot ships, as was the old 10,800-ton *Bremen*, which had started life in 1900 as the *Prinzess Irene*. In 1925 the new 15,000-ton *Berlin* joined the fleet. The service prospered, and soon NDL started thinking of reviving their 'express' service. This later resulted in the splendid 50,000-tonners *Bremen* and *Europa* appearing on the scene.

The *Columbus* suffered an unfortunate mishap on 2 August 1927 when her starboard propeller shaft fractured when in mid-Atlantic. This caused the engine to race and become damaged beyond repair. The ship had to go to the Vulkan Yard at Bremen where a much smaller triple-expansion engine was fitted as a temporary measure. This enabled the ship to continue in service at a slightly slower speed. In 1929, however, she was taken off the route for complete re-engining. This was done to increase her speed to enable her to take her place on the new 'express' service which was now a reality.

Blohm and Voss of Hamburg were given the job, and the ship's two reciprocating engines were replaced by two single reduction geared turbines. A number of watertube boilers were added to enable the extra steam to be produced. During this time alterations were made to the accommodation, and the ship's two slender funnels were replaced by larger squat ones. She now in fact rather resembled a smaller version of the two big ships, *Bremen* and *Europa*. Of course, she was not as fast as the two newcomers, but could now manage about 22–23 knots and could take her place on the 'express' service. This she did up to the outbreak of war in 1939. The ship also went cruising, especially during the winter months, and gained a great reputation. Some of these cruises were lengthy affairs; a 'Round South America' trip in 1938, for example, took 47 days.

Her end was a very sad one. The ship was on a Caribbean cruise when war broke out. She at once made for Havana, where passengers were landed. She *Columbus* then sought sanctuary in the neutral port of Vera Cruz, Mexico. On 14 December 1939 the big ship sailed, in an attempt to break through to Germany. On 19 December, however, the British destroyer *Hyperion* appeared on the scene and ordered the German liner to stop. Rather than surrender this valuable vessel which could have been most useful to Britain the crew set her on fire and opened the sea-cocks. The ship sank about 320 miles east of Cape Hatteras, her crew being rescued by the US cruiser *Tuscaloosa*.

Crown Princess

Name: **Crown Princess** (1990)

Line: P & O (Princess Cruises)

Builders: Fincantieri Cantieri Navali Italiani S.P.A. Monfalcone, Trieste, Italy, launched February 1989, completed May 1990

Dimensions: Gross tonnage 69,845/ Length 804 ft (245m)/Beam 105.8 ft (32.25m)

Machinery

Engines: 4 M.A.N/B & W medium speed diesel driving 4 alternators, 2 synchronous electric motors driving twin screws

Service speed: 19.5 knots

Regular Routes

Cruising

Passenger Capacity

1,590 one class

Sister-ships

Regal Princess (1991)

Photograph 1990

THIS ship, like the *Royal Princess* belongs to Princess Cruises, owned and managed by P & O. She is considerably bigger than the earlier vessel.

The advent of the *Crown Princess* and, in 1991 by her sister *Regal Princess* means that a couple of 70,000 tonners have been added to the cruising fleet. It is said that the design of these vessels was inspired by the image of a dolphin moving through the water (rather a large dolphin!)

The ship was built by the Fincantieri Yard at Monfalcone near Trieste, Italy. She had been originally ordered by the Sitmar Line prior to its takeover by P & O in July 1988. The vessel is Italian designed and registered. Launched in February 1989 she was completed by May 1990.

As can be seen the 'Princess' is of imposing, rather massive appearance, typical of large cruise ships of today. The hull has a well raked stem and modern type cruiser stern. Superstructure is extensive but well proportioned and the single funnel positioned well aft. The ship has eleven decks for passengers. Reading downwards these are named: Sun, Lido, Aloha, Baja, Caribe, Dolphin, Promenade, Emerald, Plaza, Fiesta and Holiday. Public rooms on the Promenade deck run the whole length of the superstructure.

There is a two-level International Show Lounge forward with other lounges, bars, shopping arcade etc and a large restaurant aft. On the Sun deck the Domed Observation Lounge above the wheelhouse gives fine panoramic views and contains a casino, cocktail bar and dance floor. There are many other amenities including a couple of swimming pools on the Lido deck, a Cinema (Emerald deck), Patisserie, Library, Gymnasium, Disco, Beauty Parlour, Medical Centre etc. The three-level Atrium extends upwards from the Plaza deck to the Promenade deck.

Passengers, all one class, are accommodated on seven decks. Cabins vary from de-luxe suites to two-berth inside. Most however are outside ones with private facilities.

It will be noticed that the lifeboats are at a lower level than usual (Dolphin deck)

Propulsion machinery is diesel-electric. Four diesel engines drive four alternators supplying current to two propulsion motors. These power the twin screws and give the ship a cruising speed of 19.5 knots. The ship has two bow thrusters and a stern one and is fitted with fin stabilisers.

After completion and trials the vessel made several initial cruises in the Mediterranean during July and August before coming to Southampton on 12 September. She then sailed to New York the next day. A vessel is usually named when launched but the *Crown Princess* was ceremoniously named in the great US port by Sophia Loren, the well known Italian film star. Then after various publicity events the ship sailed south to commence her Caribbean cruising programme.

The vessel is now employed mainly on cruises in this area. She may also be sent elsewhere if required. In short she is very fully utilised. The crew consists of Italian officers, Italian and Portuguese dining and cabin stewards, British bar and reception staff.

Deutschland

THIS ship was one of the four vessels built by HAPAG for their intermediate transatlantic service. These are generally known as the *Albert Ballin* class, this ship and our subject being the first pair to be built. The second pair, *Hamburg* and *New York*, were slightly different.

The *Deutschland* was built, like the other three, by Blohm and Voss at Hamburg. She was launched on 28 April 1923, completed by December that year, and sailed on her maiden voyage from Hamburg to New York on 27 March 1924.

They were remarkable ships, these four vessels, and all had rather remarkable histories, being much altered during their lifetime. This was always with the object of keeping them up to date and making them more economical to run.

The *Deutschland*'s design was very close to that of the *Albert Ballin*. She had a straight stem, cruiser stern, four masts and two funnels, of which one was a dummy. Blisters on either side of the hull were added for stability. Like the rest of the quartet, she underwent a re-engining programme in 1930, and lengthening in 1934, both of which substantially increased her speed.

The ship continued reliably in service until the outbreak of war, surviving a rather serious fire. During the war she became an accommodation ship for the U-boat training division at Gdynia.

By 1945 the situation in the German eastern territories had become desperate, and evacuation had to be put in hand. The *Deutschland* was used for this service in company with other large liners, including the ex-*Albert Ballin* (now renamed *Hansa*), the *Wilhelm Gustloff* and *Cap Arcona*.

All the above were sunk during these desperate days by either Russian submarines or air attack. Great loss of life ensued, especially when the *Wilhelm Gustloff* was sunk. The *Deutschland* evacuated key naval personnel and civilian refugees making a number of voyages, apparently sometimes carrying around 11,000 people. However, on 3 May 1945, a few days before the end of the war in Europe, she was bombed and sunk by British aircraft off Neustadt in Lübeck bay. In 1948 the wreck was raised and scrapped.

This ship and the three other members of the 'Ballin' class had done fine work on the transatlantic service in the twenties, and thirties. All four were sunk during the war while serving Germany, but two, the *Hansa* and *Hamburg*, were later salvaged by the Russians and put back into service.

Name: **Deutschland**

Line: HAPAG

Builders: Blohm & Voss, Hamburg; launched 28 April 1923, completed December 1923

Dimensions: Gross tonnage 20,607/ Length 627 ft/Beam 72.8 ft

Machinery

Engines: 2 sets turbines single reduction geared, twin screw, 13,500 s.h.p.

Boilers: 4 single-ended, 4 double-ended cylindrical 225 p.s.i.

Service speed: 16 knots

Major Refits

1930 Blohm & Voss, higher-powered turbines fitted, conversion to oil fuel, 29,000 s.h.p., 4 watertube boilers, 400 p.s.i., 19.5 knots
1934 Blohm & Voss, lengthening, 677 × 72.8 ft, 21,046 tons

Regular Routes

Hamburg – New York

Passenger Capacity

1923: 1st 221, 2nd 402, 3rd 935
1934: 1st 200, Tourist 360, 3rd 400

Sister-ships and near sisters
Albert Ballin (1923), **Hamburg** (1926), **New York** (1927)

Photograph 1933

Dilwara

THIS ship, and her sister *Dunera*, were both built for trooping, and were also adaptable for cruising. The *Dilwara* was launched at Barclay Curle's yard at Glasgow on 17 October 1935 and completed by January 1936. She then entered service as a troop-ship, being joined by her sister the following year.

As can be seen, the ship was a good-looking vessel, rather typical of motorships of that era. The hull had a raked stem, good sheer and a cruiser stern. It contained three decks, lower, main and upper, and a shelter deck. Superstructure above was quite low and nicely rounded at the forward end, with a squat funnel on top. There was a longish forecastle and a well forward with two pairs of lifeboats.

The ship's accommodation was for first and second class and troops. As noted above, she could also be used for cruising and had the usual range of public rooms. The vessel was not a cargo carrier as such but had six holds, four forward and two aft, which could be used for carrying army equipment.

The *Dilwara* soon became very popular as she went about her duties. She was in fact the first ship to be specifically built as a troop-ship. Her design had been prepared in close co-operation with the Sea Transport department of the Board of Trade. For trooping the first and second class accommodation was occupied by officers, warrant officers and sergeants and their families. The ship was also used for cruising on occasions in the summer months, mostly to the northern capitals. In 1930 the *Neuralia* had made a couple of cruises to these regions with parties of schoolboys. These were very successful, and the *Dilwara* took up this role in 1936. She took part in the Coronation Fleet Review at Spithead in 1937.

The outbreak of war in 1939 found the ship in the Indian Ocean heading westward. Her wartime service was very considerable. The early part of the war was spent carrying troops from South Africa to Egypt, through the Red Sea. When Italy joined the conflict the ship was often attacked by Italian aircraft, but was not hit. This did not prevent the enemy radio claiming to have sunk her! When the ship was used on occasions for ferrying Italian POWs these men could not believe they were on board the *Dilwara*, as they had been told she was on the bottom of the sea.

The ship took part in the Greek campaign in 1941. When she was taking Australian troops back to Egypt she was often attacked by German dive bombers, descending almost to mast-height. Her gunners were much in action, and she came through unscathed.

The *Dilwara* was fitted as an LSI for specific operations. As such she took part with the *Dunera* and others in the Madagascar campaign in 1942. She successfully put her landing-craft ashore at the Majunga beaches. In 1943 she was much involved in the Burma campaign, as were other BI ships, and suffered some damage when striking a mine. She continued trooping in Far Eastern waters, making many voyages with troops and stores to Singapore, Calcutta, Siam and Penang, among other places.

Her work continued after the war, and in 1949 she went for a lengthy refit to bring her up to date for post-war requirements. Accommodation was improved, hammocks replaced by three-tier standee berths and other alterations made. The forward well was built in and the funnel heightened. She now carried fewer troops in greater comfort.

The *Dilwara* took part with other ships in the Suez affair in 1956, and continued in her trooping role during the fifties. Aircraft now began to take this job over, and the ships became redundant. The vessel was acquired in 1960 by the China Navigation Co, and on 7 October sailed from Southampton to Hong Kong. She was fitted out as a pilgrim carrier at Taikoo dockyard.

In 1961, now renamed *Kuala Lumpur*, she entered this new service. She was employed carrying pilgrims from Malaysia to Jeddah, and was used on a service from Hong Kong to New Zealand. Some cruising also featured on her itinerary. She continued these activities for a further ten years, until in December 1971 she arrived at Kaohsiung, Taiwan, to be broken up.

Her sister *Dunera* became an educational cruise ship in 1961, and was scrapped in 1967.

Name: **Dilwara** (1936); **Kuala Lumpur** (1961)

Line: British India (1936-60); China Navigation Co. (1960-71)

Builders: Barclay Curle & Co., Glasgow; launched 17 October 1935, completed January 1936

Dimensions: Gross tonnage 11,080/ Length 517 ft/Beam 63.2 ft

Machinery

Engines: 2 Doxford opposed piston diesel, twin screw, 6,500 b.h.p.

Service speed: 14.5 knots

Major Refits

1949 accommodation altered, funnel heightened, 12,555 tons

Regular Routes

Malaysia — Jeddah
Hong Kong — New Zealand

Passenger Capacity

1936: 1st 104, 2nd 100, Troops, 1,150
1952: 1st 125, 2nd 96, 3rd 104, Troops 705
1960: 1st 243, Pilgrims 1,669

Sister-ships

Dunera (1937)

Photograph 1953

Dominion Monarch

SHAW Savill & Albion had long been involved in the UK – New Zealand trade. In the late 1930s it was decided to start an entirely new fast service from London to New Zealand via South African and Australian ports. An order was placed with the Swan Hunter yard on the Tyne for a large vessel, which was to be given an appropriate name for the route. The *Dominion Monarch* was launched on 27 July 1938 and completed early the following year. She ran trials in January 1939, during which she achieved the satisfactory speed of 21½ knots. The ship sailed on her maiden voyage from London to New Zealand on 16 February. On this route the round voyage took about 3½ months.

The ship had a rather unusual appearance. She had long, sweeping lines, elegant superstructure and twin funnels placed rather aft of midships. There was a foremast only, and plenty of derrick posts. A slightly raked stem and cruiser stern completed her elegant profile. She had a large cargo capacity, having six holds, and could carry nearly 13,000 tons of frozen meat or dairy produce in her refrigerated spaces, and some 3,600 tons of general cargo.

The *Dominion Monarch* was the largest vessel built on the Tyne since the *Mauretania* of 1907. She also had a good claim to be the biggest and most powerful motor liner in the world at that time. Her maiden voyage was extremely successful, and she received a very enthusiastic welcome at Australian and New Zealand ports. However, war broke out while she was nearing the end of an outward voyage, and before her homeward run she was hastily armed with a few small guns that were available. She got back to London safely. She was considered for trooping duty, but was temporarily rejected. At the time the authorities felt that her luxurious passenger accommodation would preclude her from carrying more than a small number of troops. She therefore continued on commercial service, but in August 1940 it was finally decided to fit her for trooping at Liverpool. Initially she was only able to carry about 1,500 men, a small number for such a large ship. However, over the next few years this capacity was gradually increased until she was carrying over 4,000 at a time.

The *Dominion Monarch's* first voyage was to Port Said with troops, then on to Australia and New Zealand. When she was in Australia more anti-aircraft guns were fitted, and also paravane gear for detecting mines. A good cargo of meat and dairy produce was loaded in New Zealand, and she then embarked Australian troops and took them to Egypt in January 1941. From here she returned to Liverpool. Outward bound again to Australia and New Zealand, she next proceeded to Singapore with reinforcements. Although the Japanese were proceeding rapidly down through Malaya, and air raids were taking place it was decided to put the ship in dry-dock for engine overhaul. Machinery had been partly stripped when further Japanese air raids and the deteriorating situation meant that dock workers were withdrawn or just disappeared. It was left to the ship's engineers and crew to get the machinery operational again.

Further voyages followed to such places as Bombay and Freetown. Her high speed was a great advantage when she was proceeding alone, but often she sailed with a convoy and had numerous narrow escapes both from U-boats and from enemy aircraft. On all her trooping voyages to the Middle East, India, Australia and New Zealand the best use of her invaluable cargo space was made on the homeward runs. Much transatlantic trooping was also done carrying American servicemen.

By January 1945 her main trooping duties were over, but she took Service and civilian passengers out to Australia, and was otherwise very fully employed. The ship's wartime record was most impressive: she had transported some 90,000 personnel and motored around 350,000 miles. She had also brought about 70,000 tons of invaluable cargo to this country.

The ship was eventually returned to her owners in July 1947, and sent back to the Tyne for a much-needed refit. This took some 15 months. The Doxford engines were found to be in excellent condition, and only needed a general overhaul.

In December 1948 the *Dominion Monarch* again resumed her normal Shaw Savill service sailing for Australia and New Zealand via the Cape. For the next thirteen years the ship continued on this run, becoming established as a most popular vessel. However, it was gradually becoming apparent that the passenger/cargo liner was uneconomic. Labour disputes over cargo-handling caused serious delays at ports, to the great inconvenience of passengers. Thus the *Dominion Monarch's* large cargo capacity – which had proved invaluable, especially on her wartime service – now proved to be her undoing. The ship made her final sailing from London in December 1961, and on her return in February 1962 she was sold to the Japanese Mitsui group. She was chartered to an American firm for use as a hotel ship at the Seattle World Fair, but this did not prove financially very successful. This fine ship went to the breakers in Osaka, Japan in November 1962.

Name: Dominion Monarch

Line: Shaw Savill & Albion

Builders: Swan Hunter and Wigham Richardson, Wallsend-on-Tyne; launched 27 July 1938, completed January 1939

Dimensions: Gross tonnage 27,155/ Length 682 ft/Beam 84.8 ft

Machinery

Engines: 4 sets 5-cylinder Doxford opposed piston diesel engines, quadruple screw, 32,000 total b.h.p.

Service speed: 20 knots

Major Refits

1947, Tyneside, general overhaul

Regular Routes

London – South Africa – Australia – New Zealand

Passenger Capacity

1st 517

Sister-ships

None

Photograph 1951

Dunbar Castle

Name: Dunbar Castle

Line: Union Castle

Builders: Harland & Wolff, Govan;
launched 31 October 1929, completed
May 1930

Dimensions: Gross tonnage 10,002/
Length 484 ft/Beam 61 ft

Machinery

Engines: 2 Harland/B & W 6-cylinder
diesel, twin screw, 6,300 b.h.p.

Service speed: 14.5 knots

Regular Routes

London – Cape Town – Durban

Passenger Capacity

1st 200, 3rd 260

Sister-ships

None

Photograph 1931

THIS ship was built for Union Castle's intermediate and round-Africa service from London. Constructed at Harland and Wolff's Govan yard on the Clyde, she was launched on 31 October 1929 and completed by May the following year, sailing soon afterwards on her maiden voyage.

She was a trim-looking vessel, very typical of motorships of that era. The hull had a straight stem and cruiser stern. Superstructure was well proportioned, with a square front and twin squat funnels.

The vessel had six decks, including the boat deck, and was divided into nine watertight compartments. First and third class passengers were carried. The former were accommodated amidships on the upper and bridge decks, while the latter were aft on main and upper decks. First-class public rooms were on the promenade deck, while third class were in the bridge deck. First and third dining saloons, each about the same size, were on upper and main decks respectively. Decks, reading downward, were Boat, promenade, bridge, upper, main and lower. Cargo capacity was very important, and the *Dunbar Castle* had five holds served by hatches and derricks. Much space was insulated.

The service provided by this ship and her sisters was a most useful one for passengers who were not in a great hurry and enjoyed a lengthy sea voyage. The other vessels on the route during the 1930s, in addition to our subject, are worth recording.

The oldest quartet comprised the *Llanstephan Castle* (1914), *Llandovery Castle* (1925), *Llandaff Castle* (1927), and *Llangibby Castle* (1929). These varied in tonnage from 10,000 to 12,000. The *Dunottar Castle* and *Dunvegan Castle* of 1936 were 15,000-tonners, while the *Durban Castle* (1938) and *Pretoria Castle* (1939) were each over 17,000 tons. The latter four ships were just about fast enough to deputize on the mail service if required.

The *Dunbar Castle* served well, providing a reliable service for ten years, with no untoward incidents.

On 8 January 1940 she left the Thames to join a convoy bound for Beira. Off Deal, however, the next day the ship struck a mine. The force of the explosion caused the foremast to crash on the bridge, fatally injuring the captain and killing two other crewmen. There was no panic on board, and boats were quickly got away before the ship sank about thirty minutes later. She was in comparatively shallow water, and much of the upperworks remained visible. The vessel, however, could not be salvaged and the wreck was eventually blown up some years later. The mine had been a magnetic one.

Union Castle ships, as we have noted elsewhere in this book, played a major role in the 1939–45 war, with thirteen altogether being lost. Of the intermediate ships mentioned above, in addition to the *Dunbar Castle*, the *Dunvegan Castle* and *Llandaff Castle* were both sunk.

Edinburgh Castle

THIS fine ship and her sister *Pretoria Castle* were the first two mail liners built for Union Castle after the war, to replace wartime losses. Both took shape at Harland and Wolff's yard at Belfast. The *Edinburgh Castle* was launched by Princess Margaret on 16 October 1947, completed by November 1948 and sailed on her maiden voyage from Southampton to Durban on 9 December that year.

Union Castle mailships built since 1926 had all been motor-driven, but the two newcomers were steam-powered. The *Edinburgh Castle* was a handsome ship. The hull had a cruiser stern, good sheer with a curved and raked stem. Upperworks were nicely proportioned, with a fine big funnel. Passenger accommodation for first class and tourist was spread over six decks. As usual, first class were amidships, with tourist farther aft. Decks reading downward were: Boat deck, Promenade deck and decks A to D. Public rooms were mainly on the promenade deck. These included the first-class lounge forward together with a smaller lounge and smoke room, veranda café and, farther aft, the fine tourist lounge. Tourist smoke room was on A deck, with both dining saloons on C. Each class had a swimming-pool, the tourist open-air one being aft on the promenade deck while the first-class indoor one was on D. All the usual amenities such as shops, library and gymnasiums were found on board. First-class cabins were on A and B decks, tourist on B and C. The ship had considerable cargo capacity, with seven holds served by derricks. Much of the space was insulated for cargoes of fruit.

The *Edinburgh Castle*'s maiden voyage was very successful, and over the years she steamed steadily to and fro, becoming very popular. By 1950 all the Union Castle mailships were back on the route, the *Arundel Castle* being the last one to return. At this time the mail fleet consisted of the following 'Castles': *Arundel, Athlone, Capetown, Carnarvon, Edinburgh, Pretoria, Stirling* and *Winchester*.

In January 1954 the *Edinburgh Castle* showed her paces. She was delayed by boiler trouble after leaving Southampton, and had to put into Plymouth for repairs. After these were complete she proceeded to make a record passage to Cape Town in 11 days 21 hours. When the 'Round Africa' service by the UC intermediate or slower vessels ceased in the early sixties, it meant that the London-based ships no longer called at St Helena and Ascension. Arrangements were then made for the *Edinburgh Castle* and her sister to make occasional calls at these remote islands. In the meantime three more ships

had joined the mail service, the *Pendennis Castle* in 1958. *Windsor Castle* in 1960 and *Transvaal Castle* in 1961. During the sixties the *Edinburgh Castle* had fairly extensive refits, when various improvements were made such as extensions to air-conditioning. Externally the foremast was shortened and used as a kingpost for derricks. The after mast was removed and replaced by another one just aft of the bridge.

In 1965 a further 'speeding-up' of the service took place when a new schedule came into operation. Passage time was now reduced to eleven and a half days. The *Edinburgh Castle* and her sister had no difficulty in managing the extra speed, but some of the earlier ships, such as the *Stirling Castle* and *Athlone Castle*, could not achieve this and were withdrawn. These had virtually reached the end of their economic lives in any case. In late 1965 the *Pretoria Castle* and *Transvaal Castle* were transferred to the South African Marine Corporation (Safmarine) and renamed *S A Oranje* and *S A Vaal* respectively. Both continued on the mail run. Air travel had of course begun to take its toll by this time and, the mail service now looked rather different. A couple of cargo ships, the *Southampton Castle* and *Good Hope Castle*, were included and the rest of the fleet consisted of the *Windsor Castle, Pendennis Castle, S A Orange, S A Vaal*, and the *Edinburgh Castle*.

In the 1970s the final, sad rundown of the mail fleet took place. The *Edinburgh Castle* completed her last voyage on the South African service when she arrived at Southampton on 12 April 1976. She sailed later with cargo which was discharged at Durban, and then made her way to Kaohsiung, Taiwan, for scrapping.

The ship had been on the mail route for over 27 years, and had served very well. She would no doubt have survived a few more years on the 'Cape Run' had this not been discontinued.

Name: Edinburgh Castle

Line: Union Castle

Builders: Harland & Wolff, Belfast, launched 16 October 1947, completed November 1948

Dimensions: Gross tonnage 28,705/ Length 747 ft/Beam 84 ft

Machinery

Engines: 2 sets Parsons triple-expansion turbines, double reduction geared, twin screw

Boilers: 3 oil-fired watertube, 630 p.s.i., superheated 850°F

Service speed: 22 knots

Major Refits

1967 foremast shortened, 27,489 tons

Regular Routes

Southampton – Capetown and S. African ports

Passenger Capacity

1st 214, Tourist 541

Sister-ships
Pretoria Castle (1948)

Photograph 1959

Ellinis

THIS ship was built for the Matson Navigation Company's service from San Francisco to Honolulu. She took shape at the Bethlehem Shipbuilding Corporation's Yard at Quincy, Massachusetts. Launched on 18 July 1932, she was completed by December that year. The *Lurline* set off on her maiden voyage, a Pacific Circle cruise, on 27 January 1933.

The new vessel was rather similar to the earlier *Malolo*, the pioneer 'big ship' on the route. She was in fact somewhat larger than the earlier ship, but very similar in general appearance. The vessel was the last of a series of three practically identical ships built for the Company in the early thirties. The other two were the *Mariposa*, later to become Home Line's *Homeric*, and the *Monterey*, which eventually became the *Britanis* of the Chandris Company.

After completion of her initial cruise the *Lurline* entered the San Francisco-Honolulu service, running with the *Malolo*. The other two ships also ran from San Francisco and Los Angeles to Honolulu, continuing often to Australia and New Zealand.

The ship continued steadily on the service until 1941, although she made a Pacific cruise in 1934. On the day of the infamous Japanese attack on Pearl Harbour on 7 December 1941 the ship was homeward-bound from Honolulu, and reached San Francisco safely.

The *Lurline* was now taken over for wartime duties as a troop-ship and given a coat of grey paint. She could carry over 4,000 and, like other vessels, was on demise charter, one that would last till the end of the war.

Her duties took her to many parts of the Pacific war theatre. Sometimes she sailed on her old route to Honolulu, at other times she went as far as Australia and New Zealand. Other places such as Guadalcanal, Noumea and Suva featured in her itinerary, she carried, in addition to troops, survivors, wounded men, POWs and other personnel, and sometimes also supplies, since she had a good cargo capacity. Her high speed enabled her often to sail unescorted. She came through the war unscathed, though she no doubt had a few near-misses. In fact, in July 1942 a torpedo was seen heading towards her, but fortunately passed well aft.

The war over, she was involved in bringing troops and other personnel home again. Her record was impressive – 388,847 miles sailed, nearly 200,000 personnel carried.

In 1946 the *Lurline* was decommissioned and went for an extensive overhaul and refit at the United Engineering shipyard at Alameda, near San Francisco. This took until 1948, and brought her back to her pre-war glory. She then resumed the San Francisco-Honolulu service. The earlier *Matsonia* (ex-*Malolo*) had commenced the post-war service but had not been completely refitted, and was now withdrawn. The *Lurline* was to keep up the service on a single-ship schedule for the next 15 years.

However, competition from aircraft eventually took its toll, and in September 1963 the ship was sold to the Greek Chandris Group. She went to the Smiths Dock Company at North Shields and was extensively refitted. Her bow was now more raked and her foremast was replaced by twin sampson posts. Funnels became modern and streamlined, with pipes protruding above instead of the original cylindrical type. The bridge was reconstructed, and much alteration was made to passenger accommodation. She was now renamed *Ellinis*.

The ship left the UK for Greece, and on 30 December 1963, she made her first voyage to Australia via Suez, returning to Southampton via Panama a round-the-world trip, in fact. At this time there was no shortage of passengers, many being on assisted passage. Another famous ship on a similar route was the *Australis*, formerly the *America*.

The *Ellinis*'s sailing pattern was usually Southampton-Piraeus-Suez Canal-Fremantle-Melbourne-Sydney-Auckland. She returned homeward via the Pacific and Panama Canal.

In 1973 the Australian migrant contract came to an end and the *Ellinis* then spent much more time cruising, often from Southampton to the Mediterranean, Atlantic islands and West Africa. She also went to Scandinavian ports, while making the occasional Australian voyage, besides cruising from Australia and from Cape Town.

In 1974 she suffered turbine problems, but a replacement unit from the *Homeric* was fitted in Rotterdam, and this enabled her to keep going for a few more years. The *Homeric* had been withdrawn, and was being scrapped.

At the end of the decade, however, the *Ellinis* was withdrawn and laid up in October 1980, together with many other out-of-work ships at Perama Bay, Greece. No further employment was forthcoming, and, after lying rusting and neglected, the old ship went to Taiwan breakers, arriving at Kaohsiung in April 1987.

Name: *Lurline* (1932); *Ellinis* (1963)

Line: Matson Navigation Company (1932-63); Chandris (1963-87)

Builders: Bethlehem Shipbuilding Corporation, Quincy, Massachusetts; launched 18 July 1932, completed December 1932

Dimensions: Gross tonnage 18,021/ Length 632 ft/Beam 79.4 ft

Machinery

Engines: 2 sets steam turbines, single reduction geared, twin screw, 28,500 s.h.p.

Boilers: 12 oil-fired watertube, 400 p.s.i.

Service speed: 20 knots

Major Refits

1946-48 United Engineering, Alameda, extensive overhaul, 18,564 tons
1963 Smiths, North Shields, bow raked, foremast removed, funnels modernised, bridge reconstructed
1974 Rotterdam, replacement turbines fitted

Regular Routes

San Francisco – Honolulu
Southampton – Suez – Auckland – Panama – Southampton. Sometimes from Rotterdam

Passenger Capacity

1933: 1st 550, 2nd 250
1963: 1668 one class

Sister-ships and near-sisters

Mariposa (1931), *Monterey* (1932)
Malolo (1927)

Photograph 1964

Empire Orwell

THE ship was built for the German East African Line (Deutsche Ost-Afrika Linie), which dated from 1890. Its first chairman was Adolf Woermann, who was also involved with a company which bore his name. As a result the two concerns, DOAL and Woermann Line, were practically managed as one entity. They provided mail, passenger and cargo services to and from West African, Angolan, South African, South-West African and East African ports. Sailings were via the west coast of Africa and also via Suez.

The *Pretoria* and her sister *Windhuk* were both constructed at the Blohm and Voss Yard at Hamburg. The former was launched on 16 July 1936, and completed by the end of the year. She sailed on her maiden voyage from Hamburg to Cape Town on 19 December.

Our photograph shows her later in her career as the *Empire Orwell*, but her profile had not altered greatly from the original. The hull had good sheer, a slightly raked stem and cruiser stern. It contained three complete decks and two partial ones. Superstructure above was comparatively short but nicely proportioned, with a couple of large funnels on top. The ship catered for first class and tourists and a good standard of accommodation was provided. Cargo was also carried, worked by derricks. Service speed was a fairly modest 18 knots, quite adequate for the route.

The *Pretoria* and *Windhuk* were billed by the Nazi Government as the 'prestige' ships on the African service, and they were undoubtedly fine vessels. At over 16,000 tons they were far larger than any of DOAL's other ships. The next largest was in fact the *Ubena*, with a tonnage of about 9,500.

The *Pretoria*'s usual route was Hamburg-Southampton-Lisbon-Casablanca-Las Palmas-Walvis Bay-Cape Town-Port Elizabeth-Durban-Lourenço Marques, a long, leisurely voyage.

The ship continued on the African service until war broke out in 1939. During the conflict she was at first used as an accommodation ship for the German navy at Hamburg. Later she was put to use as a hospital ship. Towards the end of the war she was used, like many other German liners, in evacuating personnel from Germany's eastern territories. Many ships were sunk at this time, with great loss of life, but the *Pretoria* survived, only to fall into Allied hands in May 1945. Taken over as a war prize, she became a troop-ship managed by the Orient Line for the Ministry of War Transport. The ship was now renamed *Empire Doon*. Later she

was laid up for a while owing to problems with her boilers. These were high-pressure ones, and had not been entirely satisfactory.

In 1948–9 the ship was extensively refitted. This included replacing her boilers by those of another type and removing two turbines. The vessel's power was reduced somewhat as a result, and service speed became 16 knots. The superstructure was extended a little, and accommodation altered and improved for troop-carrying. The ship (now renamed *Empire Orwell*) was most useful in this role. For the next few years she carried out trooping duties to various parts of the world.

In 1958 she was chartered to the Pan-Islamic Shipping Company of Karachi for pilgrimage work, but at the end of the season she was laid up for a while. In November that year she came under the ownership of Alfred Holt and Co of Blue Funnel Line, and had a further refit at Barclay Curle, Glasgow. She was now to be permanently on the pilgrimage routes between Indonesia, the Middle East and Jeddah. Her troop accommodation was replaced by Indonesian pilgrim-type beds.

In March 1959 the ship sailed for Djakarta to take up service. She was renamed *Gunung Djati*. After three years she was sold to the Indonesian government to continue the same work. In 1965 and 1966 she was sold again, on both occasions to an Indonesian company. She continued in the same trade but, because of the heavy increase in oil fuel prices, was becoming expensive to operate by the early seventies. In 1973, now 37 years old, she was given a major refit in Hong Kong. Her steam machinery was removed, and replaced by two diesel engines. In 1977 she was again classified as a troop transport and accommodation ship by the Indonesian government. Incredibly, the ex-*Pretoria* survived until 1987, when she was sold for scrapping at Kaohsiung, Taiwan. In her latter years she was used more in her accommodation role. She had been renamed yet again in 1977 as *Kri Tanjung Pandan*.

Empire Trooper

BY THE end of the 1914–18 war the fleet of the Hamburg-South America Line (HSAL) had virtually ceased to exist. New ships had to be built, to be reasonably cheap, but with good passenger and cargo capacity.

Two ships were ordered from the Vulcan Yard at Hamburg. These were the *Antonio Delfino* and her sister, the *Cap Norte*. The former entered service in March 1922, followed by the other later that year.

Launched on 8 May 1922, the *Cap Norte* was completed by August and set off on her maiden voyage from Hamburg to the river Plate on 14 September.

Our photograph shows the ship much later in her career, but her general appearance had changed little. The hull had a straight stem and cruiser stern. It contained three overall decks with a shade deck above. There were nine main bulkheads and the central, rather square superstructure was topped by a single vertical funnel. The ship catered for first class, third class and steerage, with the steerage passengers numerous and accommodated in dormitories. Numbers carried varied throughout the ship's lifetime. Cargo capacity was very important, and the vessel had six holds and hatchways worked by derricks.

The *Cap Norte* commenced the regular HSAL route to the river Plate and ports on the east coast of South America. She was, like her sister, a popular vessel, steady and reliable. The big *Cap Polonio* was also on the route, but since she was much faster she was also more expensive to operate, and had no running-mate.

In 1927 the *Cap Norte* and her sister were speeded up a little by the addition of exhaust steam turbines to their machinery. They both continued to give reliable, if unspectacular, service up to the outbreak of war. In 1932 the ship was chartered to the Norddeutscher Lloyd line (NDL) for a time, and renamed *Sierra Salvada*. However, she reverted to her original name in 1934 when the charter ended.

In September 1939 the ship was homeward-bound from Pernambuco, Brazil, when war broke out. She landed her passengers at Lisbon, then attempted to reach Germany by steaming in a wide circle well clear of the British Isles, flying the Swedish flag. She was unsuccessful, however, being intercepted by the British cruiser HMS *Belfast* north-west of the Faroe Islands. Her crew had intended to scuttle the ship, but delayed too long and the *Cap Norte* was safely escorted into Scapa Flow. She was taken down to the Tyne for conversion to a troop-ship. Now renamed *Empire Trooper* and put under the management of the British India Company, she was seen in many theatres of war.

On Christmas Day 1940 the ship was in a large troop convoy bound for the Middle East, when it was attacked by the German heavy cruiser *Admiral Hipper*. The *Hipper* fired a number of shells, securing hits on several vessels before she withdrew. The *Empire Trooper* was somewhat in the rear, and sustained hits in a forward hold and engine-room causing casualties and flooding. The convoy had scattered during this action and the ship found herself rather alone, down by the head and listing. She was stoutly built, however, and, escorted by a corvette, limped into Ponta Delgada in the Azores. Here temporary repairs were made, and she then proceeded to Gibraltar for more permanent ones before eventually continuing her voyage.

The *Empire Trooper* was present at Madagascar during the invasion of that island in 1942, and was much involved in the landings in Sicily and at Salerno during the Italian campaign the following year. In fact, she made many trooping voyages until in late 1945 she went to the Tyne for a much-needed overhaul. Next year she had a more extensive refit to make her suitable for peacetime trooping. She now had cabin accommodation and standee berths, and was used for some time on the route from Tilbury to Cuxhaven transporting BAOR personnel and families.

In 1949 the ship was further modernized at Falmouth and carried on regular trooping duties throughout the world for another five years.

On 12 April 1955 the veteran arrived back at Southampton from Hong Kong and this spelt the end of her long career. She went to breakers at Inverkeithing, Scotland, but caught fire while awaiting demolition and sank. She was later raised and broken up.

Name: Cap Norte (1922-32); **Sierra Salvada** (1932-34); **Cap Norte** (1934-40); **Empire Trooper** (1940-55)

Line: HSAL (1922-39); British India (Managers) (1939-55)

Builders: Vulcan-Werke, Hamburg; launched 8 May 1922, completed September 1922

Dimensions: Gross tonnage 13,615/ Length 526 ft/Beam 64 ft

Machinery

Engines: 2 triple expansion, twin screw, 6,300 i.h.p.

Boilers: oil-fired cylindrical boilers

Service speed: 13.5 knots

Major Refits

1927: 2 Bauer-Wach exhaust steam turbines incorporated, 8,500 i.h.p., 15 knots

1949: Falmouth, modernization, 14,106 tons

Regular Routes

Hamburg – river Plate

Passenger Capacity

1922: 1st 184, 3rd 334, Steerage 1,368
1938: Cabin 175, 3rd 956
1949: Cabin 336, Troops 924

Sister-ships

Antonio Delfino (1922)

Photograph 1949

Empress of Australia

Name: **Tirpitz** (1914); **Empress of China** (1921); **Empress of Australia** (1922)

Line: HAPAG (1914-19); Canadian Pacific (1921-52)

Builders: Vulcan, Stettin; completed 1920

Dimensions: Gross tonnage 21,498/ Length 615 ft/Beam 75.1 ft

Machinery

Engines: 2 impulse-reaction turbines, twin screw, Fottinger hydraulic transmission, 14,000 s.h.p.

Boilers: 14 watertube, German navy type, 242 p.s.i.

Service speed: 16.5 knots

Major Refits

1921 John Brown, Clyde, conversion to oil-burning
1927 Fairfield, Clyde, re-engining: 2 sets Parsons turbines, single reduction geared, twin screw, 20,000 s.h.p., 6 double-ended Scotch boilers, 220 p.s.i., speed 19 knots

Regular Routes

Vancouver – Yokohama – Shanghai – Hong Kong – Manila
Southampton – Quebec

Passenger Capacity

1922: 1st 370, 2nd 190, 3rd 415, Steerage 1000
1927: 1st 400, 2nd 150, 3rd 630
1933: 1st 387, Tourist 394, 3rd 358

Near-Sister-ships

Reliance (1920); **Resolute** (1920)

Photograph 1928

THIS ship was ordered by the Hamburg–America Line before the First World War. With her two near-sisters (later to become *Reliance* and *Resolute*) she was intended for the South American service. Work was suspended during the war, however, and not completed until hostilities ceased. In 1919 she was handed over to Britain, and after arriving at Hull was briefly used for some trooping work. In February 1921 she was laid up for a short time at Immingham, but in July of that year she was bought by the Canadian Pacific company for their trans-Pacific route. Now renamed *Empress of China*, she was dispatched to the Vulkan yard at Hamburg to be adapted to their requirements. On 2 June 1922 she was renamed *Empress of Australia*.

She left the Clyde on 16 June, bound for Vancouver via the Panama Canal. She now took her place on the regular route from Vancouver to the Far East, calling at Yokohama, Shanghai, Hong Kong and Manila.

In 1923 the *Empress* ran aground briefly at Uraga near Yokohama, but was refloated undamaged. In the autumn of that year she achieved fame for her rescue work in the great Tokyo earthquake. On 1 September she was about to sail from Yokohama when great shocks were felt. The wharf, on which many people were gathered, partly collapsed, flinging some into the water. Winds of gale-force rapidly developed, making the big ship rock violently. However, lifeboats were soon launched, and many people picked up from the water. Eventually the *Empress* managed to get outside the harbour, where she anchored. The water was covered in burning oil, for tanks in a nearby naval base had burst, but the boats continued to bring survivors to the ship for medical help. It was estimated that in her role as a hospital ship she saved about 3,000 lives. On 8 September she sailed for Kobe, fully laden with refugees.

The *Empress* then resumed her routine voyaging. However, CPR were very dissatisfied with her machinery. Since she entered their service she had been disappointingly slow, rarely able to exceed 16 knots, and extravagant on fuel. In 1926 it was decided to fit her with completely new engines and boilers, so she returned to the Clyde in September. Proceedings were held up for a while by the General Strike, but eventually the replacement was completed. In trials she achieved over 20 knots, and fuel consumption was greatly reduced. Passenger accommodation had also been renovated, and the ship was transferred to the North Atlantic service. In the winter she was to be used for cruising.

She made her first voyage from Southampton to Quebec on 25 June 1927. On the next voyage she carried the Prince of Wales, Prince George, and the Prime Minister, Stanley Baldwin, to the Diamond Jubilee celebrations of the Canadian Confederation. In December she left on a round-the-world cruise, the first of four which she was to undertake. In the Depression years of the 1930s she also regularly cruised from the UK to Scandinavia and the Mediterranean, and from New York to the West Indies. While on a South Atlantic cruise in 1935 she made a call at the island of Tristan da Cunha to land supplies. In 1939 she acted as a 'royal yacht' to take the King and Queen to Canada.

On reaching Southampton in September 1939, the *Empress* was grey-painted armed with a three-inch high-angle gun and a few machine guns, and fitted out for trooping. Her first voyage took her out to Colombo and then across the Atlantic to Halifax. Here she joined a convoy bringing the First Canadian Division to Britain. During this voyage, which was heavily escorted, the *Empress* temporarily lost the convoy in thick fog. When she was eventually sighted by the destroyers the flotilla leader signalled 'Luke 15 verse 6', which reads 'Rejoice with me for I have found my sheep which was lost'.

In April 1940 the *Empress* carried many troops for the Norwegian campaign, during which time she came under air attack. Her duties took her to and from Malaya and the East Indies, across the Atlantic and round Africa; she was greatly involved in the North African invasion. She suffered many air attacks unscathed. However, when entering Oran harbour in 1943 she was in collision with the Orient liner *Ormonde*, another troop-ship. She was holed, and soon patched up, but had to be properly repaired on her return home. In October 1944 the *Empress* made the trip to Murmansk with Russian repatriates. Her last wartime voyage was in July 1945 to Hong Kong, where she embarked POWs for the UK. She was able to carry as many as 5,000 men, and also had capacious holds for cargo, a useful feature. During the war she had steamed about 250,000 miles and transported some 140,000 personnel.

After the war the *Empress* continued as a hired transport, making many voyages to the Middle East, India and the Far East. On 30 April 1952, she arrived back at Liverpool from Hong Kong and in May went to the breakers at Inverkeithing, the end of a long and distinguished career.

Empress of Britain

Name: **Empress of Britain**

Line: Canadian Pacific

Builders: John Brown & Co., Clydebank; launched 28 November 1928, completed May 1931

Dimensions: Gross tonnage 42,348/ Length 760.5 ft/Beam 97.5 ft

Machinery

Engines: 4 independent sets single reduction geared turbines, quadruple screw

Boilers: 8 Yarrow and 1 Johnson oil-fired watertube

Service speed: 24 knots

Regular Routes

Southampton – Quebec

Passenger Capacity

1st 452, Tourist 260, 3rd 470

Sister-ships

None

Photograph 1931

THIS fine ship, built at Clydebank in 1931, was one of the most remarkable passenger liners of the century. She possessed some unique features and provided a standard of luxury which has probably not been bettered. The Canadian Pacific Company had transferred their premier passenger ships to Southampton in 1922. Among those which ran on this route in the 1920s were some well-remembered ones the *Empress of Scotland* of 25,000 tons and *Empress of Australia* (21,850 tons) were former German ships. They were accompanied by the *Empress of France* of 18,500 tons. The speeds of these ranged from 17 to 19 knots. However, the company conceived the idea of building a very large, fast vessel for the Canadian service which they hoped would also capture some of the traffic to the American middle west. Passengers to Chicago, for example, would find that a quick voyage to Quebec followed by a rail journey saved many hours compared with the route via New York. The ship would also be specially designed for long cruises during the winter months when the St Lawrence was frozen over and transatlantic traffic slight.

The resulting 42,000-ton vessel was the biggest ship built in Britain since the ill-fated *Britannic* of the White Star Line, completed in 1915. She was also the largest passenger liner ever owned by Canadian Pacific a record which still holds.

Their premier passenger vessels were mostly 'Empresses' and earned a fine reputation on transatlantic and trans-Pacific services.

The first *Empress of Britain* of 14,000 tons had been launched on the Clyde in 1906. The second, the subject of our story, was laid down at John Brown's Clydebank yard on 28 November 1928. She was launched by the Prince of Wales on 11 June 1930, and sailed on her maiden voyage from Southampton to Quebec on 27 May 1931.

As can be seen from the photograph, she was a massive ship, high out of the water and possessing three enormous funnels. This was largely because her full-load draught had to be limited to 32 feet, and her length kept to the minimum necessary to achieve the required speed. It was essential for her to be able to pass through both Panama and Suez Canals and to enter many ports both large and small in her cruising role. She had a straight, slightly raked stem and a cruiser stern. There were in all ten decks; sun deck, boat deck, promenade deck and decks A to G, the last two being partial only. Very adequate subdivision was provided, there being fourteen watertight bulkheads. Of the three large funnels only the first two were used as uptakes. The third was a dummy, serving as an engine-room ventilator.

On completion the ship undertook extensive sea trials, during which she achieved 25.52 knots, a very satisfactory figure. Her first voyage was very successful, reaching Quebec in just over five days from Cherbourg. Her high speed permitted her to sail from Southampton once a fortnight. Her fuel-consumption proved to be remarkably low, and her reliability excellent. During the winter months she transported a wealthy clientele on round-the-world cruises. These occupied about five months, and included visits to about 80 ports. Usually only about four hundred privileged passengers were carried on these luxury voyages.

The ship had certainly succeeded in capturing some of the American middle west traffic, but to take full advantage of this, two ships were needed to provide a more frequent service. CPR had planned to do this, but the depression years of the 30s put paid to the idea.

A few mishaps befell the *Empress*, none of them too serious. The worst was on 16 June 1935, when she was in collision with the 5,000 ton collier the *Kafiristan* in the Gulf of St Lawrence in fog while eastbound. The collier was damaged, and three crewmen lost their lives. The *Empress* sustained only a slightly damaged bow, and was able to continue her voyage.

In 1939 she brought the Royal Family back to the UK from their tour of Canada, leaving Halifax on 15 June and calling at Newfoundland en route. The ship's last commercial departure was from Southampton on 2 September. On arrival at Quebec she was laid up, but two months later, painted grey, she was commissioned for trooping. Her first trip brought Canadian troops to Britain. She was ideal for the trooping role, and in addition to transatlantic crossings voyaged as far as New Zealand. Usually unescorted because of her high speed, on one notable occasion she sailed in a convoy which included among others the *Queen Mary* and *Aquitania*.

It was, however, while unescorted that she met her end. En route from Suez and Cape Town to Liverpool she was attacked and set ablaze by a German Focke-Wulf bomber off the NW coast of Ireland. This was on 26 October 1940. Boats were got away and rescue ships appeared. The big ship was taken in tow by tugs but was torpedoed and sunk by U32 two days later.

Empress of Scotland

THE *Kaiserin Auguste Victoria* was designed by the HAPAG line to combine large size and capacity with a fairly moderate speed. This policy was inaugurated after their unsatisfactory experience with the *Deutschland*, built in 1900; although very fast, she was unreliable in service and suffered from vibration problems. The new ship was to be called the *Europa*, but the presence of the German Empress at the launching decided the company on her final name. Her four masts and two funnels gave her rather an impressive appearance – she was the largest passenger liner in the world at the time.

The ship had a straight stem and elegant counter stem. The hull contained four decks and superstructure above was substantial but nicely proportioned. Cargo capacity was important and the vessel had seven holds, worked by derricks and winches. First class accommodation was of a luxurious standard and at the other end of the scale the steerage was rather austere.

The maiden voyage of the *Kaiserin* was from Hamburg to New York, and she continued to serve on this route, frequently calling at Southampton, until August 1914. She arrived back in Hamburg shortly before the war broke out, and there she remained for the whole duration. She was obviously thought too big for use as an armed merchant cruiser.

At the end of the war the ship was allocated to Britain, and sailed for England in March 1919. She was immediately lent to the United States for her first duty of repatriating American forces.

In 1920 the *Kaiserin* was operated by Cunard on their transatlantic service, starting her first voyage from Liverpool to New York on 14 February. However, shortly afterwards, in May 1921, she was sold to Canadian Pacific and renamed *Empress of Scotland*. Extensive refitting in the Vulkan-Werft yard at Hamburg followed, improving accommodation and also increasing her tonnage. Trials were carried out in January 1922, and she made her first transatlantic voyage for the company to New York, from where she did a cruise in the Mediterranean on charter to the Clark Travel Agency. From then on she was used mainly on the Southampton-Cherbourg-Quebec route, occasionally starting in Hamburg. In the winter months she was used for cruising, which included a world cruise which left New York in December 1925 and took six months. This trip was repeated the following year. She was at this time the largest passenger vessel to use the Panama Canal.

In 1923 the *Empress* rescued the crew of the schooner *Clintonia*, which was sinking in the Atlantic. A few months later she struck a submerged wreck off the Nab, and had to be dry-docked for repairs. She was involved in two minor collisions, with the German steamer *Bonus* in Hamburg, and the following year with the US steamer *Scottsburg*.

Unfortunately, the depression of the late 1920s meant that the *Empress* was no longer economically viable to run. When she arrived in Southampton in October 1930, she was withdrawn from service and sold to Hughes Bolckow of Blyth for scrapping. A charity ball was to be held on board soon after arrival at the port. Sadly, however, fire broke out one morning in the early hours. The ship was well ablaze by the time the fire brigade arrived and had to be scuttled. As the scrappers raised her, she broke in two, making it more difficult to break her up.

Name: **Kaiserin Auguste Victoria** (1905); **Empress of Scotland** (1921)

Line: HAPAG (1906-19); Cunard (1920); Canadian Pacific (1921)

Builders: Vulkan of Stettin; launched 29 August 1905, completed April 1906

Dimensions: Gross tonnage 24,581/ Length 705 ft/Beam 77.3 ft

Machinery

Engines: 2 sets 4-cylinder quadruple expansion engines twin screw 17,500 i.h.p.

Boilers: 9 Scotch-type, 8 double-ended, 1 single-ended, 200 p.s.i.

Service speed: 17.5 knots

Major Refits

1921 Vulkan-Werft, Hamburg, conversion of furnaces to burn oil fuel, 25,037 tons

Regular Routes

Hamburg – Southampton – New York (also Halifax)
Southampton – Cherbourg – New York
Hamburg – Southampton – Cherbourg – Quebec

Passenger Capacity

1906: 1st 652, 2nd 286, 3rd 216, Steerage 1842
1921: 1st 439, 2nd 478, 3rd 536

Near-Sister-ships

Amerika (1905), **George Washington** (1909)

Photograph 1928

Europa

THE Europa was the second of the large 50,000-tonners built by NDL in 1929–30. The first was the *Bremen*, whose career rather sadly lasted only 12 years. The *Europa* was built at the Blohm and Voss yard in Hamburg. She was launched on 15 August 1928, just one day earlier than the *Bremen* slid into the water at Bremerhaven. However, misfortune soon occurred. In March 1929, when the ship was nearing completion, a disastrous fire broke out which almost destroyed her. This happened in the early hours of 26 March and raged throughout the day. It was not until about 7 p.m. that the fire was virtually extinguished. By this time the ship was completely flooded and sitting on the bottom. The turbine machinery which had already been installed was badly damaged, in addition to the general devastation throughout the vessel. However, after discussion between her builders and NDL it was decided the ship could be repaired. First of all she had to be salvaged a difficult job after which Blohm and Voss made monumental efforts over the next few months, working day and night. Incredibly, she was completed by February 1930 and successfully carried out her sea trials in the North Sea.

It had originally been intended that the *Europa* would enter service before the *Bremen*, but of course the disastrous fire put paid to that idea. She eventually set out on her maiden voyage to New York on 19 March 1930 and at once captured the Blue Riband from her sister by a narrow margin. In the event, such was progress in the 1930s speed stakes that the record went to the Italian *Rex* in August 1933, and later, of course, to the *Normandie* and *Queen Mary*.

Like the *Bremen*, the *Europa* was fitted with a catapult to land a small mail-carrying plane, but this arrangement was dispensed with after a few years. Nevertheless, it had been a bold experiment and by all accounts successful, although costly. Also, like her sister, the *Europa*'s funnels were heightened later to improve smoke-dispersion.

The ship settled down to regular transatlantic crossings on the Bremerhaven – New York route. Together with her sister and the *Columbus*, she provided a weekly service. The ships, although successful, did not carry quite as many passengers as had been hoped. This was no doubt due partly to the international depression of the 1930s. There was also a growing anti-Nazi feeling in other European countries and America. Nevertheless, they continued reliably in service.

In August 1939 the *Europa* was on a westbound passage when a message was received ordering her to return to Germany. She accordingly reversed course and proceeded back to Bremerhaven, where she off-loaded her passengers.

Like her sister, the *Europa* sailed round to Hamburg, where it had originally been intended to convert both of them to troop-carriers for the planned invasion of England. However, this came to naught and both returned to Bremerhaven. The *Europa* survived the war intact and the neglected and badly rusted ship was seized by the American forces in May 1945. Some temporary repairs were done, and the ex-NDL ship was put under the US flag as AP 177 USS *Europa*. She was dry-docked in New York before commencing American trooping work.

However, she was not in very good shape, needing a thorough refit, and in early 1946 was handed over to the Reparation Commission. The French had a good claim to this former express liner as a replacement for the splendid *Normandie*, lost in 1942. The ship was accordingly handed over to them and went to Le Havre. Misfortune again struck. During a severe gale in December 1946 she broke adrift, struck the wreck of the *Paris* sunk in the harbour, holed herself badly and had to be scuttled to prevent capsizing. Pictures taken at the time show her sitting on the bottom of Le Havré harbour, sunk for the second time in her career. Fortunately, she was in an upright position and was salvaged by April 1947 and towed away to St Nazaire. Here the shipyard of Chantiers de l'Atlantique set about giving her a very comprehensive refit. The ship had been renamed *Liberté* by this time.

The ship completed her maiden voyage for Compagnie Générale Transatlantique under her new name in August 1950. She had been almost completely rebuilt, and no longer retained her outstanding speed. She could still manage voyages at about 24 knots, however, good enough to be paired with the famous *Ile de France*, and in 1952 with the new *Flandre* on the Le Havre – New York route. In 1954 her funnels were further heightened and fitted with dome tops. She continued reliably in service throughout the 1950s.

The new *France* was intended to replace both the ageing *Ile de France* and the *Liberté*, and so in November 1961 the latter made her last voyage for CGT. It was then hoped she would become a floating hotel for the World's Fair at Seattle but this idea was never realized and she went to breakers in La Spezia, Italy, in January 1962.

Name: Europa (1930); **Liberté** (1946)

Line: Norddeutscher Lloyd (1930-45); Compagnie Générale Transatlantique (1946-62)

Builders: Blohm & Voss, Hamburg; launched 15 August 1928, completed March 1930

Dimensions: Gross tonnage 49,746/ Length 941 ft/Beam 102 ft

Machinery

Engines: 4 sets triple expansion single reduction geared turbines, quadruple screw, 130,000 s.h.p.

Boilers: 24 oil-fired watertube, 327 p.s.i.

Service speed: 27 knots

Major Refits

1947 Chantiers de l'Atlantique, St Nazaire, refit, 51,839 tons

Regular Routes

Bremerhaven – New York
Le Havre – New York

Passenger Capacity

1930: 1st 687, 2nd 524, Tourist 306, 3rd 507
1950: 1st 569, Cabin 562, Tourist 382

Sister-ships

Bremen (1929)

Photograph 1937

France

THE Compagnie Générale Transatlantique – usually known as the French Line or more simply as CGT – dated from 1864. The North Atlantic route was their premier passenger one.

In the early years of this century their ships were in general smaller and slower than contemporary British and German vessels. However, from 1906 to 1911, some fine ships were added to the fleet, including the 13,700-ton *La Provence* and the 12,700-ton *Rochambeau*. It was decided in 1907 that a larger vessel should be built for the express service, to be the biggest ship ever owned by the company. The ship was laid down at the Penhoet yard in early 1909. Launched on 20 September 1910, she was completed in April 1912. She set off on her maiden voyage from Le Havre to New York on 20 April.

It had originally been intended to name the ship *La Picardie*, but later it was decided to name her after the whole country rather than just a province. At 23,600 tons she was the largest passenger vessel to be built in a French yard up to that time, as well as the only four-funnelled one.

The new ship's maiden voyage passed off very successfully, although the occasion was greatly dampened by a recent catastrophic disaster. The sinking of the *Titanic* had occurred only days previously, and most people were still numb with shock when the *France* arrived in New York.

Not unnaturally, the CGT took pains to emphasize that their new ship had on board enough life-saving equipment for all passengers and crew. She in fact carried 24 lifeboats, 22 being of 52-person capacity and two smaller ones that could take 25 each.

The summer of 1912 was marred somewhat by a French seamen's strike which had its effect on the new ship's operations. When it was over the *France* settled down to normal Atlantic voyaging. She handled well, and soon became very popular. The cuisine on board was splendid indeed, the French excelling in this field.

The new vessel's running-mates on the route included the *La Provence* mentioned above and the *La Lorraine* and *La Savoie*, each of 11,150 tons.

On the outbreak of war in 1914 the *France* sailed from Le Havre to New York in early August, heavily laden with Americans anxious to return home. The big ship was, however, soon to become a unit of the French navy. Fitted out initially as an armed merchant cruiser, she was renamed *France IV*. It was soon realized,

however, that with her considerable size and coal-hungry boilers she was not really suited to this role, her only advantage being her high speed. She then became a most valuable troop-ship and was much employed in 1915 transporting troops for the Dardanelles campaign, in company with such ships as the *Aquitania, Olympic* and *Mauretania*. She could carry 4,000 troops, and performed a most useful service.

Later she was converted to a hospital ship and served in this humane role throughout 1916 and much of 1917. In the latter year she again reverted to being a trooper, transporting Americans across to Europe. The ship suffered a boiler explosion in 1918 which resulted in nine deaths, but otherwise came through the war unscathed. She had been dry-docked in Toulon a couple of times for refitting and conversion work during this time. In 1918, and for much of 1919, the ship was engaged in taking American troops from Brest to New York, sometimes carrying civilian passengers as well.

By now she was back under CGT management, and in August 1919 recommenced the Le Havre – New York commercial sailings. The ship speedily regained her popularity with transatlantic passengers. The new *Paris* joined her in 1921, and at 34,500 tons relegated the *France* to second place as regards size. She was, however, not quite so fast as the earlier ship, whose fine reputation continued during the 1920s.

In 1928 the brand-new *Ile de France* joined the service. At over 43,000 tons she was by far the largest ship in the fleet. That same year on 16 June the *France* had the misfortune to strike a wreck in the Hudson river, incurring propeller damage. This was quickly repaired, and she was soon back in service. During the slack winter months this elegant ship now, like many others, went cruising. This took her to the Mediterranean, West Indies and Norwegian fjords. Once the Depression had set in this activity became an important alternative to the declining Atlantic trade. She incurred some damage in collision with the Italian cargo ship *Carmia* off the Ambrose Lightship in July 1931. After repairs she was back in the cruising trade but, alas, not for long. She completed her final sailing in August 1932 and was then withdrawn and laid up in Le Havre, in the hope that better times would materialize. A small outbreak of fire on board in January 1933 was soon brought under control, but the shipping situation did not improve and the *France* was sold for scrapping in late 1934 and broken up at Dunkirk.

Name: France

Line: Compagnie Générale Transatlantique

Builders: Chantier et Atelier de St. Nazaire (Penhoet); launched 20 September 1910, completed April 1912

Dimensions: Gross tonnage 23,666/ Length 713 ft/Beam 75.6 ft

Machinery

Engines: 4 sets Parsons triple expansion turbines directly coupled to 4 propeller shafts, 42,000 s.h.p.

Boilers: 8 single-ended, 11 double-ended cylindrical

Service speed: 23 knots

Major Refits

1923-24 Penhoet, furnaces converted to oil-firing, accommodation improved, 23,769 tons

Regular Routes

Le Havre – New York

Passenger Capacity

1912: 1st 534, 2nd 442, 3rd 250, Steerage 800
1923: 1st 517, 2nd 444, 3rd, 510, Steerage 152

Sister-ships

None

Photograph 1912

France

Name: **France** (1961); **Norway** (1979)

Line: Compagnie Générale
Transatlantique (1961-79); Norwegian
Cruise (1979-)

Builders: Chantiers et Ateliers de St
Nazaire; launched 11 May 1960,
completed 1961

Dimensions: Gross tonnage 66,348 (1989:
70,202)/Length 1,035 ft/Beam 110.5 ft

Machinery

Engines: 4 sets Parsons geared turbines,
quadruple screw, 160,000 s.h.p.

Boilers: 8 Penhoet oil-fired watertube

Service speed: 31 knots

Major Refits

1980 Hapag-Lloyd, Bremerhaven, now 2
turbine sets, twin screw, 40,000 s.h.p., 4
boilers, 18 knots, 3 bow thrusters, 2 stern
thrusters
1990 Bremerhaven — further
reconstruction, gross tonnage 76,049

Regular Routes

Le Havre — New York

Passenger Capacity

1961: 1st 407, Tourist 1,637
1980: 1,774 one class
1990: 2,024 one class

Sister-ships

None

Photograph 1962

IN THE fifties the North Atlantic ferry service flourished. Cunard's 'Queens' continued their splendid service, and the *United States* kept the Stars and Stripes flying prominently. It became obvious that the French Line (CGT) would have to build a new ship to compete with these, and as a replacement for their two elderly vessels, *Ile de France* and *Liberté*.

The splendid *France* was the result. She was launched at the Penhoet Yard, St Nazaire, on 11 May 1960, and was completed later the following year.

The ships trials were very satisfactory, speeds in excess of 34 knots being achieved, some 3 knots above the desired service speed. After a short 'shake-down' cruise from Le Havre to the Canary Islands, the big ship set off on her maiden voyage to New York, getting a great reception on arrival. She then settled down to regular voyaging, and swiftly gained a great reputation.

The United States Lines and CGT came to an agreement whereby the sailings of the *France* and *United States* did not clash, to the benefit of both companies. Late in the decade, however, the North Atlantic trade diminished as aircraft took over. Soon winter sailings were cut out and the big ship went cruising during this time. In 1972 she went on a round-the world trip, a very spectacular affair. As she was too big to transit the Panama Canal, the ship had to circle South America. Enough wealthy passengers were forthcoming for this voyage to be repeated in 1974, lasting from January to April.

North Atlantic traffic had greatly diminished by then, and there had been an astronomical increase in fuel oil prices. The French government relinquished its subsidy, and CGT had no option but to withdraw the ship, in spite of spirited demonstrations against this by the crew. In October 1974 she was laid up at Le Havre.

There she lay until purchased by the Norwegian Cruise Line, a division of Klosters Cruise Ltd, in 1979. (An earlier plan to convert her to a sort of floating casino had rather fortunately come to naught).

An extensive refit now followed at the Hapag-Lloyd Shipyard at Bremerhaven. Brief details of work done are as follows: The three top decks were lengthened and 24 luxury cabins and eight penthouse suites were added to the sun deck (now called Fjord deck). Other cabins were added to the promenade deck (now Pool deck). Many public rooms were refurbished and altered, and new bars and a casino incorporated. The ship now has an outdoor restaurant and three swimming-pools. Externally the most noticeable additions are the two big tenders forward with large supporting davits. These can each take 400 passengers ashore when the ship is not moored alongside.

In short the ship has been greatly transformed, but is still recognizable as the ex-*France* in spite of her new colour scheme and new name of *Norway*. Incidentally, the decks have been renamed too, and reading downward are: Sun, Fjord, Oslo, International, Pool, Viking, Norway, Atlantic, Biscayne, Caribbean, and Dolphin.

In May 1980 the *Norway* crossed from Oslo to New York via Southampton and then took up station at Miami. She cruises regularly from here through the Caribbean to St Thomas and St John (Virgin Islands) and St Martin (Leeward Islands), calling at NCL's private island Great Stirrup Cay, on the return trip.

In late 1990 the *Norway* was given a further refit at Bremerhaven. Two more decks were added above the bridge deck containing de-luxe accommodation. Passenger capacity has been increased by 250 and gross tonnage is now 76,049. She shares Caribbean services with other NCL ships including the *Seaward*, *Starward*, *Skyward* and *Sunword II*.

Thus, after a few years of idleness in mid-career, the ex-*France* seems assured of many more years of operation.

Early in 1992 the *Norway* was subject to new working arrangements. Kloster Cruise Ltd and Overseas Shipholding Group (New York) were to become joint owners/operators of the big ship and several others. The *Sunward* (ex *Royal Viking Sky*), *Westward* (ex *Royal Viking Star*) *Southward*, and *Starward* were to be operated also but still owned by Kloster.

Fürst Bismarck

Name: **Fürst Bismarck** (1899); **Don** (1904); **Moskva** (1907); **Gaa** (1910); **San Giusto** (1920)

Line: HAPAG; Russian Volunteer Fleet (1906-8); Austro-Hungarian Navy (1909-19); Cosulich (1919-24)

Builders: A.G. Vulkan, Stettin; completed May 1891

Dimensions: Gross tonnage 8,430/Length 522 ft/Beam 57.6 ft

Machinery

Engines: 2 sets triple expansion, 16,400 i.h.p.

Boilers: 6 double-ended Scotch type

Service speed: 20 knots

Major Refits

1909-10 reconstruction as depot ship

Regular Routes

Hamburg – New York
Liepaja – Rotterdam – New York
Trieste – New York

Passenger Capacity

1st 420, 2nd 172, 3rd 700

Near-Sister-ships

Augusta Victoria (1889), Normannia (1890), Columbia (1889)

Photograph 1899

HAMBURG–America had very largely been content up to the 1880s with rather medium-sized ships on the Atlantic run. However, under the astute leadership of Albert Ballin, a great name in German shipping, four splendid twin-screw ships were ordered. These were the *Augusta Victoria, Fürst Bismarck, Normannia* and *Columbia*. There had always been rivalry between the great Hamburg company and the Norddeutscher Lloyd of Bremen.

The *Fürst Bismarck* did very well on her trials, averaging over 20 knots, very respectable for those days. Sailing on her maiden voyage from Hamburg to New York on 8 May 1891, she performed well, in fact setting up a new record from Southampton to the American port with an average of about 19½ knots. With all four new ships in operation HAPAG could now provide a weekly service from the home port during the summer months. The *Fürst Bismarck* was in fact the largest of the four, and the last of them to enter service. She also proved to be the fastest, by a small margin.

During the winter months, passengers being few, the ships were withdrawn from the North Atlantic run. The *Augusta Victoria* was sent cruising in the Mediterranean in the winter of 1891, and this proved successful. The *Fürst Bismarck* and the others followed suit with cruising both in the Mediterranean and to Norway. The ship also, during the period 1894–1902, made some winter voyages from Genoa and Naples to New York.

In 1892 terrible outbreaks of cholera occurred in Hamburg, severely restricting the flow of passengers from the port. Every effort was made to stamp this out, but until the situation improved the ships used Southampton as their European terminal and only carried first and second class passengers during this time. The company suffered high revenue losses which took some time to recoup. As things improved a call at Cherbourg was inaugurated.

Such was the increase in size and speed of ships on the Atlantic ferry that within a comparatively short time the HAPAG quartet were becoming outmoded and outpaced. The NDL *Kaiser Wilhelm Der Grosse* eclipsed them all, and others soon followed suit.

The Spanish–American War broke out towards the end of the decade, and in 1898 the *Columbia* and *Normannia* were both sold to Spain for use as armed transports. The *Fürst Bismarck*, however, remained with HAPAG and still continued on the Atlantic run.

In 1900 HAPAG introduced their record-breaker *Deutschland* to the service. She proved to be a fast but rather erratic performer,

suffering from excessive vibration. By this time the NDL had gained the ascendancy again with other fast, reliable ships.

The *Fürst Bismarck*'s days on the express service were clearly numbered, but she still had many useful years ahead of her, as we shall see. The Russo–Japanese War proved profitable to the Hamburg company, and much of their fleet was chartered to the Russians. Fast merchant cruisers were required. Our subject made her last HAPAG Atlantic run from Hamburg – Southampton – New York in November 1903, and in 1904 became the *Don*, an auxiliary cruiser.

The *Fürst Bismarck* did not see much, if any, active service and in 1906 was acquired by the Russian Volunteer Fleet. This association had been founded in 1878 at St Petersburg. Its purpose was to build up a fleet which could be used as auxiliary cruisers attached to the navy in wartime. In peacetime they operated on services such as Odessa – Vladivostok and from 1903 Odessa – Naples – New York. After the war the latter service was not restarted, and a new one from Libau (now Liepaja, Latvia) – Rotterdam – New York began. It was on this route that our subject, now renamed *Moskva*, operated from May 1907. This proved to be short-lived, the RVF ceasing activities in 1908. The ship in fact made only four round voyages in this service, and then spent a period laid up. However, in 1909 she was purchased by the Austro–Hungarian navy. They required a suitable vessel for conversion to a depot ship, and the ex-HAPAG liner seemed to fit the bill. The ship was reconstructed for this role from August 1909 till May 1910. She was renamed yet again, this time as *Gaa*.

In her fresh role the ship was armed with four 4.7 inch and four 12-pounder guns. Her complement was 331 officers and men. Initially the ex-liner was used as a destroyer depot ship, but later fulfilled the same role for submarines. She was based in the Bay of Cattaro throughout the 1914–18 war.

At the end of the conflict the Austro–Hungarian Navy had ceased to exist. Now 30 years old, the veteran changed hands once again, becoming a member of a newly re-established company under Italian management. The Cosulich line based at Trieste recommenced operation in 1919, and the ex-HAPAG ship, after some refitting, sailed on their Mediterranean service to New York in 1921. She was nearing the end of her career, and was soon laid up prior to being sold for scrapping. She was broken up in Italy in 1924.

Gelria

THE Royal Holland Lloyd Company (Koninklijken Hollandschen Lloyd NV) of Amsterdam dated from 1899, when it was founded as the South American Line. It changed its name in 1908. As would be expected, the company ran services from Holland to South American ports.

The *Gelria* was built on the Clyde by Alexander Stephen & Co. Launched on 20 May 1913, the ship was completed by October and sailed on her maiden voyage from Amsterdam to the river Plate on 5 November. Alexander Stephen had in fact built a couple of earlier ships for the Dutch company, the 7,300-ton *Hollandia* in 1909 and the 7,900-ton *Zeelandia* in 1910. The *Gelria* and her sister *Tubantia*, also built there, were both 14,000-tonners and in the category of luxury liners.

Our subject was a fine-looking vessel, as can be seen in the photograph, taken later in her career. The hull with its good sheer, elegant counter stern and straight stem contained two complete decks and a shelter deck. The superstructure above was fairly substantial and typically rather 'square', with a couple of tall, slender funnels atop. The ship catered for first, second, third and steerage passengers. She had a good cargo capacity also. Service speed was 16 knots, quite adequate for the route. The *Gelria* and her sister were the biggest and most luxurious vessels in the Company's service, and swiftly became popular.

The outbreak of war in August 1914 resulted in German services to South America being withdrawn and British, French and other countries' shipping being reduced. The Dutch company thus had reduced competition, and kept their ships running.

However, on 16 March 1916 the *Tubantia* was torpedoed and sunk by the German *UB-13* in the North Sea, near the Noord Hinder lightship. This was in spite of her having her name and home port painted in large letters on her sides. Passengers and crew were picked up by Dutch rescue vessels, but as a result of this totally unexpected disaster it was decided to lay up the *Gelria* and she did not recommence the service until 12 March 1919.

The Dutch made strong protests to Germany about the sinking, and secretly reached an agreement with her to take over two 19,000-ton vessels then under construction. These were the *William O'Swald* and *Johann Heinrich Burchard*.

The *Gelria* continued on the South American route in company with other vessels such as the *Zeelandia* mentioned above and the 9,700-ton *Orania* and 10,000 ton *Flandria*, both of which joined in 1922.

The company's sailings were from Amsterdam, Southampton and Cherbourg to Spanish, Portuguese and South American ports. They also ran from Hamburg and Antwerp. In 1921, for a change, the *Gelria* made a voyage to the Dutch East Indies on charter to the Rotterdam Lloyd Company. Up until 1928 the ship was a coal-burner, but that year her furnaces were converted to oil fuel.

The Depression soon began to take its toll, and in 1931 the ship was laid up. During the second half of 1933 she was chartered by an Argentine concern for conversion to an exhibition ship, sailing out to Buenos Aires for this purpose. However, the scheme fell through and the ship returned to lay up in Amsterdam.

In 1935 she was sold to Italy, and now managed by the Lloyd Triestino Company, she was renamed *Gradisca*. This was the time of the Abyssinian war, and the ship was used for trooping and also as a hospital ship. Photographs have survived showing her in the latter role, with red crosses on her funnels and sides. After that conflict was over she made further trooping voyages to East Africa.

The *Gradisca* was also employed as an Italian hospital ship during the 1939–45 war. Following the capitulation of Italy in 1943 she was taken over by the Germans for the same use.

On 28 October 1944, while on a voyage from Salonica to Trieste, the ship was stopped by a British submarine and ordered to Alexandria where, after disembarking some wounded personnel, she proceeded to Algiers. After the war the vessel eventually became a British war prize.

On 23 January 1946 while on a voyage from Port Said to Malta the *Gradisca* ran aground off the island of Gavdos. She was later salvaged and laid up in Venice, but sold in 1949 for breaking up there.

The Royal Holland Lloyd Company ceased passenger-ship operations in 1936, although they continued with cargo vessels. They are now part of the big Nedlloyd Group.

Name: **Gelria** (1913); **Gradisca** (1935)

Line: Royal Holland Lloyd (1913-35); Lloyd Triestino (1935-44)

Builders: Alexander Stephen & Co., Linthouse; launched 20 May 1913, completed October 1913

Dimensions: Gross tonnage 13,868/ Length 560 ft/Beam 65.6 ft

Machinery

Engines: 2 quadruple expansion, twin screw, 12,000 i.h.p.

Boilers: 3 double-ended, 3 single-ended cylindrical, 220 p.s.i.

Service speed: 16 knots

Major Refits

1928 furnaces converted to oil fuel

Regular Routes

Amsterdam – river Plate

Passenger Capacity

1913: 1st 250, 2nd 230, 3rd 140, Steerage 900
1928: 1st 233, 2nd 350, 3rd 704

Sister-ships

Tubantia (1914)

Photograph 1920

George Washington

Name: George Washington (1909);
Catlin (1941); **George Washington**
(1941)

Line: Norddeutscher Lloyd (1909-17);
United States (1921-31)

Builders: Vulkan Yard, Stettin; launched
November 1908, completed June 1909

Dimensions: Gross tonnage 25,570/
Length 723 ft/Beam 72.8 ft

Machinery

Engines: 2 quadruple expansion engines,
twin scrw, 21,000 i.h.p.

Boilers: 8 double-ended, 3 single-ended
cylindrical, coal-fired Howden's forced
draught

Service speed: 18.5 knots

Major Refits

1920 Hoboken, 23,788 tons
1942-3 Brooklyn, oil-fired boilers fitted,
masts reduced in height, now one funnel
only

Regular Routes

Bremen — New York

Passenger Capacity

1st 520, 2nd 377, 3rd 614, Steerage 1,430

Near-Sister-ships

Kaiserin Auguste Victoria (1906);
Amerika (1905)

Photograph 1922

THIS big ship was built for the NDL Company's 'intermediate' service on the North Atlantic. She was not intended for speedy crossings, but could carry very large numbers of passengers in reasonable comfort. She in fact performed a similar duty to the White Star quartet of *Adriatic, Baltic, Cedric* and *Celtic*.

The Vulcan yard in Stettin were the builders of this 25,000-ton vessel. Launched in November 1908, she was completed the following year and set off on her maiden voyage from Bremen to New York on 12 June 1909.

The ship had the distinction at that time of being the biggest passenger liner built in Germany, but this was only to apply for a few years. Soon vessels of twice her tonnage were to take to the water. From the very first she proved a most satisfactory vessel. An excellent sea boat, she was very popular with passengers and for the next five years gave reliable, trouble-free service, transporting many thousands of them across the Atlantic.

The outbreak of war, however, curtailed her activities. She arrived in New York on 15 August 1914, and the US authorities stopped her from leaving. She was obliged to remain laid up, with several other German vessels, until 1917. America entered the war that year, and the *George* was needed as a transport to take American troops to France. Grey-painted, she became US Naval Transport No 54, but retained her name. She was fitted with four 5-inch guns and a number of smaller ones. The ship could carry 3,000 troops, and performed excellent service in her new role, coming through unscathed. After the war in 1919 she had the distinction of bringing President Wilson and his staff to Europe for the Versailles Peace Conference, and later taking them back again. She also acted as a 'royal yacht' in transporting the King and Queen of Belgium over for a visit to America.

By 1920 she had finished her trooping duties and was transferred to the US Shipping Board. Laid up for a while, she was then given a much-needed refit at Hoboken. The ship then made one voyage for the rather ill-fated US Mail Co. in August 1921 from New York to Bremen and back. Then, together with several other ships, she was transferred to the United States Line and continued on the transatlantic route. During the next few years she found herself sailing, under the US flag, with a number of other ex-German vessels, notably the ex-HAPAG ships *Leviathan* (ex *Vaterland*), *America* (ex *Amerika*) and *Republic* (ex *President Lincoln*).

The *George Washington* again proved very popular with the travelling public and was probably the most successful of US Line's very mixed fleet at the time. Like many other vessels, she sometimes went cruising in the off-season. Prohibition, however, caused a fall-off in traffic. In 1927 the ship was converted to a cabin-class ship and continued to be popular.

However, the Depression took its toll and in October 1931 the big ship was withdrawn and later laid up in the Patuxent river. She was still there when war came. In the interim period two new ships, the *Manhattan* and *Washington*, had entered US Line's service. They were, of course, more economical to run than the big ship.

In 1941 the ship was renamed *Catlin*, and was to be used as a US Navy transport. Not surprisingly, after her long lay-up she was in poor condition, especially her boilers. She was transferred to the British government, and some further unsuccessful attempts were made to get her operational. It was not until she had a thorough refit at Brooklyn in 1942–3 that real success was achieved. New oil-fired boilers were fitted, and she was completely overhauled throughout. By this time she had reverted to her original name once more. Now, minus her forefunnel and with a shorter after one, she had also had her masts reduced in height. The ship had gained a fresh lease of life and become once again a very efficient troop-ship, capable of carrying about 7,000 men. She made numerous voyages which included trooping from US ports to the UK and Mediterranean, and visiting such places as Bombay, Cape Town and Brisbane. In short she performed an invaluable service, both trooping and repatriation work, until 1947.

In March that year, while she was still operational, a serious fire occurred on board in New York. Badly damaged, she was laid up in Baltimore. Four years later, in January 1951, fire broke out on the quay where she was moored and soon engulfed the old ship. This time she was a complete write-off and there was no alternative but to scrap her.

Georgic

T HE *Georgic* was the second of the White Star motorships to be built for the Liverpool to New York service. Like her sister *Britannic*, she was built by Harland and Wolff at Belfast. Launched on 12 November 1931, she was completed by June next year and sailed on her maiden voyage on the 25th of that month.

The vessel was similar in most respects to the *Britannic*, with some differences, of course. Externally the forepart of the *Georgic*'s superstructure and bridge were rounded instead of straight like her sister's. Internally the decor of public rooms was modern in style, whereas the *Britannic*'s was 'period'. As in the earlier ship, the forward funnel was a dummy, housing the radio room and the engineers' smoke-room. Again like the *Britannic*, she catered for cabin, tourist and third-class passengers.

The *Georgic* joined her sister on the Liverpool-New York route, and her service up to the outbreak of war in 1939 was rather similar. This involved normal transatlantic work for much of the year, followed by some winter cruising to the West Indies. In 1933 she made some voyages from Southampton to New York relieving the *Olympic*, which was being overhauled. In 1935 both ships switched to a London-New York route.

At the outbreak of war the ship continued on the transatlantic run for a while, but in March 1940 was taken over for trooping duties. The ship took part in the evacuation of troops from Norway in May, and later performed similar duties from St Nazaire and Brest. She survived plenty of air attacks during this period. Further trooping to Iceland, across the Atlantic, and to the Middle East followed. However, it was when she was at Port Tewfik that disaster struck the ship. The *Georgic* had arrived there on 7 July 1941 and unloaded troops and stores. Loading for the home voyage was in hand when, in the early hours of 14 July, German bombers attacked the harbour. Severe damage resulted to shore installations, and the *Georgic*, being the biggest ship present, was singled out for special attention. One bomb exploding nearby caused severe leakage, while another, hitting aft, penetrated five decks before exploding. Fire at once broke out, and ammunition stored below exploded. Soon the ship was well ablaze. The captain managed to beach the vessel, the engineers gallantly remaining on duty below. Passengers were taken off and the ship burned for two days.

After temporary patching and pumping out the *Georgic* was eventually refloated and towed to Port Sudan. Here she lay for several weeks while more temporary repairs were done to prepare her for the long trip to Karachi. She was towed there by the *Clan Campbell* and *City of Sydney* assisted by tugs, a 2,775-mile voyage taking 26 days. After arrival, on 1 April 1942, much work was done during an eight-month period with considerable resort to improvisation. The *Georgic* then sailed under her own power to Bombay for dry-docking and more hull work. On 20 January 1943 the ship set forth on an epic, unescorted 6,200-mile voyage to Liverpool, arriving on 1 March.

She now went to her builders at Belfast for an extensive rebuilding, to become a permanent troopship. Her gutted upperworks were completely reconstructed and her machinery overhauled, and in December 1944 she reappeared as a fine trooper. She was still all grey, but minus her forward funnel. Her mainmast had also been removed, and the foremast considerably shortened. A small signal mast was fitted abaft the bridge. She was now owned by the Ministry of War transport and managed by Cunard White Star.

The ship now trooped to the Middle East, India and Italy. After the war was over she was engaged on repatriation duties. During 1946 she took back 5,000 Italian prisoners of war, and the same year brought a similar number of RAF and RN personnel from Bombay.

This work continued until 1948. In that year she was altered to an immigrant ship and commenced a service from Liverpool to Australia. Many other ships were also on this route.

While mainly keeping to this run she did six transatlantic voyages from Liverpool for Cunard in 1950, and from 1951 to 1954 made some passages from Southampton to New York. She also made a trooping voyage to Japan in 1955.

The *Georgic*'s final voyage ended in November 1955, and she was then withdrawn. Sold for demolition she arrived at Faslane for breaking up on 1 February 1956.

Name: **Georgic**

Line: White Star, later Cunard-White Star

Builders: Harland & Wolff, Belfast; launched 12 November 1931, completed June 1931

Dimensions: Gross tonnage 27,759/ Length 711 ft/Beam 82.3 ft

Machinery

Engines: 2 Harland Burmeister & Wain 10-cylinder 4-stroke double acting air injection diesel, each 10,000 s.h.p., twin screw

Service speed: 18 knots

Regular Routes

Liverpool — New York

Passenger Capacity

1930: Cabin 479, Tourist 557, 3rd 506
1948: 1,962 one class

Sister-ships

Britannic (1930)

Photograph 1953

Glenart Castle

Name: Galician (1900); **Glenart Castle** (1914)

Line: Union Castle

Builders: Harland & Wolff, Belfast; completed 1900

Dimensions: Gross tonnage 6,575/Length 430 ft/Beam 52.2 ft

Machinery

Engines: 2 triple expansion reciprocating, twin screw

Boilers 2 coal-fired cylindrical, 180 p.s.i.

Service speed: 12 knots

Regular Routes

London – Cape Town and South African ports

Passenger Capacity

1st 55, 2nd 70, 3rd 70

Sister-ships

German (1898); Galeka (1899)

Photograph 1917

THIS vessel was one of a series designed for the Union Line's service to South Africa. She was built by Harland and Wolff at Belfast, and was completed in 1900. She then commenced sailing on the slower, intermediate service.

Our photograph depicts her as a hospital ship at a later stage of her career. Although it shows her painted in different colours, her general appearance is virtually just as built. The hull had a straight stem and counter stern. It contained three decks, and the super-structure above was quite low. Two nicely raked masts and a tall, slender funnel completed an elegant profile. The ship catered for three classes of passengers, first second and third. Accommodation and public rooms were of a quite adequate standard for what was a secondary service. The ship had a good cargo capacity also – most important on this route.

This ship and her two sisters German and Galeka were the last of the vessels known as the G class built for the Union Line. These finally numbered ten, and proved to be successful ships. The first three were 4,700-tonners named Gaul, Goth and Greek built in 1893. The Guelph of 1894 was somewhat bigger, and the Gaika, Gascon and Goorkha of 1897 were of 6,300 tons. The Galician and her two sisters were very slightly larger. The ship took her place on the route and steamed steadily to and fro. The service was a leisurely one, the voyage to Cape Town taking about 21 days.

In 1900 the Union and Castle Lines combined to form Union Castle. Actually the Galician, although ordered by the Union Line, never sailed under its flag – by the time she was completed the new company had been formed. After the amalgamation, the base for the mail ships became Southampton, while the 'intermediates' sailed from London. For this service, in fact, cargo was often loaded at Hamburg, Rotterdam and Antwerp, the ship completing loading in London before sailing to South Africa.

In November 1901 the mail ship Dunnottar Castle broke a shaft when outward-bound and had to be towed into Dakar. The Galician, together with the Lismore Castle and Braemar Castle, embarked her passengers and mails and took them on to the Cape.

The Galician left Cape Town on 28 July 1914 with about 50 passengers and a valuable cargo. While she was at Lobito Bay the news of the outbreak of war was received. The captain was advised to keep clear of the Canary Islands, as it was thought that German raiders might be in the vicinity. The ship plodded steadily northward for another week, steering farther to the westward than usual. A wireless message was sent to Tenerife asking if supplies were available there, but unknown to the Galician her message had been overheard by the German raider Kaiser Wilhelm der Grosse, and the latter was able to intercept the slow-moving Union Castle vessel. She was boarded by a party from the enemy ship, her papers examined and her wireless equipment disabled; some medical supplies were taken, and two of her military passengers were made prisoners of war. The Galician was then ordered to steam ahead of the raider with all lights extinguished throughout the night and lifeboats made ready for use. However, early next morning the Kaiser Wilhelm signalled: 'I will not destroy your ship on account of the women and children on board. You are dismissed. Goodbye.' The Union Castle ship sailed on, calling at Tenerife where she related her experience. She reached England safely.

Soon after her encounter with the enemy raider the ship's name was changed. She was given the English name of Glenart Castle. Similarly, her sister-ship German was renamed Glengorm Castle.

The vessel now became a hospital ship, with a capacity for about 450 patients. She served well in this role on the Indian route, in the Mediterranean during the Gallipoli campaign of 1915, and on cross-Channel duties. On 1 March 1917, while bringing wounded from Le Havre to Southampton, HMHS Glenart Castle struck a mine off the Owers lightship. Although badly damaged, she was towed safely into Portsmouth and repaired. No lives were lost, her passengers being taken off by rescue vessels.

However, on 26 February 1918 she was bound from Newport to Brest. She had all her Red Cross lights burning but, when west of Lundy Island at about 4 am, she was torpedoed and sank very rapidly. Some of her people managed to cling to rafts and were later picked up, but there was great loss of life. Out of about 200 on board, only 38 were saved. The ship had been torpedoed by U-56.

The G class in general had quite long lives. The Glengorm Castle survived until 1930, the Gaika and Gascon till 1928. The Galeka, however, was mined in October 1916, and became a total loss. The Greek had several name-changes, eventually becoming Royal Mail's Chignecto.

Hamburg

Name: **Hamburg** (1926); **Yuri Dolgoruki** (1954)

Line: HAPAG (1926-45)

Builders: Blohm & Voss, Hamburg; launched 14 November 1925, completed March 1926

Dimensions: Gross tonnage 21,132/ Length 635 ft/Beam 72.5 ft

Machinery

Engines: 2 sets turbines, single reduction geared, twin screw, 14,000 s.h.p.

Boilers: 4 single-ended, 4 double-ended cylindrical, 225 p.s.i.

Service speed: 16.5 knots

Major Refits

1930 higher-powered turbines, 29,000 s.h.p., 19.5 knots, 4 watertube boilers, 400 p.s.i.
1933 lengthening, 22,117 tons, 677 × 72.5 ft
1950-60 reconstructed as factory ship 25,377 tons

Regular Routes

Hamburg — New York

Passenger Capacity

1926: 1st 222, 2nd 471, 3rd 456
1933: 1st 200, Tourist 350, 3rd 400

Sister-ships and near-sisters

New York (1927); **Deutschland** (1924); **Albert Ballin** (1923)

Photograph 1930

THIS vessel was one of the celebrated *Albert Ballin* class of four vessels. These were built by HAPAG for their intermediate transatlantic service.

The ship was constructed by Blohm and Voss at Hamburg. Launched on 14 November 1925, she was completed by March the next year and set off on her maiden voyage from Hamburg to New York on 9 April.

The four ships were built in pairs. The *Albert Ballin* and *Deutschland* were the first two, followed by our subject and her sister *New York*. All four were very similar in design, having a straight stem, cruiser stern, four masts and two funnels, one of which was a dummy. Blisters on either side of the hull gave stability.

In general, too, the *Hamburg*'s career followed similar lines to the other three. She was fitted with new engines and boilers from August 1929 to February 1930 which increased her speed by about three knots. A further refit took place in 1933, when her forepart was lengthened and modernized, resulting in a further increase in speed. All four of the class were in fact improved and kept up to date during their transatlantic service. By all accounts they were sturdy, comfortable and reliable vessels. The *Hamburg* continued steadily in service until the outbreak of war in 1939. In 1940 the ship was fitted out as an accommodation vessel for the German navy and stationed at Gdynia. In 1945 she was used, as were many other vessels, for evacuating service and other personnel from Germany's eastern territories. In three voyages the ship brought out some 23,000 people.

On 7 March that year, after disembarking her passengers at Sassnitz, the *Hamburg* was being taken to another anchorage when she struck a couple of mines. Severely damaged, the vessel sank. There she remained until raised by a Soviet salvage team in 1950. The vessel was then taken round to Antwerp and then to Warnemünde for the mammoth task of repairing and refurbishing.

The first idea was to rebuild the ship as a passenger vessel, somewhat on the lines of her near-sister, the *Albert Ballin/Hansa*, which was rebuilt to become the *Sovietsky Soyuz*. However, when reconstruction was well advanced after several years' work, it was decided instead to convert the ship to a whaling 'mother ship'. She finally entered service as such in July 1960, now renamed *Yuri Dolgoruki*.

Pictures taken at this time not unnaturally reveal a very different vessel from the original *Hamburg*. She now had a rather short superstructure with a massive single funnel atop. Much additional deck gear had been fitted, with a helicopter pad aft. No doubt the ex-*Hamburg* was effectively used in her new role until 1976, when she was withdrawn, and scrapped the following year.

Hanseatic

Name: **Empress of Japan** (1930);
Empress of Scotland (1942);
Hanseatic (1958)

Line: Canadian Pacific (1930-58);
Hamburg Atlantic (1958-66)

Builders: Fairfield Shipbuilding &
Engineering Co. Ltd, Govan, Glasgow;
launched 17 December 1929, completed
June 1930

Dimensions: Gross tonnage 26,032/
Length 666 ft/Beam 83.7 ft

Machinery

Engines: 2 sets Parsons turbines, twin
screw, single reduction gearing, 34,000
s.h.p.

Boilers: 6 Yarrow oil-fired watertube, 425
p.s.i., superheated 725°F, two Scotch
auxiliary boilers

Service speed: 21 knots

Major Refits

1958 Hamburg, extensive reconstruction,
tonnage 30,030

Regular Routes

Vancouver – Yokohama
Liverpool – Quebec
Hamburg – New York

Passenger Capacity

1930: 1st 399, 2nd 164, 3rd 100, Steerage
510
1948: 1st 458, Tourist 250
1958: 1st 85, Tourist 1,167

Sister-ships

None

Photograph 1958

THIS ship had a long and distinguished career in peace and war. She was built at the Fairfield Yard, Glasgow, for the Canadian Pacific's trans-Pacific service. Launched on 17 December 1929, she was completed and delivered by 8 June 1930. On 14 June she took her maiden sailing from Liverpool to Quebec.

As built the ship looked very different from our photograph, which was taken much later in her career. She originally had three well-spaced funnels, the after one being a dummy, and the upper deck had a proliferation of cowl ventilators. In addition to her passengers accommodation and amenities there was plenty of cargo space, much of it insulated, and stowage was provided for silk.

The trials of the *Empress of Japan* were very satisfactory, and she achieved 23 knots without difficulty. Her maiden voyage was from Liverpool to Quebec, with return to Southampton. Later she sailed out to Hong Kong via Suez, and then to Yokohama and across to Vancouver.

She was now employed on the trans-Pacific service together with the other *Empresses, of Asia, Russia* and *Canada*. The new ship was the fastest, and held the speed record. Her route to Yokohama was usually via Honolulu, and regular reliable crossings became the norm for the next nine years.

The ship was in Shanghai when war broke out in September 1939. She proceeded back to Victoria (Vancouver Island). Here a couple of guns were fitted and, grey-painted, she became an armed troop transport, being officially requisitioned on 26 November 1939. For the next 8½ years the ship remained on government service. Her wartime activities would fill many pages, so a fairly brief summary will have to suffice. She made a number of voyages from Australia to the Middle East, an important run. In May 1940 she was a member of convoy US 3 from Australia, which included the *Queen Mary, Aquitania, Mauretania, Andes, Empress of Britain* and *Empress of Canada*. She left this convoy at Cape Town and proceeded to Hong Kong.

In January and June 1941 the *Empress* took troops to Singapore. After an overhaul in Vancouver she again went there, arriving in January 1942. The situation was now bad, and she evacuated some women and children to Batavia.

Her name was now considered inappropriate since Japan was an enemy, and she was renamed *Empress of Scotland* in October 1942.

During 1943 and 1944 she was mostly on the North Atlantic run, bringing troops across from the USA and Canada, before again proceeding to Australia and New Zealand. The next three years were spent on voyages to Australia and India, latterly repatriating troops and civilians. During her 8½ years of service, the *Empress* had steamed over 720,000 miles, carrying 258,000 personnel and 30,000 tons of cargo. Of course she had a few near misses. On 9 November 1940, she was attacked and bombed by enemy aircraft some 400 miles west of Ireland. One bomb exploded in the water near the stern but, although damaged she made port and was soon repaired at Belfast.

The *Empress of Scotland* was released on 3 May 1948, and after a two-year extensive refit re-entered CPR service, now on the UK–Canada route. Many alterations and improvements had been made to the ship, and she now catered for first class and tourist. She sailed on her first voyage from Liverpool to Quebec via Greenock on 5 May 1950.

From 1952 the ship continued from Quebec to Montreal, her masts being shortened to pass under the bridges. She also cruised during the winter months, often from New York or Southampton to the Caribbean, South Africa and South America. In November 1951 she brought HRH Princess Elizabeth and the Duke of Edinburgh back to the UK after their Canadian tour. In 1956 the new *Empress of Britain* entered on the scene, followed the next year by the *Empress of England*. In 1958 the *Empress of Scotland*, now 28 years old, was sold to a newly formed German company, the Hamburg–Atlantic Line. Temporarily named *Scotland*, she sailed to Hamburg for an extensive refit at the Howaldtswerke shipyard.

She emerged from this looking as she appears in our photograph and renamed *Hanseatic*. The superstructure had been largely rebuilt and many internal alterations had taken place. She had a couple of swimming pools instead of one, and was fully air conditioned. Her tonnage was increased, and she now catered mainly for tourist passengers, with just a few first class. On 19 July, 1958, she made her first Hamburg–New York voyage. The old ship continued successfully on this route and went cruising during the winter months to Madeira, the Canaries, the Caribbean and the North Cape. Alas, this all ended in 1966. On 7 September that year fire broke out on board while she was in New York. Damaged beyond economic repair, she was sold to breakers at Hamburg.

Himalaya

THIS fine ship was built by Vickers-Armstrongs at Barrow. Launched on 5 October 1948, the *Himalaya* was completed in September the following year, and set out on her maiden voyage from London to Sydney on 6 October 1949.

In many respects she was similar to Orient Line's *Orcades*. The hull was of almost identical design, and the superstructure was of a broadly similar pattern, although different in points of detail. The bridge structure was in a conventional forward position, whereas that of the *Orcades* was adjoining the funnel. This latter feature was of different design, and was later further altered. The *Himalaya* sported a fine, well-raked mast in the usual position instead of the *Orcades*' small tripod.

The ship had eight decks, seven being for passengers. These, reading downward, were boat deck, promenade deck and decks A to E. Many of the first-class public rooms were on the promenade deck, with those of tourist class on B, C and D. Dining saloons for both classes were on D (the equivalent of F deck on the *Orcades*). First-class cabins were on A to D, with tourist on D and E. A most useful feature was a distillation plant which could convert sea water to fresh.

Trials were very satisfactory, speeds in excess of 25 knots being achieved. The *Himalaya*'s maiden voyage was a great success. In fact, the fine ship soon became very popular on the mail run. Keeping smoke and soot clear of the decks was a problem, alleviated to a great extent by fitting a Thornycroft funnel top in 1953. This was similar to the one fitted to the *Chusan*, and increased the funnel height by about 12 feet.

The *Himalaya*'s career followed a rather similar pattern to that of the *Orcades*, and the other vessels on the Australian route. The P & O – Orient services became much extended to include a Pacific, West Coast USA and Far Eastern network. The service included the *Arcadia*, *Chusan* and *Iberia*, together with Orient's *Orcades*, *Oronsay* and *Orsova*. A feature of the new arrangement was the introduction of 'Round-the-world' sailing, in both directions. This involved additional calls at places such as Bermuda, Miami, Nassau, Trinidad, and other Caribbean ports.

The *Himalaya* also cruised extensively, from both Australia and the UK. In 1963 she was converted into a one-class vessel, and by the late sixties she was used more and more for cruising, proving very popular. She had been improved at various refits. Fin stabilizers were added in 1959, and she was later fully air-conditioned all adding to passenger comfort.

From 1969 the ship's home port became Southampton instead of Tilbury, and the early 1970s were almost entirely spent cruising from there and from Sydney. The ship retained her great popularity to the end.

The *Himalaya* was very reliable in service, and few mishaps befell her in her lengthy career. On 30 August 1956, however, while in the Mediterranean en route to Australia, an explosion occurred in a domestic refrigeration plant. Three of her crew were killed and two more died later. Thirteen others were injured, some seriously, and these were put ashore at Malta. This was the only major mishap in the ship's career. In July 1959 one of her propellers was damaged on leaving the Suez Canal, and she completed the voyage on one screw, being repaired at Sydney.

The astronomical rise of fuel-oil prices in the early 1970s, coupled with the advent of purpose-built cruise ships, spelt the end of this fine ship's career. She made her last cruises from the UK in the spring of 1974, then sailed for Sydney for some more. On 19 October she left the Australian port for Hong Kong with passengers. They landed there, and the *Himalaya* then departed on her final voyage to the breakers at Kaohsiung, Taiwan, arriving there on 28 November 1974.

Name: **Himalaya**

Line: P & O

Builders: Vickers-Armstrongs, Barrow; launched 5 October 1948, completed September 1949

Dimensions: Gross tonnage 27,955/ Length 709 ft/Beam 90.6 ft

Machinery

Engines: Parsons turbines single and double reduction geared, twin screw, 42,500 s.h.p.

Boilers: 4 Foster-Wheeler watertube, 525 p.s.i., superheated 850°F

Service speed: 22 knots

Regular Routes

London – Sydney and trans-Pacific

Passenger Capacity

1949: 1st 758, Tourist 401
1963: 1,416 one class

Near-Sister-ships

Orcades (1948)

Photograph 1958

151

Homeric

THIS ship was to be initially an 'intermediate' steamer for the Norddeutscher Lloyd Company, although she was albeit a big vessel for such a service. They had four splendid 'express' vessels in operation for their first-line transatlantic service at the time (1913), and the 25,500 ton *George Washington* was doing good work on the slower secondary service. It was felt that a couple of other vessels of large size but similar economic speed (about 18 knots) would be very profitable, and accordingly two such ships were ordered from the Schichau Yard at Danzig. The one we are concerned with was launched there on 17 December 1913 as the *Columbus* but she was not to be completed for a long time due to the onset of war. By August 1914 the ship was about 80 per cent complete, but work was now halted, and did not continue until peace returned once more.

The incomplete vessel was ceded to Britain, and was purchased from the government by the White Star Line in 1920. The Company needed to obtain ships to replace war losses while the *Titanic* loss had also not been made good. Construction on the *Columbus* had recommenced rather slowly in 1919, the German shipyard workers were not working very enthusiastically, knowing the ship was to be handed over to their former enemy. White Star staff went to the yard to oversee final completion, and the big ship eventually arrived at Southampton for the first time on 21 January 1922. She sailed on her maiden voyage to New York on 15 February.

The ship had by now lost her original name of *Columbus* and, in keeping with White Star nomenclature, had been renamed *Homeric*. She looked all of her 34,000 tons, a solid-looking vessel indeed, with five overall decks and an orlop. Above were the bridge deck and boat deck, with further superstructure above. Her straight stem and counter stern helped to make her quite a good-looking vessel, through perhaps not as handsome as some. Fourteen main watertight bulkheads gave her excellent subdivision, and she had considerable cargo capacity with six hatches.

Accommodation was of a high standard, and she catered for first, second and third class passengers. As usual, the first class were amidships, with the second class further aft. Most public rooms were situated on the bridge and boat decks.

After a refit in 1923 she re-entered service with her speed somewhat improved to 19½ knots. The ship had now 'stepped up a grade', being on the White Star 'express' service to New York. She was running alongside the two giants *Olympic* and *Majestic* on this route, and remained on it for the next ten years. The big ex-German was not really fast enough for an 'express' service, and had not been built for it. However, a third ship was required, and the *Homeric* fulfilled this role in spite of being the 'slow boat'. She achieved a great reputation for steadiness over the years, and was popular with passengers, voyaging steadily until the Depression years arrived and fewer ships were required on the mail run. The *Homeric* made her last transatlantic voyage in January 1932, and her remaining, alas all too few, years were devoted to cruising. She was well suited for this purpose, having good accommodation and an economical speed.

The Cunard-White Star merger came in 1934, and the ship continued her cruising activities until September 1935 when she was withdrawn and laid up. In 1936 this fine ship was sold for breaking up, being scrapped at Inverkeithing. Her sister ship, laid down somewhat later, was originally to have been called *Hindenburg*. Later, however, she herself took the name *Columbus*, and survived until 1939.

Name: **Columbus** (1913); **Homeric** (1922)

Line: Norddeutscher Lloyd (1913); White Star (1920)

Builders: Schichau Shipyard, Danzig; launched 17 December 1913, completed January 1922

Dimensions: Gross tonnage 34,351/ Length 774 ft/Beam 82 ft

Machinery

Engines: 2 sets 4-cylinder triple expansion, twin screw, 32,000 total i.h.p.

Boilers: 12 double-ended, 210 p.s.i.

Service speed: 18 knots

Major Refits

1923 Harland & Wolff, conversion of boilers to oil-firing, 19.5 knots

Regular Routes

Southampton – New York

Passenger Capacity

1922: 1st 529, 2nd 487, 3rd 1750
1932: 1st 472, Tourist 832, 3rd 659

Sister-ships

Columbus (1924)

Photograph 1922

Iberia

Name: **Iberia**

Line: P & O

Builders: Harland & Wolff, Belfast; launched 21 January 1954, completed September 1954

Dimensions: Gross tonnage 29,614/ Length 718 ft/Beam 90.2 ft

Machinery

Engines: 2 sets triple expansion geared turbines, twin screw, 42,500 s.h.p.

Boilers: 3 Foster-Wheeler oil-fired watertube, controlled superheat, 620 p.s.i.

Service speed: 22 knots

Major Refits

1961 Thornycrofts, Southampton, passenger accommodation improved

Regular Routes

London — Sydney

Passenger Capacity

1st 674, Tourist 733

Sister-ships

Arcadia (1954)

Photograph 1960

THIS vessel was a virtual sister-ship of the *Arcadia*, which entered service a short time before her. Like the earlier vessel, she was intended for the Australian service and for cruising.

The ship was built at Harland and Wolff's yard at Belfast. Launched on 21 January 1954, she was completed by September that year and set off on her maiden voyage on the 28th of the month. She was very similar to her sister *Arcadia*. By comparing photographs of the two it will be seen that about the only external difference lay in the funnel design, although both stacks looked pretty good. The *Iberia* was 3 ft shorter than her sister, and her gross tonnage was slightly less. Rather sadly, this vessel was destined for a much shorter life than the *Arcadia*.

The ship's entry into service meant that P & O's post-war modernisation programme was complete. It made possible the introduction of a fortnightly express service from London to Sydney in conjunction with Orient Line vessels. Ships employed were the *Himalaya*, *Arcadia*, *Iberia*, *Orcades*, *Oronsay*, and *Orsova*.

The *Iberia*'s maiden voyage went off satisfactorily. She arrived at Sydney via Suez and Bombay on 1 November 1954, and was given a good reception. Returning to London before Christmas, her second voyage was delayed somewhat due to a temporary closure of the Suez Canal. A tanker in transit had collided with a bridge, and shipping was held up for a few days while the obstruction was cleared.

For the first few years of her career the *Iberia* was mostly on the UK–Australia route as planned. A mishap befell her on 29 March 1956, when outward – bound off Colombo. She was in collision with a 10,000 ton tanker, the *Stanvac Pretoria*. This vessel struck the P & O liner on her port side amidships, causing considerable damage.

She received temporary repairs at Colombo, then proceeded at reduced speed to Sydney via Fremantle and Melbourne with her passengers still on board. Complete repairs were carried out here at the Cockatoo Dockyard, but the ship was not ready for sea again until 2 May.

Like her sister *Arcadia*, the ship went cruising also during her career, to the Mediterranean and other favourite cruise areas. In 1958 she made her first call at New York. The ship had a major overhaul in 1961 at Thornycrofts' yard at Southampton. Passenger accommodation was upgraded, making it more suitable for cruising, and the air-conditioning was greatly extended. The *Iberia* was now doing her share of trans-Pacific cruise duties.

After the refit she sailed to Australia, New Zealand and Japan before returning to the UK for a programme of summer cruising. During the 1960s the ship became a familiar sight with cruise passengers on the west coast of the USA, like her sister *Arcadia*. Both ships were doing fairly similar duties. The *Iberia* also became well known in Cape Town and Durban when she had to take this route due to Suez Canal closure. Unfortunately, in the late 1960s the ship was beset with mechanical and other problems. It seems that her machinery and electrical equipment was not so reliable as that of her sister. In October 1968 a breakdown in the power system delayed her at Madeira for several days while on a cruise. In December 1969 she limped into Southampton after a disastrous voyage from Australia via Panama. Among other mishaps the funnel had caught fire at Pago-Pago for a short while, raining red-hot soot on the decks. An electrical fault caused her to be a day late at Honolulu, and at Acapulco problems with the starboard engine developed which slowed her for the rest of the voyage. At Curaçao a baggage room was accidentally flooded with oil while refuelling.

She went into dry-dock at Southampton for repairs, but on her next Australian voyage further electrical problems resulted, among other things, in her stabilizers being out of action for a while during a gale. She was back in the UK for summer cruises in 1970, before again going to Australia and the Pacific.

1971 was spent on the Australian and Pacific route, followed by her last series of cruises from the UK. She left for Sydney in November, and once more cruised the Pacific. While she was there P & O announced that she would be withdrawn and sold. The jets had now taken over with a vengeance, and the big liners were no longer well patronized on this route. On arrival at Southampton on 19 April 1972 the *Iberia* was laid up in the Western Docks. Sadly, she was sold for scrapping and left for Taiwan on 28 June that year.

The ship's career had only spanned 18 years. The economic situation, coupled with her propensity for breakdowns, had no doubt caused her premature withdrawal.

Ivernia

THIS fine ship was one of the quartet built for the Cunard Canadian service. She was launched from John Brown's Clydebank yard on 14 December 1954, completed by June 1955, and set off on her maiden voyage from Greenock to Montreal on 1 July that year.

The *Ivernia* was almost identical to her sister *Saxonia*. The hull had a raked stem, good sheer and cruiser stern. Superstructure was low, with a round topped funnel amidships, and a single mast abaft the bridge.

The ship's second voyage was from Liverpool to Montreal, and this was the main route of the quartet. For the first few years the ships on the Canadian service did well, carrying plenty of passengers and cargo. During the winter months when the St Lawrence was frozen over they sailed to New York instead.

In 1957 the *Ivernia* transferred to the Southampton to Montreal route, together with her sister *Saxonia*. The other two, *Carinthia* and *Sylvania*, remained on the Liverpool service.

Like her sister, the *Ivernia* was withdrawn and refitted as a cruise liner from October 1962 to June 1963. This work was done by her builders, and she emerged with altered and improved passenger accommodation. Now with a green hull, she was renamed *Franconia*, her sister having been renamed *Carmania*. In July 1963 she made her first voyage under her new name from Rotterdam to Montreal. The ship now had full air conditioning among other improvements. Both ships were mostly on the Canadian service during the summer, switching to cruising from Florida to the Caribbean in winter. However, over the next few years there was a general falling-off in passenger trade to Canada and the *Franconia* and *Carmania* spent more and more time cruising. In 1967 both were given white hulls, and in that year the *Franconia* made the last Cunard passenger voyage from Liverpool to Montreal. In 1968 the *Carinthia* and *Sylvania* were disposed of, being sold to the Italian Sitmar Line. The *Franconia* and *Carmania* continued with Cunard, but were losing money. During the course of their careers problems with striking dock-workers from time to time had added to their financial problems.

By 1970 the *Franconia* and her sister were solely used for cruising, but in 1971 were withdrawn and laid up at Southampton. Late in 1972 they transferred to the river Fal, a favourite area for ships to lay up.

In August 1973 they were sold to the Nikreis Maritime Corporation of Panama, who acquired them for the Russian State Shipping Company. Both went to the Swan Hunter Yard at South Shields for overhaul. The *Franconia* was now renamed *Fedor Shalyapin*, her sister becoming the *Leonid Sobinov*.

On 20 November 1973 the *Fedor Shalyapin* made her first sailing under Russian ownership from Southampton to Sydney and Auckland. Subsequently she cruised in Australian and Far Eastern waters. In May 1976 she was chartered by Shaw Savill Cruises of Australia for six months. In 1979 the ships were banned from Australian ports as a protest against the Russian invasion of Afghanistan, and they had to proceed to the Russian Pacific coast. Later the *Fedor Shalyapin* was employed in a Black Sea Service.

Name: *Ivernia* (1955); ***Franconia*** (1963); ***Fedor Shalyapin*** (1973)

Line: Cunard (1954–73), Russian Companies (CTC, USSR-Far Eastern Shipping Co) (1973–)

Builders: John Brown & Co., Clydebank; launched 14 December 1954, completed June 1955

Dimensions: Gross tonnage 21,717/ Length 608 ft/Beam 80.4 ft

Machinery

Engines: 4 Parsons turbines double reduction geared, twin screw, 24,500 s.h.p.

Boilers: 4 oil-fired watertube, 550 p.s.i.

Service speed: 20 knots

Major Refits

1963 John Brown, Clydebank, conversion to cruise liner, 22,637 tons
1973 Swan Hunter, South Shields, general overhaul

Regular Routes

Liverpool – Montreal
Southampton – Montreal

Passenger Capacity

1955: 1st 110, Tourist 833
1963: 1st 119, Tourist 728

Sister-ships

Saxonia (1954); ***Carinthia*** (1956); *Sylvania* (1957)

Photograph 1958

157

Jan Pieterszoon Coen

Name: **Jan Pieterszoon Coen**

Line: Nederland Royal Mail

Builders: Nederland Shipbuilding Co.,
Amsterdam; launched 30 September
1914, completed June 1915

Dimensions: Gross tonnage 11,692/
Length 522 ft/Beam 60.4 ft

Machinery

Engines: 2 sets 3-cylinder triple-expansion
engines, twin screw, 7,400 i.h.p.

Boilers: 8 single-ended cylindrical, 215
p.s.i.

Service speed: 15 knots

Regular Routes

Holland — Dutch East Indies

Passenger Capacity

1st 200, 2nd 166, 3rd 43

Near-Sister-ships

Johan de Witt (1920)

Photograph 1927

THIS vessel was built for the Nederland Company's service from Holland to the Dutch East Indies. She was constructed by the Netherlands Shipbuilding Co. of Amsterdam. Launched on 30 September 1914, the ship was completed by June 1915 and set off on her maiden voyage to the Far East in July that year.

As can be seen, the vessel had a rather striking appearance. The hull had a straight stem, elegant counter stern and quite good sheer. It contained two overall decks and a shelter deck. Superstructure above was substantial, with a couple of rather slender funnels. Bridge and poop decks were combined, and the ship had quite a lengthy forecastle. The *J P Coen* in fact was rather similar in many respects to the slightly smaller *Johan de Witt* of 1920 which features in this book. She catered for first, second and third class passengers, and a good standard of accommodation was provided. Public rooms were light and airy. The vessel had a good cargo capacity also, as will be obvious from the many cranes and derricks. This was a very important requirement for the route.

The ship of course commenced her service during wartime. The normal route had been via Suez, but the *J P Coen* now sailed via the Cape. As she was a neutral vessel, she had her name painted in large letters on her sides, together with the flag of the Netherlands in order to discourage any attack by U-boats. In late 1916 the Dutch mail steamers changed their route, now proceeding via the Panama Canal.

The ship came through the war unscathed, and continued in service during the twenties and thirties. Her story in fact was rather similar to that of the *Johan de Witt*. Another running mate on the route was the *Prins der Nederlanden*, of 9,300 tons, dating from 1914. Other vessels joined the fleet. The *Pieter Corneliszoon Hooft* commenced in 1926, and the *Christiaan Huygens* the following year. In 1930 the 19,000-tonners *Johan van Oldenbarnevelt* and *Marnix van St Aldegonde* commenced operating.

The *J P Coen* was now a little outdated, but still continued running. When war came and Holland was invaded, many ships of the fleet made their escape. The *J P Coen*, however, was taken over by the Dutch naval authorities and sunk at Ijmuiden across the North Sea Canal, in an effort to block it. This of course brought her seagoing career to an end in a rather dramatic way, and a few years later she was broken up.

Johan de Witt

THE Dutch mail, passenger and cargo services to the East Indies were operated by two major companies, the Rotterdam Lloyd and the 'Nederland' Company of Amsterdam. Both of these ran a number of ships on this route and had a high reputation for comfort and service.

The Nederland Royal Line (Nederland Stoomvaart Maatschappij) was founded in 1870, and commenced services to the Dutch East Indies via the Suez Canal. Ships gradually increased in size over the years. The fine 11,700-ton *Jan Pieterszoon Coen* of 1915 was a good-looking vessel, and during the war a slightly smaller ship, the subject of this article, was laid down. She was not completed until hostilities had ended, and set forth on her maiden voyage in 1920.

The *Johan de Witt* was built by the Netherlands Shipbuilding Company, Amsterdam, and was quite an attractive-looking vessel. Her hull had a straight stem and cruiser stern. There were three overall decks including shelter deck, and the superstructure was nicely proportioned. Of the two funnels the aft one was a dummy.

When she sailed in 1920 on the East Indies run the *Johan de Witt* was about the smartest vessel on the route. Sailing from Amsterdam, ports included Southampton, Algiers, Genoa, Port Said, Colombo, then Singapore, Batavia (Djakarta), and East Indies ports. This was a lengthy voyage accomplished at the fairly leisurely speed of 15 knots, quite adequate for the purpose. The ship continued reliably on the route, and was later joined by some larger running-mates. These were both motorships, the first being the *Pieter Corneliszoon Hooft* of 14,600 tons which commenced the run in 1926, followed by the 16,000-ton *Christiaan Huygens* the next year.

In 1930 the Nederland Line introduced the *Johan van Oldenbarnevelt* and *Marnix van St Aldegonde*. These 19,000-ton vessels were somewhat faster than the *Johan de Witt*, and rather put her in the shade. She was in fact laid up for a short period.

The *P C Hooft* was now lengthened and given new machinery to push her speed up a couple of knots. However, very sadly, she caught fire in Amsterdam and had to be written off as a constructive total loss. This was in November 1932. Her place was taken on the route by the *Johan* once again, but the latter's speed was not now adequate, and in 1933 she was refitted in Amsterdam. Her original machinery was retained, but she now sported a Maierform bow, which increased her length by a few feet. Speed had been increased to about 16 knots. In general her appearance had been improved too. She remained on the mail run, interspersed with some cruising activity, until 1940. The *Johan de Witt* managed to get away from Amsterdam before the Germans invaded, and after sailing to the East Indies proceeded on to Sydney where she was converted into a troop-ship. She did very useful work in this role. During this time she sailed under Orient Line management.

She returned to Amsterdam in late 1945 and then made some voyages out to the East Indies. However, with the changing political situation her former trade had virtually disappeared. The Nederland Line had two passenger ships left besides the *Johan*. The *Oranje* and *Johan van Oldenbarnevelt* had both survived the war, but the *Marnix van St Aldegonde* had been lost. The former two vessels were now put on a round-the-world service, and the *Johan* put on the sales list, as she was now something of a veteran.

In December 1948 she was sold to the Greek Line and received the rather shorter name *Neptunia*. She was given a refit which considerably altered her appearance. Her after dummy funnel was removed, and the fore-funnel replaced by a larger one. The mainmast was also removed, as were some of the cranes, and considerable rebuilding took place. The ship was now to run alongside the old *Nea Hellas*, (formerly the anchor liner *Tuscania*) on the route from Piraeus to New York. She made her first voyage in 1949, and was on this for a couple of years before being transferred to the Bremerhaven-New York-Boston service. This involved calls at Southampton and Cherbourg. The *Neptunia* had been further refitted at Naples, and now catered for a small number of first-class passengers and over 700 in tourist class. In 1953 she was joined on the route by the brand-new *Olympia*.

Soon the *Nea Hellas* (which had been renamed *New York*) also entered the Bremen-New York service. Later the *Neptunia*'s route was altered to a Montreal service from Bremerhaven, calling at Southampton and Cherbourg. She now sported a white hull which if anything enhanced her appearance.

On 2 November 1957 when entering Cobh harbour she grounded on the notorious Daunts Rock. The ship was beached and all passengers and crew escaped unharmed. The old ship was very badly damaged, however, and since she was now 37 years old, it was not an economic proposition to repair her. She was sold for scrapping in Holland.

Name: Johan de Witt (1920); **Neptunia** (1949)

Line: Nederland Royal Mail (1920-48); Greek Line (1948-58)

Builders: Nederland Shipbuilding Co., Amsterdam; completed 1920

Dimensions: Gross tonnage 10,355/ Length 499 ft/Beam 59.4 ft

Machinery

Engines: 2 sets 3-cylinder triple expansion, twin screw, 7,000 i.h.p., 15 knots

Boilers: 6 single-ended, forced draught, 215 p.s.i.

Service speed: 15 knots

Major Refits

1933 Amsterdam, lengthened, 16 knots
1948 dummy funnel removed, forefunnel replaced, mainmast removed

Regular Routes

Holland — East Indies
Piraeus — New York
Bremerhaven — Boston/Montreal

Passenger Capacity

1920: 1st 197, 2nd 120, 3rd 36
1951: 1st 78, Tourist 748

Near-Sister-ship

Jan Pieterszoon Coen (1915)

Photograph 1921

Johan van Oldenbarnevelt

THE Nederland Royal Mail Line or, to give it its full title, Nederland Stoomvaart Maatschappij of Amsterdam dated from 1870. Its main service was a passenger, mail and cargo one to the Dutch East Indies via Suez. All vessels had been steamships until 1925, when a 15,000-ton motorship, the *Pieter Corneliszoon Hooft* was built, followed two years later by the *Christiaan Huygens* of about the same size. The company decided on a couple of larger, 19,000-ton vessels, which became the *Johan Van Oldenbarnevelt* and *Marnix van St Aldegonde*.

The *Johan* was built in Amsterdam by Nederland Shipbuilders. Launched on 3 August 1929, she was completed in March 1930 and set off on her maiden voyage from Amsterdam to the Dutch East Indies in May. As can be seen in the photograph, the ship was of rather unusual appearance. The hull had a slightly raked stem and cruiser stern. Superstructure was pretty substantial, with a couple of small funnels on top.

The *Johan*'s maiden voyage was in fact delayed somewhat when she collided in the North Sea Canal with the Dutch freighter *Reggestroom*. She was only slightly damaged, but had to return to Amsterdam for repairs. She was soon off again, and the voyage was very successful. The ship and her sister *Marnix* were the biggest vessels owned by the company, and soon became very popular with passengers travelling on this route. They provided a pleasant, leisurely service, the voyage from Amsterdam to Batavia (Djakarta), calling at numerous ports en route, taking about 29 days.

The *Johan* operated steadily during the 1930s with few incidents. However, during the Spanish Civil War, passing the coast of Spain was sometimes hazardous. On 31 July 1937 the ship was fired on and hit by some shells while so doing. Luckily, only slight damage resulted. In the summer of 1939 she made a trip to New York and back for the Holland-America Line, taking tourists and refugees anxious to flee from the Nazis. In September the *Johan* sailed to Batavia via the Cape. Her European port later became Genoa. Intending passengers from Holland had to travel there by rail, and the ship proceeded via Suez.

The *Johan* was on a return journey, in the Red Sea when the Nazis bombed Rotterdam in May 1940. She was ordered to turn back to the East Indies and was soon transferred to a service from Java to New York via the Cape. In January 1941 she officially joined the Allied cause and was converted in New York to a troop-ship. She could carry 4,000 troops, and was to be very usefully employed in this role throughout the war. The ship which still had Dutch officers with a Dutch and Javanese crew was put under Orient Line management. During her fine war service she motored about 281,000 miles transporting some 72,000 personnel.

Initially she did some transatlantic trooping, successfully avoiding the U-boats. The ship took part in the North African landings, putting many troops ashore for this campaign.

In February 1945 she sailed to Italy and on to Port Said, taking out and bringing back personnel. Further voyages followed, to Bombay returning with POWs, and again to India, Singapore and Penang. She returned to her owner's peacetime service in 1946.

She was now employed on her old route again, taking troops out to the East Indies, and returning with civilian personnel while the struggle for independence went on. By 1950 the political climate had changed so much that the route was no longer viable. The *Johan* now switched to taking passage-assisted Dutch settlers out to South Africa and Australia.

In the late fifties it was decided that the *Johan*, together with the company's 20,500-ton *Oranje* and Royal Rotterdam Lloyd's 23,000-ton *Willem Ruys*, should be modernized and put on a round-the-world route. The ship's appearance was considerably altered. Her funnels were increased in height and given rounded tops. The foremast had been shortened, mainmast removed and a small signal mast positioned on the bridge roof. Her hull was now a light grey.

Unfortunately, the service did not prove very successful, there being a shortage of passengers. The ship was withdrawn from it in late 1962, and for a short while took up the role of hotel ship at Fremantle for the Commonwealth Games at Perth.

The *Johan* was now sold to the Goulandris-owned Greek Line; she was in fact registered to a subsidiary, the Ormos Shipping Company. A refit followed at Genoa, and the ship was renamed *Lakonia*. She was now intended to cruise from Southampton. A series of cruises was completed, but not without some problems. Her speed was not satisfactory, and she went into dry dock at Southampton for overhaul in December 1963.

On 19 December the *Lakonia* set off on her last tragic voyage. There were 1036 passengers and crew on board. When nearing Madeira an outbreak of fire occurred which quickly spread. Rescue ships appeared but despite all efforts the death toll was 128. The burnt-out hulk was taken in tow but sank on 29 December.

Name: ***Johan van Oldenbarnevelt*** (1930); ***Lakonia*** (1963)

Line: Nederland Royal Mail (1930-62); Greek Line (1962-63)

Builders: Nederland Shipbuilding Co., Amsterdam; launched 3 August 1929, completed March 1930

Dimensions: Gross tonnage 19,040/ Length 608 ft/Beam 74.8 ft

Machinery

Engines: 2 Sulzer 10-cylinder diesel, twin screw, 14,000 total b.h.p.

Service speed: 17 knots

Major Refits

1941 New York, conversion to troop-ship
1959 Amsterdam, funnels heightened, foremast shortened, main mast removed, 20,314 tons

Regular Routes

Amsterdam – Batavia
Amsterdam – South Africa, Australia

Passenger Capacity

1930: 1st 366, 2nd 280, 3rd 64, 4th 60
1959: 1,210 one class

Sister-ships

Marnix van St Aldegonde (1930)

Photograph 1933

Kaiser Wilhelm II

Name: **Kaiser Wilhelm II** (1903);
Agamemnon (1917); **Monticello**
(1929)

Line: Norddeutscher Lloyd (1903-17); US
Shipping Board (1920-40)

Builders: Vulkan, Stettin; launched 12
August 1902, completed 30 March 1903

Dimensions: Gross tonnage 19,361/
Length 707 ft/Beam 72.3 ft

Machinery

Engines: 4 sets quadruple expansion,
44,500 total i.h.p. twin screws

Boilers: 12 double-ended, 7 single-ended
cylindrical 225 p.s.i.

Service speed: 23 knots

Major Refits

1917 Brooklyn, conversion to troop-ship

Regular Routes

Bremerhaven – New York

Passenger Capacity

1st 775, 2nd 343, Steerage 770

Near-Sister-ships

Kaiser Wilhelm der Grosse (1897),
Kronprinz Wilhelm (1901);
Kronprinzessin Cecilie (1907)

Photograph 1912

THIS ship was the third of the four-funnelled 'express' liners built for the NDL company in their very successful bid to win supremacy on the North Atlantic. She was built at the Vulcan Yard at Stettin, as were all the others, and was launched on 12 August 1902 in the presence of the Kaiser. She was completed by 30 March the following year, and went off on her maiden voyage from Bremerhaven to New York on 14 April 1903.

As can be seen from the photograph, the ship resembled in appearance the earlier Stettin-built 'flyers' *Kaiser Wilhelm der Grosse* and *Kronprinz Wilhelm*. At over 19,000 tons, she was considerably larger than the earlier two and had an additional mast. Her accommodation and public rooms were on similar lines, and have been described as luxuriously magnificent, in the heavily decorated style of that period. Like the other members of the NDL fleet, she was earmarked for naval service in wartime, and was suitably stiffened in particular areas for fitment of guns.

The ship's maiden voyage passed off satisfactorily, although it was not a record – breaking one as she struck some rough weather. Machinery performed well, but there were some vibration problems – not unusual in new ships. A change of propellers improved matters considerably: the ship was now making crossings at around 23½ knots. She settled down to reliable regular service, and by 1906 had both the eastbound and westbound records.

The fourth 'four-funneller', the *Kronprinzessin Cecilie*, joined the service in 1907, and the NDL now had a very well-balanced fleet of 'express' liners. The speed records were soon to be wrested from them by the new Cunarders *Mauretania* and *Lusitania*, but the NDL ships carried on reliably and very efficiently until the outbreak of war in 1914.

On 17 June 1914, while on a westbound crossing, the *Kaiser Wilhelm II* was struck amidships by the British steamer *Incemore* of 3,060 tons just after passing the Needles in dense fog. This necessitated repairs at Southampton and cancellation of her voyage, passengers being transferred to another vessel, HAPAG's *Imperator*. Repairs having been completed, the ship returned to her normal service. She was on her way to New York when war broke out, and on arrival at the US port on 5 August she tied up at her pier, and there she remained for nearly three years.

However, when America entered the war in 1917 the *Kaiser Wilhelm II* and several other interned German liners were taken over for use as troop transports. The big ship was renamed *Agamemnon*, and given a much-needed refit at the Brooklyn Navy Yard. She was armed with four 6-inch guns and a couple of 3-inch ones. Her sister *Kronprinzessin Cecilie* had also been interned and likewise taken over for transport work. She was renamed *Mount Vernon*.

For the next 3 years the *Agamemnon* carried many thousands of American troops to France, and then when the war ended brought them back to America again. In November 1917 she was involved in a collision with the ex-*Kronprinz Wilhelm*, her erstwhile sister-ship, causing some damage to both vessels. In fact the *Mount Vernon* was torpedoed by one of her countrymen's U-boats in September 1918 while in a fast convoy in which the *Agamemnon* was also present. She succeeded in making port safely.

Trooping service ended in 1920. The *Agamemnon* was laid up at Boston, as was the *Mount Vernon*. Both now belonged to the US Shipping Board. The ex-*Kaiser Wilhelm II*'s story now really becomes something of an anti-climax. One would have thought that the ship, only seventeen years old, still had some useful service ahead of her. But it was not to be. No doubt she would have been costly to refit. Her huge reciprocating machinery was now somewhat outdated: the great height of these engines had given stability problems, and meant that about 2,000 tons of ballast were needed during her working life. Various schemes were proposed to get the ship and her sister operational. These included conversion to geared turbine machinery with oil-fired watertube boilers. This would have lowered the centre of gravity and greatly improved the stability situation. Another alternative was to fit diesel engines. Unfortunately, nothing come of any of these proposals. The idea of using the ship as a floating trade fair also came to naught. In 1924 both ships were laid up in Chesapeake Bay and simply lay idle, deteriorating with the passing years. In 1929 the *Agamemnon* was renamed *Monticello*, but more years passed, and the ships continued to lie degenerating at their moorings. In 1940 both were offered to Britain but not accepted. That same year both of them went for scrap at Baltimore.

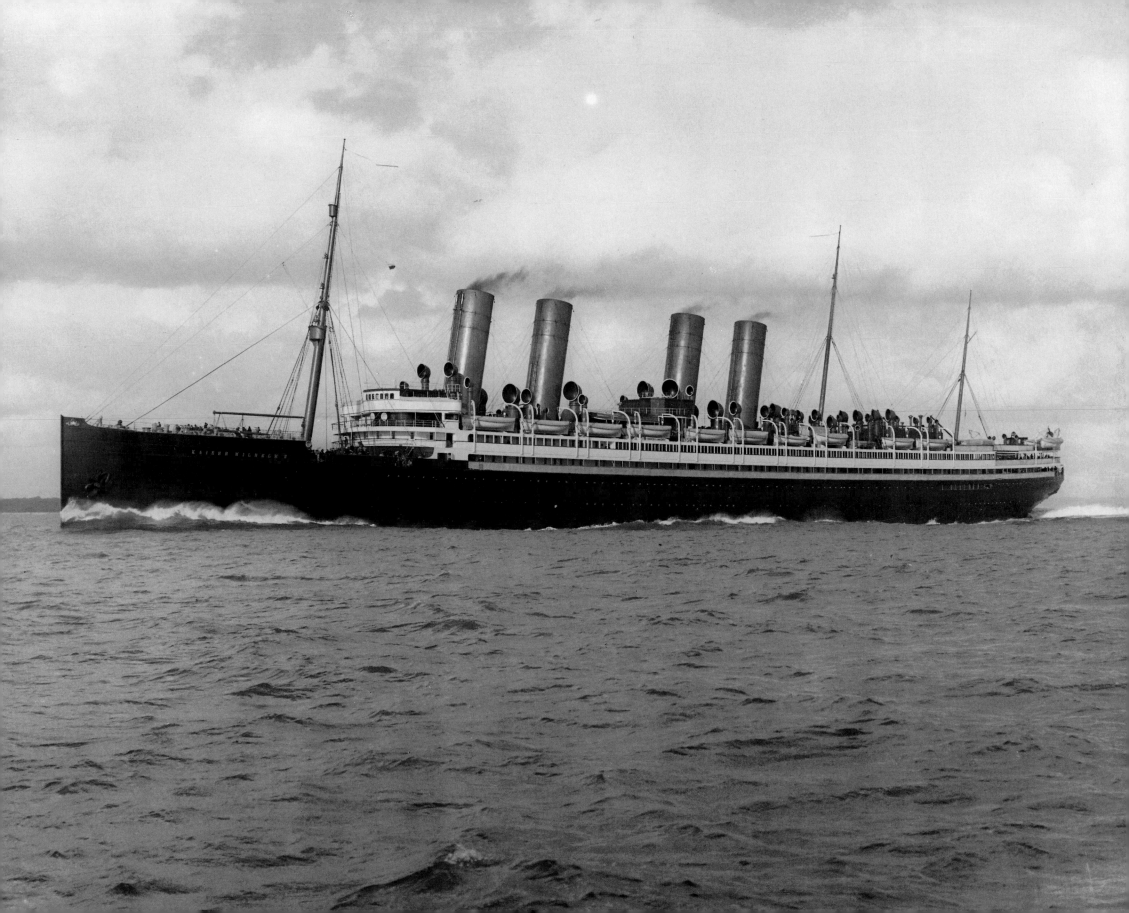

Kaiser Wilhelm der Grosse

Name: **Kaiser Wilhelm der Grosse**

Line: Norddeutscher Lloyd

Builders: 'Vulkan', Stettin; completed 1897

Tonnage: 14,349 gross

Length: 655 ft/Beam 66ft

Machinery

Engines: 2 sets of 4-cylinder triple expansion engines, i.h.p. 31,000 twin screw

Regular Routes

Bremerhaven – New York

Passenger Capacity

Numbers varied during the ship's career 1st 558, 2nd 338, Steerage 1074

Near-Sister-ships

Kronprinz Wilhelm (1901); **Kaiser Wilhelm II** (1903), Kronprinzessin Cecilie (1907)

Photograph 1912

THE two large German shipping companies, Norddeutscher Lloyd of Bremen and Hamburg-America, had always been major contenders on the North Atlantic. In the 1890s the competition was very keen and German tonnage was increasing rapidly. The Bremen company had long realised that large fast ships were likely to attract a high percentage of Continental, British and American passengers. The *Kaiser Wilhelm der Grosse* was the first of a series of 'flyers' which made a name for themselves on the transatlantic route. The conditions laid down by the company to the builders, Vulcan of Stettin, were onerous to say the least. Trials were to include the complete maiden voyage of a double Atlantic crossing. If the NDL's requirements were not fully met they had the right to reject the ship. In return the builders had a big say in the vessel's design.

The ship was launched on 3 May 1897 in the presence of Kaiser Wilhelm II and a crowd of about 30,000. The ship sailed from Stettin in 29 August 1897, but going up the river Weser to Bremen she went aground and remained stuck for about a week, eventually refloating undamaged. She sailed on her maiden voyage from Bremerhaven on 19 September bound for Southampton and New York. She was at that time the largest passenger liner in the world. Her maiden voyage was to establish her beyond doubt as a potential 'riband' holder: she averaged over 21 knots between the Needles and Sandy Hook westbound, and nearly 22 knots on the eastbound to Plymouth. Later that year the *KWDG* gained the eastbound record at 22.35 knots and in 1898 captured the westbound one with an average of about 23. These were fine performances, but her greatest distinction was to be her consistency and reliability. The result was that the ship was never short of passengers. In 1898, for example, the ship carried nearly a quarter of all transatlantic passengers landed at New York. The *KWDG* enjoyed a rather unique distinction in another way. She was the first merchant ship to be commercially equipped with ship-to-shore wireless on the Marconi system. This apparatus, fitted in February 1900, had only a range of about 25 miles, but was very useful for reporting arrival times.

In October 1907 the ship encountered heavy weather whilst on an eastbound crossing. Struck by an enormous following sea, her rudder was ripped off. But, steering by means of the twin screws, she reached Bremerhaven via Plymouth without mishap, declining assistance which was offered by several other ships.

The advent of the steam turbine, and the coming of faster ships such as the *Mauretania* and *Lusitania* of the Cunard Line, took some of the lustre away from the *KWDG* and her consorts. However, she continued reliably in service until war came in 1914. Fitted out as an armed commerce raider, she was sent out into the Atlantic. Her speed was useful for this purpose, but heavy coal consumption was a disadvantage.

She was fitted with six 10.5 cm quick firing guns and two smaller (3.7 cm) ones. 400 rounds of ammunition were carried for the larger guns and 200 for the 3.7 cm. She was thus a pretty formidable adversary when she set sail from Germany on 5 August 1914. Commanded by Fregatten-Kapitan (Captain) Max Reymann, she carried a crew of 584 officers and men.

Her first success was a pretty small one: the little British trawler *Tubal Cain* was sunk by gunfire 50 miles from Iceland after the crew had been taken on board. This was on 7 August. By mid-August she was in position near the Canaries when the *Arlanza* of Royal Mail Line was sighted, homeward-bound from Rio. The British ship was ordered to heave to, but on discovering she carried many women and children, Reymann allowed her to proceed. Later the Union Castle liner *Galician* was afforded similar treatment, but two cargo ships were not so fortunate. New Zealand Shipping Company's *Kaipara* was encountered some 170 miles from Tenerife on 16 August and sunk by gunfire after her crew had been safely taken off. Elder Dempster's *Nyanga* was captured and scuttled on the same day. Her crew were transferred to a collier and eventually reached Las Palmas.

Time was running out for the German Merchant cruiser however. Her insatiable appetite for coal proved to be her downfall. On 26 August the British cruiser *Highflyer* found her coaling off Rio de Oro on the African Coast in Spanish territorial waters. Captain Buller of the British cruiser signalled to the German to surrender but this was refused. A sharp engagement followed, and although the *KWDG* put up a good fight, scoring several hits, the issue was never in doubt. After about two hours the ex-NDL flyer had sunk, finally being scuttled when the position was hopeless and ammunication had run out. Fortunately there was little loss of life on either side. 82 of the *KWDG*'s crew escaped ashore, to be later interned. Most, however, got away on one of the nearby supply ships, the *Bethania*. Later this ship was captured by a British cruiser, HMS *Essex*, and the *KWDG*'s crew became prisoners.

Kenya

Name: Kenya

Line: British India

Builders: Barclay Curle & Co., Stobcross, Glasgow; launched 28 November 1950, completed August 1951

Dimensions: Gross tonnage 14,464/ Length 540 ft/Beam 71.2 ft

Machinery

Engines: 2 sets Parsons triple expansion geared turbines, 12,300 s.h.p.

Boilers: 3 Babcock & Wilcox oil-fired watertube, 450 p.s.i., superheated to 750°F

Service speed: 16 knots

Regular Routes

London – East African ports via Suez

Passenger Capacity

1st 194, Tourist 103

Sister-ships

Uganda (1952)

Photograph 1953

THIS ship, and her sister *Uganda*, were built for the British India service from the UK to East African ports. This had been a traditional route of this company for many years. Both vessels were built by the Barclay Curle Yard at Stobcross, Glasgow. The *Kenya* was launched on 28 November 1950, completed by August 1951 and sailed on her maiden voyage from London to East Africa on the 22nd of that month.

She was a handsome vessel, as can be seen in the photograph. (This picture, incidentally, shows her dressed overall for the Fleet Review at Spithead in 1953.) The ship had a well-raked stem and cruiser stern, plus nicely proportioned upperworks with single funnel amidships.

There were five passenger decks, and public rooms and accomodation was of a very high standard. First-class and tourist passengers were carried. All first-class public rooms were on the promenade deck comprising a smoking-room, lounge, library, writing-room, veranda, ballroom etc., also a swimming-pool. Tourist rooms were on the deck below A, as was also their swimming-pool. Much wood panelling was used in the decor of the public rooms a feature not found so much today. Both dining saloons were on C deck, and other amenities, medical facilities etc were provided. Cargo was of considerable importance on the route, and the *Kenya* had five cargo holds served by the same number of hatches. Two derricks were fitted at each hatch for handling. Propelling machinery consisted of two sets of single reduction geared turbines driving twin screws. Steam was provided by three watertube boilers. An auxiliary boiler was also fitted for domestic services.

The ship's trials were carried out successfully on the Clyde, where she achieved a speed in excess of 19 knots. This was very satisfactory, as a service speed of only 16 knots was required for this route.

The maiden voyage was successful. When she arrived at Mombasa there were no less than six other British India vessels in the port as well, sea travel being of paramount importance in those days.

In August 1952 the *Kenya* was joined by her sister *Uganda* and with these two fine ships in service, four of the smaller vessels were gradually withdrawn. These were the 9,000-tonners *Matiana*, *Mantola*, *Mulbera* and *Modasa* built in 1921–2.

The *Kenya* and her sister steamed steadily to and fro, and became very popular with passengers. In 1955 they were both given white hulls, which was perhaps more suitable for a tropical service.

The route taken varied a little from time to time according to requirements. A typical one would be London, Gibraltar, Port Said, Aden, Mombasa, Tanga, Zanzibar, Dar-es-Salaam, Beira and Durban. Calls were made at other ports, including Lourenco Marques, Malta, Naples, Marseilles and Barcelona.

During the 1960s trade dwindled on the East African route. This was due to the changing political situation. Air travel was of course increasing rapidly, and container ships began to replace conventional cargo vessels such as the *Kenya* and her sister. The closure of the Suez Canal in 1966 did not help; it meant re-routing via the Cape. Altogether the service was becoming unprofitable. For a while the sailings of the two ships were timed in conjunction with those of the Union Castle intermediate vessels *Rhodesia Castle* and *Kenya Castle*. However, all was to no avail. The *Uganda* was withdrawn in 1967 and converted into a school ship. The *Kenya* soldiered on alone, but in 1969 she too was withdrawn. She arrived back in London for the last time in June that year, and soon afterwards was sold to shipbreakers at La Spezia, Italy.

Kronprinz Wilhelm

THE *Kronprinz Wilhelm* was the second in a fleet of four ships built by the Norddeutscher Lloyd Company of Bremen to provide a transatlantic express service. Completed in 1901, she sailed on her maiden voyage from Bremerhaven to New York in September of that year. With the possibility of war in mind, she was designed to be adapted for use as an armed merchant cruiser, strengthened in places for fitment of guns. An elaborate telephone system, remarkable for those days enabled the bridge to communicate with other departments of the ship. She was also equipped with the Marconi wireless.

The service provided by the fleet was the most luxurious operating at the time, although later eclipsed by the advent of the *Lusitania* and *Mauretania*. The *Kronprinz Wilhelm* held the westbound record for an Atlantic crossing, averaging 23 knots, but later lost it to her sister-ship, *Kaiser Wilhelm II*. Until 1914 her history was largely uneventful, except for the unfortunate sinking of a small collier off Beachy Head in dense fog, when two of the collier's crew were lost. A collision with an iceberg off Newfoundland resulted in only minor damage.

On the outbreak of war, the *Kronprinz Wilhelm* found herself in New York. Her planned sailing was cancelled, and after taking on provisions and coal, she went to a secret rendezvous with the German cruiser *Karlsruhe*, east of Cuba. Supplies were transferred and two 8.8 cm guns and ammunition were placed on board the liner. Under the command of Kapitanleutnant. Thierfelder, the ship now functioned as an armed commerce raider, albeit a very vulnerable one. She was poorly armed, an easy target, and she carried a large crew, many of whom were stewards not trained as sailors. Furthermore, she consumed large quantities of coal (500 tons a day at full speed), and would need frequent refuelling. Her one great asset was her fine speed and, one should add, the resourcefulness and determination of her commander and crew.

Her rendezvous with the *Karlsruhe* was abruptly terminated by the arrival of a British cruiser, HMS *Suffolk*. Although the *Kronprinz Wilhelm* escaped, she had been unable to take on much ammunition. However, on 18 August she received further supplies and 2,400 tons of coal from the supply ship *Walhalla*, near the Azores. The two guns had been mounted on either side of the forecastle and a machine gun placed on the bridge. The grand saloon was transformed into a huge coal-bunker and the smokeroom became the ship's hospital.

For the next eight months the *Kronprinz Wilhelm* enjoyed a remarkable career raiding enemy supply ships, without once putting into port. During this time she captured and sank 14 British, Belgian and French and Norwegian ships carrying various cargoes of coal, frozen meat, timber, machinery, grain, and coffee. The British steamer *Bellevue* even provided her with twelve live oxen, as well as a fine supply of wines and whisky. Enemy ships were either rammed or sunk by gunfire, after useful provisions and crew had been taken off. Sometimes, a ship was used for scouting or towed alongside for several weeks while supplies were transferred. Occasional rendezvous with German ships allowed them to take on fresh supplies and transfer prisoners.

However, in the spring of 1915 the state of the ship was serious. A German ship from which she was due to take on coal supplies was captured by the British. In addition, engines and boilers were in need of repair, the hull was leaking from damage incurred in ramming other ships, and many of the crew were suffering from beriberi. These conditions decided the captain to make for port. After reaching Newport News on her last reserves of coal, the *Kronprinz Wilhelm* was eventually interned. She had been at sea continuously for 251 days, during which time she had steamed 3,700 miles, and sunk 58,000 tons of enemy shipping, without causing the loss of a single life.

In April 1917 the *Kronprinz Wilhelm* was taken over by the American navy. Having been refitted and renamed *Von Steuben*, the ship became an armed troop transport. She sailed to Brest in October of that year in convoy, colliding en route with the USS *Agamemnon*, and suffering a damaged bow. On her return trip she spent several days in Halifax, Nova Scotia, rendering assistance in the aftermath of the terrible explosion of the ammunition ship *Mont Blanc* in the harbour, which killed 2,000 people and practically razed the town. She served on the transatlantic route for the rest of the war, and was used after the Armistice to bring American troops back from Europe. She was finally decommissioned in October 1919. In 1923, after no suitable further employment could be found, the *Von Steuben* was sent to the breakers at Baltimore.

Name: **Kronprinz Wilhelm** (1901); **Von Steuben** (1917)
Line: Norddeutscher Lloyd
Builders: Vulkan, Stettin; launched 30 March 1901; completed August 1901
Dimensions: Length 664 ft/Beam 66 ft/ Gross tonnage 14,908

Machinery
Engines: 2 sets 6-cylinder quadruple-expansion engines, twin screw 33,000 i.h.p.
Boilers: 14 coal-fired, 12 double-ended, 2 single-ended, 200 p.s.i.
Service speed: 22.5 knots

Regular Routes
Bremen – New York

Passenger Capacity
1st 367, 2nd 340, Steerage 1,054

Near-Sister-ships
Kaiser Wilhelm der Grosse (1897), **Kaiser Wilhelm II** (1903), Kronprinzessin Cecilie (1907)

Photograph 1912

Lancashire

THE ship was built for the Bibby Company's service to Burma. She was laid down at Harland and Wolff's Belfast yard in 1914, but her construction was much delayed due to the priority given to naval work. It was not until 1917 that the ship was completed; she then sailed for a while on her owner's passenger and mail service to Rangoon.

The ship had a very elegant appearance, apparent in the photograph, which depicts her later in her long career. The hull had a straight stem, good sheer and a cruiser stern. She was in fact the first Bibby liner to have this latter feature. There were three overall decks, and the superstructure above was well proportioned with a slender funnel on top. Four nicely raked masts added to the ship's elegant appearance. She carried passengers all in one class in very comfortable accommodation. Cargo was carried as well. Speed was quite modest at 15 knots; this was economical for the long voyage to Rangoon.

On completion the *Lancashire* at once entered her owner's service to Ceylon and Burma. This had latterly been maintained by one ship only, the *Warwickshire*. Many other ships of the Bibby fleet were on war service as troopships, hospital ships and armed merchant cruisers. After the Armistice, however, the *Lancashire* operated to and from the continent taking back Belgian refugees, bringing home prisoners of war and other duties. She also transported Australian troops back to their homeland.

The ship had a refit at Belfast during which she was converted to burn oil fuel. Then it was back to the Burma service, on which she steamed steadily for the next ten years. The *Yorkshire* of 1920 was another celebrated passenger liner on the Rangoon route from Liverpool.

Because of their high tween decks designed to give good ventilation in the tropics Bibby vessels were found very useful for trooping during the 1914–18 war. From 1921 the company were awarded a series of contracts for taking troops to the Levant and to India.

In 1930 an extra vessel was required for use as a permanent troop-ship and the *Lancashire* was converted for this purpose at Cammell Laird's Birkenhead yard. During the thirties she was employed in this role, together with the *Somersetshire* and *Dorsetshire*. The troop-ships operated from Southampton, mostly to Bombay on the Indian relief service, which was seasonal. During the off-season they were usually laid up in the river Dart. From 1935 onward, however, the troopers were increasingly busy due to growing international tension.

The *Lancashire* could carry about 1,100 men and there was accommodation also for wives and families. During the Second World War the ship was very actively employed. Her wartime trooping voyages took her to India, the Persian Gulf, Italy, North Africa, East and West Africa. In fact she was seen in practically every theatre of war. During the D-Day landings the *Lancashire* acted as commodore ship. As a matter of fact, the Bibby Company were well represented on this occasion. Four of their ships, the *Cheshire*, *Devonshire*, *Worcestershire* and *Lancashire*, proceeded across to the invasion beaches, carrying in total some 10,000 men.

Soon afterwards the *Lancashire* was fitted out as an accommodation ship for the Pacific Fleet Train support group and went east once more. After the end of hostilities she spent some time in Hong Kong assisting in the restoration of the dockyard and public services. She had survived the war, no doubt having a few near-misses from time to time. The ship was more fortunate than her running-mate, the *Yorkshire*, which was sadly torpedoed and sunk on 17 October 1939. The ship then returned home and was reconverted for trooping duties. She carried these out efficiently until February 1956, when she was sold for breaking up at Barrow. In post-war days her second mast, abaft the bridge, was removed and she sailed as a three-master.

Name: Lancashire

Line: Bibby

Builders: Harland & Wolff, Belfast; launched 1914, completed 1917

Dimensions: Gross tonnage 9,445/Length 502 ft/Beam 57.3 ft

Machinery

Engines: 2 quadruple-expansion, twin screw 6,000 i.h.p. (approx)

Boilers: 2 double-ended, 2 single-ended cylindrical, 215 p.s.i.

Service speed: 15 knots

Major Refits

1919 Harland & Wolff, conversion to oil fuel
1930 Cammell Laird, Birkenhead, conversion to troop-ship, 10,331 tons

Regular Routes

Liverpool – Rangoon

Passenger Capacity

320, Troops, 1,100

Sister-ships

None

Photograph 1937

Leviathan

THE *Vaterland* was the second of Albert Ballin's three great liners for HAPAG. The *Imperator* was the first, and the *Bismarck* the final member of the trio.

This ship was built by Blohm and Voss at Hamburg. She was launched on 3 April 1913, completed at the end of April 1914 and set off on her maiden voyage from Cuxhaven to New York on 14 May that year.

Accommodation and public rooms were of the sumptuous order of her two sisters. Boiler uptakes were divided in a similar manner to the later *Bismarck*, which enabled the interior designer to take full advantage of the space available. In the big public rooms pillars were avoided where possible and the high domes were supported on roof girders. This all gave a great impression of spaciousness. Nothing was spared to make it as luxurious as befitted a ship that was the largest in the world until the *Bismarck* appeared on the scene.

Trials were completed satisfactorily soon after completion in 1914, and speeds of over 25 knots were achieved. The ship's maiden voyage passed off well at an average speed westward and eastward of over 23 knots. There had been a slight argument with some barges in New York harbour, but nothing too serious. Her two 'running-mates' on the service were the *Imperator* and *Kaiserin Auguste Victoria*.

She arrived at New York at the end of her fourth westbound voyage on 30 July 1914, just a few days before the outbreak of war. The ship prepared to sail on the return voyage next day, but a cable from Germany prevented this. The big vessel, along with several others, was interned at Hoboken. Here she remained for nearly three years. In April 1917, the United States having entered the war, the *Vaterland* was seized by the US Government and fitted out as a troop-ship. The German crew had sabotaged the ship as much as they could. However, the Americans carried out the necessary repairs and conversion work in about three months. She was armed with eight 6-inch guns and several smaller ones, and manned as an Army transport by the US navy.

The big ship was renamed *Leviathan*, and during the next couple of years made some ten trooping voyages across the Atlantic. She could carry around 10,000 men at a time, and was a very useful acquisition indeed. She finished her last voyage in September 1919, bringing back General Pershing and his Staff. Now followed a period laid up whilst her future was being decided. She was still a coal-burner, and much reconditioning would be required.

Eventually the big job was carried out by the Newport News Shipbuilding and Dry Dock Company, commencing in February 1922. William Francis Gibbs and his brother were in charge of the conversion. The ship's accommodation was renewed. Machinery was overhauled and boilers converted to oil-firing. No expense was spared, and the *Leviathan* blossomed forth as flagship of the newly formed United States Lines. She was again a very luxurious passenger vessel after her hard trooping work and subsequent long lay-up. She now sported the red, white and blue funnels of the premier US Company. Outwardly she was little changed and was now to join the *George Washington, Republic, America* and others on the service to Europe.

After successful trials she sailed from New York for Southampton on 4 July 1923. The ship was in fact the biggest American passenger ship ever. She exceeded in size even the famous *United States* of 1952.

However, the rest of the ships story makes rather sad reading. She never really paid her way, in spite of being very popular with passengers. Lack of a similar-sized running-mate may have contributed to this; she was much bigger and faster than other members of the fleet, and of course more costly to run. Prohibition in America was another great hindrance to the liner. This applied to American ships at sea, and of course thirsty passengers had no option but to avoid travelling on US vessels.

The *Leviathan*'s accommodation was modified and improved from time to time, notably in 1926 when she had a big overhaul. In 1929 P.W. Chapman and Company took over the fleet but not for long. It was, however, under this regime that two new liners of more moderate size, the *Manhattan* and *Washington*, were laid down. In 1931 the United States lines came under IMM control. The *Leviathan* spent some winter months laid up, followed by some transatlantic voyages before being again off service. She made only eleven round voyages in 1932, and in 1934 only four or five.

By this time both the *Washington* and *Manhattan* were in service, and of course they were much cheaper to run. The harsh economic realities of the Depression had hit the big ship hard. On arrival at New York on 14 September 1934 she was withdrawn.

The ship was laid up at New York for the next three years and little maintenance work was done on her. Eventually, in December 1937, she was sold to British breakers. A skeleton crew was sent from the UK to bring the ship over to Rosyth.

Name: **Vaterland** (1914); **Leviathan** (1917)

Line: HAPAG (1914-17); US Lines (1923-37)

Builders: Blohm & Voss, Hamburg; launched 3 April 1913, completed April 1914

Dimensions: Gross tonnage 54,282/ Length 948 ft/Beam 100 ft

Machinery

Engines: 4 direct drive steam turbines, quadruple screw, 90,400 s.h.p.

Boilers: 46 watertube naval type, 235 p.s.i.

Service speed: 23.5 knots

Major Refits

1917 Hoboken, conversion to troop-ship
1922 Newport News, boilers converted to oil-firing, accommodation renewed

Regular Routes

Cuxhaven – New York
New York – Southampton

Passenger Capacity

1914 1st 752, 2nd 535, 3rd 850, Steerage 1772
1931 1st 940, Tourist 666, 3rd 1402

Sister-ships

Imperator (1914), *Bismarck* (1922)

Photograph 1923

Lusitania

THIS ship and her sister *Mauretania* were the Cunard Company's answer to the German express steamers on the transatlantic service. Both were built with the aid of a government subsidy. The *Lusitania* took shape at John Brown's Clydebank yard. She was launched on 7 June 1906 and completed in August 1907. She set off on her maiden voyage from Liverpool to New York on 7 September that year.

The ship was very similar to her sister. The main external difference was that she had far fewer large cowl ventilators, which were a prominent feature on the *Mauretania*. In general, however, the two ships were very much alike, although their internal decor and furnishings differed considerably. All the funnels were 'operational' ones – unlike many four-funnelled vessels, in which one was often a dummy.

The *Lusitania* catered for first, second and third class passengers, and a good standard of accommodation was provided. Cargo could also be carried. As on her sister, provision was made for mounting twelve 6-inch guns if necessary in wartime.

Propelling machinery was by direct-drive steam turbines. The ship's trials were very satisfactory, and she achieved speeds in excess of 26 knots. Her maiden voyage was also a satisfactory one.

The *Mauretania* in fact proved to be slightly the faster, but only by a very small margin. Both ships became very popular with the travelling public.

When war came it was decided that the two big Cunarders were not after all really suitable for conversion to armed merchant cruisers.

The *Mauretania* became a hospital ship, but the *Lusitania* kept open the mail and passenger service from the UK to New York. For economy, six of her boilers were closed down, her speed accordingly being reduced to about 21 knots.

In April and May 1915 the German Embassy in New York put announcements in American newspapers warning intending passengers of the dangers of sailing in Allied ships. All carried the threat that such vessels in a war zone would be sunk.

The *Lusitania* left New York on 3 May 1915 on what was to be her last, tragic voyage. The ship had 1,959 passengers on board.

For the first few days all proceeded quite normally, the ship steaming steadily at her reduced speed. Captain William Turner was called to the bridge on the early morning of 7 May. Fog had swept down, and visibility was poor. Speed had already been reduced to 18 knots to enable the vessel to arrive at the Liverpool bar at around high tide. She could then enter the Mersey at once, without having to wait outside in a vulnerable position for possible U-boat attack. The presence of fog caused a further speed reduction to 15 knots, but this was increased to 18 again when the fog lifted just before noon. The Irish coast was well in sight, and Captain Turner moved a little closer inshore to get a good 'fix' to check his position. The *Lusitania* was not steering a zig-zag course, though Captain Turner had received a message earlier informing him that enemy submarines were active off the south coast of Ireland. That morning another message advised him to 'avoid headlands and to pass harbours at full speed. Submarines off Fastnet'. No naval escort had been provided for the big Cunarder in these dangerous waters.

The *U-20* commanded by Kapitänleutnant Walter Schwieger was in the area on the look-out for prey. In the early afternoon the *Lusitania* was sighted, about 13 miles away. The U-boat dived, and headed on a course to intercept the big vessel. A torpedo was fired at a range of about 700 yards; it was impossible to miss such a huge target. The *Lusitania* was struck on the starboard side, at a position roughly between the third and fourth funnels. There was a great explosion, followed soon afterwards by a second one. The ship at once listed to starboard and commenced to sink. Some lifeboats were got away with difficulty, but the list made it impossible to launch those on the port side. The *Lusitania* sank very rapidly and in about twenty minutes was on the bottom. Many people had jumped overboard and were picked up by rescue boats which soon arrived from shore. However, the loss of life was terrible, a total of 1,198 including 124 Americans.

Schwieger always maintained that only one torpedo was fired. The second explosion seems to have been the more damaging, and was almost certainly caused by explosives being detonated. It was later known that the ship was in fact carrying a considerable amount of explosive material. This would seem to be the reason she sank so rapidly, in a position about 11 miles off the Old Head of Kinsale.

Enquiries were held in Britain and America. Captain Turner was exonerated from any blame, but had to face hostile questioning. This fine seaman remained bitter about it all to the end of his days.

Name: **Lusitania**

Line: Cunard

Builders: John Brown & Co. Clydebank, launched 7 June 1906, completed August 1907

Dimensions: Gross tonnage 31,550/ Length 787 ft/Beam 87.8 ft

Machinery

Engines: steam turbines (Parsons type built by Shipbuilders), direct drive 76,000 s.h.p.

Boilers: 23 double-ended and 2 single-ended cylindrical, coal-fired, 195 p.s.i.

Service speed: 25 knots

Major Refits

1909 New propellers fitted

Regular Routes

Liverpool – New York

Passenger Capacity

1st 563, 2nd 464, 3rd 1,138

Sister-ship

Mauretania (1907)

Photograph (c. 1910)

Majestic

THIS huge ship was the third and biggest of Hamburg-America's giant liners, built for their luxury service across the Atlantic. The other two were the *Imperator* (later to become the Cunard *Berengaria*) and the *Vaterland*, which later sailed under the American flag as the *Leviathan*.

The *Bismarck*, being the last of the three, was able to benefit from lessons learnt from the *Imperator*, the first one to be completed. Her own completion, however, was to be very long delayed due to the war.

The big ship was built by Blohm and Voss at Hamburg and was launched on 20 June 1914 when war clouds were already beginning to gather. The Kaiser himself was there to see the great hull slide into the water. Work on the giant, however, was suspended during the war, and for some time after the Armistice. The Reparations Committee in 1919 awarded the incomplete *Bismarck* and the *Imperator* to Britain, and in 1921 the two ships were jointly acquired by Cunard and White Star. The *Bismarck* blossomed forth as the White Star *Majestic*. (Ownership in fact remained shared for ten years.) First of all, however, the big ship had to be completed, and this was done by her German builders.

With a gross tonnage of over 56,000 the *Majestic* was the largest ship in the world until the advent of the *Normandie* in 1935. She was completed in March 1922 and left Hamburg on the 28 of that month for trials in the North Sea. Going down the Elbe to Cuxhaven she stuck on the mud for a short while, but assisted by tugs reached the outer port safely where she anchored. It seems speeds of about 25 knots were achieved, but most testing was done at somewhat lower speeds. The big ship sailed for Southampton, arriving on 10 April. A strenuous month was then spent on finishing touches and preparations and the ship set off on her maiden voyage from Southampton to New York on 10 May.

The *Majestic* became the largest member of the White Star's trio of express liners operating on the Southampton–Cherbourg–New York route. The others were the *Olympic* and *Homeric*. In August 1922 the ship was visited off Cowes by King George V and Queen Mary. For the next ten years or so she continued on this prestigious route, and was a very popular ship. Together with the Cunard *Aquitania*, *Berengaria* and *Mauretania* White Star provided a twice-weekly service. The *Majestic* can claim to be the second fastest ship of the six, exceeded in the speed stakes only by the *Mauretania*. She was capable of making voyages at 24 knots.

The stresses induced by the North Atlantic gales took effect in 1924. The *Majestic*'s strength deck became fractured completely across in the midships area and a short way down the port side. The ship was in no danger, but repairs had to be swiftly done. These took the form of doubling the deck for about 100 feet fore and aft of the damaged area.

During the latter part of the decade the *Majestic*, like other White Star and Cunard vessels, did a little cruising. Between voyages she made short trips such as New York – Halifax and back. This all helped with revenue-earning. Passenger numbers varied from time to time during the ship's career, and various improvements were made to accommodation and public rooms during refits. In spite of the Depression the 'express' service continued in the early 1930s. It was now maintained by the *Aquitania*, *Berengaria*, *Olympic* and *Majestic*, the *Homeric* and *Mauretania* being used for cruising.

In 1934 Cunard and White Star merged, and sadly the big ship's days were now numbered. The world recession seriously affected shipping, and also the *Queen Mary* was due to enter service. The *Olympic* was withdrawn in 1935, and in February 1936 the *Majestic* was laid up at Southampton after she had completed her 207th Atlantic voyage. On 15 May 1936 she was sold for breaking-up, but soon resold to the Admiralty for fitting out as a training ship for some 2,000 boys. This work was carried out by Thornycroft of Southampton. The vessel now became the largest training ship ever. Her big public rooms were adapted to become lecture halls. Workshops for artificer apprentices were installed and a couple of 6 inch guns were shipped, together with two 4.7 inch and three 4 inch ones. Her funnels were reduced in height, as were her masts for passage up the Forth to Rosyth where she arrived in April 1937 and was moored alongside a wharf. She became HMS *Caledonia*.

For over two years she did duty in her new, most useful role, then when war broke out the boys were put into shore accommodation and the ship anchored in the Forth. It was announced that extensive alterations were to be carried out. The ship would in fact have made a very useful troop-ship. However, any plans which may have been in mind for her were shattered on 29 September 1939 when an outbreak of fire occurred. This was so serious and so much water was pumped on board that the ex-*Majestic* sank and was declared a constructive total loss. Sold again to the breakers in March 1940, she was partially demolished where she lay, and in 1943 towed away to Inverkeithing for final demolition.

Name: **Bismarck** (1914), **Majestic** (1922)

Line: HAPAG (1914-19); White Star (1923-36)

Builders: Blohm & Voss, Hamburg; launched 20 June 1914, completed March 1922

Dimensions: Gross tonnage 56,551/ Length 956 ft/Beam 100 ft

Machinery

Engines: 4 Parsons type direct drive turbines, quadruple screw, 86,000 s.h.p.

Boilers: 48 Yarrow watertube, 265 p.s.i.

Service speed: 23 knots

Major Refits

1936 Thornycroft, Southampton, conversion to training-ship

Regular Routes

Southampton – New York

Passenger Capacity

1st 750, 2nd 545, 3rd 850

Sister-ships

Imperator (1914), **Vaterland** (1914)

Photograph 1932

Manhattan

Name: **Manhattan** (1932); **Wakefield** (1941)

Line: United States

Builders: New York Shipbuilding Co., Camden, New Jersey; launched 5 December 1931, completed 1932

Dimensions: Gross tonnage 24,289/ Length 705 ft/Beam 86.3 ft

Machinery

Engines: 2 sets triple-expansion single reduction geared turbines, twin screw

Boilers: 6 oil-fired watertube, forced draught

Service speed: 20 knots

Major Refits

1942-4 Boston, conversion to troop-ship

Regular Routes

New York – Hamburg

Passenger Capacity

Cabin 582, Tourist 461, 3rd 196

Sister-ships

Washington (1933)

Photograph 1934

THIS ship and her sister *Washington* had the distinction when built of being the largest passenger vessels constructed in America. The *Manhattan* in fact was the first really modern vessel to be added to the fleet of the United States Lines, as this company since its formation in 1921 had relied chiefly on second-hand tonnage, particularly ex-German ships. Originally the intention had been to build two much bigger ships, rivalling the *Bremen* and *Europa* in size. The onset of the Depression had caused the plans to be changed. The US Line itself was bought by the P.W. Chapman Company in 1929, but they remained in control for only a short while. In fact before the two ships were completed the IMM Combine (International Mercantile Marine) had taken charge.

Both were built at the Camden Yard of the New York Shipbuilding Corporation. The *Manhattan* was completed in July 1932 and commenced her maiden voyage from New York to Hamburg on 10 August. The ship had a rather elegant profile, the hull having a moderately raked stem with a fairly pronounced sheer forward and attractive counter stern. She had a bulbous forefoot and semi-balanced rudder. The two funnels were well spaced. Initially they were shorter than in the photograph and had to be increased in height by over twelve feet to help keep smoke clear of the upper decks. The US Lines advertised the splendid features of their two new ships as 'built in America to provide American luxury'. The *Manhattan* kept up a regular transatlantic service interspersed with some cruises during the 1930s. When the *Leviathan* was withdrawn from service in 1935 she and her sister then indeed became the largest and fastest American North Atlantic ships. In fact the company were so impressed with their performance that they decided to order a third and larger ship in 1937. This vessel became the *America*.

The *Manhattan* reached New York on 31 August 1939 after a normal transatlantic passage. War was now imminent, and the rest of her 1939 schedule was abruptly altered. She now ran several emergency evacuation trips between New York and Bordeaux bringing back Americans and others who wished to get away from Europe. During these trips she carried considerably more than her usual complement of passengers. Although America was neutral, the *Manhattan* had her name, 'United States Lines' and two large American flags painted on her sides to deter lurking U-boats. By President Roosevelt's Neutrality Act of November 1939 all ports in Europe except those in Portugal and the Mediterranean were closed to American shipping. The *Manhattan* and her sister then ran a service from New York to Naples and Genoa for a while. This, however, only lasted for about six months since Italy then entered the war. After the *Manhattan* had made a trip in July 1940 between New York and Lisbon it was felt that her safety on the Atlantic could no longer be guaranteed. She and her sister then went on a coastal service between New York and California. The brand-new *America* also joined in this service.

An unfortunate incident befell the *Manhattan* on 12 January 1941 when she ran aground off the Florida coast. She remained fast until refloated again on 3 February. Her propellers were damaged, and she had to be towed to New York for repairs.

Wartime events were moving quickly, although the United States had not become actively involved as yet. In June 1941 the *Manhattan* and her sister were taken over for military duty. She was refitted as a troop-ship with a capacity for carrying about 7000 men. She was now renamed *Wakefield*. In this capacity she was en route to the Philippines when the Japanese attacked Pearl Harbour on 7 December 1941. In January 1942, while in Singapore evacuating personnel, she was hit during a Japanese air attack and rather badly damaged. Patched up in India, she then went to the naval yard in Philadelphia for full repairs. Returning to trooping, the USS *Wakefield* was to have further disaster befall her. On a westbound Atlantic convoy on 3 September 1942 an outbreak of fire occurred and rapidly spread. The ship had to be abandoned after all personnel had been taken off, and was towed, still burning, and beached near Halifax. She was later taken to Boston, and at the naval shipyard she was eventually repaired. This was a very lengthy job and she did not reappear until April 1944, now rebuilt as a permanent troop-ship and under US navy ownership. She again operated across the Atlantic, running from either Boston or New York to Liverpool. Other voyages to Gibraltar, Marseilles and Naples followed. Some Pacific voyaging came later still, during which she visited such ports as Tsingtao, Taku, and Guam. In May 1946 the ship was back in New York. From here she went to the Hudson to join the 'mothball fleet' of laid-up troopers and other vessels. In 1953 she was joined by her sister *Washington*, which had done wartime trooping as the USS *Mount Vernon* and had continued 'austerity' Atlantic crossings afterwards. Both ships lay there languishing, no longer suitable for commercial work, until in 1965 they were scrapped at New Jersey.

Mauretania

THE fastest passenger liners on the 'Atlantic Ferry' at the beginning of the century were the German ones. Powered by big reciprocating engines, ships such as the *Kaiser Wilhelm der Grosse, Kaiser Wilhelm II, Kronprinz Wilhelm* and *Deutschland* were all capable of speeds in excess of 23 knots.

At this time Cunard received a loan from the Treasury to construct two liners. These were to be considerably larger than any others then in service and were to be available for naval service in the event of war. After much discussion the company decided upon quadruple-screw ships of some 30,000 tons and capable of 25 knots. A contract was placed for building the *Mauretania* with Swan Hunter and Wigham Richardson of Wallsend on Tyne in May 1905. Her sister *Lusitania* was to be built on the Clyde at John Brown's yard. The two ships were of the same general design but differed in points of detail.

Work proceeded apace and the Clyde-built ship was the first to take the water, being launched in June 1906. The Tyne-built ship followed in September and was finally completed the following year, beginning her trials on November 1907 and sailing on her maiden voyage to New York on the 16 of that month. She had a straight stem with a large forecastle, low superstructure and elegant counter stern. Her four funnels were beautifully proportioned, adding greatly to her appearance. There were seven decks amidships and two orlop decks fore and aft.

The ship's maiden voyage was something of an anticlimax. Bad weather, especially fog, prevented any records being broken, but in spite of this she averaged a respectable 22 knots. On the return 'leg', however, she just beat the record which had been established by her sister a month or two earlier. The *Mauretania* eventually proved to be the faster of the two – by a very narrow margin. She was to hold on to the record for many years; it was not until 1929 that she surrendered it to the new German liner *Bremen*.

When war came the regular transatlantic service from Liverpool was interrupted and replaced by a skeleton one. The *Mauretania* continued to cross until October 1914, when she was withdrawn for potential war service. Her sister kept the service going until her tragic torpedoing in May 1915.

Although the ships had been earmarked for possible use as armed merchant cruisers in wartime, this was not now considered advisable. A much more suitable role was as troop transports over long distances. The ill-fated Gallipoli operation in 1915 provided the opportunity for the *Mauretania* to transport large numbers of troops. She was converted to a troop-ship early that year, and made three voyages to Lemnos with over 10,000 troops. Late in 1915, now fitted as a hospital ship, she commenced the task of bringing back the wounded to this country. Her large public rooms were doing duty as hospital wards. She made three return voyages, but was then laid up for a while in 1916. However, she later became a troop-ship again, dazzle-painted for camouflage. Over 6,000 Canadian troops were brought from Halifax to Liverpool in late 1916, but then rather surprisingly the ship was laid up on the Clyde for the whole of 1917.

Operational again in early 1918, she brought 33,000 American troops across in seven voyages from New York. After the war finished she transported American troops back to their homeland.

Now followed a much needed refit (albeit a rather short one), and in March 1920 she again commenced her transatlantic voyaging, this time from Southampton. The Cunard 'express service' had now been transferred to the southern port.

An outbreak of fire on board in July 1921 did considerable damage, and Cunard took the opportunity of sending her for an extensive refit which included conversion to oil-firing.

Early in 1923 she was chartered to make a lengthy Mediterranean cruise by an American company. Her machinery had been given a routine overhaul at her last refit but a much more extensive one was needed and this took place at Thornycrofts of Southampton in November. Due to a strike this had to be completed at Cherbourg. Her refit was completed, but on returning to service she had the misfortune to break an outer propeller shaft, dropping the propeller. After repair she was able once again to make 25-knot passages. Her 'running-mates' on the Atlantic Ferry were the *Berengaria* (ex-German *Imperator*) and the *Aquitania*. The *Mauretania* also continued to make cruises which were very popular, especially during the Prohibition era in America.

The veteran was becoming more and more a cruise ship by the 1930's and had a white-painted hull. However, she was not really suitable for this, not having air-conditioning, private bathrooms or swimming-pools. Nevertheless, she continued in operation until 1934. On 26 September 1934 she made her last crossing from New York. On 1 July 1935 she left Southampton for Rosyth to be broken up.

Name: Mauretania

Line: Cunard

Builders: Swan Hunter & Wigham Richardson, Newcastle-on-Tyne; launched September 1906, completed November 1907

Dimensions: Gross tonnage 31,938/ Length 790 ft/Beam 88 ft

Machinery

Engines: 6 steam turbines, direct drive, quadruple screw, 78,000 s.h.p.

Boilers: 23 double-ended, 2 single-ended Scotch, 195 p.s.i.

Service speed: 25 knots

Major Refits

1915 conversion to troop-ship
1923 Thornycroft, Southampton, extensive overhaul

Regular Routes

Liverpool – New York
Southampton – New York

Passenger Capacity

1st 560, 2nd 475, 3rd 1,300

Sister-ships
Lusitania (1907)

Photograph 1933

Mauretania

BY THE late 1930s Cunard's secondary services to the US were in need of fresh tonnage. It was decided to order a much larger vessel for the New York service, one that would provide a fine standard of accommodation and, being a little slower than the express ships, would be economical to run. She would nevertheless be fast enough to act as a relief when one or other of the 'Queens' was having a refit. The ship would also be used for cruising. The contract for the new ship was placed with Cammell Laird of Birkenhead. She was launched on 28 July 1938 and completed in May 1939. On the 31st of that month she left for trials on the Clyde. Having completed these very satisfactorily the ship set off on her maiden voyage from Liverpool to New York on 17 June. Although the ship had been built for a secondary service she was still ranked among the dozen or so largest passenger liners in the world. She carried about 1,300 passengers and the return trip was to Southampton. The new ship then went round to London and in August became the largest vessel to proceed up the Thames to the King George V dock. She left again on 11 August for Southampton and New York and on the return voyage was diverted to the Hampshire port instead of London as the international situation deteriorated. She arrived there on 3 September, the day war was declared. On 14 September the ship sailed again to New York but returned to Liverpool. She was laid up first there, but a safer place was required and on 10 December 1939 she left for New York. Here she remained, in the illustrious company of several other big ships including the 'Queens' and the *Normandie*, until March 1940.

On the 6th of that month Cunard were told by the Ministry of War Transport that the *Mauretania* was required for trooping duties. Following some quick conversion work the ship sailed for Sydney via the Panama Canal and Honolulu. In the Australian port, where she arrived in mid-April, the conversion work for trooping duties was continued and on 5 May she set off in convoy laden with about 2,000 Australian troops bound for Glasgow. This kind of work was to occupy the ship for the next six years.

For the period 1940–2 she was much engaged in ferrying troops from Australia and New Zealand to the Middle East. A typical route was New Zealand – Australia – Ceylon – Suez. From June 1941 to January 1942 she was on the Durban – Suez shuttle. Other routes included Bombay – Aden – Suez, Bombay – Durban – Suez, and, just for a change, Suez – Durban – Rio de Janeiro –

Newport News (USA). Other liners on these routes included the *Nieuw Amsterdam* and the *Ile de France*. Prisoners of war, wounded men, and evacuees were brought on the return trips. Often these ships ran unescorted, relying on their speed and zig-zagging to keep them out of trouble. When the North African campaign had been successfully concluded, the *Mauretania* reappeared on her old stamping-ground again ferrying American and Canadian troops across the Atlantic. In 1943 alone she made no less than 21 crossings. After VE day the big ship again went trooping in the East. Following VJ day she was very much occupied in bringing home many thousands of troops from India and the Middle East, and also returning Australian and New Zealand personnel.

The ship's engines had performed splendidly during this time, and had pushed her along sometimes at around 25 knots. During the war she had steamed about 540,000 miles and carried over 350,000 personnel, a splendid record. A mishap befell the ship on 8 January 1944; fully laden with troops, she collided with an American tanker the *Hat Creek* in New York harbour. Damage, however, was slight and repairs completed within twelve hours.

Reconditioning the *Mauretania* took about eight months. The ship returned to the North Atlantic ferry service in April 1947. She sailed from Liverpool to New York on 26 April. She soon moved to Southampton and settled down to steady voyaging over the next few years. During the winter months she undertook cruises from New York. These usually involved calls at Nassau, La Guaira, Curaçao, Colón and Havana.

After the first commercial jets commenced in 1958 ships like the *Mauretania* began to lose passengers. In February 1962 the ship made her first Mediterranean cruise from New York. The next year now painted in 'cruising green' she was tried on another service from Naples to New York, sailing via Genoa, Cannes, and Gibraltar. This proved rather unsuccessful, as the elderly vessel had to complete with the modern Italian and American liners. As a cruise ship too she had become a little outdated.

However, the *Mauretania* continued her cruising and Line voyages from Southampton and New York in 1964 and 1965. She made her final cruise that year when she set off on 15 September from New York on a 56-day cruise to the Mediterranean and Black Sea, returning to Southampton on 10 November. During this trip it was announced that she would be withdrawn, and on 20 November she left Southampton for the last time for the breakers at Inverkeithing.

Name: **Mauretania**

Line: Cunard

Builders: Cammell Laird, Birkenhead; launched 28 July 1938, completed May 1939

Dimensions: Gross tonnage 35,739/ Length 772 ft/Beam 89 ft

Machinery

Engines: 2 sets Parsons single reduction geared turbines, twin screw, 42,000 s.h.p.

Boilers: 6 Yarrow watertube oil-fired, 425 p.s.i., superheated to 725°F

Service speed: 23 knots

Major Refits

1940 conversion to troop-ship
1946 Cammell Laird, overhaul of boilers, machinery, improvement to accommodation
1957 Liverpool, extending air conditioning

Regular Routes

Liverpool – New York
Southampton – New York

Passenger Capacity

1939: Cabin 486, Tourist 390, 3rd 502
1947: 1st 475, Cabin 390, Tourist 304

Sister-ships

None

Photograph 1964

Milwaukee

Name: **Milwaukee** (1929); **Empire Waveney** (1945)

Line: HAPAG (1929-45); Cunard-White Star (Managers) (1945-46)

Builders: Blohm & Voss, Hamburg; launched 20 February 1929, completed June 1929

Dimensions: Gross tonnage 16,699/ Length 575 ft/Beam 72.5 ft

Machinery

Engines: 2 MAN diesel engines, twin screw, 12,600 b.h.p.

Service speed: 16 knots

Major Refits

1935-36 Blohm & Voss, conversion to cruise ship
1946 conversion to troop-ship (destroyed by fire)

Regular Routes

Hamburg – Boulogne – Southampton – New York

Passenger Capacity

1929: Cabin 270, Tourist 259, 3rd 428
1936: 1st 559

Sister-ships

St Louis (1929)

Photograph 1938

THIS fine ship was built for HAPAG's intermediate service and also for cruising. Like many of their other vessels, she was constructed at the Blohm and Voss yard at Hamburg. Launched on 20 February 1929, she was completed by June that year and set off on her maiden voyage from Hamburg to New York on the 18th of that month.

The *Milwaukee* had a sister, the *St Louis*, built at the Bremer Vulcan Yard at Vegesack. Both vessels were motorships of nearly 17,000 tons. They were thus unlike the larger *Albert Ballin* quartet which were powered by steam turbines. Both had American names, appropriate enough for ships on the trans-Atlantic route.

As can be seen, the *Milwaukee* was a striking looking vessel, with two rather short, vertical funnels and upright masts. The hull had a vertical stem and cruiser stern. It contained five decks and the superstructure was compact and well proportioned. Accommodation was provided for cabin, tourist, and third-class passengers to a good standard. The ship also had considerable cargo capacity.

Propelling machinery consisted of a couple of diesel engines driving twin screws through reduction gearing. Service speed was an economical 16 knots. Both the *Milwaukee* and her sister were stated to be good sea boats and comfortable to travel on. Since they were economical to run, they were very suitable for cruising as well as line voyages. For the latter the *Milwaukee*'s route was typically Hamburg–Boulogne–Southampton–New York. She often called also at Cobh and Halifax.

The ship and her sister motored steadily to and fro and went cruising. For the latter activity her hull was painted white with red boot topping from 1934. In 1935–6 she was thoroughly refitted as a cruise ship by her builders. The vessel was now in fact a luxury liner and could offer spa-type facilities on board. She was advertised as a 'floating spa' a rather unusual description for a cruise ship, but this no doubt helped to attract passengers. Scandinavian cruising featured prominently in the ship's itinerary. Many photographs taken in the 1930s depict this fine white-hulled vessel amid the magnificent scenery of the Norwegian fjords.

During the war the *Milwaukee* was converted for use as an accommodation ship by the German Navy, stationed at Kiel. She survived the conflict, and in 1945 was surrendered to Britain, being transferred to the Ministry of Transport. Under Cunard–White Star management she became a troopship renamed *Empire Waveney*. However, luck now deserted the ship.

She was being refitted at Liverpool when on 1 March 1946 she was destroyed by fire. She sank, was salvaged and taken away for scrapping the next year. The ship then had a sad ending. She had, however, served well on the North Atlantic and in her cruising role in the 1930s had been a very popular vessel.

The *Milwaukee*'s sister *St Louis* also did a good deal of cruising. She was at sea when war broke out but succeeded in reaching Germany via Norwegian territorial waters. Like her sister, she was also an accommodation ship at Kiel, but was badly damaged and beached in an air raid in August 1944. After the war her remains were towed to Hamburg and converted to a floating hotel-restaurant in the harbour. She continued in this role until 1950, being eventually broken up in 1952.

Monarch of the Seas

THE Royal Caribbean Cruise Line (operating company Royal Caribbean Cruises Ltd) dates from 1968. It was founded by three shipping companies, I.M. Skaugen, Anders Wilhelmsen & Co., and Gotaas Larsen Shipping Corporation. Head Office is at Oslo, Norway and operational headquarters at Miami, Florida.

In addition to the American market the company makes a feature of fly/cruise holidays for passengers from the UK and Europe. They also carry out cruises on the West Coast of the USA and to the Mediterranean. In 1991 the cruising fleet numbered eight vessels ranging in size from the *Sun Viking* (18,500 tons) to the *Sovereign of The Seas* and our subject which are of 74,000 tons. Others include the *Song of America* (37,000 tons) and *Nordic Empress* (44,300 tons). A further 74,000 ton vessel the *Majesty of The Seas* is due to join the fleet in 1992.

The Monarch of The Seas was build at St Nazaire by the same yard that built the *Normandie* in 1935. She was completed by the Autumn of 1991. As can be seen she has the striking appearance typical of modern cruise ships. The shapely hull has a well raked and flared bow and modern stern. Upperworks are extensive and the funnel with its 'wrap around' 'Viking Crown' lounge is placed well aft.

The ship has a total of fourteen decks and passengers are accomodated on nine of them. Reading downwards these are designated 'Bridge', 'Commodore', 'Mariner', 'Promenade', 'Tween', 'Showtime', 'Main', 'A', and 'B' decks. Above are the 'Sun' and 'Compass' decks Accommodation is luxurious indeed, cabins are mostly twin bedded, all with private bathrooms, T.V., radio, and of course are air conditioned. Many are outside ones. There are some luxury suites as well. As is usual in modern cruise ships of the 'MEGA' type the *Monarch of the Seas* has facilities to suit all tastes. These may be briefly summarised: There are 12 lounges/public rooms with varying passenger capacities. The largest is the 'Sound of Music' lounge which extends through 2 decks (Showtime/Promenade) and can accommodate 1,050 persons. On a smaller scale the 'Touch of Class' and 'Card/Conference Room' both on the Promenade deck cater for 50 and 80 people respectively. There are two dining saloons, the 'Brigadoon' on 'A' deck accommodates 706 diners and the 'Flower Drum Song' on the main deck caters for 666.

The magnificent 'Centrum' contains the embarkation lobby and other amenities. Extending through four decks it has glass elevators, fountains and grand staircases, the virtual 'hub' of shipboard activities. Amongst other rooms may be noted the 'April in Paris' lounge (Mariner deck) 'Dancin' Lounge' (Promenade deck) and 'Ain't Misbehavin' Nightclub' (Commodore deck). There is a cinema on 'B' deck and the 'Windjammer Cafe' is high up on Sun and Compass decks. There are a couple of outdoor swimming pools where passengers may disport themselves. They can also indulge in a little gambling in the Casino, do some golf driving, play shuffleboard, or beautify themselves in the beauty saloon. There are of course numerous shops, gymnasiums, library, and full medical facilities.

Propelling machinery for this giant cruise vessel consists of four Pielstick diesel engines coupled to twin screws. Maximum speed is 22 knots, cruising-speed a little less. The ship has two bow thrust units forward to aid manoeuvrability and is fitted with fin stabilisers. Needless to say she is fitted with the latest in navigational equipment. A feature claimed by the owners is that the ship is 'environment-friendly'. She has very advanced waste treatment and disposal plants on board. This is very important especially when cruising in the Caribbean.

In short the *Monarch of the Seas* is very up to date in all respects.

The ship arrived at Southampton on 17 October 1991 and was open for inspection by travel agents etc. She sailed the next day on a transatlantic voyage to Boston before proceeding to her base port of San Juan, Puerto Rico. Her packed schedule for 1992 includes cruises of 8–15 days from here around the Leeward Islands etc. Her sister *Sovereign of the Seas* built in 1987 cruises mostly from Miami, Florida.

Name: Monarch of the Seas

Line: Royal Caribbean Cruise Line

Builders: Chantiers de L'Atlantique, St Nazaire, completed 1991

Dimensions: Gross tonnage 74,442/ Length 880 ft (268.32 m)/Beam 106 ft (32.2 m)

Machinery

Engines: 4 Pielstick 9-cylinder diesel engines with flexible couplings and geared to 2 screw shafts, total b.h.p. 27,840, twin screws with controllable pitch propellers

Service speed: 22 knots

Regular Routes

Caribbean cruising

Passenger Capacity

2,766

Sister-ships

Sovereign of the Seas (1987), *Majesty of the Seas* (1992)

Montrose

Name: Montrose (1922); **HMS Forfar** (1939)

Line: Canadian Pacific

Builders: Fairfield Shipbuilding & Engineering, Glasgow; launched 14 December 1920, completed March 1922

Dimensions: Gross tonnage 16,402/ Length 575 ft/Beam 70.2 ft

Machinery

Engines: 2 sets turbines, double reduction geared, twin screw 14,000 s.h.p.

Boilers: 10 single-ended cylindrical, 215 p.s.i.

Service speed: 16 knots

Major Refits

1931 Harland & Wolff, Belfast, turbines replaced by single reduction geared units
1939 Portsmouth, conversion AMC

Regular Routes

Liverpool – Montreal
Hamburg – Montreal

Passenger Capacity

Cabin 542, 3rd 1,268

Sister-ships

Montcalm (1921), Montclare (1922)

Photograph 1929

THIS ship was built for Canadian Pacific's Transatlantic service, being constructed by the well-known Fairfield Yard at Glasgow. Launched on 14 December 1920, the vessel was completed by March 1922 and sailed on her maiden voyage from Liverpool to Montreal on 5 May that year.

As can be seen, the *Montrose* was quite an attractive-looking ship. The hull had a slightly raked stem and a cruiser stern. It contained two decks and a shelter deck, with a further partial one below. Superstructure above was fairly low, with a couple of rather slender funnels atop. Perhaps the ship's profile was marred somewhat by the special boat-launching davits which show up rather prominently, as do the cowl ventilators. Like her two sisters *Montcalm* and *Montclare* (both built by John Brown & Co., Clydebank), she had considerable cargo capacity with six holds, served by derricks.

The ship catered at first for cabin class and third-class passengers. For a 16,000-ton vessel she carried a large number, about 1,800. The usual type of public rooms were found on board. Cabin class were in 2 and 4 berth accommodation, while third class had 2, 4, and 6-berth cabins. Later this became cabin, tourist, and third class.

The ship and her twin sisters all had gun rings and platform stiffenings built in so that in the event of war they could be quickly armed for naval use. All of them were to be later taken up for this purpose.

The name originally intended for the ship was *Montmorency*, after a great waterfall in Quebec, but this was changed to *Montrose* before the ship was launched. She soon settled down on the Canadian route, and both her sisters started on it also in 1922. They provided a most useful service, which in 1923 was extended to include a call at Greenock. Calls were occasionally made at Belfast also.

An unfortunate mishap befell the *Montrose* on Easter Monday 1928 when she was in collision with an iceberg near St John's, Newfoundland. The ship was steaming slowly in thick fog at the time and her bows were badly crunched. Unfortunately, heavy lumps of ice fell on board and killed two seamen. The vessel, however, was able to continue her voyage to Liverpool.

By the late 1920s the three 'Monts' had been somewhat eclipsed by the advent of the four 20,000-ton 'Duchesses', of *Bedford*, *Atholl*, *Richmond* and *York*. Also the original turbine machinery fitted to the three was not entirely satisfactory, and all were eventually re-engined. The *Montrose* had her new turbines fitted by Harland and Wolff at Belfast in 1931. This resulted in lower fuel-consumption and generally improved performance. After the advent of the 'Duchesses' on the Liverpool route the 'Monts' made many of their summer sailings from Antwerp and Hamburg, calling at Southampton and Cherbourg. The *Montrose* in fact made her first sailing from the German port to Montreal in May 1929. In that year also she called at Cardiff a couple of times to pick up emigrant passengers.

From 1932 onward she made cruises from UK ports to such places as the Canary Islands and North Africa. Up to the outbreak of war cruising was in fact to be her main occupation, interspersed with some North Atlantic voyages from Hamburg, Antwerp, Southampton or Liverpool. In May 1937 the *Montrose* was chartered to make a four-day cruise from Liverpool to Spithead for the Coronation Fleet Review.

The ship returned to Liverpool from Canada on 11 September 1939 and was soon requisitioned for conversion to an armed merchant cruiser. She went to Portsmouth for this to be done and emerged with eight 6-inch guns and a couple of 3-inch anti-aircraft weapons. Since there was already a destroyer of the same name in the Navy, the Canadian Pacific ship was renamed *Forfar*, and given pennant number F30. She then joined the Northern Patrol, where she did very useful service for the rest of the year and most of 1940.

However, in the early hours of 2 December that year, while about 400 miles west of Ireland on her way to meet a convoy from Halifax, she was torpedoed. She was struck amidships, flooding the engine-room. About half an hour later a couple more torpedoes struck the disabled vessel, but it took another two, five in all, to finally sink this stoutly built ship. Unfortunately, 185 of her crew were lost including the captain, but many survivors were picked up by the destroyers HMS *Viscount* and HMCS *St Laurent*, together with a tramp steamer. HMS *Forfar* thus had a tragic ending, but she had served well in peace and war for some 18 years. The submarine which sank her was U-99.

Her two sisters were more fortunate. HMS *Montclare* became an AMC and later a submarine depot ship, eventually being broken up in 1958. The *Montcalm* was renamed HMS *Wolfe* and became in succession an AMC, submarine depot ship and then a destroyer depot ship. She finally went to the breakers in 1952.

Mooltan

AFTER the 1914–18 war the P & O fleet had to be built up again, and a number of vessels were constructed in the 1920s. These included the *Mooltan* and *Maloja*, sister-ships both coming from Harland and Wolff's yard at Belfast. They were destined for P & O's Australian service.

The *Mooltan* was launched on 15 February 1923 and completed by September the same year. On 5 October 1923 she sailed on a voyage to Bombay and back, before commencing the Australian service in December.

She was a handsome vessel, as can be seen, rather typical of P & O vessels of that era. The hull had a straight, almost vertical stem, good sheer and cruiser stern. It contained five decks, three being continuous, and eleven bulkheads. Superstructure was nicely proportioned with a couple of large funnels on top. Originally the ship had two masts, but one was removed in wartime and never replaced.

The *Mooltan* soon settled down to the service, sailing via Marseilles, Port Said, Aden, Colombo, Fremantle, Melbourne and Sydney. Later a call at Bombay was introduced. Other P & O ships on the route included her sister *Maloja*, and four 16,000-tonners, the *Mongolia*, *Moldavia*, and the *Naldera* and *Narkunda*. The *Mooltan* and her sister, at over 20,000 tons, were the biggest ships built for P & O up to that time, and were in fact about the largest which could go through the Suez Canal as it was then. The *Mooltan* was a very steady ship in a seaway, and became very popular with passengers. However her speed was a bit less than desired. This meant she worked to a rather tight schedule, and sometimes could not remain in port long enough fully to utilize her large cargo capacity. Matters were improved a little in 1929 when she was fitted with exhaust steam turbo-electric machinery coupled to each shaft. This augmented her power, and increased speed by about a knot.

Newer, faster ships entered the service, and in the 1930s the *Strathnaver* appeared on the scene, followed in due course by four others. These ships had service speeds of 20 knots. However, the *Mooltan* and her sister plodded steadily on, still popular. In the mid-thirties the ship's second class became known as tourist.

When war came in September 1939 the *Mooltan* was taken over, to be fitted as an armed merchant cruiser. This conversion was done by the builders Harland and Wolff, and the ship was given an armament of eight 6-inch guns and a couple of 3-inch AA guns.

In order to give the latter pair a better arc of fire the aft (dummy) funnel was removed.

HMS *Mooltan* (now based at Freetown) spent much time on the important work of convoy escort. The U-boat menace was ever present, as was the likelihood of air attack. However, all her convoys reached the UK safely.

Such large vessels of moderate speed were rather vulnerable, and in 1941 she was converted for trooping. Often she took troops to Egypt via the Cape, and was much involved in the North African landings. P & O ships were well represented in this campaign in November 1942. In addition to the *Mooltan* and *Maloja*, others taking part included the five 'Straths', the *Narkunda*, *Cathay*, *Ettrick* (built as a troop-ship) and the *Viceroy of India*. The two Orient liners *Otranto* and *Orion* were also involved. The *Mooltan* in fact was in the first convoy carrying American assault troops for the initial landings. Sadly, the *Cathay*, *Ettrick*, *Strathallan* and *Viceroy of India* were lost. The *Mooltan* and *Maloja* survived and later were to play important roles in the landings in Sicily and then on the Italian mainland, often under air attack.

Trooping work continued. After the war in Europe ended the *Mooltan* made voyages to India and the Far East. She was then engaged in the humane work of repatriating prisoners of war.

Released from war service in 1947, the ship had a complete refit at Belfast. She became a one-class vessel capable of carrying a large number of passengers. Many people wished to emigrate to Australia, and the *Mooltan* was one of the ships that transported them to their new country during the next few years. She set off on her first post-war voyage to Sydney in August 1948. Her dummy funnel had long been replaced and the ship was once more in P & O colours with black hull.

The ship continued on the Australia run until 1954. By this time the rush of emigrants had eased somewhat. Now thirty years old, this fine vessel had reached the end of her economic life. On reaching Tilbury on 7 January 1954 she was withdrawn and soon sold to the breakers at Faslane, where she arrived in April.

Name: Mooltan

Line: P & O

Builders: Harland & Wolff, Belfast; launched 15 February 1923, completed September 1923

Dimensions: Gross tonnage 20,847/ Length 625 ft/Beam 73.2 ft

Machinery

Engines: 2 4-cylinder quaruple expansion, twin screw, 16,000 total i.h.p.

Boilers: 6 double-ended, 2 single-ended oil-fired, 215 p.s.i.

Service speed: 16 knots

Major Refits

1929 LP turbo-electric machinery added, 17 knots
1939 Harland & Wolff, conversion to AMC
1941 R H Green and Silley Weir Ltd, conversion to troop-ship
1947 Harland & Wolff, reconstruction after war service

Regular Routes

Southampton – Sydney via Suez

Passenger Capacity

1924: 1st 327, 2nd 329
1948: Tourist 1030

Sister-ships

Maloja (1923)

Photograph 1946

Neuralia

THIS elegant ship was built for British India's service from the UK to India. Constructed by Barclay Curle & Co on the Clyde, she was launched on 12 September 1912 and completed by November that year. The ship was then put on the London-Calcutta service.

As can be seen from the photograph – which shows the vessel later in her career – she was a fine-looking one. The hull had good sheer, a straight stem and an elegant counter stern. It contained three decks and a shade deck. Superstructure above was well proportioned, with a single funnel nicely raked, as were the two masts.

The *Neuralia* had a sister, *Nevasa*, built by the same yard and completed in March 1913. These two fine vessels were, at over 9,000 tons each, the largest owned by British India up to that time.

Both ships had been built with the idea of their use as troop-ships in the event of war. This was soon to occur, and the *Neuralia* found herself in October 1914 bringing Indian troops to Marseilles. The next year she was much employed transporting troops to the eastern Mediterranean for the ill-fated Gallipoli campaign. Later on she became a hospital ship with 630 beds, and saw service in the Mediterranean and Indian Ocean. In late 1918 the ship performed duty as an ambulance transport.

The vessel returned to her owners' service after being refurbished in 1919. She spent the next few years back on commercial work, mostly on the route from the UK to East Africa. Her sister *Nevasa* had performed rather similar duties during the war, and recommenced BI sailings afterwards.

In 1925 the *Neuralia* and her sister were converted to become permanent troop-ships. At this time, of course, the British Empire extended over a vast area, and Service personnel had to be transported world-wide.

Until 1927 both ships retained their BI livery of black hull and black funnel with two white bands. In 1928 they were painted in standard troop-ship colours with white hull, blue riband and yellow funnel. The *Neuralia* appears thus in our photograph. Her trooping duties took her to many ports in India, Singapore, Egypt, Malta and the West Indies.

A different assignment befell the ship in 1932 when she made an educational cruise from Leith to Baltic ports, sailing via the Kiel Canal. She carried a large complement of students on this, the first such cruise handled by BI. It was a type of cruising which was to prove popular. Trooping work continued throughout the thirties, and when war came in 1939 the *Neuralia* and *Nevasa* were very actively involved.

In 1940 the *Neuralia* spent much time bringing Australian troops to Suez. One troop convoy, for example, which left Australia on 13 April consisted of the *Neuralia* and *Nevasa* together with BI's *Dunera*, P & O's *Ettrick* and *Strathaird*. After her troops had gone ashore to join those guarding the Canal, the *Neuralia* went to Cyprus and returned with people who wished to leave, as their island was threatened.

The ship then sailed through the Mediterranean and on to Dakar to bring French colonial troops to France. However, during this voyage the country surrendered to the Germans, so the troops were returned to Dakar.

The ship carried troops from Southampton to Bombay, and made voyages from the latter port to Basra, and from Madras to Rangoon. She also helped with the evacuation of the latter port when Burma was invaded by the Japanese. After the fall of Rangoon the *Neuralia* sailed from Madras to Port Blair in the Andaman Islands to take off those who wished to leave.

During 1943 the ship was much involved in the Far East and Mediterranean. Among other duties she carried troops to Taranto, Naples, Augusta (Sicily) and Tripoli. In May 1944 she had a quick refit at Glasgow before joining other ships at London preparing for the invasion of Normandy. Sailing on 5 June, she took troops across to the beaches and continued to do so until October.

Sadly, however, the *Neuralia* did not survive the war. In April 1945 she took some 1,700 Yugoslav refugees back from Egypt to their homeland. Sailing from Port Said, she landed them safely at Split, then set off for Taranto to embark some German POWs. She never arrived there. As the ship was entering the Gulf of Taranto in the early morning of 1 May she struck a mine. The engine-room flooded rapidly and lights went out. The order was given to abandon ship, and all on board took to the boats. When dawn broke the ship was seen to be still afloat. It was hoped to reboard her, and possibly arrange for her to be towed into port. As the boats got near, however, the *Neuralia* listed heavily and soon afterwards sank beneath the waves.

Name: Neuralia

Line: British India

Builders: Barclay Curle & Co., Glasgow, launched 12 September 1912, completed November 1912

Dimensions: Gross tonnage 9,082/Length 499 ft/Beam 58 ft

Machinery

Engines: 2 quadruple-expansion, twin screw, 6000 i.h.p.

Boilers: 7 single-ended cylindrical, coal-fired, 180 p.s.i.

Service speed: 14.5 knots

Major Refits

1925 conversion to troop-ship

Regular Routes

London – Calcutta
London – East African ports

Passenger Capacity

1st 218, 2nd 98
1,000 Troops

Sister-ships

Nevasa (1913)

Photograph 1937

Nevasa

THIS vessel was built as a permanent troop-ship in the days when practically all trooping was done by sea. She was constructed on the Clyde by Barclay Curle and Co. Launched on 30 November 1955, the ship was completed by July the following year.

This vessel and the similar-sized *Oxfordshire* of Bibby Line were in fact the last troop-ships to be built, and represented the final development of this once numerous class of ship. Accommodation on board was of a high standard.

The hull had six decks, and above were the promenade, boat, and forecastle decks and navigating bridge. Three classes, first, second and third, had cabin accommodation while the main body of troops were in dormitories. Officers, their wives and families occupied first class, with warrant officers and families taking second class. Third class was often taken by Servicewomen, senior NCOs etc. The dormitories for the main body of ORs were very spacious. There were lounges, drawing-rooms, dining saloons, libraries, childrens' nurseries etc., with a large cafeteria and a big recreation room among the many amenities on board. Plenty of space was available for recreation, film shows etc. In short, the *Nevasa* was designed to make long trooping voyages as pleasant as possible.

Propelling machinery consisted of two steam turbines geared to twin propeller shafts. Service speed was a nominal 17 knots, but the engines were powerful enough to provide 21 knots if required. She in fact achieved this on her trials. This extra power was a factor which helped to lead to her premature demise after a rather short career. The *Nevasa* was fitted with Denny Brown fin stabilizers, the first troop-ship to have them.

The ship was soon employed transporting troops to and from the UK and overseas possessions. She became very popular with Servicemen for her excellent amenities. However, after some six years of operation the government decided that future trooping was to be done by aircraft. The *Nevasa* was withdrawn, and laid up in the river Fal in 1962. Nevertheless, she was soon to get a fresh lease of life. British India had been much involved with educational cruise ships. Pupils were taken to places of interest while still having normal classroom lessons on board. The ships also provided separate accommodation for adult passengers as well, who paid higher fares – an arrangement which worked out very well economically. The *Dunera* and *Devonshire* (renamed *Devonia*), both ex-troopships, had been doing this for some time, but were now becoming elderly and

due for replacement. British India dispatched the *Nevasa* to Silley Cox & Co's yard at Falmouth to be converted for school cruises. This was done in 1964/5, and she sailed on her first educational trip from Southampton on 28 October 1965.

For the next few years she was very busy in her new role transporting scholars and 'paying guests' to the Mediterranean and elsewhere, proving to be extremely popular. The *Uganda*, owned by the same company, was doing similar work at this time.

During the late sixties and early seventies both vessels were very successful and popular. In December 1972 both came under P & O ownership.

In 1973 things started to go wrong. The steep rise in oil prices began to have a very adverse effect on operating costs. The *Nevasa*, in fact, with her rather powerful turbine machinery was something of a 'fuel-guzzler', and became uneconomical to run. In January 1975 she was withdrawn from service. Apparently no buyer was forthcoming to acquire her for further operations, and in April that year she was sold for scrap and proceeded to Kaohsiung, Taiwan, where she was broken up.

Her near-sister *Oxfordshire* was much more fortunate. Withdrawn from trooping about the same time as the *Nevasa*, she became the cruise ship *Fairstar* of Sitmar Cruises and is still in service today.

Name: Nevasa

Line: British India (1956-72); P & O (1972-75)

Builders: Barclay Curle & Co., Glasgow; launched 30 November 1955, completed July 1956

Dimensions: Gross tonnage 20,527/ Length 609 ft/Beam 78.1 ft

Machinery

Engines: 2 sets Parsons steam turbines, double and single reduction gearing, twin screw, 20,280 s.h.p.

Boilers: 4 oil-fired watertube, 500 p.s.i., superheated to 800°F

Service speed: 17 knots

Major Refits

1964-5 Silley Cox & Co., Falmouth, conversion to school cruise ship

Passenger Capacity

1956: 1st 220, 2nd 100, 3rd 180, Dormitories 1,000
1965: Cabins 307, Dormitories 783

Sister-ships

None (Near-sister *Oxfordshire* (1957)

Photograph 1959

New York

Name: New York

Line: HAPAG

Builders: Blohm & Voss, Hamburg;
launched October 1926, completed
March 1927

Dimensions: Gross tonnage 21,455/
Length 635 ft/Beam 72.5 ft

Machinery

Engines: 2 sets steam turbines single-
reduction geared, twin screw, 14,000
s.h.p.

Boilers: 4 single-ended, 2 double-ended,
225 p.s.i.

Service speed: 16 knots

Major Refits

1930 higher-powered turbines, 29,000
s.h.p.; 4 watertube steam pressure
boilers, superheated with forced and
induced draught, 400 p.s.i.; service speed
19.5 knots
1934 lengthened and improved, 22,337
tons

Regular Routes

Hamburg — New York

Passenger Capacity

1927: 1st 247, 2nd 321, 3rd 464
1934: 1st 247, 2nd 350, 3rd 400

Sister-ships and near-sisters

Albert Ballin (1923), *Deutschland*
(1924), *Hamburg* (1926)

Photograph 1930

THIS ship was the final member of the HAPAG quartet to enter service, the *Albert Ballin* being the first. Like the other three, the *New York* was built by Blohm and Voss at Hamburg. Launched in October 1926, she was completed in March 1927 and set off on her maiden voyage from Hamburg to New York via Southampton and Cherbourg on 1 April that year.

The *New York* and her sister *Hamburg* were in general very similar to the *Albert Ballin*. The latter pair were in fact slightly longer and of greater tonnage than the *Albert Ballin* and *Deutschland*. The main visual difference was that they had two masts instead of four. The photograph rather clearly shows up the blister on the side of the ship glistening in the sunlight. These bulges, one each side, coupled with the Frahm tanks made the quartet steady vessels. As with the *Ballin*, the *New York*'s funnels varied in height from time to time during her career. The picture depicts her with short ones. She underwent the same re-engining programme as her sisters in 1930, and like them was lengthened and improved in 1934. The four ships had gained good reputations on the Atlantic service, and continued to do so up to the outbreak of war.

One or two incidents befell the *New York*. On 18 December 1934, while homeward bound from the USA, she picked up an SOS call from the Norwegian cargo ship *Sisto*, drifting and in danger of sinking. The German ship arrived on the scene to find the British tanker *Mobiloil* already there. Several other vessels appeared. In heavy seas the *New York* launched a boat, and succeeded in taking off the Norwegian crew before their ship sank. On 7 May 1936 in thick fog she collided with and sank the Dutch steamer *Alphard* in the Channel, but managed to rescue the crew.

In August 1939 the liner was at New York, and on the 28 of that month she left without passengers. She sailed on a northerly route, and succeeded in reaching the Russian port of Murmansk. She lay there for some months, later making a dash down the Norwegian coast to reach Hamburg on 13 December. The ship was now used as an accommodation vessel for the German navy. In 1943–4 the *New York* was stationed in the Altenfjord in Norway, still acting in the same role for workmen repairing the damaged battleship *Tirpitz* after she had been attacked by British midget submarines. Later the ship was used for moving troops and supplies to the Eastern Front and evacuating refugees, as were her sisters also. On 3 April 1945 her career came to an abrupt end when she was bombed and sunk at Kiel by the RAF. In 1949 the wreck was raised and towed to the UK for scrapping.

The ship had served well for twelve years on the North Atlantic, during which time she had an enviable record of reliability and was comfortable to travel on. She had been progressively improved during this period as in fact had all the quartet, and had done much to rejuvenate HAPAG's fortunes on the Atlantic ferry. No doubt they had done useful service for Germany during the war as well.

Nieuw Amsterdam

THE world depression of the early 1930s had damaged the fortunes of many shipping companies – including the Holland-America Line. However, with the help of some funding from the Dutch Government, it was decided to build a large liner. This ship would be a running mate to the 29,000 ton *Statendam* built in 1929. She was built by the Rotterdam Drydock Company. Laid down in January 1936 and launched on 10 April 1937, the ship was completed the following year and set off on her maiden voyage from Rotterdam to New York on 10 May 1938. This proceeded satisfactorily and the new ship now joined the *Statendam* and the older 24,000 ton *Rotterdam* on the main transatlantic service. She had been designed for cruising in the winter months from New York to Bermuda or the Caribbean.

When war broke out in 1939 there was no shortage of passengers fleeing from Europe to America, but soon it became obvious that it was dangerous to keep the big ship running when U-boat activity was taking a steady toll. The *Nieuw Amsterdam* was therefore laid up in New York. (The *Statendam* was laid up in Rotterdam but was not so fortunate: set on fire during the Nazi invasion of Holland in 1940, she became a total loss.)

The *Nieuw Amsterdam* was eventually chartered to Britain's Ministry of War Transport and put under the management of Cunard – White Star. The liner was converted to a troopship at Halifax. She was to carry about 8,000 personnel, and much of her furniture and fittings had to be removed and stored. She was to cover vast distances during her wartime career transporting thousands of troops. Being fast, she could travel unescorted when required and in fact did so for much of the time. From mid 1941 until the end of 1942, the ship made no less than 23 troop voyages. These included runs from New Zealand/Australia to India, South Africa and Suez, and the Durban-Suez, and Suez-Durban-Capetown shuttle service. She also made voyages from India to and from the Middle East. In short, the ship was very actively employed. She also served in the Pacific Ocean making voyages from west coast ports of the US to Australia and New Zealand. Later, the ship returned to her home ground, bringing US and Canadian troops to Britain. Then followed some repatriation work. The big ship came through the war unscathed and finally returned to Rotterdam on 10 April 1946 to a great welcome. The Dutch were very proud of their flagship's splendid war effort. She had steamed over 530,000 miles and carried some 378,000 personnel.

Reconversion for Atlantic ferry duty took some eighteen months. Passenger accommodation was modified and brought up to date; machinery and boilers were given a thorough overhaul after their arduous war service. Most of this work was done by her original builders the Rotterdam Dry Dock Company but the finishing touches were done at Southampton in the King George V drydock.

On 29 October 1947, the *Nieuw Amsterdam* once again commenced the North Atlantic ferry service Rotterdam-Le Havre – Southampton – New York and swiftly won back her fine reputation with trans-Atlantic passengers. In the winter months she again went cruising from New York to the West Indies. She was so much bigger and faster than the other H A ships (both *Ryndam* and *Maasdam* were 15,000 ton, 16 knot vessels) that the company decided later to build two larger running mates. This was the time, in the 1950s, before air competition had reached serious proportions. The 24,000 ton *Statendam* and 38,000 ton *Rotterdam* eventually joined the fleet in 1957 and 1959 respectively, both having about the same speed as the *Nieuw Amsterdam*.

And so the ship continued reliably on the Atlantic service and cruising. In 1961 she was converted to a two-class vessel to bring her into line with the two new ships. Our subject had now been ousted from her position of the largest Dutch passenger ship by the new *Rotterdam*.

By the mid-sixties, the *Nieuw Amsterdam*'s boilers were giving trouble and she suffered a severe breakdown in 1967. The ship was now approaching her 30th birthday, but fortunately she was still considered good for a few more years and five suitable boilers were speedily found and fitted to the veteran. At the same time, a little further modernisation took place. She was back in service in 1968, but trans-Atlantic trade had fallen off badly by now. At first, she continued on the regular run combined with cruising but by late 1971 had reverted to being solely a cruise ship based at Port Everglades. In this service, the old ship spent her twilight years carrying out cruises of from 8 to 14 days' duration.

Proposals were put forward to preserve her statically at Rotterdam; this would have been a splendid conclusion to her fine career but, sadly, nothing came of it. On 9 January 1974, the *Nieuw Amsterdam* left Port Everglades for the breakers at Taiwan, sailing via the Panama Canal.

Name: **Nieuw Amsterdam**

Line: Holland-America

Builders: Rotterdam Drydock Company, completed 1938

Dimensions: Gross tonnage 36,287 (1938), 36,982 (1961)/Length 758 ft/Beam 88 ft

Machinery

Engines: 2 sets of quadruple-expansion Parsons turbines single reduction geared, twin screws, 34,000 s.h.p.

Boilers: 6 Yarrow watertube, steam pressure 630 p.s.i.

Service speed: 20.5 knots

Major Refits

1940 Halifax Conversion to troopship
1946/47 Rotterdam Drydock/ Southampton re-conversion for peacetime duty
1967 Schiedam Replacement of boilers

Passenger Capacity

1938: Cabin 568, Tourist 465, 3rd 209
1947: 1st 552, Cabin 426, Tourist 209
1961: 1st 574, Tourist 583

Regular Routes

Rotterdam – New York

Photograph 1952

Normandie

Name: **Normandie**

Line: Compagnie Générale
Transatlantique

Builders: Chantiers et Ateliers de Saint
Nazaire (Penhoet); launched 29 October
1932, completed May 1935

Dimensions: Gross tonnage 79,280/
Length 1,030 ft/Beam 117.8 ft

Machinery

Engines: 4 sets Zoelly impulse turbines, 4
electric propulsion motors, quadruple
screw, 160,000 s.h.p.

Boilers: 29 Penhoet 3-drum watertube oil-
fired, 400 p.s.i.

Service speed: 29 knots

Major Refits

1935-36 Le Havre, propeller replacement,
stiffening of hull, 83,423 tons
1938 replacement of propellers

Regular Routes

Le Havre – New York

Passenger Capacity

1st 848, Tourist 670, 3rd 454

Sister ships

Photograph 1935

THIS magnificent ship was the first of the 'thousand-footers' to go into service across the North Atlantic. The next two were of course the British *Queen Mary* and *Queen Elizabeth*.

The hull was designed on a rather revolutionary principle for that time, the brainchild of Vladimir Yourkevitch, a Russian then living in France. The stem was well rounded, almost clipper-like, while the stern was of a special semi-counter pattern. In plan view the hull tapered from amidships to each end with no parallel portion. Above the shapely bow was a whaleback forecastle with a breakwater of V-shape at the after end. Beneath the whaleback were the capstans and deck machinery, effectively screened. The superstructure was beautifully proportioned, and the nicely raked funnels were well spaced and receded in height from forward to aft. The after funnel was in fact a dummy one but added enormously to the ship's profile.

Public rooms and accommodation were on a lavish scale. The first class dining saloon for example was 300 feet long and three decks high. Other amenities included lounges, reading and writing rooms, smoking rooms, gymnasium and swimming pool.

The *Normandie*'s propelling machinery was perhaps the most daring innovation of all. Before this giant ship, turbo-electric propulsion for merchant vessels had been confined to ships of up to about 22,000 tons. It possesses the advantage that full power is available astern as well as ahead and all four screws can still be driven, even if a turbine has to be shut down for any reason. Also it was claimed that turbo-electric drive was quieter and smoother than turbines with reduction gearing.

The trials of the *Normandie* went off very satisfactorily. She reached speeds of over 32 knots, and fuel consumption figures were very good. The French giant broke the speed record westbound, crossing from Bishop Rock to the Ambrose Light in 4 days 3 hours 2 minutes at an average speed of 29.98 knots, faster than the Italian *Rex*. The eastbound record was also achieved at an average of 30.31 knots, about a couple of knots faster than the *Bremen*'s record. The ship had a few 'teething troubles', as would be expected from such a revolutionary design. On the westward leg, in fact, vibration problems in the after part had caused concern to the engineers and some discomfort to passengers. Some running repairs were required when a condenser tube fractured – this necessitated stopping one turbo alternator for a while, but the ship continued on all four screws. From the end of October 1935 until April 1936 she was at Le Havre having her vibration troubles sorted out. The *Queen Mary* arrived on the scene in 1936 and was to take the speed record from the *Normandie*. The French giant got it back again later, but the British ship regained the honours in 1938.

The ship continued her service reliably, and in July 1938 had completed her hundredth crossing. Prior to this CGT had investigated the possibility of using their giant ship for cruising purposes. The result was a lengthy cruise from 5th to the 27th February 1938 from New York via Nassau and Trinidad to Rio de Janeiro. She stayed here five days before returning via Fort de France (Martinique) to New York.

In April 1938 the *Normandie* received another set of four – bladed propellers which were an even bigger improvement on the earlier set. She continued to run successfully, and in February 1939 carried out another cruise on similar lines to the previous year. About a thousand passengers went on it.

All this was soon to come to an end. War clouds were gathering. The *Normandie* sailed on her last eastbound voyage from New York on 16 August 1939 and arrived back again on 28 August. She moored at Pier 88 as usual. She was never to sail again.

Many of the crew left the ship in September to return to France, but a considerable number remained on board to carry out care and maintenance duty. On 12 December 1941, a few days after the Pearl Harbour attack by the Japanese, the US Government took possession of the big ship. Later that month she became a unit of the US navy. She was renamed *Lafayette*, and work commenced to fit her out as a troop-ship. This proceeded apace with over 2,000 men on board. On February 1942 an outbreak of fire occurred which destroyed this splendid ship.

In the Grand Lounge a lot of materials had been stored, including some 1,140 burlap bales containing life-jackets, a potential fire hazard. These became accidentally ignited by sparks from a cutting torch. Despite all efforts the fire rapidly spread. So much water was pumped on board that the big ship finally capsized.

After cutting away her superstructure and funnels the great vessel was eventually refloated on 27 October 1943. Much discussion took place about her future. In the end it was decided that it was not economically viable to rebuild this once splendid vessel. She went for scrapping at Port Newark in 1946.

Northern Star

THE *Southern Cross* had been so successful that it was decided to build a similar, somewhat larger vessel for the 'round-the-world' service. She would replace the very popular *Dominion Monarch* and would incorporate various improvements based on the experience of operating the earlier 'engines aft' ship. The contract was awarded to the Tyneside yard of Vickers Armstrong. The ship was launched by Queen Elizabeth the Queen Mother in June 1961, completed a year later and commenced her maiden voyage from Southampton on 10 July 1962.

As can be seen in the photograph, the ship was very similar in appearance to the *Southern Cross*. Externally there were slight differences in the shapes of the funnel, mast, upperworks and stern, but no drastic alteration had been carried out. She had a greater tonnage by about 4,000, was longer and wider, and her machinery was a little more powerful to give her the same service speed as the earlier vessel.

The *Northern Star* had a few anxious moments when leaving the Tyne for her trials. She was to sail round Scotland to carry out these over the measured mile off Arran. Like her sister, with her massive superstructure she possessed a deal of 'windage'. Her funnel being well aft also caused problems, acting somewhat like a sail. In the rather strong wind the ship was in danger of being blown on to a breakwater, but managed to anchor in time and all was well. Trials were then completed satisfactorily.

However, the ship's maiden voyage was fraught with machinery problems. Without going into technicalities, this was due to the failure of some of some of the turbines rotor bearing pads. However the engine-builders eventually sorted out the problem, which was due to the use of the wrong sort of lubricating oil. The ship's second voyage passed off successfully.

She was then settled down into the round-the-world route with the *Southern Cross*. The *Dominion Monarch* had now been withdrawn. Shaw Savill had been realistic in not expecting the ships to make a great deal of money, but they were expected to pay their way reasonably well. Alas, it was not to be for very long. The era of the liner voyage was coming to an end. The airlines, which could of course offer much quicker transport, were making heavy inroads into the passenger trade. Both the *Northern Star* and her sister interspersed their liner voyages with cruising as well, the *Northern Star* making her first cruise in 1968. By March

1973, however, the *Southern Cross* had been sold. Shaw Savill had purchased the *Empress of England* in 1970 from the Canadian Pacific Company. She made one voyage to Australia, and was then refitted as a cruise ship. She had been renamed *Ocean Monarch*, and made her first cruise in 1971. Although the Company was now down to these two ships, a quite extensive programme was arranged for that year. Unfortunately, the *Ocean Monarch* had proved to be mechanically rather unreliable, and was withdrawn and sold for scrap in June. This left the *Northern Star* as the company's only cruise liner. She had had further mechanical problems during 1974, which included an engine-room explosion in June while she was in the Mediterranean. By all accounts she had never achieved the reliability of the *Southern Cross*. In May 1975 the company announced that the ship would be withdrawn after she had completed her cruising programme for that year. They felt it uneconomic to operate one cruise ship only. The ship still had eleven cruises to complete, and by all accounts these went off very successfully, with upward of 1,000 passengers on each one. Sadly no buyer could be found for this elegant vessel and she was sold to breakers in Taiwan, arriving at Kaohsiung on 11 December 1975.

Name: **Northern Star**

Line: Shaw Savill & Albion

Builders: Vickers-Armstrongs, Wallsend on Tyne; launched June 1961, completed June 1962

Dimensions: Gross tonnage 24,733/ Length 650 ft/Beam 83.5 ft

Machinery

Engines: 2 sets Parsons compound double reduction geared turbines, twin screw, 22,000 s.h.p.

Boilers: 2 oil-fired Babcock & Wilcox, 665 p.s.i., superheated to 900°F

Service speed: 20 knots

Regular Routes
Round-the-world

Passenger Capacity
1,412 one class

Near-Sister-ship
Southern Cross (1955)

Photograph 1962

Oceanic

THIS ship was the second White Star liner to have this rather famous name. The first *Oceanic*, a 3,700-ton vessel built in 1870, achieved a good reputation on the North Atlantic route, later transferring to the Pacific. She was sold for breaking up in 1896, and it was not long before White Star decided to give this name to another vessel.

The second *Oceanic* was much larger than the first one, being over 17,000 tons, and faster too. She may be considered as the British company's answer to the German express liners of that period. She was, however, not intended to be a record-breaker, being a few knots slower than they were. The ship was built by Harland and Wolff at Belfast. Launched on 14 January 1899, she commenced her maiden voyage from Liverpool to New York on 6 September that year. At that time she was the largest and most luxurious liner afloat, but only held this distinction for about two years.

As can be seen in the photograph, the *Oceanic* was an elegant-looking vessel. Her long, shapely hull had four decks, a slightly raked stem amd a counter stern. Above the fairly low superstructure were two very tall funnels, nicely raked and well spaced.

The new ship soon became popular on this Atlantic route, on which she remained until the outbreak of war in 1914 apart from a brief spell as a troop-ship during the Boer War. She sailed from Liverpool until 1907, transferring to Southampton that year when the White Star express service moved to that port. In the meantime other, bigger ships had joined the fleet. The big four, *Celtic, Cedric, Baltic* and *Adriatic*, entered service in 1901, 1903, 1904 and 1907 respectively. These varied in size from 21,000 tons to 24,500, but were slower than the *Oceanic*. They represented a change in policy of the company to sizeable ships of moderate speed which were thus more economical to run.

The *Oceanic*'s running-mates on the Southampton to New York route were the *Teutonic* and *Majestic*, both 20-knot vessels of around 10,000 tons. The *Adriatic* too joined her for a while; she had been given a bit more power than her three sisters, and could manage around 18 knots, just adequate for the express service. She in fact took the first sailing on the Southampton route on 6 June 1907, although the *Celtic* had made an experimental voyage in May. The latter ship was of course too slow for the express service, and continued on the Liverpool route. In 1907 plans were set in motion for three giant ships to be built for the Southampton-New York run. The *Olympic, Titanic* and *Britannic* would replace existing vessels, but the *Oceanic* would be retained. She would act as relief ship, taking sailings when one or other of the big three were being overhauled. Alas, these plans went badly astray.

By 1911 the *Adriatic* had returned to the Liverpool service. In that year also the *Teutonic* was relieved by the brand-new giant *Olympic*, and the *Majestic* was laid up that winter pending the advent of the *Titanic* in 1912. The tragic loss of this vessel meant that the older ship re-entered the service.

The *Oceanic* continued steadily on the route. A few mishaps befell her during the course of her career: in September 1901 she collided with the British coaster *Kincora* in fog off the Tuskar rock near Rosslare, Ireland. The latter vessel sank with the loss of seven lives. In 1905 there was a mutiny by the ship's firemen on board. Thirty-three of the men were convicted as a result.

An unusual accident occurred in 1911 when the ship was struck by lightning while in the river Mersey. Part of a mast was lost and some minor damage resulted, but fortunately no injuries.

In August 1914 the *Oceanic* was taken over for quick conversion to an armed merchant cruiser. She had in fact been strengthened in specific areas for possible gun-fitment when built. Her career as a warship was to be tragically short. She was allocated to Northern patrol duties with the celebrated Tenth Cruiser Squadron. Her regular master remained on board, but the ship was now commanded by a naval captain.

On 8 September 1914 faulty navigation put her aground off the island of Foula, some 20 miles west of the Shetlands. Fortunately, no lives were lost but the ship remained fast, all attempts to refloat her failed and she became a total loss. Some guns and fittings were removed, and over the years much was recovered from the wreck, providing work for salvage operators and divers.

Name: Oceanic

Line: White Star

Builders: Harland & Wolff, Belfast; launched 14 January 1899, completed August 1899

Dimensions: Gross tonnage 17,274/ Length 704 ft/Beam 68.3 ft

Machinery

Engines: 2 4-cylinder triple-expansion, twin screw, 28,000 i.h.p.

Boilers: 12 double-ended, 3 single-ended, cylindrical 192 p.s.i.

Service speed: 19.5 knots

Major Refits

1914 conversion to AMC

Regular Routes

Liverpool – New York
Southampton – New York

Passenger Capacity

1st 410, 2nd 300, 3rd 1,000

Sister-ships

None

Photograph 1912

Ohio

Name: München (1920); **Ohio** (1923); **Albertic** (1927)

Line: Norddeutscher Lloyd (1914-19); Royal Mail (1920-27); White Star (1927-34)

Builders: A.G. 'Weser', Bremen; launched 23 March 1920, completed March 1923

Dimensions: Gross tonnage 18,940/ Length 615 ft/Beam 71.5 ft

Machinery

Engines: 2 quadruple-expansion reciprocating, twin screw, 16,000 i.h.p.

Boilers: 6 double-ended, 1 single-ended cylindrical, coal-fired

Service speed: 17 knots

Regular Routes

Hamburg/Southampton – New York
Liverpool – Quebec – Montreal

Passenger Capacity

1923: 1st 229, 2nd 523, 3rd 690
1927: Cabin 270, Tourist 1,100
1929: Cabin 218, Tourist 496, 3rd 565

Sister-ships

None

Photograph 1923

THIS ship was intended for the Norddeutscher Lloyd Co. of Bremen, but never entered their service. She was laid down in 1914 at the A.G. Weser yard at Bremen, but no further work was done on her during the war. In 1919 she was ordered to be completed and then handed over to Britain. Not unnaturally, the Germans did all they could to retain the valuable but incomplete ship. They needed tonnage themselves to make up for war losses, but they were finally forced to surrender the vessel. Eventually launched on 23 March 1920, she was purchased soon afterwards by the Royal Mail Group. Her final completion was supervised by the British company. Due to material shortages and general chaos in the shipbuilding industry, the vessel was not completed until March 1923. She had been launched with the name *München*, but Royal Mail changed this to *Ohio*. After successful trials the ship commenced her maiden voyage from Hamburg to New York on 4 April 1923.

As can be seen, the *Ohio* was quite an attractive looking vessel. The hull had a straight stem, quite good sheer and elegant counter stern. It contained three overall decks with a fourth one in the holds and there were ten main watertight bulkheads. Superstructure above was quite well proportioned, with a couple of rather slender funnels on top.

The ship catered for three classes of passengers, first, second and third. She had a good cargo capacity also, with six holds and hatchways.

Propelling machinery consisted of two sets of reciprocating engines driving twin screws. This was a very conventional arrangement for pre-war vessels, but a little outdated in the 1920s. Service speed was a fairly modest 17 knots. Steam was provided by seven coal-fired cylindrical boilers, again a little outdated.

For a while after the war there was a complete cessation of German sailings on the North Atlantic and the Royal Mail decided to open a service from Hamburg. They started this in 1921 using the 15,500-tonners *Orduna*, *Orbita* and the slightly smaller *Oropesa*. The *Orca* joined in 1922, and the *Ohio* the following year. The service was quite successful at first, but German companies began to get back on their feet and competition mounted. Often the *Ohio* and others omitted Hamburg, with Southampton becoming the terminal. American restrictions on immigration also made things more difficult. Experimental sailings were made from Plymouth and Greenock with calls at Queenstown. The ship also sometimes called at Halifax on westward crossings.

In 1925 the *Ohio*, like the other 'O's, added cruising to her itinerary. She was reputedly a steady, comfortable ship to travel on.

The Royal Mail took control of the White Star Line in 1927 and the four 'O's were dispersed. The *Orbita* and *Orduna* went to the Pacific Steam Navigation Co., within the group, while the *Orca* and *Ohio* were transferred to White Star's Canadian service. The *Orca* was now renamed *Calgaric*, while the *Ohio* became the *Albertic*. There was no outward change in the ship's appearance, apart from new White Star colours, but soon afterwards her masts were shortened by some 37 feet.

On 22 April 1927 the *Albertic* left Liverpool on her first voyage to Quebec and Montreal. In May 1928 she was transferred to the service from London and Southampton to Canada, running with the 15,000-ton *Megantic*.

In 1929 she took the place of the wrecked *Celtic* on the Liverpool – New York route for a while, but the next year she was back on the Canadian service from Liverpool, where she remained for the next three years.

The Depression was beginning to bite, however, and many ships were withdrawn in the early thirties. Sadly, the *Albertic* was one of these. Laid up in the Holy Loch in March 1933, she was sold for scrapping in Japan the next year, arriving at Osaka on 29 November 1934.

The ex-*Ohio*'s career cannot be called very satisfactory. She was yet another sad victim of adverse economics in the shipping trade. Under more favourable conditions this fine ship would undoubtedly have given much longer service than the ten years she achieved.

Olympic

Name: Olympic

Line: White Star

Builders: Harland & Wolff, Belfast;
launched 20 October 1910, completed
May 1911

Dimensions: Gross tonnage 45,328/
Length 882.75 ft/Beam 92 ft

Machinery

Engines: 2 4-cylinder triple expansion,
each 15,000 h.p., exhaust steam turbine
16,000 h.p., triple screw

Boilers: 24 double-ended, 5 single-ended,
215 p.s.i.

Service speed: 21 knots

Major Refits

1913 Harland & Wolff, new safety
measures incorporated
1915 conversion to troop-ship
1919 Harland & Wolff, conversion of
boilers to oil, modernization of
accommodation

Regular Routes

Southampton – New York

Passenger Capacity

1911: 1st 735, 2nd 674, 3rd 1026
1928: 1st 675, Tourist 561, 3rd 819
1934: 1st 618, Tourist 447, 3rd 382

Sister-ships

Titanic (1912), **Britannic** (1915)

Photograph 1934

THE *Olympic* was the largest ship afloat at the time of her completion by the Harland and Wolff yard at Belfast in May 1911. Together with her sisters *Titanic* and *Britannic*, she had been designed as a rival to the Cunard 'express' liners *Mauretania* and *Lusitania* which had set a new standard in Atlantic travel. Unlike these two, however, the White Star ships, considerably larger, were built for comfort and moderate rather than high speed. Proceeding then to Southampton, she commenced her maiden voyage to New York on 14 June 1911.

Public rooms were luxurious indeed. The first class dining saloon was in Jacobean style and there was a Louis Quinze lounge and a Georgian smoke room reading and writing rooms, a gymnasium and swimming pool were among other amenities on board.

On 20 September 1911 the big ship was involved in a collision with the British cruiser HMS *Hawke*. The *Olympic*, outward bound, had passed down Southampton Water and had just completed a tight turn to port off the Bramble Bank to take her into Spithead. The cruiser coming up from the West Solent struck the liner on her starboard side about 80 feet from the stern. This opened up a gash about 40 feet long, while the *Hawke*'s bows were badly crumpled. The cruiser managed to limp into Portsmouth Harbour, and the *Olympic* anchored in Osborne Bay. Later she moved off Cowes, where many passengers were taken off by tender and the ship then proceeded back to Southampton. The voyage, of course, had to be cancelled. The big ship had to return to Belfast, and repairs took about six weeks.

On 15 April 1912 her sister *Titanic* sank after striking an iceberg. The *Olympic* at the time was over 500 miles away homeward-bound from New York, so was unable to render assistance. She completed five more voyages then was sent back again to Belfast. Some fairly extensive alterations were put in hand as a result of lessons tragically learned from the *Titanic* disaster. Perhaps most important of all was the provision of many more lifeboats, more than enough to accommodate all passengers and crew.

The *Olympic* returned after her extensive refit and was back on the Atlantic run.

An adventure befell her in October 1914 when she went to the assistance of a stricken warship near Lough Swilly, Northern Ireland, while on an eastbound passage. HMS *Audacious*, a battleship of some 23,000 tons, was a unit of the 2nd Battle Squadron,

and with others had been carrying out firing practice when she struck a mine. At first it was thought she could steam to Lough Swilly, but eventually all power was lost and she lay helplessly. The *Olympic* appeared in early afternoon and made a strenuous attempt to tow the stricken battleship. Unfortunately, the tow-line broke. Further attempts by the cruiser *Liverpool* and collier *Thornhill* were equally unsuccessful. The big White Star ship had taken risks in entering the minefield, the extent of which was unknown, but she took off most of the battleship's crew. The big warship later sank after the remainder of her crew had been rescued.

In September 1915 the *Olympic* became a troop-ship hoisting the White Ensign of the Royal Navy. Troops were needed for the Gallipoli campaign and the big ship made four voyages to Mudros. She spent the rest of the war bringing American and Canadian troops across the Atlantic. By the time the war ended the great liner had steamed some 184,000 miles, transporting many thousands of troops and civilian passengers. She had been attacked again by a submarine in May 1918 when well laden with troops near the Lizard. The *U-103*, however, had got too close for her own safety. A quick helm movement and ramming by 46,000 tons of steel proved fatal to the enemy submarine, which was dispatched to the bottom. Most of her crew were rescued.

The *Olympic* then spent some time in 1919 repatriating troops back across the Atlantic, before returning to Belfast for an extensive refit. She then resumed the Southampton-Cherbourg-New York route, and was soon joined by two new consorts. These were two ex-German liners, the giant 56,000-ton *Majestic* (ex *Bismarck*) and the smaller 34,000-ton *Homeric* (ex *Columbus*).

With the onset of the Depression the profitable days disappeared. Short cruises were undertaken. One more sad mishap befell the ship on 16 May 1934 when she rammed and sank the Nantucket lightship in thick fog; with the tragic loss of the lightship's seven crew.

White Star merged with Cunard in February 1934 to form Cunard-White Star. Several of the former company's ships were now placed on the disposal list, including the *Olympic*. She lay at Southampton for some time in the hope that a buyer might be found to give her further employment she was by no means worn out, and her hull was in very good condition. Sadly, none was forthcoming and eventually she was sold for breaking up at Jarrow, to help relieve unemployment in that distressed area.

S.A. Oranje

Name: **Pretoria Castle** (1948); **S.A. Oranje** (1965)

Line: Union Castle (1948-66); Safmarine (1966-75)

Builders: Harland & Wolff, Belfast; launched 19 August 1947, completed July 1948

Dimensions: Gross tonnage 28,705/ Length 747 ft/Beam 84 ft

Machinery

Engines: 2 sets of Parsons type triple expansion turbines, double reduction gearing, twin screw

Boilers: 3 oil-fired watertube 630 p.s.i. superheated to 850°F

Service speed: 22 knots

Regular Routes

Southampton — Cape Town and South African ports

Passenger Capacity

1st 214, Tourist 541

Sister-ships

Edinburgh Castle (1948)

Photograph 1970

THIS ship and her sister *Edinburgh Castle* were the first two mail liners built for Union Castle after the last war. Unlike the previous six mailships which were diesel-driven this pair were powered by steam turbines.

The *Pretoria Castle* was built by Harland & Wolff at Belfast. She was launched on 19 August 1947, completed by July 1948 and set off on her maiden voyage from Southampton to Durban on the 22nd of that month.

The naming and launching of this ship was rather unusual. It was performed by Mrs Jan Smuts, wife of the Prime Minister of South Africa. She did this from her home some 6,000 miles away near Pretoria. By pressing a button, electrical impulses were sent out by land line to Cape Town. From here they were directed by radio link to London, and thence by land line to Belfast. These impulses were arranged to cause a bottle of South African wine to break on the bows of the new ship and to activate the launching gear. A unique ceremony.

The *Pretoria Castle* was almost identical to her sister. The hull had a cruiser stern, good sheer with a curved and raked stem. Upperworks were well proportioned, with a large funnel. There were six decks for passenger accommodation, and cargo capacity of seven holds, much of it insulated for carrying fruit. After a successful maiden voyage, she settled down to steady steaming to and from South Africa.

On 15 June 1953 the ship was amongst those assembled at Spithead for the Coronation Review of the fleet. One of the largest merchant ships present on that historic occasion, she looked resplendent indeed.

The *Pretoria Castle* continued reliably in service throughout the 1950s. In the early sixties she was altered in the same way as her sister, her foremast being shortened and mainmast removed. In 1966 the ship was transferred to the South African Marine Corporation (Safmarine). At Cape Town on 2 February she was renamed *S.A. Oranje*.

This elegant vessel continued on the route until her last arrival at Southampton on 8 September 1975. She was sold for breaking up and sailed on 19 September for Kaohsiung, Taiwan, taking some cargo which she off-loaded at Durban en route.

Incidentally, an 'intermediate' vessel of the same name had joined the Union Castle fleet in 1938. After serving during the war as an armed merchant cruiser and escort carrier, she rejoined the Union Castle Company. She was then renamed *Warwick Castle* so that her original name was available for the new mailship.

Oranje Nassau

Name: **Oranje Nassau** (1957); **XX Aniversario** (1973)

Line: Royal Netherlands

Builders: Sheepsbouwwerf Gebroeders Pot, Bolnes; launched 26 January 1957, completed August 1957

Dimensions: Gross tonnage 7,214/Length 431.5 ft/Beam 56.5 ft

Machinery

Engines: 1 Stork 9-cylinder diesel, single screw, 4,500 b.h.p.

Service speed: 15 knots

Regular Routes

Amsterdam – Caribbean

Passenger Capacity

116 one class, 68 group

Sister-ships

Prins der Nederlanden (1957)

Photograph 1965

THIS ship, and her sister *Prins der Nederlanden*, were built for the Royal Netherlands Steamship Co. (Koninklijke Nederlandsche Stoomboot Mij Nv). They were both for the company's Caribbean service, which was flourishing at the time. This Dutch company had owned steamships since 1856, and ran extensive services, especially to the Caribbean, and South America.

The *Oranje Nassau* was built by the Dutch yard of Sheepsbouwwerf Gebroeders Pot, Bolnes, and completed in August 1957, entering service shortly afterwards. As can be seen, the ship was a very attractive one. The hull had a spoon-type cruiser stern, a well-raked bow and good sheer. It contained two full decks and a partial one. Superstructure above was nicely proportioned, with a modern streamlined funnel on top. The ship catered for a comparatively small number of passengers in one class. There was also some 'group' accommodation for troops, immigrants, students etc. Cargo capacity was of great importance, and the ship had five holds, three forward and two aft with a couple of tween decks. Considerable space was insulated for refrigerated cargo. Derricks were fitted for handling this.

The ship's sister, the *Prins der Nederlanden*, was built by P. Smit Jr at Rotterdam. She was practically identical to the *Oranje Nassau*, and was completed by September 1957.

Both ships entered service on the Holland-Caribbean route and soon became very popular. Passengers greatly appreciated the homely atmosphere on board. Ports of call varied from time to time, but a typical route would be Amsterdam – Southampton – Barbados – Trinidad – La Guaira – Curaçao – Aruba-Puerto Limon – Kingston – Santiago de Cuba – Port-au-Prince, returning to Plymouth and Amsterdam. It was intended initially for one-way traffic, for passengers proceeding from Holland or Britain out to their various destinations. However, the route became very popular, especially during the winter season, as a round-trip cruise of some 34 days. Many passengers took advantage of voyages on these fine vessels. In the late 1960s, during a reshuffling of the Royal Netherlands passenger fleet, the *Oranje Nassau* was transferred to the Surinam service.

The ships continued running for the remainder of the sixties and early seventies. However, containerization was now making 'conventional' cargo ships redundant, and of course air travel was taking over the passenger traffic. All this spelled the commercial demise of these two sisters. They were withdrawn, and laid up in 1972 in Amsterdam. The next year they were acquired by the Cuban Government for use as military transports and training ships. The *Oranje Nassau* was now renamed *XX Aniversario*, apparently commemorating the twentieth anniversary of one of Castro's attacks on the barracks at Santiago de Cuba in the 1950s.

The ship was renamed *Ani* in 1989 and was sold for breaking up in India in 1990. Her sister was renamed *Vietnam Heroico* when taken over. Sadly, she was declared a constructive total loss as a result of damage sustained when she capsized against the quay at Havana on 1 October 1984.

Oranjefontein

THIS ship was one of a trio built for Holland-Africa's service to South and East Africa. The other two were the *Klipfontein* and the *Rietfontein*, the latter to be renamed twice, as we shall later note. All three had varied experiences before eventually coming together as a trio on the service for which they had been built.

The *Oranjefontein* was launched from the yard of P.Smit Junior at Rotterdam during wartime, on 21 March 1940. Completed by December that year, she was soon taken over by the Germans for their own use. She did not in fact sail on her first voyage to South and East Africa until after the war.

As can be seen, the ship had an attractive appearance, rather typical of passenger-cargo liners of that period. The hull had good sheer, a cruiser stern and nicely raked stem. It contained three decks, and the fairly short superstructure above was well-proportioned, with a single vertical funnel on top. Passenger accommodation was for first class and tourist. Public rooms were good, and there was plenty of deck space, with a swimming pool at the aft end of the promenade deck. First class occupied the midships superstructure on four decks, while tourist class were accommodated on the aft structure. The ship had considerable cargo capacity with holds forward and aft worked by derricks.

As noted, the ship was taken over by the German navy during the war, and seems to have had a somewhat chequered career. On 17 March 1941 she was put under the management of the German African line. She was damaged in Rotterdam by Allied bombing in August 1941, necessitating repairs. She was used for training purposes as a target vessel for U-boats and the Luftwaffe. In the latter part of the war, in 1945 she is reported to have been used as a refugee transport for evacuation of Germany's eastern territories. She was apparently named *Pionier* for a while.

In July 1945 the *Oranjefontein* was returned to her rightful owners. She was in reasonable shape, but of course required a refit. Dutch yards were unable to do the work at this time, so the ship was overhauled on the Tyne. She then made some repatriation sailings, taking back displaced citizens to the Dutch East Indies and bringing Dutch people back to Holland from the Caribbean. The ship then at last commenced sailing to South and East Africa, the service for which she had been built.

Her two sisters eventually joined her also. The *Klipfontein* had in fact been completed first, and had voyaged on the service in 1939. She later served during the war as a transport for the US War Shipping Administration. She returned to her owners for the African service after the war. The *Rietfontein*'s name was changed to *Elandsfontein* before launching. She too had a chequered career in the German navy during the war, ending up sunk off the mouth of the Vistula. However, she was raised, rebuilt and entered Holland-Africa service in 1950, now renamed *Jagersfontein*. During the late forties the service was maintained by our subject together with her sister *Klipfontein* and the *Bloemfontein* of 1934 vintage. This latter vessel originally had a sister, a previous *Jagersfontein*, sunk in July 1942.

By the time the rejuvenated *Jagersfontein* joined the fleet the service was going well. The ships were popular with passengers, and motored steadily to and fro. Sadly, however, in 1953 the *Klipfontein* was lost. On 8 January that year she struck submerged rocks or some underwater object off Cape Barra, Mozambique, and sank in about 45 minutes. Fortunately, passengers and crew abandoned the ship and were picked up by the Union Castle liner *Bloemfontein Castle*.

The *Oranjefontein* and the two others continued the service. They were joined in 1959 by the new *Randfontein*. The *Bloemfontein* was withdrawn for scrapping in that year after a distinguished career in peace and war.

The service went into decline in the sixties. In 1967 the *Jagersfontein* was withdrawn, and went to Taiwanese shipbreakers. The *Oranjefontein* went for scrapping in Spain that same year. For her final voyage to Bilbao where she arrived on 11 August she was named *Fontein*.

The Holland – Africa Line is now but a memory. Part of the Netherlands Steamship Co. (VNSM), this was eventually merged with the great Nedlloyd Group and lost its identity. However, the passenger cargo service it once ran to South and East Africa had a very high reputation indeed.

Name: **Oranjefontein**

Line: Holland-Africa

Builders: P. Smit Jr., Rotterdam, launched 21 March 1940, completed December 1940

Dimensions: Gross tonnage 10,544/ Length 527 ft/Beam 62.7 ft

Machinery

Engines: 2 Burmeister & Wain diesel, twin screw

Service speed: 17 knots

Major Refits

1945 Tyneside, post-war overhaul

Regular Routes

Rotterdam – South and East Africa

Passenger Capacity

1st 100, Tourist 60

Sister-ships

Klipfontein (1939). *Rietfontein* (later *Jagersfontein*) (1950)

Photograph 1946

Orcades

DURING the last war the Orient Line suffered heavy losses. Their eight passenger liners had all been requisitioned for trooping duties, and four had been lost. These were the *Orama*, *Oronsay*, *Orford* and an earlier *Orcades*. The latter ship had only entered service in 1937, and it was rather fitting that the first new ship to be built after the war should receive this name.

The earlier vessel had proved very successful in her short life before being torpedoed by *U-172* in the South Atlantic on 10 October 1942. The new ship was to be somewhat bigger and a little faster, to suit the requirements of the Australian trade. She was built by Vickers-Armstrongs at Barrow. Launched on 14 October 1947, she was completed by November the following year, and set off on her maiden voyage from London to Sydney on 14 December.

She was a good-looking vessel. The hull had a raked stem and cruiser stern, and superstructure above was well proportioned. The central feature of the ship's profile was the structural group comprising the elegant funnel, casing and superstructure with which it was integrated. This latter consisted of three short bridge decks which included the navigating bridge, wireless room and officers' accommodation. Atop was the single tripod mast. The whole group rather resembled the control tower of a warship and all helped to give the ship an elegant profile. The funnel initially fairly plain later had a 'welsh hat' top added to improve smoke-dissipation.

The trials of the *Orcades* were very satisfactory, a speed of 24.74 knots being achieved. The maiden voyage was a great success and she was given a splendid welcome at Sydney and Melbourne. It had been a quick passage too, London to Melbourne in 26 days.

The ship then settled down to regular Australian voyaging, interspersed with some cruising. In the early 1950s, for instance, she made a number of these from Tilbury to the Mediterranean. She could make four complete round voyages to Australasia in a year.

In June 1953 the *Orcades* was one of the liners present at the Great Coronation Fleet Review at Spithead. During the actual review the despatch vessel HMS *Surprise* was used by the Queen since the Royal Yacht *Britannia* had not been completed. A number of other vessels were in the procession carrying Government guests and these included the *Orcades*, *Pretoria Castle* and *Strathnaver*.

During the 1950s the ship cruised also from Sydney, becoming very popular. However, by the mid-fifties the number of passengers to Australia had diminished somewhat and there was competition from other lines. In 1954 some of P & O's sailings were continued across the Pacific to Vancouver and San Francisco. The *Orcades* made her first departure on this service on 17 December 1954, proceeding from Sydney to San Francisco and returning to Australia. On 22 August 1955 she sailed from Tilbury out to Australia via the Panama Canal and back through Suez.

In 1956 the *Orcades* was berthed at Melbourne as a floating hotel for a couple of weeks during the Olympic Games. In 1959 she had a major refit at Harland & Wolff's Belfast yard. All accommodation was now air-conditioned, a new swimming-pool added and other improvements made.

During another refit in 1964 her accommodation become all one class and her hull was painted white. In 1962 the ship was registered under P & O ownership, and later in the decade the name 'Orient Line' vanished from the shipping scene.

The *Orcades* continued on the Australian/Pacific service, but was spending more time now cruising from Australia and the UK. The ship had proved very reliable in service, and not many 'incidents' befell her. However, on 7 May 1952 she ran aground in Port Philip Bay while leaving Melbourne. She was pulled free by four tugs later that day, and her strong hull was found to be undamaged.

On 17 April 1972, while she was in Hong Kong on a cruise, fire broke out in her boiler-room, causing considerable damage. Repairs were soon put in hand, and she continued the cruise.

After the P & O – Orient lines merger the *Orcades* had moved from London to Southampton for operational purposes, and some of her refits took place in that port. Her UK cruises remained popular. During the summer of 1971, for example, these varied from six to fifteen days. The shorter ones included visits to Lisbon and Ceuta, while longer ones took her into the Mediterranean or Madeira.

In 1972 the company announced the ship would soon be withdrawn. On 3 June that year she left Sydney for the last time. On arrival in the UK she made a series of cruises which lasted until 13 October. She was then laid up, until she finally left for Taiwan breakers in January 1973.

219

Name: Orcades

Line: Orient (1948); P & O (1964-73)

Builders: Vickers-Armstrongs, Barrow; launched 14 October 1947, completed November 1948

Dimensions: Gross tonnage 28,164/ Length 709 ft/Beam 90.6 ft

Machinery

Engines: Parsons turbines, single and double reduction geared, twin screw, 42,500 s.h.p.

Boilers: 4 Foster-Wheeler watertube, 525 p.s.i., superheated to 850°F

Service speed: 22 knots

Major Refits

1959 Harland & Wolff, air-conditioning fitted
1964 accommodation altered to one class

Regular Routes

London – Sydney

Passenger Capacity

1948: 1st 733, Tourist 772
1964: 1,635 one class

Near-Sister-ships

Himalaya (1949)

Photograph 1952

Oriana

Name: **Oriana**

Line: P & O – Orient

Builders: Vickers-Armstrongs, Barrow; launched 3 November 1959, completed 1960

Dimensions: Gross tonnage 41,915/ Length 804 ft/Beam 97.1 ft

Machinery

Engines: 2 sets Pametrada double reduction geared turbines, twin screw, 80,000 s.h.p.

Boilers: 4 Foster-Wheeler oil-fired watertube, 750 p.s.i., superheated to 950°F

Service speed: 27.5 knots

Regular Routes

Southampton – Sydney

Passenger Capacity

1960: 1st 638, Tourist 1,496
1973: 1,700 one class

Sister-ships

None, but **Canberra** (1961) similar in size

Photograph 1960

During the 1950s the P & O – Orient Line management decided on a couple of bigger and faster vessels for the Australian route. From 1958 this was to extend across the Pacific to the west coast of America. Cruising was also very much a requirement, and this resulted in the building of the *Oriana* and *Canberra*.

The *Oriana* was built by Vickers–Armstrongs at their Barrow yard. She was launched on 3 November 1959 by Princess Alexandra and completed a year later, sailing on her maiden voyage from Southampton to Sydney on 3 December 1960.

The ship was of rather unusual appearance. She had a graceful hull with rounded, curved stem and well-proportioned super structure. The funnel arrangement was unusual. Only the forward one was operational, the after 'flower-pot' serving as a ventilation outlet for the engine-room. The hull had a pronounced knuckle, extending about 200 feet back from the bow. Underwater it had a bulbous forefoot. A noteworthy feature was the mooring deck, below the forecastle. Lifeboats were carried farther down than usual, rather as on the *Canberra*. There were eleven passenger decks for first class and tourist. The superstructure above the strength deck was almost entirely of aluminium. Topmost here was the short bridge deck and compass platform. Then the 'tennis deck', bathing deck, stadium deck, veranda deck, and A deck, the strength deck being B.

The ship had fine lounges and restaurants together with the usual amenities – cinemas, shops, hairdressing salons and two swimming pools.

On trials the *Oriana* exceeded 30 knots, which was very satisfactory. The maiden voyage passed off very well, the ship being given a great welcome in Sydney. From here she made a cruise before proceeding to Auckland and across the Pacific to visit Vancouver and San Francisco. She then returned to Sydney, and sailed back to Southampton via Suez. For her second voyage she returned via Panama, and this was the general pattern of employment. The *Canberra* soon joined, and together with others in the fleet, a fine service was provided. 'Line' voyages were combined with cruising, the latter being very important.

A few mishaps befell the *Oriana*. On 3 December 1962 she was in collision near Long Beach, California with the US aircraft carrier *Kearsage* of the *Essex* class, (displacement 33,000 tons). Both vessels suffered damage but no casualties. A small fire on the *Oriana*

in a paint locker was swiftly put out. The ship had to go into a local shipyard for repairs to a large gash high up on her bow and some buckled plating. The collision had occurred in dense fog, and even radar and modern navigational equipment had not prevented it. A court of enquiry found the big liner to blame for this mishap.

The ship continued successfully in her operations for the next few years. In 1964 her corn-coloured hull was repainted white. In September 1966 she was the victim of a bomb hoax, but nothing was found after a careful search. In April 1968 her starboard propeller was damaged by striking the bank in the Panama Canal. With only one screw operational she arrived back in Southampton several days late, and was dry-docked for repairs.

In June 1970 a boiler-room fire occurred while she was cruising in the Pacific. This was soon extinguished, but on 11 August that year a more serious one occurred while outward-bound off Calshot. For a while the ship lay helpless, all power lost. The fire was eventually put out, thanks to the fine efforts of the crew and the fire-fighting tugs which were fortunately nearby in Southampton Water. Serious damage had occurred this time, and repairs took several weeks, the ship eventually sailing on 27 August.

By 1972 the *Oriana* was spending much of her time cruising, soon becoming a one-class ship. She usually cruised from Southampton during the summer months, going to Australia around November to cruise from Sydney. In May 1978 another bomb warning was received while she was on a Caribbean cruise from Southampton, again proving to be a hoax.

The *Oriana* made her last cruises from Southampton in 1981, making her final departure from the port on 12 November. From now on she was to be permanently based at Sydney. She was replaced at Southampton by the *Sea Princess* in 1982, the latter having been Australia-based since 1979.

The *Oriana* was very popular with passengers. However, competition from Russian – subsidized vessels, and other economic factors, meant that the ship was not so financially successful as had been hoped. She completed her last cruise on 27 March 1986 and was later sold to a Japanese company for use as a floating hotel at Oita, near Beppu on the island of Kyushu. She was towed to Japan and refitted for this new role. She is still there.

Orinoco

Name: *Orinoco* (1928); ***Puebla*** (1941);
Olympia (1947); ***Juan de Garay***
(1947)

Line: HAPAG (1928-41); Cia
Transoceanica Argentina (1947-63)

Builders: Bremer Vulkan, Vegesack;
completed 1928

Dimensions: Gross tonnage 9,660/Length
480 ft/Beam 60.9 ft

Machinery

Engines: 2 MAN diesel, twin screw

Service speed: 15 knots

Major Refits

1942 San Francisco, conversion to troop-
ship
1946 Brooklyn, reconversion to passenger
liner

Regular Routes

Hamburg — West Indies
Argentina — Portugal, Spain, Italy

Passenger Capacity

1928: 578
1947: 850 Tourist

Sister-ships

Magdalena (1928)

Photograph 1934

THIS fine-looking ship was built for the Hamburg America Company's service to the West Indies. Her builders were the Bremer Vulkan Yard at Vegesack, near Bremen, and she was completed in 1928. She sailed on her maiden voyage from Hamburg to the West Indies in April that year.

As can be seen in the photograph, she was a handsome looking vessel, very typical of the motorships of that era. The hull with its slightly raked stem and cruiser stern contained three complete decks and a partial one. Superstructure above was well proportioned, with two funnels on top. Accommodation and public rooms on board were very good. There was considerable cargo capacity also, with holds fore and aft worked by derricks.

Propelling machinery consisted of two diesel engines driving twin screws. Service speed was 15 knots.

The ship and her sister *Magdalena*, built by the Schichau yard at Danzig, maintained regular sailings in Hapag's service between Europe and West Indian ports throughout the 1930s. The *Orinoco* ran on other routes from time to time, making the occasional North Atlantic passage to New York. Hapag services were very extensive during this period. From now on, however, the ship had a rather chequered career.

In 1941 the vessel was seized by the Mexican government while she was in the Caribbean area, and was renamed *Puebla*. In 1942 she was chartered to the US for service as a troop-ship. She sailed round to San Francisco, where she was given an extensive refit. Trooping voyages then took her to Honolulu, Noumea, and various Pacific islands. By December 1943 her machinery was giving problems, and she was out of service for about a year while repairs were carried out. In January 1945 she resumed her Pacific trooping duties, and this continued until 1946. Released from duty, she was returned to the Mexican government. She had a refit at Todd's Brooklyn Shipyard.

In early 1947 she made a voyage from New York to Naples and Piraeus and back for the South African Olympian Line. Her name was in fact changed to *Olympia* for a short while, but soon reverted to *Puebla*.

Later that year she was sold to the Cia Transoceanica Argentina of Buenos Aires. Renamed *Juan de Garay*, she was employed principally between Argentina and Portuguese, Spanish and Italian ports. She was managed by the Spanish Ybarra concern.

Pictures taken of the ship at this time show her still looking very much the same as in our photograph. A small radar mast had been added abaft the bridge, and of course she was in different colours, but little altered externally.

She continued on the service until she was eventually withdrawn and laid up in Barcelona prior to going to Spanish shipbreakers at Castellon and being broken up in 1963.

Her sister *Magdalena* eventually became the Russian *Pobeda*, and had one funnel only from 1934.

Oronsay

THIS fine vessel was built for Orient Line's Australian service and for cruising. Laid down in early 1949 at Vickers-Armstrong's Barrow Yard, the ship was launched on 30 June 1950 and completed, after some setbacks, by May 1951. She set off on her maiden voyage from London to Sydney on the 16 of that month.

The ship's design was very similar to that of the *Orcades* although the *Oronsay* was in fact slightly smaller than the earlier ship. Like her, she was fitted with Denny-Brown fin stabilizers.

Construction had proceeded well on the ship until some four months after her launching. On 28 October 1950 fire broke out on board in number two hold. The Vickers, Barrow, Dalton and several other fire brigades were quickly on the scene, but it was not until three days later that the conflagration was finally put out. So much water was pumped on board that it was felt at one time the ship would capsize. Due to prompt remedial action, however, this did not happen. Fortunately, the damage was not so bad as at first feared, but it delayed the ship's completion by about two months. On investigation the fire was found to have started in cork insulation, following welding operations.

There were plenty of amenities for first class and tourist passengers on board, such as lounges, ballrooms and swimming-pools, and the *Oronsay*, like her sisters, was always a most popular vessel. Like the others, she was used extensively for cruising in addition to Australian voyaging, and made her first cruise from Tilbury in the summer of 1952. Her career in fact followed a similar pattern to the other P & O and Orient liners on the route to Australasia.

During the Suez crisis of 1956 she had to be routed, like the others, via Cape Town for a while.

In 1959 the ship had a fairly extensive refit at Liverpool. This included extending the air conditioning throughout passenger and crew accommodation and other improvements. In 1954 her profile had been altered slightly by the addition of a 'top hat' to her funnel to improve smoke-dispersal. In that year also the *Oronsay* sailed from Sydney across the Pacific to the west coast of America, and this soon became a regular feature. She also cruised from the Australian port. The ship made her first Panama Canal transit in 1956 as Orient Line introduced the round-the-world service.

In 1964 the *Oronsay*, like other Orient vessels, came under the P & O houseflag and her hull was painted white instead of being corn-coloured. In January 1970 there was an unfortunate outbreak of typhoid on board, and the ship had to be placed in quarantine at Vancouver for a while. There were a few fires on board, none of them very serious. In October 1958 a small one in a hospital ward was soon extinguished, while in July 1967 a fire broke out in an aft hold. Several cabins were damaged, but there were no casualties. The ship spent a few days in Hong Kong for thorough examination before continuing her voyage to the UK.

By late 1972 the *Oronsay* had become a one-class ship and was cruising all the year round, especially from Australia. In April 1975 P & O announced that she would be withdrawn. The ship made her last cruise from Southampton in July, and on 4 August left the Hampshire port for the last time. She was given a tremendous send-off, the vessel having always enjoyed great popularity both in Britain and Australia. She sailed via Panama to Sydney, from where she made her final cruise to Hong Kong, arriving on 28 September. Having disembarked her passengers here, she then sailed to Kaohsiung and the breakers' yard.

Name: **Oronsay**

Line: Orient (1951-64); P & O (1964-75)

Builders: Vickers-Armstrongs, Barrow; launched 30 June 1950, completed 1951

Dimensions: Gross tonnage 27,632/ Length 708 ft/Beam 93.5 ft

Machinery

Engines: Parsons, single and double reduction geared, twin screw, 42,500 s.h.p.

Boilers: 4 Foster-Wheeler watertube, 525 p.s.i., superheated to 850°F

Service speed: 22 knots

Major Refits

1959 Liverpool, extension of air-conditioning

Regular Routes

London – Sydney
Sydney – West Coast USA

Passenger Capacity

1951: 1st 688, Tourist 833
1960s: 1,400 Tourist

Near-Sister-ships

Orcades (1948) **Orsova** (1954)

Photograph 1965

Orontes

THIS ship was the last of a fine series of five 20,000 ton vessels. These were all built during the 1920s for the Orient Line's service to Australia. The others were the *Orama* (1924), *Oronsay* and *Otranto* (1925) and the *Orford* (1928).

The *Orontes* was built at Barrow by Vickers-Armstrongs. Launched on 26 February 1929, she was completed in July, and after sundry other activities sailed on her maiden voyage from London to Brisbane on 26 October that year.

She was an attractive-looking ship, as indeed were all her four near-sisters. The hull had a cruiser stern and nicely raked stem. She differed from the others in this respect, as they had straight stems. Superstructure was well proportioned, with two slender funnels on top. Cargo capacity was of great importance on this route and there were six holds, much space being insulated.

The *Orontes* carried out successful trials and after her arrival at Southampton sailed on a rather unusual charter. Both she and her sister *Orford* became the official vessels for guests visiting the 1929 Schneider Trophy air races held at Calshot. They were stationed off Ryde Pier, a good viewing point. The contest was won by Britain.

After a 'shakedown' cruise to the Mediterranean the *Orontes* took her place on the Australian route and became very successful and popular. She remained on this service until the outbreak of war, interspersed with cruising during the northern summer. In 1933, for example, she did a six-week West Indies cruise, and the next year visited the Mediterranean. On this latter occasion she ran aground on the Gallipoli coast, but was refloated without damage.

For the first few months of the war the *Orontes* continued on the Australian route. Her cargo capacity was especially useful at this time. However, in April 1940 she was taken over for trooping. Her first voyage in this role was a familiar one to Australia, from whence she took troops to Singapore. The ship then returned to the UK, and became very actively engaged. Voyages were made to the Middle East with urgently needed troops, coupled with transatlantic ones. In late 1942 she was much involved transporting troops for the North African campaign, landing them at Oran. The ship was for a time fitted as an LSI(L) carrying assault craft. This enabled her to put troops ashore quickly. She took an active part in July 1943 in the invasion of Sicily, landing troops at the Avola beach. The ship was often under attack during these operations but escaped unscathed. In fact her own anti-aircraft gunners were credited with downing at least one enemy aircraft. She was involved with landings on the Italian mainland, at Salerno in particular, while under US control. Later she reverted to long-distance trooping to Bombay and elsewhere. The year 1945 saw her out in Australia, and she also took French troops to Saigon. A humane task was bringing back prisoners of war to the UK.

In April 1947 the *Orontes* was released from trooping duties. During her seven years under government control she had steamed over 370,000 miles, carrying about 125,000 troops.

The ship now underwent a long and extensive reconditioning during 1947–8 by Thornycroft at Southampton. This resulted in little outward change to her appearance, but much alteration and improvement had been made to passenger and crew accommodation.

The ship now resumed the Australian service from Tilbury, making her first sailing on 17 June 1948. She steamed steadily to and fro, and in 1953 was converted to a one-class ship, taking tourist passengers only. She was now much involved in taking immigrant settlers to Australia and New Zealand and sailed on a separate service from the mail one. Her sister *Otranto* was likewise employed, and both omitted the Mediterranean ports. The *Orontes* still went cruising from time to time, especially from Sydney. She remained popular, and retained her black hull to the end. She made her last sailing from Tilbury to Australia on 25 November 1961, and on her return was withdrawn. Sold to Spanish shipbreakers, she arrived at Valencia on 5 March 1962.

Of her four sisters, the *Orama*, *Oronsay* and *Orford* became war losses.

Name: **Orontes**

Line: Orient

Builders: Vickers-Armstrongs, Barrow; launched 26 February 1929, completed 1929

Dimensions: Gross tonnage 19,970/ Length 664 ft/Beam 75 ft

Machinery

Engines: 2 sets Parsons triple expansion, single reduction geared turbines, twin screw, 20,000 s.h.p.

Boilers: 6 double-ended, 2 single-ended oil-fired Scotch, 215 p.s.i.

Service speed: 20 knots

Major Refits

1942 conversion to LSI(L)
1947-8 Thornycroft, Southampton, alteration to accommodation 20,186 tons
1953 conversion to one-class ship

Regular Routes

London – Brisbane

Passenger Capacity

1929: 1st 500, 3rd 1,112
1948: 1st 502, Tourist 610
1953: Tourist 1,410

Near-Sister-ships

Orama (1924), Oronsay (1925), Otranto (1925), Orford (1928)

Photograph 1946

Orsova

Name: **Orsova**

Line: Orient (1954-64); P & O (1964-73)

Builders: Vickers Armstrongs, Barrow; launched 14 May 1953, completed March 1954

Dimensions: Gross tonnage 28,790/ Length 723 ft/Beam 90.2 ft

Machinery

Engines: 2 sets Parsons turbines, single and double reduction geared, twin screw, 42,500 s.h.p.

Boilers: 3 Foster-Wheeler watertube, 525 p.s.i., superheated to 850°F

Service speed: 22 knots

Major Refits

1960 Vickers-Armstrongs, air-conditioning installed
1972 Thornycroft, upgrading of accommodation

Regular Routes

London – Sydney

Passenger Capacity

1st 681, Tourist 813

Near Sister-ships

Orcades (1948), **Oronsay** (1951)

Photograph 1965

LIKE her near-sisters *Orcades* and *Oronsay*, this ship was built for the Orient Line's service to Australia and for cruising. Like the other two, she was constructed at Vickers-Armstrongs' Barrow yard. Launched on 14 May 1953, the vessel was completed by March the following year and set off on her maiden voyage from London to Sydney on 17 March 1954.

By comparing photographs it will be seen that the *Orsova* bore a great resemblance to the two earlier ships. However, she lacked the stumpy mast abaft the bridge, the funnel instead being rigged to carry wireless aerials, radar scanner etc. Her nicely raked and curved stem differed also from those of her running-mates. She was in fact a most attractive-looking vessel, the first large passenger liner to be built without a mast. Although the three ships were nominally of the same class, the *Oronsay* was an improvement on the *Orcades*, and the *Orsova* was better still.

Improvements in welding techniques enabled her hull to be all welded, and thus less resistant to the flow of water past it. This undoubtedly helped her to achieve a higher speed on trials, 26.07 knots against the *Oronsay*'s 25.23 and the 24.74 of *Orcades*.

In general, however, she was fairly similar internally to the earlier vessels and tourist class was of the same high standard, with all the amenities likely to be required on long voyages and for cruising. Like the others, she was fitted with Denny-Brown fin stabilizers. Her career also followed a similar pattern.

In spring 1955 the *Orsova* made her first voyage into the Pacific. Leaving Tilbury on 27 April, she sailed via Gibraltar, Naples, Port Said, Aden, Colombo, Freemantle, Adelaide and Melbourne to Sydney. She then proceeded to Auckland and across the Pacific to Suva, Vancouver, San Francisco and Los Angeles. She returned to Tilbury via the Panama Canal, calling en route at Trinidad and Cherbourg. Round the world voyaging such as this was to be very much the order of the day, coupled with cruising from Sydney and Southampton.

Not surprisingly, the *Orsova* broke a speed record in 1955 which had stood for about 30 years. She steamed the 2,100 miles between San Francisco and Honolulu in 3 days 17 hours, beating the previous best time by about 3 hours.

In 1960 the ship had an extensive refit at Vickers-Armstrongs yard at Newcastle. Air-conditioning was installed throughout, and other improvements made to keep her thoroughly up to date. Like the other ships, she was transferred later to the P & O flag, and her hull was painted white. She got caught up in the disastrous seamen's strike of 1966, and lay idle at Tilbury for several weeks.

Due to the decline in passenger traffic to Australia, the *Orsova* was used extensively for cruising during her later years. Southampton was her UK base, and she made many cruises from there. In 1972 she had a major refit by Vosper Thornycroft at the port, which upgraded her accommodation, making it even more suitable for cruising, but she still retained her two passenger classes. In 1973 the announcement was made that the *Canberra* would be withdrawn from service as she was not considered suitable for cruising and that the *Orsova* would take over her 1974 programme. However, this decision was later reversed, and the *Orsova* was the one to be withdrawn. Apparently the company felt that 'one-class' cruising was the better bet. Presumably the cost of converting the ship was considered too high. Thus, in spite of her recent refit, the *Orsova* was withdrawn from service on 25 November 1973, on completion of her final cruise. A few weeks later she left Southampton bound for Kaohsiung, Taiwan, and the breakers' yard.

Pacific Princess

THE considerable development in the cruise industry, particularly in the Caribbean, led to the creation of Norwegian Cruiseships A/S, to be better known as Flagship Cruises. This was formed by several well-known shipping concerns, notably Oivind Lorentzen and Fearnley and Egar. A couple of 20,000-ton vessels were built in West Germany for the company, and named *Sea Venture* and *Island Venture*. Each could take over 600 passengers in one class.

The *Sea Venture* was built at the Nordseewerke Yard at Emden. Launched on 9 May 1970, she was delivered a year later. The ship set off on her maiden voyage from New York to Hamilton, Bermuda, in June 1971. The *Island Venture*, built at the same yard, entered service in January 1972.

As can be seen, the ship has a somewhat similar profile to many other contemporary cruise vessels. She has a clipper bow, streamlined upperworks and funnel well aft.

There are seven decks for passengers, and all the usual amenities are found on board. She has lounges, bars, casino, library, a couple of swimming-pools, gymnasium, sauna, hairdressing salon, etc, together of course with a medical centre. The ship is air-conditioned, and in fact has all the facilities that cruise passengers can expect.

Propelling machinery consists of four diesel engines in pairs driving twin screws through gearing. Cruising speed is 20 knots; the ship is fitted with stabilizers and a bow thrust unit.

The *Sea Venture* sailed initially mostly on the New York to Bermuda route, a seven-day cruise. Her sister *Island Venture* was usually on longer runs to the Caribbean.

However, in October 1974 the ship was sold to P & O with delivery in April 1975. She was then renamed *Pacific Princess*. In the meantime the British company had acquired Princess Cruises from the Americans, and also had bought our subsect's sister ship which had been renamed *Island Princess*.

P & O now had three ships based on the west coast of the USA and all were to be busily employed. The *Pacific Princess* in fact went to Australia for a spell in December 1975, remaining until May 1976, during which time she cruised from Sydney to the Pacific.

Returning to the west coast, over the years she has cruised extensively from there. The vessel is still an important member of P & O's luxury 'Princess' fleet operated by 'Princess Voyages', the holiday division of the company launched in 1986. The numbers of ships have increased over the years, and now consist of the following 'princesses' – *Royal, Sea, Island, Pacific, Star, Sky, Dawn, Fair* and *Crown*

The *Pacific Princess* and her sister have been based principally at San Francisco and Los Angeles. Cruises to Alaska are very popular during the summer months. The Mexican Riviera, and the Caribbean via the Panama Canal, feature regularly in the ship's itinerary.

She has been kept up to date at various refits and remains very popular in spite of the advent of much larger and more modern vessels to the fleet.

At the present time the ship's passenger decks reading downward are: Observation, Sun, Promenade, Riviera, Aloha, Fiesta and Coral. The promenade deck contains deluxe suites and cabins, while the Riviera deck has the main public rooms: the Carousel Lounge, bar and dance floor, Princess Theatre, International, Bridge and Caribbean Pacific Lounges are here. There is also a casino, a gymnasium and a swimming-pool. The Starlight Lounge and Casino are on the Sun deck, while the Aloha, Fiesta and Coral decks contain passenger cabins, most being outside ones. The dining saloon and medical centre are on the Coral deck.

Her programme includes a cruise to Rio. Sailing from San Juan, the ship visits Barbados, Trinidad, Davis Island (the former French penal colony), Fortaleza (Brazil), Recife, Salvador and Rio de Janeiro.

Since she is comparatively small, the *Pacific Princess* can sail right up the Amazon, and she does in fact proceed up this great river for 1,000 miles on the 'Heart of the Amazon' cruise. After calling at Caribbean ports such as St Thomas, Martinique and Barbados the ship enters the river, and calls en route at Santarem, Alter do Chao and Boca do Valerio before reaching Manaus, a marvellous trip.

The above cruises have been described in the 'southbound' direction. They of course also operate the other way round. Passengers from the UK or elsewhere may fly to and from San Juan and/or Manaus depending on which direction they take.

The ship also continues the popular Caribbean cruises, and goes via the Panama Canal to Acapulco. Alaska cruises in the summer months remain popular.

Name: **Sea Venture** (1971); **Pacific Princess** (1975)

Line: Flagship Cruises (1971-4); P & O (1975-)

Builders: Nordseewerke, Emden; launched 9 May 1970, completed 1971

Dimensions: Gross tonnage 20,636/ Length 554 ft/Beam 80.7 ft

Machinery

Engines: 4 Fiat diesel, 10-cylinder 4SCSA, twin screw, CP propellers

Service speed: 20 knots

Passenger Capacity

626 one class

Sister-ships

Island Venture (1972)

Photograph 1987

Pendennis Castle

THIS fine ship was a most useful addition to the Union Castle Mail fleet. She was built by Harland and Wolff at Belfast, who were responsible for many of the Company's vessels. The ship was named on 10 December 1957, but could not be launched until 24 December due to a strike. She was completed by November 1958, and sailed on her maiden voyage from Southampton to Durban on 1 January 1959.

She was a good-looking vessel, as can be seen from the photograph. The hull had a cruiser stern and curved stem. Upperworks were well proportioned and with an attractive funnel on top. There was a short foremast and a signal mast abaft the bridge. This was in like manner to the arrangements on the modified *Edinburgh Castle* and *Pretoria Castle* after their 1960s' refits.

The *Pendennis Castle* was the first ship to be completed after the merger of Union Castle with Clan Line to form British and Commonwealth Shipping. The new management had in fact altered her design somewhat after construction had commenced. It was decided to fit Denny-Brown fin stabilizers, making her the first Union Castle vessel to have them. This necessitated lengthening the vessel amidships. To get increased speed the forward hull section required fining in addition to lengthening. This all resulted in considerable improvement.

The hull had twelve bulkheads and there were five decks for passengers. These, reading downwards, were; boat deck, E deck (promenade) D, C and B decks. The ship catered for first class and tourist passengers, many cabins being interchangeable. As usual first class were amidships and tourist farther aft. The promenade deck contained the first-class lounge, smoke-room, writing/card room, library etc. Also here were the lido, gymnasium and open-air pool. Farther aft on the same deck were the tourist lounge, lido and pool. The tourist smoke-room, library, etc were on D deck, both dining saloons being on B. Decor was modern, light and airy, with plenty of deck space. All the usual amenities were available. First-class suites and cabins were on D and C decks, tourist being on C and B.

A unique feature for that time was the bridge-control console. This extended the width of the wheelhouse, and most of the vessel's services could be controlled from this. Cargo was of course of great importance, and the ship had seven holds, three forward and four aft, with much insulation space. Seven hatches and appropriate derricks were fitted for handling.

The *Pendennis Castle* was a replacement for the fine old *Arundel Castle*, which had reached the end of her 36 year-long career. The new ship soon became a very popular member of the mail fleet as she steamed steadily to and from South Africa. When the new accelerated service came into operation in the mid-sixties she had no difficulty in meeting the revised schedule. As a matter of fact, due to a loading delay in Cape Town in February 1968 she had to make up time, and steamed from the South African port to Southampton in 10 days 15 hours a remarkably fast passage. The ship proved very reliable, and few mishaps befell her. However, in May 1968 she was damaged by fire while in Southampton, necessitating considerable repairs. The following year, when diverted to Antwerp due to a dock strike at her home port, she collided with a quay and was delayed about a fortnight while damage was repaired.

The mail service was run down in the mid-seventies. The *Pendennis Castle*'s last voyage in this role ended when she arrived at Southampton on 14 June 1976. She was still less than eighteen years old, about half the age of the vessel she had replaced. Sadly, her final few years were to be very dismal ones. She was sold to a Philippine-owned company, the Ocean Queen Navigation Corporation, registered in Panama. The ship was intended for use as a cruise liner, which would seem to be very appropriate. Renamed *Ocean Queen*, her hull was painted white and her funnel golden-brown. She arrived at Hong Kong on 9 August 1976, but was then laid up. In late 1977 the ex-*Pendennis Castle* was again sold, to the Kinvarra Bay Shipping Co and renamed *Sindbad*. Later she became *Sindbad I*, but apparently never traded, under this name and in April 1980 this former mail ship went to the breakers at Kaohsiung, Taiwan.

Name: **Pendennis Castle** (1958); **Ocean Queen** (1976); **Sinbad** (1977)

Line: Union Castle (1958-76); Ocean Queen Navigation (1976-77); Kinvarra Bay (1977-80)

Builders: Harland & Wolff, Belfast; launched 24 December 1957, completed November 1958

Dimensions: Gross tonnage 28,582/ Length 763 ft/Beam 83 ft

Machinery

Engines: 2 sets compound double reduction geared turbines, twin screw, 46,000 s.h.p.

Boilers: 3 oil-fired watertube, 680 p.s.i., superheated to 850°F

Service speed: 22.5 knots

Regular Routes

Southampton — Cape Town and South African ports

Passenger Capacity

1st 197, Tourist 473

Sister-ships

None

Photograph 1959

Pennland

THIS 16,000-ton vessel was ordered originally for the American Line, one of the members of the International Mercantile Marine (IMM) Combine. She was one of a similar pair built by Harland and Wolff, the other being the *Regina* for the Dominion Line. The *Pittsburg* was built at Belfast, while the *Regina* was constructed at their Govan yard on the Clyde, but finally completed at Belfast.

Although laid down in November 1913, the ship was not completed until after the war. She was launched in November 1920 and finished by May 1922. She sailed on her maiden voyage from Liverpool to Boston in June that year. She was a distinguished-looking vessel. The hull had four decks and contained twelve watertight bulkheads. Above, the superstructure with promenade and boat decks was comparatively low. As will be noted, there was a gap between the navigating bridge and officers' deck and the main midships superstructure. Hatchways and derricks occupied this space. The ship in fact had a considerable cargo capacity with seven holds. The two funnels were nicely proportioned and spaced, the after one being a dummy.

The *Pittsburgh* was completed in White Star colours, since the American Line had virtually ceased to function by then. She started on the Liverpool to Boston and Philadelphia run in June 1922, but soon switched to the Bremen – New York service.

While on an eastward crossing on 14 November 1922 the ship received a distress signal from the 7,400 ton Italian cargo ship *Monte Grappa*. This vessel, built in 1920 and owned by the Navigazione Libera Trestino Company (Trieste), was on a voyage from Montreal to Venice laden with 9,200 tons of grain. The grain boards shifted due to heavy rolling in the very rough seas, and the ship developed a dangerous list. Despite all efforts by the crew, she was in imminent danger of sinking. The *Pittsburgh* arrived on the scene, and succeeded by fine seamanship in launching two boats and saving all 45 of the Italian ship's crew, a splendid effort. The city of Pittsburg later presented the ship with a plaque commemorating this gallant rescue.

One of the ship's running-mates on the route was the 12,200-ton White Star *Canopic* built in 1900. The German terminal was changed in November 1923 to Hamburg, and in 1925 the *Pittsburgh* was transferred to the Red Star route from Antwerp via Southampton to New York.

In 1926 the ship blossomed forth in Red Star colours and was renamed *Pennland*. She is best known under this name, which she retained for the rest of her career. The White Star *Arabic* was also on the route at this time as were the *Lapland* and the big 27,000 ton *Belgenland*. In 1930 her accommodation became tourist and third. The vessel's sister ship *Regina* (now renamed *Westernland*) was also on the route. By 1934 the trading situation for the Red Star Line was bad, but the *Pennland* and *Westernland* still made a few voyages. However, the sailing of the latter vessel in December marked the virtual end of the company's active career.

Early in 1935 the two ships were bought by the German shipowner Arnold Bernstein of Hamburg. In conjunction with a New York company, the Red Star Line GMbh was formed. The German company is often referred to as the Bernstein (Red Star) Line. The white bands on the ship's funnels were increased in depth, and a red star painted on them. Our photograph shows the *Pennland* in this rig.

In 1937 Arnold Bernstein was arrested by the Nazis and thrown into prison. His shipping interests were entrusted to other hands, and the *Pennland* and *Westernland* continued running until late 1938. In May 1939 they were both acquired by the Holland America Line. They were now painted in the Dutch company's colours, and continued on the North Atlantic route. When war came the ships as neutrals had their names and Rotterdam painted in large letters on their sides and continued in operation.

In April 1940 the *Pennland* took a large number of passengers to New York and then returned to Liverpool. Chartered by the British Ministry of War Transport, she was now converted to a troop-ship. As Holland was now under German occupation, a number of other Dutch vessels, including the *Nieuw Amsterdam*, *Volendam*, and *Westernland*, were also taken over as troopers under the control of Cunard White Star.

The *Pennland* did most useful work in this new role. Early voyages took her to Jamaica with prisoners of war and to Canada to bring troops to the UK. Further voyages took her to Suez, after which she transported Australian troops from Alexandria to Greece for what was to be a desperately unsuccessful campaign. Later she was involved in evacuating troops from there when the situation had become hopeless. On 25 April 1941 this fine ship met her end. Off Piraeus in the Gulf of Athens she was attacked by enemy aircraft. Hit by numerous bombs, she was abandoned and later sank, fortunately without loss of life.

President Harding

THIS vessel was one of the US Shipping Board's 535-ft class of standard ships. She was built at the New York Shipbuilding Corporation's Yard at Camden, New Jersey. Launched on 3 December 1920, the ship was completed by March 1922. She sailed on her first voyage from New York to Bremerhaven on 25 March under the management of the United States Lines.

The vessel cannot be described as handsome. The hull had a straight stem and cruiser stern. It contained two decks, shelter and shade deck, and the 'square' superstructure above was rather short, with a vertical funnel on top. There were four 'goalposts' for cargo-handling, as the ship had a good capacity for this with eight holds. The actual masts were signal posts fitted on the second and third 'goalposts'. She catered for first and second class passengers, but nomenclature varied from time to time.

The United States Lines in the 1920s operated a number of 'standard' ships, including the *Lone Star State*'s sister *Peninsula State*. Apparently these names were criticized on the grounds that no one outside the USA would know what they signified. (*Lone Star State* was in fact the nickname for Texas, while *Peninsula State* meant Florida.) It was decided to name the vessels after American Presidents. Our subject was therefore renamed *President Taft* in May 1922, but three months later became *President Harding*. She retained this name for the next eighteen years. The *Peninsula State* was likewise renamed *President Roosevelt*, after a brief spell as *President Pierce*.

The ship continued transatlantic sailings together with her sister and other units of the US Lines. The great *Leviathan* had commenced on the express service in 1923.

The *President Harding* was a steady ship by all accounts, and steamed to and fro at an economical speed. Together with her sister, she made three voyages from New York to the Mediterranean in 1928, but generally remained on the Atlantic ferry. Itinerary varied from time to time. Initially Cherbourg had been the French port used, but Le Havre was substituted from 1932.

The ship sailed on her last voyage from Hamburg to New York on 16 August 1939. War clouds were gathering and there were many Americans stranded in Europe who wished to return home. The *President Harding* voyaged in September from New York to Pauillac (Bordeaux) to repatriate them. The *President Roosevelt* was similarly employed. In October the ship made a round voyage from New York to Southampton, but on 4 November the American Presi-dent signed the Neutrality Act, which among other things banned American shipping from virtually all European ports except those of Portugal and neutral nations of the Mediterranean.

In February 1940 the *President Harding* and seven of the US Lines' other ships were sold to a new Belgian company called the Société Maritime Anversoise of Antwerp (Antwerp Navigation Company). Apparently 60 per cent of this company's capital was Belgian, the remainder held by US Lines. The reason given for the sale was that the ships could no longer trade profitably under the American flag. The *President Harding* was now renamed *Ville de Bruges*. This company started their operations at an extremely unfortunate time. Within a few months Belgium and Holland were overrun by the Germans. Very soon afterwards the *Ville de Bruges* was bombed near the mouth of the river Scheldt while attempting to get from Antwerp to Southampton. She was beached and burnt out, becoming a total loss, and later demolished.

This was a tragic ending for the ship after only eighteen years. The seven other US vessels taken over by the Belgian company were also former standard ships of about 7,500 tons, with 'American' names, such as *American Traveller*, *American Trader*. Only one survived the war, the remainder being sunk between 1940 and 1941. The survivor was the *American Banker* renamed *Ville d'Anvers* which later became the *Arosa Kulm*.

Queen Elizabeth

THIS splendid ship was the second of the great passenger liners to be built for the weekly express service from Southampton to New York. As it happened, it was to be six long years before she entered it, but the ship had a long and distinguished career in war and peace.

Externally the *Queen Elizabeth* was of the same elegant profile as her near-sister the *Queen Mary*, the most obvious differences being that she sported two funnels instead of three. The main deck had no well forward, being flush right to the bows. It was decided to fit an additional anchor, and this – in the centre of the bow – meant the latter had to be given a greater rake

Work proceeded apace, even when war had broken out. As is well known, it was decided to dispatch the new ship, without any trials being undertaken, across the Atlantic to New York.

The new vessel found herself laid up in New York harbour, in company with the *Queen Mary, Normandie* and *Mauretania*. A fortnight after she arrived, in fact, her older sister was called up for conversion to a troop-ship and sailed away on 21 March 1940 for this to be done. The QE in turn got her call-up in November and set sail for Singapore, where she was dry-docked. Some of the conversion work took place here before she sailed for Sydney for the final completion.

In April 1941 the *Queen Elizabeth* made her first trooping voyage, with over 5,000 on board, to Suez, returning to Sydney. For the rest of 1941 she was based at Sydney, trooping to the Middle East. In February 1942, since Singapore was about to fall to the Japanese, she sailed to Esquimault, British Columbia, for dry-docking. On leaving here she loaded American troops at San Francisco, and took them to Sydney. (At this time the fear of Japanese invasion of Australia was ever present.) A voyage to New York via Rio followed, and then across the Atlantic to the Clyde.

After another long trip from here to Suez and back to New York the big ship proceeded to do North Atlantic trooping for the rest of the war. Like the *Queen Mary*, she carried around 15,000 troops on most eastbound passages rarely taking less than 13,000 even during the winter months. On Westbound voyages she carried wounded men, prisoners of war, diplomats etc. After peace in Europe she was busily engaged in returning American and Canadian personnel back home.

On 6 March 1946 the *Queen Elizabeth* returned to Southampton.

Her war service had involved sailing about half a million miles and transporting over 811,000 'passengers'. The ship stayed at Southampton having work done on her for about three weeks. She then sailed for the Clyde, where the major part of reconversion to an Atlantic passenger liner took place. Public rooms and amenities on this splendid ship were superb.

On 16 October 1946 the QE set off from Southampton on her maiden passenger voyage to New York. She had 2,288 passengers on board – a small number compared with her wartime sailings. Now was to follow some 22 years of transatlantic voyaging in company with the *Queen Mary*. For the first time the two great ships were on the service for which they had been designed.

In April 1947 the *Elizabeth* with a full quota of eastbound passengers on board, grounded on a sandbank near the entrance to Southampton Water. She remained fast for 26 hours, until tugs eventually pulled her free. Only very minor damage resulted, soon remedied at her next dry-docking.

Like her sister, the *Queen Elizabeth* went cruising in the 1960s, and like her lost money in the process. The big ships were not really suitable for this. However, Cunard tried hard to make a success of it. The QE was given an extensive overhaul on the Clyde in 1965–6 when various improvements were made, but, the situation did not materially improve, although some cruises were well booked.

The *Queen Mary* finished her Atlantic service in September 1967, and on 5 April 1968 Cunard announced that the *Queen Elizabeth* had been sold to an American group of businessmen. She sailed out to Florida arriving in early December. In August 1970 the ship was sold yet again, to Mr C.Y. Tung. Renamed *Seawise University*, she was to be completely refitted at Hong Kong. She would then be used as a floating university carrying students and also cruise passengers. The ship would sail world-wide in this role.

The final phase of the *Queen Elizabeth*'s story makes very sad reading. Much work was done on her while she was anchored in Hong Kong harbour, and this was virtually completed by January 1972. On Sunday, 9 January, however an outbreak of fire occurred on board which swiftly engulfed the vessel. She eventually capsized and became a total loss. A very sad ending for a wonderful ship. She was broken up in situ.

Name: Queen Elizabeth

Line: Cunard

Builders: John Brown & Co., Clydebank; launched 27 September 1938, completed 1940

Dimensions: Gross tonnage 83,673/ Length 1029 ft/Beam 118.4 ft

Machinery

Engines: 4 sets Parsons single reduction geared turbines, quadruple screw, 200,000 s.h.p.

Boilers: 12 Yarrow watertube, 425 p.s.i., superheated to 750°F

Service speed: 28.5 knots

Major Refits

1940 Singapore/Sydney, conversion to troop-ship
1946 Southampton/Clyde, reconversion to passenger liner

Regular Routes

Southampton – New York

Passenger Capacity

1st 823, Cabin 662, Tourist 798

Near-Sister-ship

Queen Mary (1936)

Photograph 1960

Queen Elizabeth 2

THIS fine ship took shape at Upper Clyde Shipbuilders, Clydebank, the former John Brown's yard. Much thought had been given by Cunard to her design over a long period. Unlike her illustrious predecessors the *Queen Mary* and *Queen Elizabeth*, she was introduced with cruising very much in mind, in addition to normal transatlantic voyaging.

The ship was laid down on 5 July 1965, launched on 20 September 1967 by the Queen, and virtually completed by November 1968. However, owing to sundry problems she was not finally in service until the following year, setting off on her maiden voyage from Southampton to New York on 2 May 1969.

The vessel's shapely hull, well-proportioned upperworks and very unusual funnel have become familiar to most people, and are clearly shown in the photograph. The ship has a total of thirteen decks which are, reading downwards, signal, sports, boat, upper, and quarter decks followed by one deck, two deck – down to seven deck. Public rooms are within the top five. The hull is divided into 15 watertight compartments. Two classes of passenger are catered for – first and tourist when on transatlantic duty but all one class when cruising.

The ship was delayed in entering service due to turbine problems. Very briefly – blade failures occurred in the high pressure rotors of both turbines. The trouble was cured by making new ones to a modified design for the turbine stages affected and with wire lacing at mid-point.

The ship's maiden voyage on 2 May 1969 was a great success. At Le Havre and New York she got a tremendous reception. Since then she has travelled far and wide, on transatlantic crossings and cruises to many parts of the world. A few incidents have befallen her.

In January 1971 she took part in a rescue operation in the Caribbean. The French liner *Antilles*, owned by CGT, struck a reef off the island of Mustique, rupturing her oil tanks and catching fire. The *QE2* quickly came to the scene, and took many of the stricken liner's passengers on board, conveying them to Bridgetown, Barbados. Other vessels helped as well. Sadly the *Antilles*, (20,000 tons, and built in 1953) became a total loss.

In May 1972 a bomb threat resulted in four experts being flown out to the ship in the Atlantic. They dropped by parachute and were taken on board, but no bombs were found. The hoaxer was later arrested in New York.

That same year in April the *QE2* met a violent storm in the Atlantic with winds of 100 mph, but rode it out without damage.

The ship made a great contribution to the Falklands campaign of 1982. She was swiftly converted at Southampton for troops; much alteration took place, including fitment of two helipads and refuelling at sea equipment. The ship sailed on 12 May with about 3,000 troops and tons of stores. She eventually arrived at Cumberland Bay, South Georgia, where her troops were transferred to the *Canberra* and *Norland*. The *QE2* then embarked survivors from the frigates *Antelope*, *Ardent* and *Coventry*, which had been sunk, and brought them back to Southampton, arriving back on 11 June.

The vessel was now converted back to passenger duty. This took about nine weeks, and some modifications and improvements were made. She returned to service with her hull painted light grey and her funnel red with black bands. However, in June 1983 she reverted to her original dark grey hull.

Since then the *QE2* has been fully employed on Atlantic crossings and cruising. Although her initial turbine problems were cured satisfactorily in 1969, boilers and machinery had proved expensive to maintain. There had been a number of breakdowns over the years. In April 1974 problems with contaminated boiler feed brought her to a standstill in the Atlantic. In 1976 an engine room blaze caused damage and put a boiler out of action, and in 1982 a breakdown occurred off Falmouth. Incidents such as these, coupled with the ever-increasing cost of oil, led to the decision to re-engine the ship. In October 1986 the ship went to the Lloyd-Werft Yard at Bremerhaven to be re-engined. Turbines and boilers were removed and nine diesel engines driving the same number of generators were fitted instead. These provide power for two large propulsion motors driving the screws. The ship is now diesel-electric, and propels the *QE2* at about the same speed as before, with considerable savings in fuel costs. On trials in the North Sea the re-engined ship reached speeds of over 33 knots.

The year 1990 marked the 150th year of Cunard's operations, and a great series of cruises were arranged for the *QE2* in celebration. From July to December there were 22 of them, including visits to the Norwegian fjords, Caribbean and the Mediterranean.

Name: **Queen Elizabeth 2**

Line: Cunard

Builders: Upper Clyde Shipbuilders, Clydebank; launched 20 September 1967, completed November 1968

Dimensions: Gross tonnage 65,863/ Length 963 ft/Beam 105 ft

Machinery

Engines: 2 sets double reduction geared turbines, Pametrada design, twin screw, 110,000 s.h.p.

Boilers: 3 Foster-Wheeler ESD, 850 p.s.i., superheated to 950°F

Service speed: 28.5 knots

Major Refits

1986 Lloyd-Werft, Bremerhaven, 9 6-cylinder, 4-stroke MAN B & W diesel engines, driving 9 GEC generators, 2 GEC propulsion motors driving 2 CP propellers, 130,000 b.h.p., 67,139 tons, 28.5 knots

Regular Routes

Southampton – New York

Passenger Capacity

1st 564, Tourist, 1,441
1,400 one class cruising

Sister-ships

None

Photograph 1987

Queen Mary

IN THE mid-1920s Cunard began plans for two ships capable of maintaining a weekly transatlantic service, replacing the three ships operating on the route, the *Aquitania, Berengaria* and *Mauretania*. This necessitated a special design which would enable them to carry large numbers of passengers at high speed, in considerable luxury. The requirements were a service speed of at least 28 knots and a minimum size of 80,000 tons – very much larger than any other liner in existence. Work began on the first ship on Clydeside in December 1930, but a year later Cunard was forced to suspend the building, as the Depression made itself felt. The situation was only resolved two and a half years later, when Cunard merged with the White Star Line and took out a large loan to enable the ship to be completed. She was launched by Queen Mary on 26 September 1934. Her maiden voyage was from Southampton, where the King George V graving dock had been specially built for her, to New York in May 1936.

After teething troubles with the turbines and excessive vibration, the *Queen Mary* settled down to steady Atlantic voyaging. In August 1936 she took the westbound and eastbound records for the crossing from the French ship *Normandie*, with whom she was evenly matched in speed.

In August 1939 the *Queen Mary* sailed to New York with a large complement of passengers, most of whom were Americans returning from war-threatened Europe. She lay there for some months while a decision was made as to how best she could be employed. On 21 March 1940, now painted grey, she sailed to Sydney to be fitted as a troop-ship. Many of her elegant furnishings and fittings were removed and stored, so that bunks and hammocks could be installed to accommodate 5,000 troops. She sailed on 5 May 1940 with Australian troops bound for the UK, in convoy with six other liners now serving as troop-ships.

Throughout 1941 she was based in Sydney, and employed in transporting troops to the Middle East, returning with wounded and prisoners. The ship was only lightly armed, with a 4-inch gun and a 3-inch AA weapon, together with a few machine guns. She later acquired a 6-inch gun, but her real defence lay in her high speed.

In January 1942, the *Queen Mary* returned to New York via Trincomalee, Cape Town and Trinidad. She was dry-docked at Boston for an overhaul and adaptation to increase her passenger capacity. For the remainder of the year she ferried American troops to Australia and the UK, and allied troops to the Middle East in readiness for the battle of El Alamein. She was now able to carry 15,000 men. In October she was involved in a tragic accident off the coast of Ireland, when the cruiser *Curacoa* (which formed part of her escort), came too close to the liner, and was cut in two. There were 338 men lost.

In late December, the *Queen Mary* took part with several other big liners in the transport home of 31,000 Australian troops, to counter the threat of Japanese invasion. In 1943 she continued with her transatlantic trooping, twice taking Winston Churchill over to Halifax, Nova Scotia, for conferences. The westbound crossings carried many wounded, and required special medical staff aboard.

In April 1945 the liner spent several months in New York being overhauled; her next duties were to take American personnel back to the States, and in 1946 GI brides and their children. Her last voyage on war service was completed on 29 September 1946. At Southampton work began to convert her back to civilian use. By July 1947 she was ready to resume operations, and for the next twenty years, with the *Queen Elizabeth*, she provided a regular transatlantic express service.

In 1949 a serious mishap befell the *Queen Mary* when she was attempting to leave Cherbourg harbour. The starboard anchor became fouled in some cables and grounded the ship on a shoal for the night. The next day she was refloated, and after emergency repairs was able to resume her voyage. In February 1953 a tugmen's strike in New York forced her to dock unaided, a feat which demonstrated her excellent handling qualities.

The 1960s proved difficult years for Cunard. The *Queen Mary* and *Queen Elizabeth* began to operate at a loss. They were unsuitable for cruising, as their size prevented them from entering many ports. The *Queen Mary* did make some short cruises from New York to the Bahamas, and from Southampton to the Canary Islands, but these too were uneconomic. After the seamen's strike of 1966 – when she lay idle for six weeks at Southampton, incurring heavy losses – Cunard decided to withdraw her from service.

The *Queen Mary* was eventually sold to the city of Long Beach, California, where she has a variety of uses as a convention centre, hotel and tourist attraction. She left Southampton on her last voyage on 31 October 1967.

Name: Queen Mary

Line: Cunard

Builders: John Brown & Co., Clydebank; launched 26 September 1934, completion April 1936

Dimensions: Gross tonnage 80,773/ Length 1,019.5 ft/Beam 118 ft

Machinery

Engines: 4 sets Parsons single-reduction geared turbines driving four screws, 180,000-210,000 s.h.p.

Boilers: 24 Yarrow watertube, superheated to 700°F, 400 p.s.i.

Service speed: 28.5 knots

Major Refits

Jan-June 1937 structure stiffened to reduce vibration, new propellers fitted
1958 2 sets Denny-Brown fin type stabilizers fitted
1967 81.237 tons

Regular Routes

Southampton – New York via Cherbourg

Passenger Capacity

1936: Cabin 740, Tourist 760, 3rd 579
1967: 1st 642, Cabin 694, Tourist 562

Near-Sister-ships

Queen Elizabeth (1940)

Photograph 1966

Randfontein

Name: Randfontein (1958); **Nieuw Holland** (1971); **Yu Hua** (1974); **Hai Xing** (1981)

Line: Holland-Africa (1958-71); Royal Interocean (1971-74)

Builders: Wilton-Fijenoord, Schiedam; launched 28 June 1958, completed November 1958

Dimensions: Gross tonnage 13,694/ Length 585 ft/Beam 70.2 ft

Machinery

Engines: 2 Wilton-MAN diesel, twin screw, 15,400 total b.h.p.

Service speed: 18 knots

Regular Routes

Amsterdam – Lourenço Marques
Melbourne – Japan
China – East Africa

Passenger Capacity

1st 123, Tourist 166

Sister-ships

None

Photograph 1963

THIS ship was the last large passenger vessel built for the Holland-Africa Line for their service to South and East Africa. She was constructed at the Wilton-Fijenoord shipyard at Schiedam, Holland. Launched by floating out in her building berth on 28 June 1958, she was completed by November that year and sailed on her maiden voyage from Hamburg to Lourenço Marques on 6 January 1959.

As can be seen, the ship had an attractive appearance. The hull had good sheer, cruiser stern and a well-raked, flared bow. It contained two complete decks, and the superstructure above was well proportioned, with an attractive funnel on top. She carried first class and tourist class passengers in comfortable accommodation. Public rooms were of a good standard, and there were a couple of swimming pools. The ship was also a large cargo-carrier, with six holds and tween decks. The equipment for working this shows up clearly, especially the large foremast with its derricks. A good deal of space was for refrigerated cargo, and the ship had deep tanks for carrying vegetable oils.

The Holland-Africa Line was part of the United Netherlands Navigation Co. or to give it its Dutch name, the Vereenigde Nederlandsche Sheepvaart Maatschappij (VNSM) Passenger cargo ships on this route had names ending in – 'fontein'. At the time our subject entered service there were three others, the 10,500-tonners *Bloemfontein* of 1934, the *Jagersfontein* of 1950 and the *Oranjefontein* of 1940. The first named was scrapped in 1959 after a distinguished career on the African service and as a wartime transport.

The *Randfontein* and her two running-mates motored steadily to and fro. The route was usually Amsterdam-Southampton-Las Palmas-Cape Town-Port Elizabeth-East London-Durban-Lourenço Marques, returning by the same route. Sometimes the ship started at Hamburg, and sometimes called at Antwerp.

The *Randfontein* carried a greater proportion of tourist passengers than did the *Jagersfontein* and *Oranjefontein*. She was the largest passenger vessel ever owned by the Holland-Africa Line.

The service was, however, in gradual decline. The ship's two running-mates were both withdrawn and scrapped in 1967. The *Randfontein* herself continued on the route for another four years, teamed up with several twelve-passenger cargo ships. Nevertheless, the passenger trade by now had greatly decreased due to competition from the airlines. The ship completed her final round voyage in April 1971. A few months later she was transferred to another Dutch concern, the Royal Interocean Lines. She was required for operation on a quite different service from the Australian ports of Melbourne and Sydney to Japan, returning via the Pacific Islands. She was renamed *Nieuw Holland*, and photos taken of the vessel at this time reveal little alteration to her appearance, apart from being painted in different colours. The foremost pair of Samson posts had gone, replaced by a single large deck crane.

The ship continued in Dutch-flag service until 1974. By this time passenger requirements on the route had declined, and freight services were becoming 'containerized'. She was now sold to the Chinese, and her home port became Canton. Renamed *Yu Hua*, the ship ran for a while on a route from China to East Africa. She carried mostly materials and construction workers who were involved on a railway project there. When this had been completed the ship switched to the shorter route across to Hong Kong. Her movements in recent years are a little obscure. She was renamed *Hai Xing* in 1981, and is still listed in Lloyds Register. Her owners are stated to be the Shanghai Hai Xing Shipping Co Ltd.

Rangitane

THIS ship, like her sister *Rangitoto*, was built for the NZSC's service from London to New Zealand. Constructed at John Brown's Clydebank yard, she was launched by the Duchess of Gloucester on 30 June 1949 and completed by December that year. The ship sailed on her maiden voyage on 27 January 1950.

The New Zealand Shipping Company dated from 1883. In 1912 they took over the Federal SNCo. although both continued to have their own funnel colours and flag. Later they came under P & O ownership, but continued to maintain their separate colours and operations.

As can be seen, the *Rangitane* was a very fine-looking vessel. The hull had good sheer, a nicely raked stem and cruiser stern. It contained four decks, and the superstructure above was well proportioned, with a large funnel. Passenger accommodation was provided for a comparatively small number in one class only. Much of the hold was insulated for refrigerated cargoes, in particular New Zealand lamb.

The ship's maiden voyage was from London to Southampton, and then to Wellington via the Panama Canal. Her sister *Rangitoto* was also on the route, as were the two older ships *Rangitiki* and *Rangitata*. The New Zealand Maori names were all rather pleasant-sounding ones.

The *Rangitane* was at once a popular vessel on the service as she motored steadily to and fro. On the homeward voyage most passengers landed at Southampton, the ship then proceeding to London where cargo was unloaded. The route usually followed was from the UK to Curaçao (where refuelling took place), then through the Panama Canal to Wellington and Auckland, returning the same way.

A few incidents befell the vessel. In February 1956 she developed engine trouble as she neared Panama en route from Wellington to the UK. This was caused by a defective crankshaft, and the ship had to go back to John Brown's yard for repairs. In general, however, the Doxford engines performed well over many years of long voyaging.

The new *Ruahine* had joined the service in 1951. Departures from London were now every four weeks; at this period most passengers were immigrants seeking a new life in Australia or New Zealand.

During the sixties passenger numbers decreased as aircraft began to take over. In 1962 the old-timers *Rangitata* and *Rangitiki* were withdrawn after splendid service of 36 and 33 years respectively.

The 13,600-ton *Remuera*, (ex-Cunard *Parthia* of 1948), joined the fleet, but was withdrawn from the service in 1965. By this time only the three post-war vessels were on the route. In that year both the *Rangitane* and her sister were given extensive refits, when their mainmasts were removed and accommodation altered. At this time their funnels were painted in Federal Line colours. It was still the case, however, that the three-ship operation was unprofitable. The company had no real option but to withdraw from the passenger/cargo trade. Air competition and containerization had made their impact. There had also been problems with strikes, which often meant cargoes being left behind at ports in order to keep to advertised schedules.

The *Rangitane* was the first to go. She completed her last voyage on the route when reaching London in May 1968. Shortly afterwards she was sold to the Astroguarda Cia Nav of Piraeus. The ship was given the very short name of *Jan*, and went to Genoa to load a cargo for Australia. The voyage was delayed somewhat by engine problems, but she reached Sydney and then sailed to Formosa (now Taiwan), having been sold to shipbreakers there. However, the ship was less than twenty years old, and fortunately had further seagoing service ahead. Before breaking-up could commence the ex-*Rangitane* was again sold to the C Y Tung Group, and under ownership of the Oriental Latin American Lines, was refitted at Hong Kong. Here her foremast was removed and more alteration made to passenger accommodation. Renamed *Oriental Esmeralda*, she crossed the Pacific to San Diego, which was to be her terminal in a new round-the world service. Her first voyage commenced on 4 June 1969. She now sailed with ORIENT OVERSEAS LINE prominently painted on her sides, and with an attractive flower on her funnel. The *Rangitoto* and *Ruahine* had also joined the C Y Tung Group, being renamed *Oriental Carnaval* and *Oriental Rio* respectively. All seemed set for many more years service. Unfortunately, the great increase in oil prices from 1973 curtailed their activities. The ex-*Ruahine* was withdrawn that year. In 1974 the *Oriental Esmeralda* and her sister made cruises from San Diego and Los Angeles to the Mexican coast and the Far East. Sadly, this did not last long. On 10 February 1976 the ex-*Rangitane* was withdrawn and laid up in Hong Kong. She went to shipbreakers in Kaohsiung, Taiwan, in April. Her sister had gone to Hong Kong breakers earlier that year.

Name: **Rangitane** (1949); **Jan** (1968); **Oriental Esmeralda** (1968)

Line: New Zealand Shipping Co. (1949-68); Astroguarda Cia Nav (1968); Oriental Latin American (1969-76)

Builders: John Brown & Co., Clydebank; launched 30 June 1949, completed December 1949

Dimensions: Gross tonnage 21,867/ Length 609 ft/Beam 78.1 ft

Machinery

Engines: 2 Doxford opposed-piston diesel, twin screw, 15,500 b.h.p.

Service speed: 17 knots

Major Refits

1965 removal of main mast, accommodation altered
1969 Hong Kong, foremast removed, accommodation altered

Regular Routes

London – Wellington via Panama Canal

Passenger Capacity

416 one class

Sister-ships

Rangitoto (1949)

Photograph 1961

Reina del Mar

THIS ship was built to operate on the PSNC service to the west coast of South America. This was a regular run from the UK, France and Spain to Bermuda, the Bahamas, Cuba, Jamaica, Panama, Columbia, Ecuador, Peru and Chile. Altogether a lengthy run, and with her running-mate the *Reina del Pacifico* she was to make five round voyages a year.

The Pacific Steam Navigation Company (founded in 1840) had been long involved in this service, and some fine ships had been included in their fleet. Among the larger units may be mentioned the 15,500-tons *Orduna* of 1914, the similar-sized *Orbita* of 1915 and the 14,000-ton *Oropesa* of 1929. The *Reina del Pacifico* was built in 1931, and at 17,702 tons was the largest in the fleet. She was possibly unique at that time, being a quadruple-screw motorship, and became very popular and successful. Some twenty-five years were to elapse before another large passenger ship was built for this route.

The *Reina del Mar*, or (*Queen of the Sea*), was built at Belfast by Harland and Wolff. She was launched in June 1955, and completed in April the following year. She started her maiden voyage from Liverpool to Valparaiso on 3 May 1956. She had a very attractive appearance. Her hull had nice sheer, a well-raked and slightly curved rounded stem and cruiser stern. With a foremast and single streamlined funnel of rather distinctive design, she looked elegant indeed. The hull had four complete decks with a lower deck fore and aft of the machinery space, and there were ten watertight bulkheads.

Public rooms and accommodation were of a high standard. Much wood panelling featured therein. There were two swimming pools.

As noted earlier, the ship's normal itinerary was the lengthy run from the UK to the west coast of South America. This was not an 'express' service, and the ship had the fairly modest service speed of 18 knots. Many ports were visited en route; a typical voyage from Liverpool including: La Rochelle, Santander, Corunna, Bermuda, Nassau, Havana, Kingston, La Guaira, Curaçao, Cartagena, Cristobal, La Libertad, Callao, Arica, Antofagasta, and Valparaiso. Calls were often made at Plymouth and Vigo as well.

However, like all passenger shipping companies the PSNC was to suffer from air competition. The *Reina del Mar* continued on the run for some seven years, but by the early 1960s the South American passenger trade had fallen off badly. Her running-mate the *Reina del Pacifico* had been withdrawn for scrapping in 1958. In 1963 it was announced that the ship was to be chartered by the Travel Savings Association, to be handed over to them in March 1964 after her last South American voyage.

The ship arrived at Liverpool on 5 March and was then sent back to Harland and Wolff at Belfast for conversion to a permanent cruise liner. This involved quite a lot of alterations. The cargo holds were turned into extra accommodation and public rooms. On the promenade deck the forward lounge was considerably enlarged, as was the forward restaurant. The boat deck was also extended aft. Sundry other alterations resulted in an increased passenger capacity. Accommodation was either 'one class' or first and tourist.

On 10 June 1964 she sailed from Liverpool to New York on her first voyage as a cruise ship. Her programme was for seven transatlantic voyages, five to New York and two to Montreal, the ship being used as a hotel while she was in port.

By late 1964 she was running under Union Castle management, and was painted in UC colours. Now began her final and successful career as a cruise liner. She usually made about sixteen cruises a year from both Southampton and, during the winter months, Cape Town. She became very popular in her new role, and as far as I am aware no untoward incident befell her during this time, although she was strikebound at Southampton during the seamen's dispute of 1966. In 1973 she was purchased outright by the Union Castle Company. Rather surprisingly, in mid-1974 the Company then announced that the ship would be withdrawn the following year. Oil-fuel prices had risen dramatically, and Union Castle contended that increased operating costs had made the ship no longer viable. She made her last cruise from Southampton in late October 1974, and after a series of winter cruises from Cape Town to South America, she arrived back at the Hampshire port in March 1975. She was soon sold to breakers in Taiwan, arriving at Kaohsiung in late July that year.

Name: **Reina del Mar**

Line: Pacific Steam Navigation Co. (1956-73); Union Castle (1973-5)

Builders: Harland & Wolff, Belfast; launched June 1955, completed April 1956

Dimensions: Gross tonnage 20,234/Length 601 ft/Beam 78.4 ft

Machinery

Engines: 2 sets Parsons double reduction geared turbines, twin screw, 17,000 s.h.p.

Boilers: 2 Babcock & Wilcox watertube, 525 p.s.i.

Service speed: 18 knots

Major Refits

1964 Harland & Wolff, conversion to cruise liner, 21,501 tons

Regular Routes

Liverpool — Valparaiso

Passenger Capacity

1956: 1st 201, Cabin 216, Tourist 343
1964: 1047 one class/951 two classes

Sister-ships

None

Photograph 1964

Reina Maria Cristina

Name: _Reina Maria Cristina_

Line: Compania Transatlantica

Builders: William Denny, Dumbarton; Launched 3 Nov 1888 completed March 1889

Dimensions: Gross tonnage 4,381/Length 408.5 ft/Beam 48 ft

Machinery

Engines: 3-cylinder triple expansion, single screw

Boilers: 3 double-ended cylindrical, natural and forced draught, coal-fired, 170 p.s.i.

Service speed: 15 knots

Regular Routes

Santander – New York
Barcelona – Vera Cruz

Passenger Capacity

1st 248, 2nd 52, 3rd 500

Sister-ships

Alfonso XIII (1889)

Photograph 1929

I N THE 1850s a Spanish shipping company was started by Don Antonio Lopez Y Lopez who commenced a service to Mediterranean ports and later to the colonies in the West Indies. By the early 1860s a twice-monthly service from Cadiz to Havana via Tenerife and Puerto Rico was in operation. From small beginnings the company steadily developed, and became known as the Compania Transatlantica by 1881. It is usually simply called the Spanish Line. A 'feeder' service from Havana to New York was established in 1886, and later a direct route to the US port came into being. The Company's vessels also sailed on numerous other routes, to Central and South American ports, the Canary Islands and even to the Philippines. It received the name Compania Transatlantica Española in 1953, but ceased passenger-ship operations in 1974.

The _Reina Maria Cristina_ looked rather like a large private yacht, at any rate in her final years of operation as depicted in our photograph. The 4,800-ton vessel was built by William Denny of Dumbarton and completed in 1889. This well-known firm also built several other ships for the Spanish company around this time. The _Buenos Aires_ of 5,200 tons was completed in 1887 and the _Reina_'s sister ship _Alfonso XIII_ also dated from 1889. The _Montevideo_ of 5,000 tons took to the water that same year.

The _Reina Maria Cristina_, with her clipper bow and elegant counter stern, was a handsome vessel, nicely proportioned. The hull had three decks and eight watertight bulkheads. As built she had four masts, with provision for sails on all of them. Rather surprisingly for such an attractive vessel, she was strengthened at various points to enable eight guns to be fitted should she be required for use as an auxiliary cruiser in wartime. She catered for first, second and third class passengers, and also had a considerable cargo capacity. Propelling machinery consisted of a triple expansion engine driving a single screw. Steam was provided by three cylindrical coal-fired boilers. The _Reina_ achieved a trial speed in excess of 17 knots, and service speed was 15.

Information on this elegant little ship is rather scanty, since the Spanish Line's records were lost in the Civil War. She was evidently intended originally for the South American route, but there is no evidence that she actually ran upon it. No doubt she operated on various routes as required. In 1920 she ran on the transatlantic route from Santander to New York via Corunna, Vigo and Havana. Later she transferred to Barcelona – Valencia – Cadiz – New York – Havana, continuing to Vera Cruz, Mexico. Later still the ship maintained a summer service between Santander and Southampton.

The _Reina Maria Cristina_ had a long life, surviving until 1931, when she went to the breakers at Genoa.

Her sister ship _Alfonso XIII_ foundered in Santander harbour in February 1915, possibly as a result of sabotage.

Reliance

Name: *Johann Heinrich Burchard*
(1914-20); *Limburgia* (1920);
Reliance (1922)
Line: Royal Holland Lloyd (1920-2); United
American (1922-6) HAPAG (1926-40)

Builders: J.C. Tecklenborg, Geestemunde;
completed November 1915

Dimensions: Gross tonnage 19,980/
Length 615 ft/Beam 71.9 ft

Machinery

Engines: 2 4-cylinder triple expansion
driving wing propellers, exhaust steam
turbine driving central screw, 17,000 total
i.h.p.

Service speed: 17 knots

Major Refits

1922 alteration for transatlantic service
1937 Blohm & Voss, modernization,
funnels rebuilt

Regular Routes

Amsterdam – river Plate, Hamburg –
New York

Passenger Capacity

1920: 1st 315, 2nd 301, 3rd 850
1922: 1st 290, 2nd 320, 3rd 400
1934: 1st 500
1947: 1st 633, 2nd 186

Near-Sister-ships

William O'Swald (1920) (later
Resolute); *Tirpitz* (1920) (later
Empress of Australia)

Photograph 1926

THIS ship's early story closely resembles that of her near sister, which later became the *Resolute*. Like her, she was originally laid down for HAPAG, but became a member of the Royal Holland Lloyd line until sold to the United American Lines in 1922.

The ship was built by J.C. Tecklenburg AG at Geestemünde, and had in fact been completed by November 1915, when she was secretly sold to the Dutch company. She was never to make a voyage under her original name of *Johann Heinrich Burchard*.

The two near-sisters were very much alike, as will be noted by comparing the photographs. A few minor points of difference may be noted, however. The funnels of the *Resolute* were round in cross-section, but those of the *Reliance* were oval and of larger section. (It is convenient to refer to these ships under the names by which they were best known.) The cowls of the latter, especially around the fore-funnel, were rather large and of rectangular section, whereas her sister had conventional round ones.

As the *Limburgia* the ship operated on the Amsterdam – river Plate service from 1920 to 1922, when with her sister she was sold to the United American Line and was refitted for transatlantic service. She was now renamed *Reliance*, and was to retain this name for the rest of her life. For the next few years her activities followed a similar pattern to that of the *Resolute* – transatlantic voyaging interspersed with cruising. Her first voyage with UAL from Hamburg to New York was on 3 May 1922, and she became a popular vessel and a good sea boat. Like her sister, she transferred to Panamanian registry in 1923 to combat Prohibition, and in 1926 once again came under HAPAG ownership. She continued on the North Atlantic service, but from 1928 she became almost exclusively devoted to cruising, transatlantic line voyages becoming a rarity. Again like her sister, she carried out some lengthy ones of over 130 days' duration. Passenger accommodation varied considerably over the years, as indeed it did in most passenger vessels. Her hull was painted white for cruising.

In 1937 the *Reliance* was refitted and modernised at the Blohm & Voss yard. She was given thicker funnels at this time, but she was not to reap much benefit from this reconstruction. On 7 August 1938 an outbreak of fire occurred on board while she was in Hamburg, preparing for a Scandinavian cruise. Damage was so severe that the ship was considered a total loss and after being laid up in Hamburg she was sold for breaking up in 1940.

Remuera

Name: *Parthia* (1948); *Remura* (1962); *Aramac* (1964)

Line: Cunard (1948-61); New Zealand Shipping Co. (1961-65); Eastern and Australian Steamship Co. (1964-69)

Builders: Harland & Wolff, Belfast; launched 25 February 1947, completed April 1948

Dimensions: Gross tonnage 13,362/ Length 532 ft/Beam 69.9 ft

Machinery

Engines: 2 turbine sets double reduction geared, twin screw 15,000 s.h.p.
Boilers: 2 oil-fired watertube, 450 p.s.i., superheated to 750 F
Service speed: 18 knots

Major Refits

1961 Alexander Stephen, Glasgow, alteration of accommodation

Regular Routes

Liverpool – New York, London – Wellington, Australia – Hong Kong, Japan

Passenger Capacity

1948: 1st 251
1962: 350 one class

Sister-ships

Media (1947)

Photograph 1962

THIS ship and her sister *Media* were built for the Cunard Company's fortnightly passenger/cargo service to the USA, her builders being Harland and Wolff of Belfast. Launched on 25 February 1947, she was completed by April 1948 and sailed on her maiden voyage from Liverpool to New York on the 10th of that month.

The ship was most attractive. The hull with its well-raked bow and cruiser stern contained three complete decks and two partial ones. Above was the short superstructure, with a single nicely raked funnel. She carried a comparatively small number of first class passengers, and the entire promenade deck was devoted to their public rooms, which were air-conditioned throughout. Cargo was very important for this service and the ship had a large capacity with six hatches, three forward and three aft. These were served by derricks. As originally completed, the *Parthia* had a foremast only. Propelling machinery consisted of two sets of steam turbines geared to twin screws. Service speed was a respectable 18 knots, and steam was supplied by a couple of watertube boilers.

The *Parthia* and her sister ran reliably on the New York service carrying passengers and cargo. In 1953 she was fitted with Denny Brown fin stabilizers. The *Media* had likewise been fitted earlier, and these two vessels were in fact the first transatlantic liners to have these anti-rolling fins. However, the passenger/cargo service for which the ships were built declined in the early 1960s and the two vessels became surplus to Cunard's requirements. In 1961 both were sold.

The *Media* went to the Italian Cogedar Line and was renamed *Flavia*. The *Parthia* was sold on 1 November to the New Zealand Shipping Company and went to the Glasgow shipyard of Alexander Stephen and Sons for a complete refit. This mainly consisted of increasing passenger accommodation to her new owners' requirements, and installation of air-conditioning throughout. The ship was no longer a North Atlantic vessel, and would be sailing through tropical seas. The main external difference was the extension of the promenade deck farther aft: this enabled a sports area to be provided, and also a swimming-pool. A new smoke-room was also added. Bunker capacity had to be increased to enable more oil fuel to be carried for much longer voyaging. A mainmast was also added which if anything rather improved her appearance. During this refit a fire broke out on board, fortunately doing comparatively little damage.

The ship, now renamed *Remuera*, sailed on 1 June 1962 from London on her first voyage to New Zealand. The service during the 1960s, with four ships operating, was every six weeks. The *Remuera* seems never to have really fitted in on this route. She was a lone steamship in a fleet of motor vessels. She was also considerably smaller than her running-mates the *Rangitoto*, *Rangitane*, and *Ruahine*, although she carried about the same number of passengers. The trade was also declining, and so in 1964 she was transferred within the P & O group to the Eastern and Australian SS Co. She was now renamed *Aramac*, her funnel was painted black and she sailed from Australian ports to Hong Kong and Japan. She remained on this route until she was replaced on it by the *Cathay* in October 1969. She was then sold to breakers and arrived at Kaohsiung, Taiwan for scrapping on 22 November. The ex-*Parthia* had thus a seagoing career of only some 21 years, not a long time for such a fine steamer. She probably suffered from being a 'hybrid' vessel with a little too much cargo capacity.

The demise of the NZSC's passenger/cargo service to New Zealand was due mostly to the growth of air competition and containerization. The alteration of sailings from once every four weeks to once every six weeks must also have lost them many passengers.

Republic

Name: Servian (1903); **President Grant** (1907); **Republic** (1924)

Line: HAPAG (1906-17); United States (1924-31)

Builders: Harland & Wolff, Belfast; launched 1903, completed December 1906

Dimensions: Gross tonnage 18,072/ Length 616 ft/Beam 68.2 ft

Machinery

Engines: 2 quadruple expansion, twin screw, 7,650 i.h.p.

Boilers: coal-fired

Service speed: 14.5 knots

Major Refits

1923-4 Newport News, Virginia, superstructure extended, alteration to accommodation, boilers converted to oil fuel

Regular Routes

Hamburg – New York
New York – Bremerhaven

Passenger Capacity

1907: 1st 326, 2nd 152, 3rd 1,004, Steerage 2,348
1924: Cabin 619, 3rd 1,332

Sister-ships

Scotian (1907) (later President Lincoln)

Photograph 1928

THE SHIP WAS originally ordered from Harland and Wolff's Yard at Belfast for the Wilsons and Furness-Leyland Company and launched as the *Servian* in 1903. However, the company withdrew from the contract and the ship was completed and purchased in December 1906 by HAPAG. They named her *President Grant*, and she sailed on her maiden voyage from Hamburg to New York on 4 September 1907, having been completed in August.

She was a striking, if not particularly handsome vessel. The hull had a straight stem and counter stern. It contained four decks and an awning deck and was subdivided by eleven main bulkheads. Superstructure above was rather 'square', with a single slender funnel. In total there were seven decks for passengers, of which a large number were carried in four classes, first, second, third, and steerage. The ship also had a large cargo capacity, with seven holds and eleven hatches.

The ship had an identical sister built at the same time at Harland and Wolff, also intended for the same British company and originally named *Scotian*. She too came into HAPAG ownership and was renamed *President Lincoln*. The *President Grant*'s maiden voyage was Hamburg-Boulogne-Southampton-New York, and for the next few years she and her sister steamed steadily to and fro at a sedate pace. This was the period of great immigration to the United States, and the ships carried large numbers of passengers on westbound crossings.

When war came both 'Presidents' were in American waters, and both were interned and laid up in New York. In July 1917 they were taken over by the US authorities and used for trooping duties. USS *President Grant* made many transatlantic crossings with American troops. She was armed with four 5-inch guns. During the remainder of the war she transported about 77,000 personnel in eastbound and westbound directions. She came through unscathed, but her sister was not so fortunate. USS *President Lincoln* was torpedoed and sunk on 31 May 1918 by her former country's U-90. Twenty-six lives were lost.

When the war was over the *President Grant* made a couple of voyages bringing Czechoslovak troops from Siberia to Trieste. The ship was not returned to Germany but was handed over to the US Shipping Board in March 1921. She then lay idle for about three years. The name *President Buchanan* was assigned to the ship for a short while, and she had an extensive refit and reconstruction at the Newport News Shipbuilding Yard, Virginia. Her third and fourth masts were removed and the superstructure extended forward to join with the previously isolated bridge structure. Many other alterations and improvements were made to passenger accommodation – she was now to carry fewer numbers. Her furnaces had been converted to burn oil fuel.

The ship did not retain her new name for long, and received her final one, *Republic*, in 1924. Now in the colours of the United States Lines, she made her first voyage for her new owners on 29 April to Bremerhaven. She sailed, still at a sedate pace, on the transatlantic route, sometimes to Hamburg for the next few years. All US Lines ships suffered badly from Prohibition laws in America which prevented them selling liquor to passengers. The *Republic* nevertheless still transported large numbers until the Depression began to take effect. Our photograph shows her as rebuilt, a general improvement on her original appearance.

The ship continued on the route, also doing some cruising until 1931. These cruises were often from New York to the West Indies; transatlantic voyaging became less frequent as the general Depression made its effects felt. The ship made her last voyage from Hamburg to New York on 17 July 1931, and was soon afterwards taken over as a troop transport for the US army. After reconversion she sailed on 4 November that year for San Francisco and on to Honolulu, Guam and Manila with Service personnel. For the next ten years she was employed in this role, usually transporting troops across the Pacific to Honolulu and elsewhere. She could normally carry over 1,000 people.

In July 1941 the ship was turned over to the US navy for the same duties. As USS *Republic* (AP33) she could now transport some 3,500 at a time to the various Pacific theatres of war. Her cargo capacity was also much utilized for taking supplies. The ship bore a charmed life, plodding steadily along at 14½ knots. She would have made an easy target for enemy submarines and aircraft, but she came through unscathed, as she had done during the earlier war. Towards the end she was converted yet again, at Mobile, Alabama, to a hospital ship. However, she remained only a short time in this role before again becoming a trooper.

When the war was over the *Republic*, like many more ships, was laid up. She remained so until sold for scrapping in 1951. This involved towing her a long distance, from Olympia in the state of Washington to the breakers at Baltimore via the Panama Canal.

Resolute

Name: William O'Swald (1914); **Brabantia** (1920); **Resolute** (1922); **Lombardia** (1935)

Line: HAPAG (1916) and (1926-35); Royal Holland Lloyd (1920-2); United American (1922-26); Lloyd Triestino (1935-43)

Builders: A G Weser, Bremen; completed 1920

Dimensions: Gross tonnage 20,200/ Length 616 ft/Beam 72.2 ft

Machinery

Engines: 2 4-cylinder triple expansion driving wing propellers, exhaust steam turbine driving central screw, 17,000 i.h.p.

Boilers: 16 Schulte oil-fired watertube

Service speed: 17 knots

Major Refits

1935 conversion to troop transport

Regular Routes

Amsterdam – river Plate
Hamburg – New York

Passenger Capacity

1920: 1st 335, 2nd 284, 3rd 469, Steerage 857
1922: 1st 290, 2nd 320, 3rd 400
1934: 497
1935: 1st 103, Troops 4,420

Near Sister-ships

Johann Heinrich Burchard (1920) (later **Reliance**), **Tirpitz** (1920) (later **Empress of Australia**)

Photograph 1922

THIS ship was one of three medium-sized three-funnel liners laid down for the Hamburg America Line, HAPAG. The other two were the *Tirpitz*, which finished up as the CPR *Empress of Australia*, and the *Johann Heinrich Burchard*, later to become the *Reliance*. HAPAG, more noted for their North Atlantic service, became involved in the South American trade in about 1900.

The *William O'Swald* was laid down at the A.G.Weser Yard at Bremen. She was in fact launched with this name, but never actually sailed under it. It is as the *Resolute* that she is best remembered. All three ships were intended for the company's South American service, but of course the outbreak of war delayed their completion. There was in fact a German-Dutch agreement in operation whereby the former country made reparation to the latter in respect of Dutch ships sunk by German U-boats. The incomplete *William O'Swald* and her near-sister *J.H. Burchard* thus became members of the Royal Holland Lloyd Company in 1916. The former was now renamed *Brabantia* and the latter *Limburgia*. However, when the war ended a complication arose when the Allies would not recognize this transaction and insisted that the two ships should be handed over. A good many arguments took place before this happened. In the meantime our subject had been completed in July 1920 and as *Brabantia* ran from Amsterdam on the service to the river Plate for the Dutch company, commencing on 1 September.

The United American Lines were formed in 1922 to operate a transatlantic service. This company, owned by the American Ship and Commerce Corporation, came to an agreement with HAPAG to operate jointly. The *Brabantia* and her sister were sold to the United American Lines in January 1922 and refitted to make them suitable for North Atlantic operation. Apparently Royal Holland Lloyd were glad to sell them by now, as they had been losing money on the South American route. Our subject was now renamed *Resolute*, and her sister became the *Reliance*. These perpetuated the names of two famous American yachts which had successfully retained the celebrated 'America's' Cup.

As can be seen in the photograph, the *Resolute* was a good-looking ship. Her hull had a traditional 'straight' stem and counter stern with good sheer. It contained four overall decks with orlops in three of the five holds and there were ten main bulkheads. Superstructure was well proportioned, and the three funnels nicely spaced. (The after one was a dummy, as was common practice at that time to improve the ship's appearance.)

The *Resolute* left Hamburg on her first UAL voyage under the American flag on 11 April 1922, calling at Southampton and Cherbourg en route to New York. She proved to be an excellent sea boat and gained a high reputation for comfort. Our photograph shows her sailing in UAL colours, the funnels being buff-coloured with two narrow dark blue bands.

Prohibition in America was something of a problem at this time. To get round it the *Resolute* and her sister were transferred to the Panamanian flag in 1923, so that they were no longer 'dry' and thus became more profitable. The ship like many others went cruising during the winter months.

By 1926 HAPAG had well and truly re-established itself on the route, and a deal was struck with United America for the German company to purchase the *Resolute*, *Reliance* and *Cleveland*. The UAL then closed operations and the three ships came under the German flag. The *Resolute* made her first voyage for HAPAG on 10 August 1926. At this time the company's funnel colours were plain buff, but in 1927 tops of black, white and red were added. By 1928 the *Resolute* had become much more of a cruise liner, but still carried out some transatlantic sailings during the summer months. Later she became almost exclusively used for cruising, and was very popular in this role. However, the recession was taking its toll, and no doubt the ship's rather outdated machinery had become a little uneconomic. Her hull had been painted white, as was the practice for many cruise liners at the time.

By 1935, however, the *Resolute* was redundant. Atlantic trade was at a low ebb, and HAPAG had a surplus of vessels. She was sold to the Italians and placed under Lloyd Triestino management. Renamed *Lombardia*, she was fitted out as a troop transport. The Abyssinian campaign was in progress, and the ship made trooping voyages to that country and to Italian Somaliland. She was also used in the Mediterranean on various government voyages, taking settlers to Libya, for instance. Sometimes she was laid up. When Italy entered the war the ship was available for trooping. On 4 August 1943, while in Naples taking troops on board, she came under an Allied air attack, was bombed, set on fire and sank. Some four years later she was raised and towed away to the scrapyard.

Rotterdam

THE Holland America Line had engaged in much post-war fleet replacement, and the *Rotterdam* was the largest ship to be built. Constructed by the Rotterdam Dry Dock Company, she was launched on 13 September 1958 by Queen Juliana and completed by July 1959. She sailed on her maiden voyage from the Dutch port to New York on 3 September that year.

The ship has an elegant profile, as can be seen. With a nicely curved and raked stem, the hull has a modern cruiser-type stern. Superstructure is well proportioned, and in place of a conventional funnel there are twin uptakes well towards the stern. These are bridged across near the top, and a small mast is fitted there to carry the aft navigation light. Amidships, where a 'conventional' funnel would normally be fitted, is a low structure of short decks almost in fact resembling a funnel. Much use has been made of aluminium in the superstructure.

Apart from some short upper decks – navigation bridge deck, upper bridge deck etc., the remainder reading downwards were named Sun, Boat, Upper Promenade, Promenade, Lower Promenade, Main, and decks A to D. The ship in her transatlantic role catered for first class and tourist. Later these were to be all one class when she became a permanent cruise ship.

For North Atlantic voyaging there was an ingenious arrangement to prevent the two classes from mingling when using public rooms. This consisted of a trick staircase in the style of the overlapping spiral one found in the Château de Chambord, Orleans.

Public rooms are on the promenade deck and upper promenade deck and consist of lounges, smoke-rooms, library, theatre etc. The Carlton Ritz on the upper promenade deck has been described as the most beautiful on board. Two decks high and facing aft, it has a large dance floor. The splendid theatre, forward on the promenade deck, has an auditorium two decks high and can seat 607. At the time she entered service the ship was the fifth largest passenger liner in the world, and the biggest one to be built in Holland. She was exceeded in size only by the two Cunard 'Queens', the *United States* and the *Liberté*.

The maiden voyage included a call at Southampton. One important passenger on board was 21-year-old Princess Beatrix, heiress to the Dutch throne. She went ashore here for a New Forest tour before rejoining the ship. A fine reception awaited the new vessel at New York.

She now sailed in conjunction with the famous *Nieuw Amsterdam* and the *Statendam* during the early 1960s. As planned she went cruising during the winter months, and by 1966 this cruising role had become the most important activity. That year she made cruises from New York to the Caribbean and Pacific and also a round-the-world one. She had done lengthy cruises in earlier years – in December 1959, for example, she completely circumnavigated South America. This took 49 days, and later in January 1961 made her first world cruise which was to become an annual event. Its itinerary varies from time to time, but usually takes over 80 days.

Holland America pulled out from the transatlantic ferry service in the late sixties, and the *Rotterdam* has been exclusively used for cruising since then, being especially converted in 1969. She has remained very popular in this role. The ship has been renovated and updated from time to time, but her essential character has remained relatively unchanged, Cruises in addition to the Caribbean route have included summer ones from Vancouver to Alaska.

One or two mishaps have befallen the ship from time to time. In January 1976 she was struck by a tremendous wave while off Casablanca. She was thrown about violently, and there was damage to furniture. Fortunately, although some passengers suffered broken limbs and bruises there were no fatalities. The strongly built ship suffered only superficial damage, she has come unscathed through the worst Atlantic storms also.

In October 1973 she was having her annual overhaul in dry dock at the Lisnave Shipyard in Lisbon. The *Rotterdam* shared this big dock with a large supertanker, which was being repaired after an explosion. The operation of a large crane lifting heavy weights, caused part of the dock wall to collapse, and there was danger of the dock flooding. This could have caused the ship to crash into the opposite wall. Fortunately, this did not happen.

As noted, the ship has been kept up to date. Her refurbishment at Portland, Oregon, in 1989 included extensions to the upper promenade deck and fitment of a bow thruster to aid manoeuvring. She continues in service.

The ship is now operated by Carnival Cruise Lines Inc. but the Holland America name is retained.

Royal Princess

THIS vessel is the flagship of Princess Cruises, owned and managed by P & O. The company had for long been involved in cruising, and the building of this ship showed their determination to remain in the forefront of the passenger cruise market. Princess Cruises, acquired by P & O in 1974, was a company which had become the leading cruise operator on the west coast of the USA.

In 1982 P & O invited tenders to build a 45,000-ton vessel which would have good fuel economy and a capacity for 1,200 passengers. The *Royal Princess* was the result. She was built at the Wartsila Yard in Helsinki, Finland, and floated out (the equivalent of launching) on 18 February 1984 and delivered in November that year. She was named at Southampton on the fifteenth of that month by HRH the Princess of Wales, and on the 19th sailed on her inaugural voyage to Miami. As can be seen, she is of striking appearance with clipper bow, massive superstructure and funnel well aft. The usual arrangement of accommodation and public rooms is reversed on this ship. Traditionally the latter have been on the upper decks, with accommodation below. On the *Royal Princess* most public rooms are lower down, utilizing the full width of the ship. Above, where the superstructure narrows, at promenade deck level, there is a five-deck block of staterooms. Each has a window, and some have private verandas. This concept is known as 'all outside cabin'. The ship has twelve decks in all, nine being for passengers. Reading downward these are: Observation, Sun, Lido, Aloha, Baya, Caribe, Dolphin (promenade) Riviera and Plaza decks.

Main public rooms are on the Riviera deck. These include the International Lounge with stage and dance floor, Princess Theatre, Princess Court, a boutique, casino and Riviera Club. The Plaza deck below contains a huge dining-room and the big main foyer. Here is included a splendid modern 'seagull' sculpture in stainless steel entitled *Spindrift*. On the sun deck, 'wrapped round' the funnel, the Horizon Lounge affords 360° views and is used as a discotheque also. Recreational facilities on board include four swimming-pools, jacuzzis, sauna and gymnasium, while there are also shops, beauty salons and medical facilities. The ship is fully air-conditioned.

Propelling machinery consists of four Pielstick diesel engines arranged in pairs. Each pair drives a controllable-pitch propeller through reduction gearing. All engines also drive alternators for electrical power, there being also a couple of standby diesel alter-nators. Control and monitoring of the machinery is by sophisticated microprocessor equipment in the control-room. The ship is fitted with stabilizers. On trials the *Royal Princess* achieved a speed of 22 knots, quite adequate, since she cruises at about 20 knots.

The ship sailed fully booked from Southampton on 19 November 1984 for her maiden voyage to Miami. By all accounts this was a lively trip as the weather was rough and the ship pitched and rolled considerably. She was, of course, not designed for North Atlantic voyaging, and normally operates in calmer waters.

Since then she has cruised to many glamorous locations – along the Mexican Riviera, among the Caribbean Islands and along the coasts of Canada and Alaska. Typical cruises are from Acapulco down the coast and through the Panama Canal to Aruba, Martinique, St Thomas, and San Juan. Passengers fly to join the ship at Acapulco and leave by air from San Juan. Other cruises are undertaken as well, and the ship has achieved considerable popularity.

Name: **Royal Princess**

Line: P & O Princess Cruises

Builders: Wartsila Shipyard, Helsinki; launched 18 February 1984, completed November 1984

Dimensions: Gross tonnage 44,348/ Length 758.4 ft/Beam 95.7 ft

Machinery

Engines: 4 Pielstick 6-cylinder 4-stroke SA diesel, each pair driving controllable pitch propeller, 39,600 total b.h.p.

Service speed: 20 knots

Passenger Capacity
1,260

Sister-ships
None

Photograph 1984

Royal Viking Sky

T HE Royal Viking Line was founded in 1970 by three well-established Norwegian shipping firms, the Bergen Line, and the Nordenfjeldske and Klaveness companies. The latter group withdrew later, and in 1984 RVL was acquired by Klosters Cruise Ltd, one of the country's oldest and most respected cruise companies.

RVL introduced the *Royal Viking Star* in 1972; she was built expressly for world-wide cruising. She was joined the following year by the *Royal Viking Sky* and *Royal Viking Sea*. All three were sisters built at the same yard, Wartsila, at Helsinki, Finland.

The *Sky* was launched on 25 May 1972 and completed by June 1973. As can be seen in the photograph, she is typical of modern cruise vessels. The hull has a clipper bow, cruiser stern, sizable but well-proportioned superstructure, streamlined mast, and funnel towards the rear. As originally built she catered for 536 passengers, but was enlarged in 1982 by inserting a 93-foot prefabricated midsection to increase her capacity to over 700. Her two sisters were similarly treated.

There are eight passenger decks, and the Scandinavian influence is apparent throughout the ship. The usual amenities expected by cruise passengers are found on board. There are lounges, bars, theatre, cinema, casino, with of course shopping facilities, beauty parlour, a couple of swimming-pools, launderette, a hospital etc. The Trondheim Lounge and main dining saloon are on the Scandinavian deck, while the Prins Olav Lounge is on the appropriately named Sky deck. Many rooms on the Promenade deck include the Finlandia bar, Casino and library. The ship is completely air-conditioned throughout, and now has 374 staterooms including nine luxury penthouse suites.

Propelling machinery consists of four Sulzer diesel engines driving twin screws. Service speed is 21.5 knots. Seven diesel generators supply electrical power and the ship is fitted with fin stabilizers and two bow thrust units.

Since coming into service the *Royal Viking Sky* and her sisters have done world-wide cruising. These have varied from comparatively short trips of seven days or so up to round-the-world voyages taking over 100 days. The latter if going westabout may start from Port Everglades, Florida, and so via the Caribbean and Panama Canal to the Mexican Riviera, California, Hawaii, and perhaps Fiji and Tahiti. They then proceed to New Zealand, Australia, Hong Kong, Singapore, India, South Africa, South American ports and back to Florida.

In short the *Sky* and her sisters are now well known from New York to the North Cape, and from Southampton to Sydney. They have become very popular for their comfort and cuisine. Passengers are extremely well catered for, whether on a short seven day cruise from New York to Bermuda or on a longer voyage.

In 1987 all RVL ships, together with those of their sister division Norwegian Cruise Line, were transferred from Norwegian to Bahamian registry. In a related action Klosters Cruise Ltd become a Bermudian company. In 1988 the latter carried out a restructuring whereby the managements of RVL and NCL were centralized, RVL's management was moved from San Francisco to Coral Gables, Florida, where all operational, marketing and financial activities for both companies are now consolidated.

It seems likely that the *Royal Viking Sky* and her sisters have a good many more useful years of service left in them, in spite of the advent of considerably larger cruise ships. The 38,000-ton *Royal Viking Sun* in fact joined the fleet in 1988. The *Sky*'s 1990 programme included, among other trips, a seventy day 'Circle South America' cruise. In November 1991 the Royal Viking Sky was transferred to the Norwegian Cruise Line fleet and renamed *Sunward*.

Name: **Royal Viking Sky** (1973) **Sunward** (1991)

Line: Royal Viking (1973-91) NCL (1991)

Builders: Wartsila Shipyard, Helsinki; launched 25 May 1972, completed June 1973

Dimensions: Gross tonnage 21,891/ Length 583 ft/Beam 83 ft

Machinery

Engines: 4 Wartsila-Sulzer, twin screw, controllable pitch propellers

Service speed: 21.5 knots

Major Refits

1982: insertion of midsection to increase capacity, 28,078 tons, 676 × 83 ft

Passenger Capacity

1973: 536
1982: 710

Sister-ships

Royal Viking Star (1972), *Royal Viking Sea* (1973)

Photograph 1984

Ruahine

THIS SHIP was built for the NZSC's service to New Zealand. Constructed at John Brown's Clydebank yard, she was launched on 11 December 1950 and completed by May 1951. She set off on her maiden voyage from London to Wellington on the 22nd of that month. Completion of the *Ruahine* had enabled a four-weekly service from London to be operated, with departures every fourth Friday.

The vessel was in fact a somewhat smaller version of the earlier pair *Rangitane* and *Rangitoto*. Like the earlier ships, the *Ruahine* catered for first-class passengers only. These were mainly accommodated in three decks A(boat), B and C. There was also a sports deck above, and a dining saloon on D deck below. Public rooms and accommodation were rather similar to that of the earlier pair, With lounge, smoke-room, verandah café. Plenty of deck space was available for recreation, and there was an open-air swimming-pool.

The ship had six cargo holds worked by derricks. As usual in these ships, much space was insulated for carriage of refrigerated dairy products and lamb. Propelling machinery consisted of a couple of Doxford-type diesel engines driving twin screws, and the ship had a service speed of 17 knots.

The *Ruahine* motored steadily to and fro for many years on the long run to New Zealand. She proved reliable, and had a career fairly free from incidents. She suffered a starboard engine breakdown in September 1954 when nearing Panama en route to the UK, and this delayed her for a few days while repairs were made.

Towards the end of 1965 the NZSC decided to adopt the funnel colours of their subsidiary, the Federal Steam Navigation Company. The *Ruahine* had a refit at this time, and like her two older sisters, emerged from this with her main-mast removed. Alterations had been made to passenger accommodation also.

However, the service was now in decline and the ship made her final departure from London in late April 1968. On her return to the UK she was briefly laid up before being sold to the C.Y. Tung Group. She then proceeded out to Hong Kong, where she was given another refit. Further alterations were made to passenger accommodation, and her foremast was removed.

Early in 1969 the ship was transferred within the C.Y. Tung Group to the Chinese Maritime Trust, registered in Taiwan. Now renamed *Oriental Rio* and with ORIENT OVERSEAS LINE painted on her sides, she set off across the Pacific to San Diego. The vessel was now on a round-the-world service using both Panama and Suez Canals. Her ex-running mates the *Rangitane* and *Rangitoto* also joined the service, as the *Oriental Esmeralda* and *Oriental Carnaval* respectively.

However, after a few years it all came to an end. The world oil crisis of 1973 helped to make the service uneconomical. The *Oriental Rio* was laid up in Hong Kong during that year, and was sold to shipbreakers in Kaohsiung, Taiwan, in December. Like many another vessel, the ex-*Ruahine* had a comparatively short career. Her sea-going service lasted about 22 years, but she had served well during that time. With more favourable economics she would undoubtedly have been usefully employed for many more years.

Name: ***Ruahine*** (1951); ***Oriental Rio*** (1968)

Line: New Zealand Shipping Co. (1951-68); Chinese Maritime Trust (1968-73)

Builders: John Brown & Co., Clydebank; launched 11 December 1950, completed May 1951

Dimensions: Gross tonnage 17,851/ Length 584 ft/Beam 75.1 ft

Machinery

Engines: 2 Doxford opposed-piston diesel, twin screw, 14,200 b.h.p.

Service speed: 17 knots

Major Refits

1965 main-mast removed, alteration to accommodation
1968 Hong Kong, foremast removed, alteration to accommodation

Regular Routes

London – Wellington

Passenger Capacity

267 one class

Sister-ships

None

Photograph 1960

Sea Goddess I

THE luxury type of cruise offered by the Royal Viking Line and others encouraged more Norwegian companies to enter the cruising trade. KS/AS Norske Cruises, itself a new company, created *Sea Goddess* Cruises in the early 1980s. The purpose was to serve a very 'affluent and discriminating section of the market that had been ignored by other cruise lines seeking to attract more passengers from the mass market'.

The *Sea Goddess I* and her sister *Sea Goddess II* were built for this purpose. They are both small, 4,000-ton vessels, but are the last word in luxury. In August 1986 Sea Goddess Cruises Ltd was acquired by Cunard, and become known as Cunard Sea Goddess.

Our subject was built at the Wartsila Yard at Helsinki in Finland. She was launched in April 1984, and completed later that year. Her sister, from the same yard, followed in 1985. As can be seen, she has a somewhat similar profile to many of the larger cruise vessels built by Wartsila. With clipper bow, streamlined superstructure, and funnel aft, she is almost like a miniature Royal Viking ship. She in fact reminds one of a large private yacht, and has been described as one of the most expensively priced cruise ships ever to sail. There are five decks for passengers, ranging from the sun deck (deck 6) down to deck 2. General amenities on board include a swimming-pool, sauna, several bars and saloons, casino, outdoor cafe, gymnasium, beauty salon, hospital etc. The club salon (deck 4) is adjoined by the casino, piano bar and library. The dining saloon (deck 2) is very spacious and splendidly decorated. Pictures of this room show luxury indeed. Cabins are described as 'outside suiterooms'. A typical one has a bedroom, sitting area (convertible to private dining area) full-sized bath, television, stereo system and a private bar. There are 58 of them, the ship carrying only 116 passengers.

A unique 'tailgate' platform fitted to the stern can be lowered to enable swimming and various water sports to be undertaken from the ship. Equipment is provided for this, including a couple of speedboats. Passengers can also indulge in clay-pigeon shooting if they so desire.

The ship is propelled by two diesel engines driving twin screws. Service speed is 17.5 knots. Three diesel generators supply electrical power, and there is a bow thruster.

Their small size enables the *Sea Goddess* and her sister to visit smaller ports and remote places where the larger vessels cannot go. They often visit marinas, coves and quiet beach areas in addition to the more popular cruising venues. They can also be chartered out for private parties. Consequently they get a varied itinerary. *Sea Goddess I* has spent a good deal of time in the Mediterranean, visiting French and Italian Rivieras, Balearic Islands, Malaga, Monte Carlo, Piraeus and numerous other places. Other itineraries for the two ships have included the Caribbean, South American coast and Pacific Ocean. The *Sea Goddess I* was chartered for nearly five months from October 1986 to serve as a review and hotel ship for the America's Cup races in Perth, Australia. No doubt she and her sister have many more years of luxury cruising ahead of them.

Name: **Sea Goddess I**

Line: KS/AS Norske Cruises (1984-86); Cunard (1986-)

Builders: Wartsila Shipyard, Helsinki; launched April 1984, completed December 1984

Dimensions: Gross tonnage 4,253/Length 340 ft/Beam 47 ft

Machinery

Engines: 2 12-cylinder diesel, twin screw, 2 CP propellers, 4,800 total b.h.p.

Service speed: 17.5 knots

Passenger Capacity

116

Sister-ships

Sea Goddess II (1985)

Photograph 1988

Southern Cross

Name: **Southern Cross** (1955); **Calypso** (1973); **Azure Seas** (1980)

Line: Shaw Savill & Albion (1955-73); Ulysses (1973-80); Western Cruise (1980-90); Azure Seas inc. (1990-)

Builders: Harland & Wolff, Belfast; launched 17 August 1954, completed 1955

Dimensions: Gross tonnage 20,204/ Length 604 ft/Beam 78 ft

Machinery

Engines: 2 sets Parsons compound double reduction geared turbines, twin screw, 20,000 s.h.p.

Boilers: 3 oil-fired Yarrow watertube, 550 p.s.i., superheated to 800°F

Service speed: 20 knots

Major Refits

1973 Piraeus, reconstruction of hull, refurbishment

Regular Routes

Southampton – Curaçao – Wellington – Cape Town – Southampton

Passenger Capacity

1955: 1,160 one class

Near Sister-ships

Northern Star (1962)

Photograph 1955

THIS SHIP, as can be seen from the photograph, was of a rather revolutionary design. Until she was built it was very unusual for a passenger liner to have her engines aft. She was in fact the result of much planning and forward thinking by her owners; they had decided that passengers and cargo did not mix very well due to delays in cargo-handling and labour disputes, so a passenger-only vessel for the Australia and New Zealand service was proposed. Also, it was agreed that a round-the-world service would be more satisfactory than going outward via the Cape and back the same way, as had been the custom.

The hull had a good sheer, nicely raked and rounded stem and cruiser stern. Altogether there were eight decks for passengers. The superstructure was well proportioned, with a streamlined bridge, and the whole impression was of a sleek, elegant vessel. The usual black livery for the hull was discarded by Shaw Savill for this splendid ship. Instead it was painted light grey with a white band, while the upperworks were pale green. Since the ship carried no cargo there was plenty of space for passenger accommodation and public rooms. These included lounges, smoke room, cinema and many others. There were two swimming pools on board.

The maiden voyage went off very well indeed, and the ship was given a great reception at ports en route. She went out via Panama to Wellington and returned via Australian ports and the Cape. She joined the *Dominion Monarch* on the round-the-world service, sometimes taking a westbound route and sometimes eastbound. The advent of the new ship meant that four older vessels could be withdrawn from the service, since the *Southern Cross*'s large capacity and higher speed meant that she could cope with all likely passenger requirements.

The new ship settled down to steady, fairly uneventful voyaging. So successful was she that a few years later Shaw Savill decided on a running-mate for her to replace the *Dominion Monarch*. She was of course to be a passenger-only vessel, and was named *Northern Star*. This ship joined the round-the-world service with the *Southern Cross* in July 1962. Throughout the 1960s the ships continued in operation.

The route normally taken by the ship was from Southampton to Trinidad, Curaçao, through the Panama Canal, Tahiti, Fiji, Wellington, Auckland, Sydney, Melbourne, Fremantle, Durban, Cape Town, Las Palmas to Southampton. This voyage lasted 76 days. In her earlier years she sometimes sailed in the opposite direction.

However, during the sixties the ubiquitous jet air-liner was taking over from the passenger ships. From 1968 the *Southern Cross* and her near-sister undertook some cruising from Southampton and Sydney, in addition to their normal round-the-world passages.

The ship also did some cruises from Liverpool. However, although comfortable she was not really well suited for cruising. Her cabins had between one to six berths, and did not have private facilities, as was expected by many cruise passengers of the 1970s.

Inevitably the liner voyages had to come to an end; there was the steep rise in the cost of oil fuel and operating costs in general to contend with. It was announced in 1971, while the *Southern Cross* was on a series of cruises, that she was to be withdrawn from service. After her final voyage for Shaw Savill she was laid up in Southampton's western docks, and later, in April 1972, she moved to the river Fal in Cornwall. The company had no doubt considered the option of converting the ship to a full-time cruise liner, but had decided the cost would be too high for this to be an economical proposition.

The ship lay rusting at her mooring with only a skeleton crew on board until Shaw Savill sold her in March 1973 to Greek buyers. Her new owners were the Compania de Vapores Cerulea S A of Panama, usually known as the Ulysses Line. She was registered in Ithaca under the Greek flag and given the name of *Calypso*. She was given a very extensive refit at Piraeus, Athens, during which the entire hull was stripped and reconstructed. All cabins were refurbished and fitted with bath and toilet facilities. She started her cruising service in spring 1975, and was soon to become a familiar sight again at Southampton: 950 passengers could be carried. She sailed to the Atlantic Islands, the Baltic ports, and from Edinburgh and Rotterdam to the North Cape and the northern capitals ports that she had not visited in her liner voyaging. Mediterranean and South African cruising followed, and later Caribbean. She even went from Los Angeles up to Alaska.

The ship changed hands again in September 1980 when sold to the Panamanian flag Western Cruise Lines. Now renamed *Azure Seas*, some alterations were made by her new owners, including replacing the forward swimming-pool by a casino, but photographs show her still recognizable as the Shaw Savill *Southern Cross*. She operated short cruises from Los Angeles to Mexico. The ship remains in operation.

Spirit of London

THIS SHIP was purchased as a partially built vessel, and became the P & O Company's first 'custom-built' cruise liner. She is still afloat today, under different ownership. At that time many of the company's ships on 'line' service to Australia and the Far East also undertook cruising as well, but these had not been built with this purpose specifically in mind.

The Norwegian Caribbean Line, owned by Klosters Reederi of Oslo, had ordered a couple of 17,000-ton cruise liners to be named *Southward* and *Seaward* from the Italian shipyard Cantieri del Terreno e Riuniti, Genoa. Apparently increased construction costs caused the Norwegians to lose interest in the second vessel (*Seaward*), although they put the *Southward* into operation, and in fact she is still in service. Hence the other vessel, was purchased on the stocks by P & O, and renamed *Spirit of London*.

The naming ceremony took place on 29 April 1972, but due to weather conditions the ship could not be launched until several days later. She was delivered in October that year and set off on her maiden voyage from Southampton to San Juan in Puerto Rico on 11 November.

The hull has a well-raked 'clipper' bow with bulbous forefoot below water. It has a pronounced 'knuckle' and a modern cruiser stern. Upperworks are streamlined, with funnel placed well aft. A small radar pole above the bridge and a well-raked mast amidships makes for quite an attractive profile. There are seven decks for passengers, and accommodation and public rooms are all very good.

As would be expected, the names of some of the latter reflected the 'Spirit of London'. The 'Thames Restaurant', and 'Churchill Room' were a couple of them, while the 'Globe' theatre was situated on the 'Chelsea' deck. All amenities such as nightclubs, lounges, cinema, theatre, swimming-pool, health centre feature on board, and the ship is fully air-conditioned. Propelling machinery consists of four Fiat diesel engines single reduction geared to twin screws. These give her a service speed of 19 knots. The ship is stabilized, and also fitted with a bow thruster.

After reaching San Juan the *Spirit of London* made a couple of Caribbean cruises before sailing to San Francisco, where she arrived in January 1973. This was to be her home port, and she cruised extensively from here for many years. She visited the Mexican coast, Caribbean, Canada and Alaska and became very popular with passengers.

When P & O acquired the Los Angeles based Princess Cruises in 1974 the ship operated under this banner together with the *Island Princess*. She was then renamed *Sun Princess*.

On 30 March 1979 the *Sun Princess* was at St Thomas, Virgin Islands when the Italian *Angelina Lauro* caught fire there and burnt out. The P & O ship took on board some passengers from the unfortunate vessel.

She continued cruising through the seventies and eighties, usually spending summers in Alaska and winters in the Caribbean. She will no doubt continue operating in the nineties, although she is no longer in P & O ownership. In 1989 she was sold to Premier Cruises Ltd of the Bahamas, and has had another name-change, to *Starship Majestic*.

In July 1991 she had an outbreak of fire on board whilst on a cruise from Port Canaveral. There were no casualties. The ship arrived back a day late.

In 1991 Carnival Cruise Line Ltd took over Premier Cruises.

Name: **Spirit of London** (1972); **Sun Princess** (1974); **Starship Majestic** (1989).

Line: P & O (1972-89); Premier Cruises (1989-91); Carnival Cruiseline (1991)

Builders: Cantieri del Terreno e Riuniti, Genoa; launched April 1972, completed October 1972

Dimensions: Gross tonnage 17,370/ Length 536 ft/Beam 75 ft

Machinery

Engines: 4 Fiat 10-cylinder 4 SCSA diesel, single reduction geared, twin screw, 18,000 b.h.p.

Service speed: 19 knots

Passenger Capacity

736

Sister-ships

Southward (1971)

Photograph 1973

St. Louis

IN 1873 the American (Keystone) Line came into being. This represented an attempt by the USA to launch a transatlantic passenger-carrying company using iron steamships. Service was from Philadelphia to Liverpool. Much of the capital had come from the Pennsylvania Railway, and since Pennsylvania was the 'Keystone State', the line was often known by this name. Financial results were not too good, and in 1884 the Keystone was sold to the International Navigation Company. Later, in 1893, came a further merger with INC's new American Line which had started life as the British Inman Line. As two of its ships were British-built, Congress had to make a special dispensation to enable them to be transferred to the American register. A further stipulation was that two similar ships of about 11,500 tons were to be built in an American yard to run with them on the Atlantic route. These two ships were to become the St Louis and St Paul. Both were built at Cramp's Yard, Philadelphia. They were in fact to be the last 'express' passenger liners built in the United States until the advent of the Manhattan and Washington in the 1930s.

The St Louis was completed in May 1895 and commenced her maiden voyage from New York to Southampton on 5 June. Both ships were to the same general design and possessed the stately elegance of 'express' liners of that period. Each had a slender hull with graceful counter stern and two slender funnels.

It is interesting to note that there were enough lifeboats, including 'collapsible' ones, for the entire complement in the event of disaster. In this respect they were well ahead of their time.

In February 1898 the St Louis performed a splendid rescue service on the Atlantic. She sighted distress rockets from the Holland America Line's Veendam, which was in difficulty in heavy seas about 500 miles west of the Scillies. The 3,700-ton Dutch vessel, formerly the White Star Baltic, had struck some underwater derelict and was sinking. Despite the mountainous seas, the St Louis launched her lifeboats and succeeded in rescuing all 212 passengers and crew before the Veendam sank.

That same year the Spanish-American war broke out and the St Louis and her sister were taken over for war duties. They were both employed as armed merchant cruisers. The St Louis was fitted with small six-pounder guns, and did some very useful work with the blockading force off Cuba. One of her main tasks was destroying communications by cutting the underwater telegraph cables. While grappling for a cable off the island near Morro Castle in May 1989

she came under fire from a shore battery and six-inch shells fell around. The AMC fired back with her small guns and eventually silenced the enemy. She later came under mortar fire as well, but succeeded in cutting the cable. She cut several more cables before returning to New York for additional guns to be fitted. The ship was also present at the main battle of Santiago when the Spanish fleet was utterly defeated. The Spanish Admiral Cervera, together with many other prisoners, was taken on board the St Louis.

The war was soon over, and the St Louis, after a general refit and removal of her armament, was back again on the Atlantic service, making her first sailing from New York to Southampton in October 1898.

In 1899 the ship and her sister were both fitted with wireless installations, the brainchild of Guglielmo Marconi, but by 1903 the ship's boilers were giving trouble. She sailed from Southampton that year with these boilers in such poor condition that the crossing to New York was made at less than 10 knots. She was at once sent for reboilering. By now the ship and her running-mates were getting outdated by bigger and faster ships.

In 1913 the St Louis and St Paul were both relegated to carrying second class and third class (steerage) only. With the outbreak of war in 1914, however, the ships found themselves a new lease of life. America was neutral for the first few years, and the two US ships, with the 'Stars and Stripes' flag and their names prominently painted on their sides, continued to ply the Atlantic carrying large numbers of passengers. Their route was now New York – Liverpool, once again carrying first, second and third class passengers. After America entered the war in 1917 the St Louis once more entered naval service as an armed troop transport. She was renamed Louisville, and was able to carry around 2,000 troops. She did useful service in this role, and when the war ended reverted once more into being a passenger liner.

In January 1920, however, while undergoing a refit in a Hoboken shipyard she was accidentally set on fire. The conflagration was so serious that the ship had to be scuttled to put the flames out. Eventually refloated, her days as an Atlantic liner were over. Various ideas for employing the old-timer were mooted, including use as an exhibition ship, but these came to naught. She lay a rusty, blackened hulk at Hoboken for three years. Eventually, in May 1924, the old liner was towed away for breaking up in Italy, thus ending a long career not without incident.

Name: **St Louis**

Line: American

Builders: Cramp. Philadelphia; launched Nov 12 1894, completed May 1895

Dimensions: Gross tonnage 11,269/ Length 554 ft/Beam 63 ft

Machinery

Engines: 2 sets 6-cylinder, quadruple expansion, 20,000 i.h.p.

Boilers: 6 double-ended, 4 single-ended, 200 p.s.i.

Service speed: 18.5 knots

Major Refits

1896 Cramp's, machinery modifications, improved draughting, removal of cowl funnel tops, 20 knots
1898 conversion to AMC
1903 new boilers fitted

Regular Routes

New York – Southampton

Passenger Capacity

1st 320, 2nd 220, 3rd 800

Sister-ships

St Paul (1895)

Photograph 1914

St. Paul

THIS SHIP was the sister of the *St Louis* and was built in the same yard, Cramps of Philadelphia. She was launched in March 1895, and caused an initial problem by sticking on the ways. It was about a fortnight before she eventually took the water. Completed late that year, she began her maiden voyage from New York to Southampton on 9 October. Her speed was initially unsatisfactory, and she received treatment from the shipyard to improve it. When this had been done she settled down to successful voyaging, her performance being about the same as the *St Louis*.

During the Spanish-American War the ship became an armed merchant cruiser, and did some good work in this guise with the blockading fleet off Cuba. A British collier laden with coal for the Spaniards was captured, and she also engaged a Spanish destroyer and sloop in action.

After the war she resumed her transatlantic service. In 1899 the *St Paul* and her sister were both fitted with the new wireless apparatus produced by Marconi. The great Italian inventor was in fact on board the ship when clear contact was made with a station set up near the Needles, Isle of Wight, as she steamed up the Channel towards Southampton. This was on 15 November 1899, and communications were exchanged over a distance of some 66 miles. It was on this occasion that a newspaper was published on board the ship containing news received by wireless, and it was the first time this had ever been done at sea –, a notable achievement.

During a voyage in November 1900 the *St Paul* had the misfortune to strike a submerged object with her starboard propeller. The latter broke off, and the subsequent 'racing' of the engine severely damaged it, necessitating a shipyard visit for repairs.

The *St Paul* had new boilers fitted in 1907. Since both ships had suffered from steaming problems it would appear the original boiler installation was not particularly satisfactory. The ship's funnels were also lengthened.

On 25 April 1908 the ship was involved in a major disaster off the Isle of Wight. That year wintry conditions prevailed for a long time. It was snowing as she left Southampton, and visibility deteriorated as she approached the narrow Hurst Channel separating the Isle of Wight from the mainland. HMS *Gladiator*, a cruiser of some 5,700 tons displacement, had left Portland earlier in the day and was on her way to Portsmouth. When first observed from the *St Paul* the warship was about half a mile away. The liner altered course to starboard, sounding one short blast. To the dismay of Captain Parson, however, he saw the *Gladiator* swing to port into the liner's path. Despite last-minute evasive attempts, the big ship struck the cruiser in the region of the aft boiler room on the starboard side. (It would seem that sound signals had been misheard in the adverse weather conditions.) Badly damaged, the *Gladiator* managed to struggle into shallow water before rolling over to starboard and sinking, roughly parallel with the shore. Gallant rescue operations were carried out by the *St Paul* and soldiers from nearby Fort Victoria. Sadly, however, 27 sailors were lost from the stricken cruiser. She was eventually salvaged and then scrapped. The liner, with a badly damaged stem, had to limp back to Southampton for repairs. She was off service for some time.

Comparatively uneventful voyaging continued for several more years, and in 1913, like her sister, she ceased to carry first-class passengers, catering for second and steerage only. During much of the First World War she continued to operate on the New York – Liverpool route, but in 1918 however she was renamed *Knoxville* and was sent to a shipyard for fitting out as an armed transport for the US navy. With conversion nearly complete the ship was being manoeuvred alongside Brooklyn berth when she suddenly capsized, rolling over on her port side. This catastrophe occurred on 25 April, the tenth anniversary of the *Gladiator* disaster. Spectators gazed with amazement as the big ship slowly rolled over, masts striking the quay and snapping off like matchsticks. In a short time thousands of tons of mud had gushed through open ports on her submerged side, and soon she had settled down between two quays a problem indeed for the salvagers. The refloating operations proved difficult and prolonged, but eventually the ship was pumped out and pulled upright.

Tonnage was desperately short and passengers numerous, and the ship was reconditioned and put into service once more. By March 1920 she was again operational on the New York – Southampton route. New funnels had been fitted and she looked much the same as before, though with shorter masts. Rather surprisingly, this service ended later that year and the ship lay in idleness apart from a few odd voyages. In 1922, however, she joined with a rather mixed fleet which included the *Manchuria*, *Mongolia* and *Kroonland* in a service from New York to Hamburg. By this time, however, her machinery was becoming unreliable and uneconomic, and in the autumn of that year the old ship was honourably retired. In September 1923 she went to the breakers' yard in Germany, being broken up at Wilhelmshaven at the old German navy dockyard.

Name: **St Paul** (1895); **Knoxville** (1918) **St Paul** (1920)

Line: American

Builders: Cramp's, Philadelphia. Launched April 9 1895, completed October

Dimensions: Gross tonnage 11,629/ Length 554 ft/Beam 63 ft

Machinery

Engines: 2 sets 6-cylinder quadruple expansion, 20,000 i.h.p.

Boilers: 6 double-ended, 4 single-ended, 200 p.s.i.

Service speed: 18.5 knots

Major Refits

1896 Cramp's, machinery modifications, improved draughting, 20 knots
1907 new boilers fitted
1918 converted to troop transport but capsized

Regular Routes

New York – Southampton

Passenger Capacity

1st 320, 2nd 220, 3rd 800

Sister-ships

St Louis (1895)

Photograph 1912

Statendam

Name: **Statendam** (1957); **Rhapsody** (1982); **Regent Star** (1987)

Line: Holland America (1956-82); Paquet Cruises (1982-86); Regency Cruises (1986-90); Shining Cruises SA (1991-)

Builders: Wilton-Fijenoord, Schiedam; launched 12 June 1956, completed December 1956

Dimensions: Gross tonnage 24,294/ Length 642 ft/Beam 81 ft

Machinery

Engines: 2 sets Parsons turbines reduction geared, twin screw, 22,000 s.h.p.

Boilers: 2 oil-fired watertube, 610 p.s.i., superheated to 840°F

Service speed: 20 knots

Major Refits

1987 Piraeus, conversion to diesel propulsion, now has four Pielstick engines with flexible couplings, SR geared to screw shafts, 2 CP propellers, 21,992 b.h.p.

Regular Routes

Rotterdam — New York

Passenger Capacity

1957: 1st 84, Tourist 867
1990: 900 one class

Sister-ships

None

Photograph 1957

THIS SHIP was built as mainly a tourist class vessel for Holland America's transatlantic service. Two smaller vessels the *Ryndam* and *Maasdam*, had proved very successful in this role, and the company decided on a larger one designed on similar lines, to be used for both line voyages and cruising. The vessel was built by the Wilton-Fijenoord shipyard at Schiedam. She was 'launched' by floating her out of her building dock on 12 June 1956, but was unnamed at that time. Completed by the end of the year, she set off on her maiden voyage from Rotterdam to New York on 6 February 1957.

The hull has good sheer with a nicely raked stem. It contains four decks, and the superstructure above is well proportioned, with a streamlined funnel. Passenger accommodation was, as noted, mainly for tourists but a few first class were catered for also. Amenities on board included a theatre, gymnasium and indoor swimming pool. Propelling machinery consisted of two steam turbines driving twin screws. Service speed of this elegant vessel was 20 knots.

There were some machinery problems when the ship set off on trials in December 1956, but these were sorted out, and on her next series in January 1957 she was named by Princess Beatrix. This was done in a rather unusual way by pouring a glass of champagne over the ship's bell! This was in fact the fourth time that the name *Statendam* had been used for a Holland America liner.

The ship's maiden voyage to New York passed off satisfactorily, although she had to dock at the US port without tugs due to a tugmen's strike.

The *Statendam* now spent the summer season on normal transatlantic voyaging, while going cruising during the winter period. For the latter she operated as a one-class ship. The Caribbean was a favourite cruise area for this fine vessel, but she also did round-the-world cruising. Some of the latter voyages were lengthy ones of 110 days. By 1960 Holland America had three big liners on the transatlantic route, the *Nieuw Amsterdam*, the new *Rotterdam* and our subject in addition to smaller ships.

However, the jet aircraft soon began to make inroads into transatlantic voyaging. The *Statendam* was the first of the three to be withdrawn from this and transferred to permanent cruising. In 1966 she commenced running from the US west coast ports of San Francisco and Los Angeles. Sometimes she crossed the Pacific to Hawaian, Australian and New Zealand waters. She also proceed to Oriental ports, the Mexican coast and through the Panama Canal to the Caribbean. Later she cruised also from New York to Scandinavia, the Mediterranean, Bermuda etc.

In 1971–2 she had a big refit which further improved her amenities. She was now to be mainly on the New York cruise circuit. In 1973, in company with other Holland America ships, she was re-registered at Willemstad in Curaçao. Week long cruises from New York to Bermuda were now her main occupation. Her former running-mate the *Rotterdam* was doing similar work. During the winter months the *Statendam* usually cruised from Florida to the Caribbean.

In 1981 the ship went to Vancouver to make the ever popular summer cruises to Alaska. It seems that her machinery now began to cause a few problems requiring emergency repairs from time to time, causing delays.

In 1982 the company sold the ship to Paquet Cruises, a French-based company registered in the Bahamas. She still continued cruising in much the same areas. Now named *Rhapsody*, she also did Mexican Riviera cruises from Los Angeles. Seemingly these operations were not too successful, for in 1986 the ship was sold to the Greek-owned Regency Cruises. The ex-*Statendam* left in July that year for an extensive refit at Piraeus. This was the biggest she had ever had, and included converting her from steam to diesel propulsion. She was now named *Regent Star*, and returned to cruising service again in June 1987, mostly in the Caribbean. On 10 January 1989 she had the misfortune to strike a wreck in Santo Domingo harbour, suffering propeller damage and having to cancel several cruises.

The ship's owners became World Pioneer S.A. of Bahamas in 1990. Later in 1991 she transferred to Shining Cruises SA of Nassau.

Stefan Batory

WITH THE recovery of Dutch shipyards after the war the Holland America Company were able to plan new ships for the North Atlantic service. The service had restarted in 1946, and some well-remembered liners were back on it, such as the *Westerdam*, *Noordam* and *Veendam*. The splendid *Nieuw Amsterdam* returned to it also in 1947 after her fine war service.

The company now decided on a couple of smaller vessels catering mostly for the tourist trade. Two passenger cargo liners (to be named *Dinteldyk* and *Diemerdyk*) were laid down in 1949, but the company decided to redesign them as Atlantic passenger liners. This resulted in the *Ryndam* (ex-*Dinteldyk*) in 1951, followed by the *Maasdam* the next year. The ship was built by the Wilten-Fijenoord yard at Schiedam. She was launched on 5 April 1952, completed in July and set off on her maiden voyage from Rotterdam to New York on 11 August. The trim hull had nicely proportioned – if a trifle bulky – superstructure with a single funnel. This latter was aerodynamic in shape, known in fact as a 'Strombus Aerofoil'. Viewed from broadside it looked normal, but viewed from fore and aft it was very narrow.

The *Maasdam*'s maiden voyage was quite a lengthy one. She went from Rotterdam via Le Havre and Southampton to Montreal before proceeding to New York. Both she and her sister *Ryndam* became popular and well patronized on the North Atlantic: they offered very economic rates of travel for passengers who appreciated a leisurely voyage. Sometimes the *Maasdam* called at Cobh and/or Galway on the route to New York. While she was mostly on the New York route, her sister sailed mainly to Canada.

From 1963 the ship started her voyages from Bremerhaven with Rotterdam the first port of call. Her inaugural visit to the German port on 15 February was something of a disaster as she struck a submerged wreck in the mouth of the Weser and suffered underwater damage. Repairs had to be made at the North German Lloyd yard before she set off on her first Bremerhaven-New York voyage on 16 April.

The ship, being comparatively short and stumpy, was not a particularly good sea boat, having a propensity to pitch and roll. Fitting Denny-Brown fin stabilizers in 1965 helped matters, and her sister later received the same treatment.

By the mid-1960s North Atlantic passengers were becoming fewer, and Holland America experimented with sending the *Maasdam* and her sister on a round-the-world service, taking a somewhat similar route to that of the P & O ships. She made her first voyage in October 1965, sailing eastabout – out via Suez, returning via Panama. She kept this up until April 1968, coupled with North Atlantic sailings. She replaced the *Ryndam* on the Canadian route in October 1966, when the latter was transferred to the Europe–Canada Line, a German subsidiary of Holland America.

Not surprisingly, the round-the-world service was not really competitive with P & O and other companies, who had bigger and faster ships. In May 1968 it was announced that the *Maasdam* had been sold to Poland, as a replacement for the fine old *Batory*, now 32 years old. The Dutchman filled the bill nicely, and in October that year she was handed over and appropriately renamed *Stefan Batory*. An extensive refit at Gdansk in two stages now followed, the ship's appearance being considerably altered. The promenade deck was extended, new masts were fitted and there was much interior modification and improvement. A different, rather more attractive 'winged' funnel replaced the 'Strombus' one.

The ship now resumed transatlantic operation coupled with much cruising and proceeded to enjoy a further successful career. She had a few 'political' problems from time to time due to Poland's domestic unrest, but sailed steadily on. The route was usually Gdynia–Rotterdam–Tilbury–Montreal. Her cruising activities were very important. The Caribbean, Mediterranean, Norwegian fjords, and Atlantic Islands featured in her itinerary.

The *Stefan Batory* made her last Canadian voyage in 1987. She arrived in Montreal on 5 October and sailed on the 7. This last eastbound trip was not uneventful. Soon after embarking the Thames pilot she ran into the hurricane which caused so much damage that year. Forced to anchor, the ship dragged and lost both 'hooks', but eventually reached Tilbury landing stage escorted by tugs. After getting anchors and chain replaced she finally reached Gdynia on 21 October.

The ship was bought by Hellenic-Polish Shipping and Trading Enterprises Ltd, Piraeus (Panamanian flag). She sailed for Flushing in June 1988, and later in November sailed for Piraeus. In 1991, temporarily renamed *Las Delicias* she took part in a film. She has recently been renamed *Stefan*.

The ship is now an accommodation vessel at Gothenburg.

Name: Maasdam (1952); **Stefan Batory** (1968); **Stefan** (1989)

Line: Holland America (1952-68); Polish Ocean (1968-88); Hellenic-Polish (1988-89); Stena A/B 1989

Builders: Wilton-Fijenoord, Schiedam; launched 5 April 1952, completed July 1952

Dimensions: Gross tonnage 15,024/ Length 503 ft/Beam 69.2 ft

Machinery

Engines: 2 general electric steam turbines, double reduction geared, single screw shaft, 8,500 s.h.p.

Boilers: 2 Foster Wheeler oil-fired watertube, 525 p.s.i., superheated

Service speed: 16.5 knots

Major Refits

1965 Denny-Brown fin stabilizers fitted
1968 Gdansk, new masts and funnel, interior improvements

Regular Routes

Rotterdam – New York
Gdynia – Montreal

Passenger Capacity

1952: 1st 39, Tourist 842
1968: 1st 39, Tourist 734
1976: one class 779

Sister-ships

Ryndam (1951)

Photograph 1969

Stirling Castle

THIS ship and her sister *Athlone Castle* were built as part of the company's rebuilding programme in the 1930s. They were given reserves of speed in anticipation of a new, faster mail service. A ten-year contract was in fact signed early in 1936 whereby the voyage time from Southampton to Cape Town was to be reduced from 16 days 15 hours to not more than 14 days. This speeded-up service was to commence in 1938.

Both sisters were built by Harland and Wolff at Belfast. The *Stirling Castle* was launched on 15 August 1935, completed by January 1936 and set off on her maiden voyage on 7 February that year. As can be seen, she was a splendid, streamlined vessel. The hull had good sheer, a cruiser stern with well-raked and curved stem. Upperworks were beautifully proportioned, with a large pear-shaped funnel instead of the two smaller ones customary in previous big motorships. She was about 5,000 tons bigger than any other ship in the fleet, and was the first to be completed in the new building programme.

The ship catered for first class and cabin class (later to be known as tourist). She in fact introduced the cabin class into the Union Castle service. There were six decks for passengers, with a short sun deck above. These were lettered upward from A to F, A being the lowest.

First class were accommodated amidships, with cabin class farther aft. The usual lounges, smoke-rooms etc. were found on board this fine ship. The big first-class lounge was forward on E (promenade) deck offering splendid sea views. This deck also contained the first-class smoke room, drawing room, café, while farther aft on it was the main cabin class lounge, verandah, and open-air swimming pool. The dining saloons were on B. There was a first-class indoor swimming-pool on A. First-class staterooms and cabins were on D and C, cabin class being on C and B. All usual amenities were found on board: gymnasium, shops hospital etc. Plenty of deck space was available and accommodation and public rooms were light and airy. The *Stirling Castle* had very considerable cargo capacity, as was a requirement on the route. She had seven holds with a good deal of insulated space. Propelling machinery consisted of two Harland – B & W diesel engines driving twin screws. Service speed was 20 knots.

The new ship's maiden voyage was very satisfactory. She kept to normal scheduled time of 16½ days, and was given a good reception. At a special lunch held on board, General Smuts, the South African Prime Minister, made the formal announcement about the accelerated service soon to come into force.

The *Stirling Castle* was quick to show her paces. When sailing from Southampton on 21 August 1936 she completed the voyage to Cape Town in 13 days 6 hours 13 minutes, returning in 13 days 9 hours 31 minutes. This in fact beat the record set up by the famous *Scot* way back in 1893.

The new ship would obviously have no difficulty in keeping to the new schedule when this came into being. She was soon joined by the *Athlone Castle*. This ship was in fact the one to inaugurate the new speeded-up service in 1938.

When war came the *Stirling Castle*, like the other mail ships, was soon taken over for naval duties, being quickly converted to a troop-ship. She was ideal for this purpose, being designed for long voyages at high speed. Swiftly the ship's capacity for under 800 passengers was increased to around 5,000 personnel.

In this role the *Stirling Castle* did a fine job, and was seen in many theatres of war. For a while during this time she was fitted as an LSI(L) to carry assault craft, but her most important role was as a conventional trooper, especially on transatlantic voyaging, bringing US troops across. Sometimes she exceeded her 5,000 capacity, and on one voyage in 1943 brought 6,160 men across from New York. On another occasion she sailed as commodore ship with a convoy from Rio de Janeiro. This was the first one to leave Brazil after that country had declared war on the Axis Powers.

The *Stirling Castle* steamed over half a million miles on her war service, transporting 128,000 personnel, a fine record. She was released from duty in 1946, and soon returned to her builders at Belfast for complete reconditioning. She emerged from this looking much as before externally, but with internal improvements.

The rest of the ship's story is of steady voyaging on the Cape Run. A reliable ship, she continued on the route throughout the 1950s and much of the 1960s, a very popular vessel with passengers. She arrived back in Southampton on her last voyage from South Africa on 30 November 1965, and after a few more weeks cruising went to shipbreakers in Japan, arriving at Mihara on 3 March 1966.

Name: Stirling Castle

Line: Union Castle

Builders: Harland & Wolff, Belfast; launched 15 August 1935, completed January 1936

Dimensions: Gross tonnage 25,550/ Length 725 ft/Beam 82 ft

Machinery

Engines: 2 Harland B & W 10-cylinder diesel, twin screw, 24,000 b.h.p.

Service speed: 20 knots

Major Refits

1939 conversion to troop ship
1946 Harland & Wolff, reconditioning

Regular Routes

Southampton – Cape Town

Passenger Capacity

1936: 1st 297, Cabin 492
1947: 1st 245, Tourist 538

Sister-ships
Athlone Castle (1936)

Photograph 1958

Strathaird

THIS ship was the second of the 'Straths' to be built. She took shape at Vickers Armstrongs yard at Barrow. Launched on 18 July 1931 and completed by January 1932, the *Strathaird* set off on her maiden voyage from London to Sydney on 12 February that year.

She was a sister to the *Strathnaver* having the same raked stem and cruiser stern; her original three funnels were later reduced to one. She had six cargo holds and considerable insulated space.

Her career ran on very similar lines to the earlier vessel, steaming steadily to and from Australia, coupled with a little cruising. Like her sister, she was originally completed with three funnels, and our picture shows her in this rig.

When war came, like the *Strathnaver* she was requisitioned as a troop-ship and did fine work in this role. Early trooping was from New Zealand to the Middle East. On 13 April 1940 the *Strathaird* sailed from Australia to the Middle East in company with the regular troopships *Dunera*, *Nevasa*, *Neuralia* and *Ettrick*. All went well on this voyage, but during the course of the war the latter two ships were to be lost in 1945 and 1942 respectively.

Returning to Liverpool in late May 1940, she was being further refitted for trooping when she was dispatched hurriedly to France to assist with the evacuation. At Brest she took on board about 6,000 troops, together with civilians, children, and De Gaulle supporters. She also carried about 200 cadets from the military school at Brest. They were no doubt very glad to see the big three-funneller arrive to take them away. The ship was in a somewhat unfinished state, one of her four boilers being out of action and other services not in working order. Her only weapons for the cross-Channel trip were the machine guns and rifles of the troops. As cargo she also took on board gold from the British banks of Paris. Fortunately, all went well and the *Strathaird* arrived safely in Plymouth on 18 June.

Like the *Strathnaver*, the ship made trooping voyages to Australia, the Middle East, South Africa and India. In early 1942 she brought US troops across the Atlantic, and later that year was much involved in the North African campaign. Again like her sister, she was fitted for a while as an LSI(L).

After the defeat of Germany in May 1945 the ship was occupied in repatriating troops back to New Zealand. She had done a splendid wartime job, carrying some 129,000 personnel and steaming 387,745 miles. She had come through unscathed, though no doubt had a few near-misses from time to time. She also received some damage in collision with the *Stirling Castle* in March 1941, but was soon repaired.

The ship was returned to P & O in 1946, and underwent a refit and reconditioning at her builders at Barrow. She emerged from this with one funnel only, and re-entered the Australian service.

The *Strathaird* sailed on her first post-war voyage from London on 22 January 1948. Her cruising speed was now 17.5 knots, making her more economical to run. Later, with the advent of more modern tonnage (such as the *Himalaya*, *Arcadia*, *Iberia*) she was to be 'downgraded', becoming a one-class ship in 1954.

The *Strathaird* continued on the route, still retaining her popularity until 1961. On arrival at Tilbury on 18 June that year she was withdrawn and sold for scrapping at Hong Kong. A fine career in peace and war had come to an end.

Name: **Strathaird**

Line: P & O

Builders: Vickers Armstrongs, Barrow; launched 18 July 1931, completed January 1932

Dimensions: Gross tonnage 22,544/ Length 664 ft/Beam 80.1 ft

Machinery

Engines: turbo-electric, twin screw, 28,000 s.h.p.

Service speed: 20 knots

Major Refits

1946 Vickers Armstrongs, two funnels removed, 17.5 knots

Regular Routes

London – Sydney

Passenger Capacity

1931: 1st 498, Tourist 668
1946: 1st 573, Tourist 496
1954: 1,242 one class

Sister-ships

Strathnaver (1931)

Photograph 1934

Strathmore

THIS ship was the third 'Strath' to be built. Like all the others, she was constructed by Vickers Armstrongs at Barrow. The *Strathmore* was launched on 4 April 1935 by the Duchess of York (now the Queen Mother). Completed by September that year, she set off on her maiden voyage on 26 October.

The ship was very similar in design to the earlier 'Straths'. Of course, there were small differences in points of detail, some improvements having been made as a result of the earlier ships' operations. However, passenger accommodation, public rooms and amenities were substantially the same as on the *Strathnaver* and *Strathaird*. The main external difference, of course, was that she had one funnel only. Internally, the propelling machinery was different. P & O had used turbo-electric propulsion for the earlier two 'Straths', and also for the *Viceroy of India*. Although these installations had been satisfactory, there had apparently been no significant savings in running costs. The capital cost of turbo-electric equipment was higher than geared turbines, and the machinery had to be built by an electrical firm (British Thomson-Houston). The latter type could be constructed by the shipbuilders themselves. Consequently, this machinery was chosen for the *Strathmore* and the following two 'Straths'. Steam was provided by six watertube boilers, four large and two small. Service speed, 20 knots, was the same as for the earlier ships.

Before setting off on her first service voyage the new ship undertook a cruise to the Canary Islands. Then, although she was intended for the Australian route, her first voyages were in fact to Bombay. In 1936 she took out the new Viceroy, Lord Linlithgow, and brought back the returning one, Lord Willingdon, to Britain. On 1 October 1937 the ship made her appearance on the Australian route, sailing via Bombay, Colombo and Melbourne to Sydney. She continued on this service, interspersed with a little cruising, until the outbreak of war.

The *Strathmore* was soon requisitioned for use as a troop-ship, as were all the 'Straths' She saw service in most theatres of war in a rather similar manner to the *Strathnaver* and *Strathaird*. One of her many voyages found her in March 1941 a member of a vast convoy to the Middle East. There were 23 troop-ships in all, including all five 'Straths', the *Viceroy of India*, four Orient liners and ships of the Royal Mail, Cunard, Union Castle, CPR together with Dutch and French liners. P & O were thus well represented. When the convoy called at Table Bay harbour en route it was the largest ever to visit the port. The *Strathmore* in fact made a detour to Bombay, but eventually reached Suez. The ship spent part of her wartime service as an LSI(L) being used for amphibious operations, but mainly she did trooping. Nearing the end of the war in Europe, the ship left Bombay in April 1945 with nearly 4,000 troops on board bound for Britain. She arrived at Port Said on 'VE day', and no doubt there were celebrations on board. Later that year she left Liverpool and picked up New Zealand troops at Taranto and Suez, returning them to their homeland. A tremendous welcome awaited at Wellington. Then it was once again to Bombay to take troops back to Southampton.

The war was now over but the ship was still fully employed in repatriation work visiting Europe, the Far East, Canada, and Australia and New Zealand. She was released after completion of her final service in May 1948, and went to Vickers Armstrongs on the Tyne for refitting for P & O service once more.

On 27 October 1949 the *Strathmore* set off on her first post-war voyage to Australia. She was to carry this on successfully for the next 14 years, more or less incident-free. Some engine problems delayed her a few days in 1953, and in October 1956 she collided in the Thames estuary with a small Norwegian vessel, the *Baalbek*, but fortunately without injuries and only slight damage.

In 1961 she was converted to 'one class'. Like her sister *Stratheden*, she was periodically used for cruising, including charter sailings for the Travel Savings Association, a fairly short-lived organization.

However, on 27 October 1963 she docked for the last time at Southampton: she had been sold to the Greek shipowner John S Latsis of Piraeus. She was now renamed *Marianna Latsis* and used for occasional pilgrim voyages, such as from West Africa and Libya to Jeddah and as a hotel ship at Jeddah. In 1966 she was renamed *Henrietta Latsis*, and in 1967 was laid up in Eleusis, Greece. This fine ship went to Italian breakers at La Spezia in May 1969.

287

Name: **Strathmore** (1935); **Marianna Latsis** (1963); **Henrietta Latsis** (1966)

Line: P & O (1935-63); Latsis (1963-69)

Builders: Vickers Armstrongs, Barrow; launched 4 April 1935, completed September 1935

Dimensions: Gross tonnage 23,428/ Length 665 ft/Beam 82 ft

Machinery

Engines: 2 triple expansion Parsons turbines single reduction geared, twin screw, 28,000 s.h.p.

Boilers: 4 large 2 small Babcock & Wilcox oil-fired watertube, 450 p.s.i., superheated to 725°F

Service speed: 20 knots

Major Refits

1948 Vickers Armstrongs, Tyne, conversions to peacetime use

Regular Routes

London – Sydney

Passenger Capacity

1935: 1st 445, Tourist 665
1949: 1st 497, Tourist 487
1961: 1,200 one class

Sister-ships

Stratheden (1937), *Strathallan* (1938)

Photograph 1961

Strathnaver

Name: **Stratchnaver**

Line: P & O

Builders: Vickers Armstrongs, Barrow; launched 5 February 1931, completed September 1931

Dimensions: Gross tonnage 22,547/ Length 664 ft/Beam 80.1 ft

Machinery

Engines: Turbo-electric, twin screw, 28,000 s.h.p.

Boilers: 4 Yarrow oil-fired watertube, 425 p.s.i., superheated to 725°F

Service speed: 20 knots

Major Refits

1943 conversion to LSI
1948 Harland & Wolff, removal of dummy funnels, 17.5 knots
1934 accommodation altered to one class

Regular Routes

London — Sydney

Passenger Capacity

1931: 1st 498, Tourist 668
1948: 1st 573, Tourist 496
1954: 1,252 one class

Sister-ships

Strathaird (1932)

Photograph 1953

THE famous P & O 'Straths' were built during the period 1931–8 for the London-Australia service. The *Strathnaver* was the first, followed in chronological order by the *Strathaird, Strathmore, Stratheden* and *Strathallan.* They all had long, successful careers, with the exception of the last-named one, which was torpedoed and sunk in the Atlantic on 22 December 1942.

The *Strathnaver* was built by Vickers Armstrongs at Barrow, as indeed were all the other 'Straths'. In fact, her sister *Strathaird* was under construction at the same period, entering service a short time after.

The *Strathnaver* was launched on 5 February 1931 and completed by September that year. She set off on her maiden voyage from London to Sydney on 2 October. The 'Straths' introduced the white hulls and upperworks with buff funnels to the P & O passenger fleet. This was a break with tradition, since black hulls and funnels, with stone colour upperworks, had long been the standard rig for this old-established company. The new colour scheme was more suitable for ships plying in tropical waters. Temperatures inside the hull were reduced by several degrees.

The *Strathnaver* had an elegant profile with nicely raked stem and cruiser stern. The well-proportioned upperworks originally had three funnels, later reduced to one, as we shall note. There were in all nine decks, with passenger accommodation and public rooms on eight of them.

The ships trials were very satisfactory, and speeds in excess of 23 knots were obtained. Her maiden voyage was also a satisfactory one, sailing out to Sydney via Marseilles, Suez, Bombay, and Colombo. For the next eight years she steamed steadily to and fro, being gradually joined by the other 'Straths'. By 1939 the fortnightly Australian service was being operated by the five 'Straths' plus the *Cathay, Comorin, Maloja, Mooltan* and *Narkunda.* The *Strathnaver,* and her sister *Strathaird,* also went cruising from time to time.

When war came the *Strathnaver,* like other P & O passenger vessels, became a troop-ship. Her wartime activity ranged far and wide. She was fitted with a 6-inch and 3-inch gun and a number of smaller weapons. An early voyage was from Sydney to the Middle East with Australian troops, and in 1941 and 1942 she was much occupied with trooping to South Africa, the Middle East and India. Her relatively high speed and capability of long voyaging made her and the other 'Straths' very suitable in this role. The *Strathnaver* was much involved too in the North African campaign in late 1942. During this time she came under heavy air attack at Algiers and Bougie. She put up a spirited anti-aircraft fire as she carried on unloading, and came through this operation unscathed, but several other P & O ships were lost, including the splendid *Viceroy of India, Cathay, Narkunda,* and the regular troopship *Ettrick.*

In March 1943 the *Strathnaver* sailed as Commodore ship in a convoy to Suez, and on arrival in the Red Sea engaged in troop exercises preparing for the invasion of Sicily and Italy. The ship had been specially fitted for this as an LSI(L), carrying assault landing craft in special davits. Troops could be quickly put ashore by this method. She then sailed laden with troops, in a convoy for the invasion of Sicily. Her troops were put ashore successfully near Cape Passaro, despite attention from enemy coastal guns and aircraft. She then proceeded to Malta, having taken some casualties on board. The big ship continued her work during the Italian campaign, landing troops at various ports during this hard-fought affair. In 1944 she was trooping to the Middle East and India and was in fact retained on government service until 1948, both trooping and repatriating. During her service she steamed some 352,000 miles, transporting about 129,000 personnel.

When she was released the ship went to Harland and Wolff's yard at Belfast in November 1948 for refitting to peacetime requirements. During this refurbishment her two dummy funnels were removed and various improvements were made. The ship then reappeared with a single taller funnel as in our photograph. She resumed Australian voyaging on 5 January 1950, now with the more economical cruising speed of 17½ knots. In June 1953 the *Strathnaver* was present at the Coronation Fleet Review at Spithead; she was one of the ships taking government guests round the assembled warships. In 1954 she and her sister *Strathaird* were refitted as one-class vessels.

She continued on reliable service until in 1962, on completion of her last voyage on 23 February, she was withdrawn and went to Hong Kong breakers, arriving there at the end of March.

Titanic

THIS tragic ship, as everyone knows, was lost on her maiden voyage after colliding with an iceberg. The *Titanic* was one of three giant White Star liners built for comfort and moderate speed. She was not intended to break any records, but nevertheless could manage some 22 knots. The vessel, like her sisters, was built by Harland & Wolff at Belfast. She was launched on 31 May 1911, completed 2 April 1912 and sailed on her ill-fated maiden voyage on 10 April.

The vessel was very similar to her sister, the *Olympic*, although her accommodation was more luxurious. All this gave her a slightly greater gross tonnage than the *Olympic* and made her the largest passenger liner in the world at that time.

The ship sailed on 10 April 1912 under the command of Captain E.J. Smith. The cross-Channel run to Cherbourg was soon accomplished, and more passengers taken on board at the French port. The ship then crossed to Queenstown in Southern Ireland, anchoring off Roche's Point. Many passengers who joined here, arriving by tender, were immigrants, mostly young men and girls travelling steerage to seek a new life in America. A few passengers also left the ship here; they had elected to take passage to Ireland on the big new giant.

Leaving Queenstown, the *Titanic* steamed steadily westward. The next few days passed uneventfully, the weather was fairly calm and passengers settled down to shipboard life. Sunday 14 April found the ship still proceeding steadily westward, making about 22 knots. The fine weather still continued, the sea was smooth and there was a moderate south-westerly wind. Commencing on the 12th, a number of ice reports had been received by the ship. These became more numerous on the 14th, and contained information about icebergs seen by a number of vessels. However, the weather was still good and the big ship continued to press steadily onward, speed unabated. More ice warnings came through during the evening, including one from the Leyland line *Californian*, which was stopped at the time due to the presence of icebergs.

Altogether some seven messages were received that day, and some, including the *Californian*'s, appear not to have reached the bridge. At 11.40 p.m. the two lookouts in the crows' nest spotted an iceberg right ahead, and immediately rang the warning bell and informed the officers on watch. The ship was immediately turned to port, but it was all too late. The *Titanic* struck the iceberg a glancing blow on her starboard side, and several tons of ice fell on the well deck. A few minutes later she became stationary, as engines had been reversed, then stopped. Reports from below revealed that the first five watertight compartments had been breached. Wireless distress calls were sent out, and rockets were fired. Plenty of vessels picked up these messages, and the Cunard liner *Carpathia*, which was 58 miles away, headed rapidly towards the stricken liner.

Meanwhile lifeboats were being lowered – initially only partially full, as passengers were not unnaturally reluctant to leave the ship, not realizing that she was sinking. Later, as she sank deeper by the head, the danger became obvious and the later boats were well filled. Eventually all boats had got away, but still over 1,500 people remained on board the doomed vessel. She sank deeper and deeper, and by 2.05 am the stern started to lift clear of the water. By 2.20 she had gone. The ship stood almost vertical for perhaps 30 seconds before plunging into the depths of the ocean. The after part of the hull broke off just before the *Titanic* disappeared and the two parts sank separately to the ocean floor, about 2½ miles down.

Meanwhile the Cunard *Carpathia* was speeding towards the scene. Normally a 14-knot ship, she succeeded in working up to about 17, and managed to avoid numerous icebergs in her mercy dash. She eventually arrived in the vicinity about two hours after the *Titanic* had sunk, and at once commenced rounding up the lifeboats and taking survivors on board. Eventually the *Californian* too arrived on the scene and was told to stay in the vicinity searching for any more possible survivors.

The *Titanic* had a total of 2,206 passengers and crew on board, of whom 1,503 were lost. Two extensive enquiries were held into the cause of the disaster, one in America and one in Britain. Both came to the same general conclusion – the tragedy was due to excessive speed in the presence of ice. Various recommendations were made, including improved watertight division, supplying lookouts with binoculars (incredibly, they had none on the *Titanic*) and most important, ensuring that enough lifeboats were available to accommodate all on board.

The wreck of the *Titanic* was found on 1 September 1985 by an expedition led by Dr Robert Ballard of Woods Hole Oceanographic Institute. In 1986, using the small submersible *Alvin*, many descents were made and photographs taken. The wreck was found to be some 13½ miles east-south-east of the last position reported by the tragic ship 73 years earlier.

Name: **Titanic**

Line: White Star

Builders: Harland & Wolff, Belfast; launched 31 May 1911, completed April 1912

Dimensions: Gross tonnage 46,329/ Length 883 ft/Beam 92.5 ft

Machinery

Engines: 2 4-cylinder triple expansion, 1 exhaust steam turbine, triple screw, 46,000 total i.h.p.

Service speed: 21 knots

Passenger Capacity

1st 905, 2nd 564, 3rd 1134

Sister-ships

Olympic (1911), **Britannic** (1915)

Photograph 1912

Uganda

LIKE her sister *Kenya*, this ship was built for the BI service to East Africa. She was launched on 15 January 1952, completed in July, and set off on her maiden voyage on 2 August.

The ship's general design was similar to that of the *Kenya*. About the only noteworthy external difference was the funnel, which was taller than that of her sister.

Until 1967 the *Uganda*'s career was very similar to that of the earlier ship. She proceeded steadily to and from East Africa, calling at similar ports and providing a useful service. That year, however, she was withdrawn from the route on completion of her last voyage on 14 January. She was dispatched to the Howaldtswerke AG of Hamburg for conversion to an educational cruise ship. This involved a rather radical alteration which somewhat spoiled her 'classic' appearance. Her mainmast was removed, and her foremast shortened. Immediately aft of it was now a swimming-pool surrounded by a screened verandah with a couple of lifeboats in davits above. Farther aft the cargo holds were converted to dormitories with two-tier bunks. Fourteen well-equipped lecture rooms now featured, and the tourist-class dining-saloon had become the students' mess room in cafeteria style.

The *Uganda* sailed from Southampton on her first educational cruise to the Mediterranean on 27 February 1968 well laden with students and 'ordinary' passengers. Over the next few years many such cruises were carried out to a variety of areas. These included the Baltic, Northern capitals, Atlantic Isles, Mediterranean, and also British ports. Sometimes she operated fly-cruises when Mediterranean-based. By 1972 all BI ships had been transferred to P & O ownership, although livery remained the same. The *Uganda*'s annual overhauls were sometimes done at Marseilles or Malta. She spent a good deal of time based in the Mediterranean.

The programme continued until 1982, when the ship received a call for a different type of duty. Argentina invaded the Falkland Islands in April that year, and a British task force was despatched to the South Atlantic. The Royal Navy had no hospital ship, although the Royal Yacht *Britannia* had been intended as one in wartime. She was considered too small for such an extensive operation, however, and the *Uganda* was selected. At the time she was in Alexandria on an educational cruise, so she was ordered to Naples, where her youthful passengers disembarked and the ship sailed to Gibraltar. Here a rapid conversion to her new role took place. Much adaptation had to be done. Recreation areas, rooms and dormitories were quickly converted for casualty reception, operating theatre, intensive care unit, wards and accommodation for medical staff. A helicopter deck was fitted aft.

The ship sailed for the South Atlantic on 19 April, and arrived at the special holding ground near the Falklands on 11 May. She was in time to receive casualties from the ill-fated HMS *Sheffield*. HM Survey Vessels *Hydra*, *Herald* and *Hecla*, converted to ambulance ships, worked closely with her. They could take non-critical casualties to Montevideo for flights back to the UK The *Uganda* often moved close inshore to make it easier to take on casualties and Argentinian wounded also were treated on board. The vessel co-ordinated the work of three Argentine hospital ships, and acted as a base for the International Red Cross. She was affectionately known as NOSH (Naval Ocean Going Surgical Hospital). Although the Argentinian garrison surrendered on 14 June, casualties from booby traps and mines continued to occur.

By mid-July the *Uganda*'s work as a hospital ship was over and the red crosses on funnel and hull were painted out. She now became a troop-ship, and brought back the Gurkhas and their equipment to Southampton, arriving on 9 August to a great welcome.

The ship was now reconverted to her educational/cruise ship role by Smith Ship-repairers at North Shields. In September she sailed from Southampton to the Mediterranean well laden with students and other passengers. P & O chartered her to the Government for a period as a Falklands troop-ship, while a new landing strip was being built there. Converted back to this role by Vosper Thornycroft at Southampton, she sailed once more to the South Atlantic on 14 January 1983. Her job was transporting personnel from Ascension Island to Port Stanley, and this service lasted until April 1985. She had a much needed refit at Falmouth in late 1983. Once the new runway was complete troop-ships were no longer needed. The *Uganda* arrived back at Falmouth on 25 April 1985. Very rust-streaked, she was laid up in the river Fal looking rather a sorry sight.

Despite some attempts to preserve the ship – a *Uganda* society was formed – she was sold for demolition. Renamed *Triton*, she arrived at Kaohsiung, Taiwan, in July 1986. While anchored outside the port, she was driven ashore on 22 August in a typhoon and lay on her side, a total loss.

Name: Uganda

Line: British India (1952-72); P & O (1972-86)

Builders: Barclay Curle & Co., Stobcross, Glasgow; launched 15 January 1952, completed July 1952

Dimensions: Gross tonnage 14,430/ Length 539 ft/Beam 71.2 ft

Machinery

Engines: 2 sets Parsons triple expansion geared turbines, twin screw, 12,300 s.h.p.

Boilers: 3 Babcock & Wilcox oil-fired watertube, 450 p.s.i., superheated to 750°F

Service speed: 16 knots

Major Refits

1967 Howaldtswerke, Hamburg, conversion to educational cruise ship, 16,907 tons
1982 Gibraltar, conversion to hospital ship
1982 Smiths, North Shields, reconversion for cruising
1983 Thornycroft, Southampton, conversion to troop-ship

Regular Routes

London – East African ports

Passenger Capacity

1952: 1st 194, Tourist 103
1968: 1,224 schoolchildren

Sister-ships

Kenya (1951)

Photograph 1969

United States

THIS fine ship was in many ways the most remarkable passenger liner built this century. She had, however, the great misfortune to enter on the North Atlantic scene rather late in the day.

The vessel was built for the United States Lines with the aid of a big Government subsidy. A condition of this was a requirement that she could be taken over in the event of war and used as a troopship. Defence features were incorporated in her design and she could be rapidly converted into a military transport able to carry a fully equipped division, around 14,000 men, for 10,000 miles without refuelling.

The vessel was laid down in a thousand-foot dry dock at the Newport News Shipbuilding and Drydock Company. She was the brainchild of a noted naval architect, William Francis Gibbs, who had been much involved with several other well-known American ships. The ship was launched by filling the dry dock on 23 June 1951 and towed to her fitting-out berth. Delivered in June 1952, she set off on her maiden voyage from New York to Southampton on 3 July.

As is well shown in the photograph, she gives the impression of power and speed. The sleek hull has a well raked stem and modern type cruiser stern. Superstructure above is nicely proportioned and surmounted by two enormous funnels. A radar mast and crows nest was fitted abaft the bridge. The ship had twelve decks in all and catered for first, cabin, and tourist class passengers. Since few details about the ship's engines were available in 1952, it was usually assumed that she was about the same power as the two 'Queens' i.e. some 180,000 s.h.p. Many years later, it was revealed that her huge turbine installation could develop power in excess of 240,000 s.h.p if required. The new vessel set off for her sea trials in mid-May 1952. A minor problem arose at first – overheating in the reduction gearing – necessitating a brief return to her builders. She set out again on 9 June and carried out extensive trials well out to sea. These included an eight-hour full power run. Naval engineers were on board and results were not made public at the time but some details were revealed many years later. A top speed of 38.32 knots is stated to have been achieved with machinery developing 241,785 s.h.p. It was afterwards claimed that the big ship was capable of even greater speeds, even as much as 45 knots.

The ship then made a 'shakedown' cruise with invited guests on board and was then open for public inspection in New York. Next she set off on her maiden voyage filled to capacity with passengers.

The vessel made the passage from Ambrose to Bishop Rock in 3 days 10 hours 40 minutes, at an average of 35.59 knots. This comfortably beat the *Queen Mary's* record of 1938, by about 10 hours.

Not surprisingly, the return voyage to New York was also a record-breaking one. Her time of 3 days 19 hours 20 minutes gave an average speed of 34.48 knots. Subsequent voyages were carried out at a slightly more leisurely pace of 30–31 knots. In November that year, the ship received the Hales Trophy for the Blue Riband of the Atlantic. No other passenger liner has wrested it from her and it is unlikely that this will ever happen.

For the next few years the *United States* enjoyed great success; she became very popular, as befitted the fastest Atlantic liner, and carried about the same number of passengers as each of the 'Queens'. Cunard, of course, offered the better balanced service since the *Queen Mary* and *Queen Elizabeth* were each about the same size and speed. The running mate of the *United States*, the *America*, was much smaller and slower: on average the bigger ship would complete about 22 round voyages a year and the smaller vessel about 15. In her first four years of operation the *United States* made 89 Atlantic voyages and carried 278,000 passengers.

Often the ship's voyages terminated at Southampton but at other times she proceeded to Bremerhaven. By the early 1960s the big ship was losing money as were most of her contemporaries. In 1964 the *America* was withdrawn. US Lines entered into an agreement with the French CGT that their ship and the *France* would combine sailings so as to maintain a weekly service.

From January 1962 the *United States* had gone cruising in the off-season. These cruises were often from New York to the Caribbean, a favourite route.

Labour problems both ashore and afloat plagued the ship during the 1960s and this caused her to lose more money. She was withdrawn in 1969 and laid up. Sadly, she has not sailed since. Many schemes have been forthcoming to get this splendid vessel operational again but so far these have come to naught. The US Lines ceased passenger operations with the withdrawal of the vessel in 1969. The ship had been put up for sale on sundry occasions: her owners at present are United States Cruises Inc of Seattle.

S.A. Vaal

Name: **Transvaal Castle** (1961); **S A Vaal** (1966); **Festivale** (1978)

Line: Union Castle (1961-66); Safmarine (1966-77); Carnival Cruises (1977-)

Builders: John Brown & Co., Clydebank; launched 17 January 1961, completed December 1961

Dimensions: Gross tonnage 32,697/ Length 760 ft/Beam 90.2 ft

Machinery

Engines: 2 sets Pametrada double reduction geared turbines, twin screw, 44,000 s.h.p.

Service speed: 22.5 knots

Major Refits

1977 Kobe, conversion for cruising, extension of superstructure

Regular Routes

Southampton – Durban

Passenger Capacity

1962: 728 one class
1978: 1,432 for cruising

Sister-ships

None

Photograph 1968

THE *Transvaal Castle* was built for the Union Castle Mail route to South Africa, being constructed at the yard of John Brown & Co., Clydebank. Launched on 17 January 1961, the ship was completed by December that year and sailed on her maiden voyage from Southampton to Durban on 18 January 1962.

The vessel as built had an attractive profile. The hull had a nicely raked stem with bulbous forefoot below. Upperworks were well proportioned, mainly grouped amidships with a rather pleasing funnel. Passenger accommodation and public rooms were on six of the ship's decks. Reading downward, these were: observation, promenade or recreation, and decks A to D. The shorter ones above contained officers' accommodation. The ship was known as a 'hotel class' vessel, the public rooms being common to all passengers. Fares varied with the type of cabin chosen, varying from a suite to a four-berth one. Main public rooms were on the promenade or recreation deck, and included the big Assembly Room decorated in pastel shades, smoke-room, writing-room, orangery and golden room (Verandah Cafe). The swimming-pool was also on this deck. The usual amenities – cinema, shop, hairdressing salons, beauty parlour and hospital – were found on board. The ship had a gymnasium and plenty of deck space for recreation. The large dining saloon was on C deck, and contained fine murals depicting a South African homestead. The ship was air-conditioned throughout.

The *Transvaal Castle* had a large cargo capacity, with seven holds and much insulation space for perishable goods. Cargo-handling equipment included an electrically operated traversing deck crane forward, with a couple of 10-ton derricks after. There was also a garage for passengers' cars.

The new ship soon settled down to regular mail-ship operation, steaming steadily to and fro. Voyage time from Southampton to Cape Town was 13½ days. Her running-mates in the fleet included the *Edinburgh, Windsor, Stirling, Pretoria, Capetown, Pendennis, Athlone* and *Carnarvon Castles*. The last named was withdrawn later in 1962 after completing 36 years of service.

In January 1966 the *Transvaal Castle* was transferred to the South African Marine Corporation (Safmarine) and renamed *S.A. Vaal*. She continued to fly the British flag until 1969, when the South African one was hoisted. The vessel continued on the mail run, and was equipped with special tanks to enable her to bring South African wine to Southampton.

For much of the seventies the 'Cape Run' continued, but the mail and passenger service which had been in operation for so long was coming to an end. The aeroplane and containerization had taken over.

The *S.A. Vaal* made her final mail and passenger sailing in 1977, when she arrived at Southampton on 10 October for the last time. On 29 October she set off for Kobe, Japan, to be converted for cruising. She had been sold to the Festivale Maritime Corporation, an American concern who operate Carnival Cruise Lines Inc. They provide cruising from Miami to the Caribbean, and also along the Mexican coast.

After extensive refitting the ship was renamed *Festivale* and was recommissioned in the autumn of 1978. In her new guise she is still recognizable as the former *S.A. Vaal*. Gone are the deck crane and derricks and the superstructure has been considerably extended both fore and aft. She has a bow thruster to aid manoeuvrability. The ship now cruises in the above-mentioned areas, and over the years has become a very popular vessel.

Warwick Castle

THIS ship was built by Harland and Wolff at Belfast for Union Castle's mail service to South Africa. She was a near sister of the *Winchester Castle*. The ship was launched on 29 April 1930, completed by January 1931, and set off on her maiden voyage from Southampton to Cape Town on the 30th of that month.

The ship was generally very similar to her sister. Like the *Winchester Castle*, her hull contained four decks with straight stem and cruiser stern. Well-proportioned superstructure above had two 'motorship' squat funnels on top. The ship catered for first, second and third class.

The *Warwick Castle* motored steadily to and fro on the Cape Run at a fairly modest 16 knots during her first years on the route. In July 1935 she was present at the Silver Jubilee Fleet Review at Spithead. When the time came for 'speeding up' the service she went back to Harland and Wolff in 1938 for fitment of more powerful machinery. She emerged from this treatment looking very much like her sister. Now with one large funnel in place of the two squat ones, the ship could achieve 20 knots.

At the outbreak of war the *Warwick Castle*, like many other liners, was taken over for trooping. She was well suited for this, now having a useful turn of speed.

The ship served well in this role during the early part of the war. In the North African landings in 1942 Union Castle were well represented. The *Winchester Castle, Durban Castle, Llangibby Castle* and *Warwick Castle* were all involved in this great campaign. The latter had in fact earlier in the year left Java just as the Japanese moved in – a lucky escape. With a full load of American troops on board she was now destined for the assault on Oran. This mission was successfully accomplished, and a few days later the troop-ships returned to Gibraltar. They sailed in a homeward convoy from there on 12 November. There was rough weather in the Atlantic, and the escorting destroyers were finding things very difficult. On the morning of Saturday 14 November the *Warwick Castle* was torpedoed, when about 200 miles off the coast of Portugal, by U-413. Seas were very rough at the time, and rescue operations difficult. The ship sank about one and a half hours after being attacked, and despite valiant efforts 63 lives were lost.

The *Warwick Castle* was one of thirteen Union Castle ships lost during the war.

Name: **Warwick Castle**

Line: Union Castle

Builders: Harland & Wolff, Belfast; launched 29 April 1930, completed January 1931

Dimensions: Gross tonnage 20,445/ Length 677 ft/Beam 75.5 ft

Machinery

Engines: 2 sets 8-cylinder 4-stroke diesel, twin screw, 13,800 b.h.p.

Service speed: 15 knots

Major Refits

1938 Harland & Wolff, 2 sets 10-cylinder 2-stroke diesel engines, 26,000 b.h.p., 1 funnel, 20 knots

Regular Routes

Southampton – Cape Town and South African ports

Passenger Capacity

1931: 1st 260, 2nd 245, 3rd 254
1938: 1st 262, 2nd 228, Tourist 209

Near-Sister-ships

Winchester Castle (1930)

Photograph 1931

Warwick Castle

THIS fine ship was originally built for Union Castle's intermediate and Round-Africa service. Launched at Harland and Wolff's yard, Belfast, on 12 October 1938, she was completed by April the following year and set off on her maiden voyage from London round Africa on the 20th of that month.

She was a good-looking vessel. The hull had a raked stem and cruiser stern. It contained three complete decks and a partial one, and there were nine main bulkheads. The superstructure above was well proportioned, with a single large funnel on top. Two classes of passengers were carried, first class and tourist, in a good standard of accommodation. The ship had a large cargo capacity too, with five holds and tween decks, two forward and three aft. A good deal of space was insulated for carrying refrigerated produce such as fruit. Propelling machinery consisted of two diesel engines driving twin screws. The ship had the respectable service speed of 18½ knots.

The *Pretoria Castle* joined her sister *Durban Castle*, which had entered the service a few months earlier. Although intermediate ships, they were intended also to run on the mail service when required. For this purpose they had been given sufficient tonnage and high enough speed to replace temporarily a mail ship which was being refitted or otherwise out of action. The earlier, somewhat smaller intermediates *Dunvegan Castle* and *Dunnottar Castle* of 1936 had also been built with this in mind. They had proved to be very successful vessels.

The *Pretoria Castle* had only made a couple of voyages when war broke out. She was taken over for conversion at Belfast to an armed merchant cruiser. The ship was given an armament of eight 6-inch guns and a couple of twelve pounder anti-aircraft weapons. In November 1939 HMS *Pretoria Castle* took station in the South Atlantic, based on Freetown.

Her work as an AMC involved convoy escort duty, coupled with long periods of patrolling; other members of the Union Castle fleet were similarly employed. These included the above-mentioned intermediates *Dunvegan Castle* and *Dunnottar Castle* and the mailship *Carnarvon Castle*. The first-named was sunk in 1940, but the others survived the war.

In December 1940 the German pocket battleship *Admiral Scheer* was ranging around in the South Atlantic, sinking many ships. HMS *Pretoria Castle* and several other warships, including the cruisers *Neptune*, *Dorsetshire*, *Dragon* and the aircraft-carrier *Hermes*, made an extensive search for the enemy. She eluded them, however, and spent a few more months in the South Atlantic and Indian Oceans sinking more ships.

In the summer of 1941 the *Pretoria Castle* was equipped with a catapult, crane and a couple of Fairey 'Seafox' float planes. These were for reconnaissance use and proved most useful, although hoisting them back on board was sometimes a tricky operation.

Later in the war, however, the need for AMC's diminished. In July 1942 the ship was purchased by the Admiralty and converted into an escort carrier. This was done at Swan Hunter's yard, the ship's superstructure being cut away and a flight deck fitted. The vessel was now completely unrecognizable as a former passenger liner. She now had a small 'island' bridge on her starboard side.

Her 6-inch guns had been removed, and she carried four 4-inch AA guns, sixteen two-pounder and twenty 20 m/m AA weapons. She had a capacity for fifteen aircraft. For the rest of the war, commencing in March 1943, she was used for training purposes to enable pilots to practise deck landings. HMS *Pretoria Castle* was released from government duty in January 1946 and became a Union Castle liner once again. She was converted back to her original build by Harland and Wolff. Our Photograph shows her thus, virtually identical to her 1939 appearance.

She was now renamed *Warwick Castle*, since her original name was to be used for a new mailship soon to enter service. The rejuvenated vessel now served on the mail service, while some of the mail fleet were being refitted after their various wartime duties. She made her first post-war sailing in March 1947 and continued on the run from Southampton until 1950. The ship then reverted once more to London and her pre-war intermediate route round Africa. Throughout the 1950s and early sixties the *Warwick Castle* continued reliably on this run. During most of this time the service was in full swing, operated by six ships. The *Warwick Castle*, *Dunnottar Castle* and *Kenya Castle* usually went out via Suez and returned via the west coast. The other three, *Durban Castle*, *Rhodesia Castle* and *Braemar Castle*, proceeded in the opposite direction. Another vessel, the *Bloemfontein Castle*, was on the London-Beira route.

The *Warwick Castle*'s last arrival in London was on 1 June 1962. By this time the intermediate service was in decline, or she would probably have survived longer. The ship was sold to Spanish breakers, and arrived at Barcelona in July that year for demolition. The famous round-Africa service had ceased by 1967.

Name: **Pretoria Castle** (1939); **Warwick Castle** (1946)

Line: Union Castle

Builders: Harland & Wolff, Belfast; launched 12 October 1938, completed April 1939

Dimensions: Gross tonnage 17,392/ Length 594 ft/Beam 76.1 ft

Machinery

Engines: 2 Harland B & W diesel, twin screw

Service speed: 18.5 knots

Major Refits

1939 Harland & Wolff, conversion to AMC
1942 Swan Hunter, conversion to escort carrier
1946 Harland & Wolff, reconversion to passenger liner

Regular Routes

London — Round Africa

Passenger Capacity

1939: 1st 220, Tourist 335
1947: 1st 180, Tourist 359

Sister-ships

Durban Castle (1939)

Photograph 1950

Willemstad

Name: Socrates (1938); **Willemstad** (1950); **Moor B** (1967)

Line: Royal Netherlands Steamship Co. (1938-67); Saudi Lines (1967-73)

Builders: Van der Giessen, Krimpen; completed 1938

Dimensions: Gross tonnage originally 3,000/Length 378 ft/Beam 50 ft

Machinery

Engines: 1 Stork 7-cylinder diesel, single screw, 3,400 s.h.p.

Service speed: 14.5 knots

Major Refits

1950 Netherlands Shipbuilding, Amsterdam, conversion to passenger/cargo liner, 5,088 tons

Regular Routes

Amsterdam – Surinam

Passenger Capacity

94 one class, 64 group accommodation

Sister-ships

Pericles (1938) (later Orangestad)

Photograph 1963

THIS small ship together with her sister *Oranjestad*, started life in 1938 as a conventional cargo vessel. They were built by the Dutch shipyard of Van der Giessen at Krimpen, Holland.

The *Willemstad* was originally named *Socrates*, and her sister *Pericles*. In their original guise they were of about 3,000 gross tons. They had a rather short, stumpy superstructure and four masts.

The Royal Netherlands Company, often referred to as KNSM, the initials of its Dutch name, provided services to the Caribbean and South America, in addition to several others. It suffered heavy war losses, and to augment its passenger/cargo fleet decided to rebuild the two ships mentioned above, giving them passenger accommodation. The *Willemstad* then appeared as in our photograph, with considerably increased tonnage, more extensive upperworks and a rather more attractive appearance. Her hull had a nicely raked bow, good sheer and cruiser stern. It contained two decks and a shade deck, and superstructure above was nicely proportioned with a stumpy 'motorship' funnel on top.

The ship carried a comparatively small number of passengers in one class. There was also some 'group' accommodation for troops, students etc. Public rooms were very good. The dining saloon was air-conditioned. There was considerable cargo capacity, as well, worked by derricks. Propelling machinery consisted of a diesel engine driving a single screw. Service speed was a modest 14½ knots. The *Oranjestad* was very similar to her sister, and both became popular vessels. They ran on the service from Holland to Surinam, a pleasant, leisurely voyage. The route usually followed was Amsterdam – Southampton – Pointe à Pitre (Leeward Islands) – Fort de France (Martinique) – Bridgetown (Barbados) – Port of Spain (Trinidad) – Paramaibo (Surinam) – Georgetown (Guyana), then returning to Plymouth and Amsterdam. Sometimes a call was made at Funchal (Madeira). This round voyage took about 38 days. Most passengers were of course proceeding to their destination in the Caribbean or South America, but some also made the round voyage as a very enjoyable cruise. The atmosphere on board was pleasantly informal.

Sometimes the ports of call varied a little, but the *Willemstad* and her sister motored steadily on the route for about 15 years. They were comparatively small vessels, but had a high reputation. By the mid – 1960s the passenger and cargo requirements had changed and the newer *Oranje Nassau* was switched to the Surinam route. The *Willemstad* for a short while carried out cruising from Amsterdam and Southampton to Madeira. In 1967 both she and the *Oranjestad* were sold to Saudi Lines, Saudi Arabia, for use as pilgrim ships. The *Willemstad* was renamed *Moor B* and her sister became the *Miriam B*. Several more years of service in this role followed. In July 1973 the ex-*Willemstad* was sold to Taiwan shipbreakers and her sister followed the next year. Both ships therefore had long useful careers.

Winchester Castle

THE *Winchester Castle* was an improved version of the *Carnarvon Castle* of 1926, the first of the Union Castle mail liners to be propelled by diesel machinery. A typical motor liner of her day, she had a cruiser stern, compact upperworks not rounded at the forward end and a straight stem. A large cargo capacity was required, especially for the export of South African fruit. The *Winchester Castle* had seven cargo holds, and her refrigerated capacity was some 216,000 cubic feet.

She set off on her maiden voyage to Cape Town on 24 October 1930. This was performed satisfactorily, and the ship then settled down as a member of the mail fleet, sailing regularly on the 'Cape Run'. In 1936 a new mail agreement was signed which required the service to be speeded up. In the case of the *Winchester Castle* this involved replacing her original 4-stroke diesel engines with 2-stroke cycle ones of much greater power. Her hull lines were found to be satisfactory for the increased speed and her straight stem was retained. However, her two rather squat funnels were replaced by a single one which rather improved her appearance. She now had a service speed of 20 knots, and this had been achieved by nearly doubling her original power.

The *Winchester Castle* was the last of the mail ships to be returned to service after the re-engining programme, but she was not on the run for long. Like many other liners, she was requisitioned for war service as a troop-ship, and did good work in this role. However, she was soon to be used for somewhat different purposes. Early in 1941, after returning from a long trooping voyage to Bombay, she was adapted on the Clyde for use as an assault training ship. Her davits now supported landing craft assault boats (LCAs), and she carried fourteen of them. She now proceeded up to Loch Fyne, and from here and elsewhere in the region the Royal Marines carried out their assault training with the LCAs on remote Scottish shores.

In March 1942 the *Winchester Castle* and other LSIs embarked a large detachment of Commandos, and joined a great troop convoy. Their destination was Madagascar. Since Japan had entered the war in December 1941, this island had become of strategic importance. It would be a good base for enemy submarines. The Governor there was known to be pro-Vichy, and it was essential for the Allies to occupy the island to deny the fine port of Diego Suarez to the enemy. The troop convoy sailed on 23 March, heavily escorted and accompanied by the battleship HMS *Ramillies*.

The vessels destined for the Madagascar operation arrived in Durban on 22 April and sailed again a few days later, the slower supply ships on 25 April and the *Winchester Castle* and other LSIs with their assault troops on the 28th. The final ninety miles or so to the selected anchorage off the north coast of the island for the assault were made in almost complete darkness. This was hazardous for the big LSIs and attendant forces, since reefs abounded. However, all went well and in the early hours of 5 May the LCAs were successfully launched and, laden with troops, moved ashore to three selected beaches. Little opposition was met, and by 6.30 am some 2,000 troops were ashore. Later some stubborn defence was met from the French garrison in one or two places, but by 7 May Diego Suarez had been completely occupied. The *Winchester Castle* and the other vessels were now able to enter the harbour.

The conquest of the rest of Madagascar then proceeded without too much opposition during the next few months.

The *Winchester Castle* with other vessels later fetched some African troops from Mombasa to the island. She then embarked her original assault troops again and took them to Bombay, where they took part in the Burmese campaign. The ship herself then made the long voyage to New York, where she was overhauled before bringing a contingent of American troops to Britain. In November 1942 the *Winchester Castle* was much involved with the North African landings, successfully landing her troops off Algiers in spite of enemy air attacks. In July 1943 the ship was in the Mediterranean landing troops for the invasion of Sicily and later the landings at Anzio and Salerno in Italy.

The war eventually ended and the ship could once again get back to peacetime voyaging. After her release from government service in 1946 she became an emigrant ship taking settlers out to South Africa. In 1948 she returned to Harland and Wolff for a much-needed refit. Considerable alteration was made to her accommodation.

The ship returned to the mail run in September 1949 and continued steadily in service throughout the next decade. On 31 January 1956 Union Castle combined with Clan Line to form British and Commonwealth Shipping Co. Ltd. The advent of the new *Windsor Castle* in 1960 meant that the career of the *Winchester Castle* was now at an end. She completed her final mail voyage on 23 September and was then sold to Japanese breakers, where she arrived on 5 November.

Name: Winchester Castle

Line: Union Castle

Builders: Harland & Wolff, Belfast; completed 1930

Dimensions: Gross tonnage 20,109/ Length 637 ft/Beam 75.5 ft

Machinery

Engines: 2 sets 8-cylinder 4-stroke double acting air injection diesel, 13,800 s.h.p.

Service speed: 16 knots

Major Refits

1938 2 sets 10-cylinder 2-stroke double acting diesel engines, 26,000 s.h.p., one funnel removed, 20 knots
1948 Harland & Wolff, alteration to accommodation

Regular Routes

Southampton – Cape Town and South African ports

Passenger Capacity

1930: 1st 259, 2nd 243, 3rd 254
1948: 1st 189, Tourist 398

Near-Sister-ship
Warwick Castle (1931)

Photograph 1935

Windhuk

THIS ship was built at the Blohm and Voss yard at Hamburg for the German East Africa Line. Launched on 21 August 1936, she was completed by March 1937 and set off on her maiden voyage from Hamburg to Cape Town on 12 April that year.

The *Windhuk* was practically identical to her sister *Pretoria*. The latter ship's photograph depicts her as a troopship late in her career, but the *Windhuk* is shown in DOAL colours, and very attractive she looked. Like her sister, the ship continued on the African service until the outbreak of war in 1939. At that time she was at Lobito in Angola, and it was deemed inadvisable for her to proceed back to Germany. On 16 November 1939 she sailed for South America, disguising herself as the Japanese vessel *Santos Maru*. (This cannot have been very effective. The Japanese ship, built in 1925 was of only some 7,000 tons and was single-funnelled!) However, the *Windhuk* arrived safely at the Brazilian port of Santos on 7 December and remained laid up until seized by the country's government in January 1942. In May that year she was sold to America, and eventually blossomed forth as the US armed transport A P 74 named *Le Jeune*. She was extensively refitted, and eventually could accommodate 4,660 troops, more than nine times her peacetime passenger capacity. Armament consisted of a 5-inch and four 3-inch guns, together with eight 40 mm weapons. Now with only one funnel (the after one had been removed) and with numerous liferafts adorning her sides amidships, she looked every bit a ship of war.

She performed trooping duties very satisfactorily for the rest of the war and for some years afterwards. However, in early 1948 she was laid up, as were many other vessels at that time.

The rest of this fine ship's story is rather a sad anticlimax. Unlike her sister *Pretoria*, which had a seagoing life of over fifty years, the ex-*Windhuk* remained inactive. Handed over to the US Maritime Commission in 1957, she remained laid-up until sold for scrapping in 1966. Her career was thus not a very satisfactory one.

Windsor Castle

THIS ship was practically identical to her sister *Arundel Castle*. She was built at the famous shipyard of John Brown and Company at Clydebank, and the vessel had the distinction of being launched on 9 March 1921 by HRH the Prince of Wales, later to become King Edward VIII. Completed in March 1922, the ship set off on her maiden voyage from Southampton to Cape Town in April that year.

The ship was very similar to the *Arundel Castle*. About the only external difference were the two tall ventilators forward of the bridge, which were lacking in the *Windsor Castle*.

In general both ships were enthusiastically accepted by the travelling public as being a great advance on previous mail vessels. There were a few criticisms, however. Coal-firing was a bit outdated, as were the compound turbines fitted. 'Astern' power was rather limited, and caused a few headaches with the pilots who had to manoeuvre the ships in confined waters. By all accounts both ships were rather awkward to steer as well. The uptakes from the boilers passed through several public rooms, a rather unfortunate feature while the 'gantry' arrangement aft was criticized also. Admittedly it was proved capable of launching from either side of the ship all of the dozen lifeboats clustered nearby, but this was found to take a very long time. In an emergency the ship might well have sunk before all these could be got away! (There were of course plenty of other lifeboats as well.)

However, none of the above could be called very major problems, and the ship soon settled down to steady voyaging. Together with her sister, she steamed steadily to and fro at 16 knots or so. Unspectacular, perhaps, but good, reliable service. This was to continue for many years. Occasionally, it seems, passengers were 'roped in' to assist the stokers in shovelling coal into the hungry furnaces! In 1935 the ship had to make a detour to Lobito to pick up Prince George (later to become the Duke of Kent) who had completed a tour of Angola. To make up for lost time passengers helped with the stoking, even the Prince is said to have lent a royal hand to feeding the fires!

The *Windsor Castle* underwent the same reconstruction and re-engining as her sister. This work was completed in 1937, and after it both ships still looked very much alike. They could now steam at 20 knots.

When war came the two vessels were quickly requisitioned for use as troop-ships and operated world-wide in this role. The *Windsor Castle* had an unpleasant experience in November 1940 when she was attacked by a Focke-Wulf 'Condor' off the Irish coast. Her anti-aircraft gunners put up a spirited defence, and although several bombs were dropped, only one hit the ship. Fortunately, this failed to explode, and the vessel reached Greenock where the bomb was safely removed.

The ship continued her most useful trooping work during 1941 and 1942, but on 23 March 1943 this fine ex-mail liner's luck run out. She was in convoy some 110 miles north-west of Algiers, bringing troops for the Tunisian campaign. It was a moonlit night when a German torpedo bomber appeared and dropped a deadly 'tin fish' which scored a direct hit. The ship's engine-room and some holds were soon flooded, but she remained afloat, which enabled destroyers and other craft to take off the 2,000 or so troops on board. Eventually only Captain J.C. Brown and a handful of crew remained on the ship, hoping the damaged vessel could be towed into port. The situation worsened later, and all were taken off, but, the stoutly built ship still remained afloat and later on more naval vessels appeared on the scene, hoping to arrange a tow. Indeed, the captain and other personnel went on board again but had to leave quickly as the ship began to sink by the stern. She soon made her final plunge.

The name *Windsor Castle* was reintroduced to the Union Castle fleet in 1960 with the advent of the new 37,000-ton flagship.

Name: Windsor Castle

Line: Union Castle

Builders: John Brown & Co., Clydebank; launched 9 March 1921, completed March 1922

Dimensions: Gross tonnage 18,967/ Length 661 ft/Beam 72.5 ft

Machinery

Engines: compound single reduction geared turbines, 15,000 total s.h.p., twin screw

Boilers: 9 double-ended, 2 single-ended Scotch, 220 p.s.i.

Service speed: 17 knots

Major Refits

1937 2 triple expansion Parsons single reduction geared turbines, 4 Babcock-Johnson watertube boilers, 425 p.s.i., 19,141 tons, 686 × 72.5 ft, 20 knots

Regular Routes

Southampton — Cape Town and South African ports

Passenger Capacity

1922: 1st 235, 2nd 360, 3rd 275
1937: 1st 219, 2nd 191, Tourist 194

Sister-ships

Arundel Castle (1921)

Photograph 1922

Windsor Castle

THIS fine vessel was the largest passenger liner ever owned by Union Castle. She was built by Cammell Laird of Birkenhead. Launched on 23 June 1959 by the Queen Mother and completed in June 1960, the ship set off on her maiden voyage from Southampton to Durban on 18 August that year.

She was a fine-looking vessel, as can be seen in the picture, with a nicely shaped hull with raked stem and well-proportioned upperworks. There were eight decks for passengers' use, comprising bridge, boat, and promenade ones and decks A to E. Above was accommodation for captain and officers, radio room etc. First class and tourist were carried, and the promenade deck contained most first-class public rooms. The splendid lounge was right forward here, and there were also a smoke room, drawing-room, library, veranda café and a swimming-pool. First-class cabins were on A, B and C decks. Their dining saloon was on D, as was the tourist one. Most other tourist rooms were on A deck, including lounge, library and writing-room, smoke-room and verandah cafe. Their swimming-pool was also here, while tourist cabins were on B, C, D, and E decks.

All amenities featured on this fine vessel such as hairdressing salons, shops, gymnasium, cinema, beauty parlour, hospital, while one unique facility on board was a health spa. There was plenty of deck space for recreation, and the ship was fully air-conditioned. Cargo capacity was very considerable with seven holds and much refrigerated capacity for fruit cargoes. Handling was served by a deck crane forward and a couple of derricks aft. A garage for passengers' cars also featured.

Propelling machinery consisted of double reduction geared turbines driving twin screws. Service speed was 22.5 knots and steam was supplied by three watertube boilers. The ship was fitted with Denny-Brown fin stabilizers.

A preliminary short cruise to the Scottish islands and Rotterdam had to be cancelled due to strike problems but the ship's maiden voyage was very successful. She soon became a most popular vessel on the route, as befitted the flagship of the fleet. Scheduled time for the voyage out was 13½ days, but the ship was capable of doing it in 11½.

She continued reliably on the Cape run for seventeen years. However, in 1977 the passenger and mail service to the Cape ceased.

The *Windsor Castle* in fact made the last outward sailing by a Union Castle passenger liner in August 1977, and on 6 September she made her last departure from Cape Town. She was given a tremendous send-off. It was in fact her 124th voyage on the Cape Run. This service had lasted for 120 years.

The *Windsor Castle* was now sold to the Latsis Group, a Greek shipping concern. She left Southampton for the very last time on 3 October 1977, flying the Greek flag, and with her funnel now painted yellow with a black top. With the name *Margarita L*, she has become a hotel ship-cum-floating leisure centre moored at Jeddah, Saudi Arabia. Her cabins, which in her seagoing days were full of passengers going to South Africa, are now occupied by construction workers.

Name: **Windsor Castle** (1960); **Margarita L** (1977)

Line: Union Castle (1960-77); Latsis (1977-)

Builders: Cammell Laird, Birkenhead; launched 23 June 1959, completed June 1960

Dimensions: Gross tonnage 37,640/ Length 783 ft/Beam 93 ft

Machinery

Engines: 2 sets Pametrada turbines, double reduction geared, twin screw, 49,000 s.h.p.

Boilers: 3 oil-fired watertube, 600 p.s.i., superheated to 950°F

Service speed: 22.5 knots

Regular Routes

Southampton — Cape Town and South African ports

Passenger Capacity

1st 191, Tourist 591

Sister-ships

None

Photograph 1960

List of Shipping Lines, with ships featured

AMERICAN: *St Louis, St Paul*

AMERICAN MERCHANT LINES: *American Banker*

AROSA: *Arosa Kulm*

ASTROGUARDA CIA NAV: *Jan*

BERNSTEIN RED STAR: *Pennland*

BIBBY: *Lancashire*

BLUE FUNNEL: *Empire Orwell*

BLUE STAR: *Arandora Star*

BREMEN-AMERICA: *Berlin*

BRITISH INDIA: *Dilwara, Empire Trooper, Kenya (1930), Kenya (1951), Neuralia, Nevasa, Uganda*

CANADIAN PACIFIC: *Empress of Australia, Empress of Britain, Empress of Japan, Empress of Scotland, Montrose*

CARNIVAL CRUISES: *Festivale*

CASTLE LINE: *Braemar Castle, Carisbrook Castle*

CHANDRIS: *Australis, Ellinis, Queen Frederica, Regina Magna*

CHINA NAVIGATION COMPANY: *Kuala Lumpur*

CHINESE MARITIME TRUST: *Oriental Rio*

CIA TRANSOCEANICA ARGENTINA: *Juan de Garay*

COMPAGNIE DE NAVIGATION SUD ATLANTIQUE: *Pasteur*

COMPAGNIE GÉNÉRALE TRANSATLANTIQUE: *Antilles, France (1912), France (1961), Liberté, Normandie*

COMPAGNIE MARITIME BELGE: *Jadotville*

COMPANIA TRANSATLANTICA ESPAÑOLA: *Begoña, Reina Maria Cristina*

COSULICH: *Gaa*

CUNARD: *Andania, Aquitania, Ascania, Ausonia, Berengaria, Carinthia, Carmania, Caronia, Empire Waveney, Ivernia, Lusitania, Mauretania (1907), Mauretania (1939), Parthia, Queen Elizabeth, Queen Elizabeth 2, Queen Mary, Sea Goddess I*

DEUTSCHE OST-AFRIKA: *Pretoria, Windhuk*

EASTERN & AUSTRALIAN SHIPPING COMPANY: *Aramac*

EUROPE AUSTRALIA: *Brittany*

FLAGSHIP CRUISES: *Sea Venture*

FLOTTO LAURO: *Angelina Lauro*

FURNESS WITHY: *Monarch of Bermuda*

GDYNIA AMERICA: *Batory*

GREEK: *Arkadia, Lakonia, Neptunia*

HAMBURG AMERICA: *Albert Ballin, Bismarck, Deutschland, Fürst Bismarck, Hamburg, Imperator, Kaiserin Auguste Victoria, Milwaukee, New York, Orinoco, President Grant, Reliance, Resolute, Tirpitz, Vaterland, William O'Swald*

HAMBURG ATLANTIC: *Hanseatic*

HAMBURG SOUTH AMERICA: *Cap Polonio, Cap Norte*

HELLENIC-POLISH: *Stefan*

HOLLAND AFRICA: *Oranjefontein, Randfontein*

HOLLAND AMERICA: *Maasdam, Nieuw Amsterdam, Pennland, Rotterdam, Statendam*

HOME LINES: *Atlantic*

KINVARRA BAY: *Sindbad*

KS/AS NORSKE CRUISES: *Sea Goddess I*

LATSIS: *Margarita Latsis, Marianna Latsis*

LLOYD TRIESTINO: *Gradisca, Lombardia*

MATSON NAVIGATION COMPANY: *Lurline, Matsonia*

NEDERLAND: *Johan de Witt, Johan van Oldenbarnevelt, Jan Pieterszoon Coen, Oranje*

NEW ZEALAND SHIPPING COMPANY: *Rangitane, Remuera, Ruahine*

NOEL SHIPPING: *Starship Majestic*

NORDDEUTSCHER LLOYD: *Bremen (1929), Bremen (1939), Columbus, Europa, George Washington, Kaiser Wilhelm II, Kaiser Wilhelm der Grosse, Kronprinz Wilhelm*

NORWEGIAN CRUISE: *Norway*

OCEAN QUEEN NAVIGATION: *Ocean Queen*

ORIENT: *Empire Orwell, Orcades, Oronsay, Orontes, Orsova*

ORIENTAL LATIN AMERICA: *Oriental Esmeralda*

PACIFIC STEAM NAVIGATION COMPANY: *Reina del Mar*

PAQUET CRUISES: *Rhapsody*

PENINSULAR & ORIENTAL: *Arcadia, Canberra, Cap Polonio, Carthage, Chitral, Chusan, Crown Princess, Fair Princess, Himalaya, Iberia, Mooltan, Nevasa, Orcades, Oriana, Oronsay, Orsova, Pacific Princess, Royal Princess, Spirit of London, Strathaird, Strathnaver, Strathmore*

POLISH OCEAN: *Batory, Stefan Batory*

PREMIER CRUISE LINE: *Starship Majestic*

RED STAR: *Belgenland, Pennland*

REGENCY CRUISES: *Regent Star*

ROYAL CARRIBEAN CRUISE LINE: *Monarch of the Seas*

ROYAL HOLLAND LLOYD: *Brabantia, Gelria, Limburgia*

ROYAL MAIL: *Alcantara, Almanzora, Andes (1913), Andes (1939), Arlanza, Asturias, Avon, Chignecto, Ohio*

ROYAL NETHERLANDS: *Oranje Nassau, Willemstad*

ROYAL INTEROCEAN: *Nieuw Holland*

ROYAL VIKING: *Royal Viking Sky*

SAFMARINE: *S.A. Oranje, S.A. Vaal*

SAUDI: *Moor B*

SHAW SAVILL AND ALBION: *Dominion Monarch, Northern Star, Southern Cross*

SILVER MOON FERRIES: *Alferdoss*

SITMAR: *Castel Bianco, Castel Felice, Fairland*

SOCIÉTÉ GÉNÉRALE DE TRANSPORTS MARITIMES À VAPEUR: *Bretagne*

SOCIÉTÉ MARITIME ANVERSOISE SA: *Ville d'Anvers, Ville de Bruges*

SWEDISH-AMERICAN: *Gripsholm*

UNION: *Greek*

UNION CASTLE: *Arundel Castle, Athlone Castle, Balmoral Castle, Braemar Castle, Capetown Castle, Cap Polonio, Carisbrook Castle, Carnarvon Castle, Dunbar Castle, Edinburgh Castle, Glenart Castle, Greek, Pendennis Castle, Pretoria Castle (1939), Pretoria Castle (1948), Reina del Mar, Stirling Castle, Transvaal Castle, Warwick Castle (1931), Winchester Castle, Windsor Castle (1922), Windsor Castle (1960)*

UNITED AMERICAN: *Reliance, Resolute*

UNIVERSAL: *Caribia*

UNITED STATES: *America, American Banker, George Washington, Leviathan, Manhattan, President Harding, Republic, United States*

VENTURE CRUISES: *America*

WESTERN CRUISE: *Azure Seas*

WHITE STAR: *Albertic, Belgic, Britannic (1915), Britannic (1930), Georgic, Homeric, Majestic, Oceanic, Olympic, Pittsburgh, Titanic*

Bibliography

1 Passenger Liners on North Atlantic Service

BONSOR, NRP, *North Atlantic Seaway* (6 Vols), David & Charles, (Vol 1, 1975), Brookside Pubs (Vol 2-6), 1978-80).

BOWEN, FC, *A Century of Atlantic Travel, 1830-1930*, Little, Brown & Co Boston, 1930.

BRINNIN JM, *The Sway of the Grand Saloon*, Arlington Books, 1986.

COLEMAN, T, *The Liners*, Allen Lane, 1976.

EMMONS, F, *The Atlantic Liners*, David & Charles, 1972

FRY, H, *History of North Atlantic Steam Navigation*, Sampson Low, 1896.

GIBBS, CRV, *Western Ocean Passenger Lines & Liners 1934-1969*, Brown Son & Ferguson, 1970.

GIBBS, CRV, *Passenger Lines of the Western Ocean, Staples Press, 1957*

HUGHES, T, *The Blue Riband of the Atlantic*, Patrick Stephens, 1973.

MAGINNIS, AJ, *The Atlantic Ferry*, Whittaker & Co, 1900.

MAXTONE-GRAHAM, J, *The North Atlantic Run*, Cassell, 1972.

MILLER, WH, *The Last Atlantic Liners*, Conway, 1985.

RANSOME-WALLIS, P, *North Atlantic Panorama*, I Allan, 1977.

WHITE, AGH, *Ships of the North Atlantic*, Sampson Low, 1937.

2 Passenger Liners on Services to South Africa, South America, Australia and The Far East

BONSOR, NRP, *South Atlantic Seaway*, Brookside Pubs, 1983.

BREMER, S, *Home and Back* (UK-Australia etc), Dreamweaver Books, Sydney, 1984.

EMMONS, F, *Pacific Liners 1927-72*, David & Charles, 1973.

GORDON, M, *From 'Chusan' to 'Sea Princess'*, Allen & Unwin (Aust), 1985.

MABER, JM, *North Star to Southern Cross*, Stephenson, 1967.

MCLACHLAN, GW, *Famous Liners of the Eastern Oceans*, Sampson Low, c1937.

MURRAY, M, *Ships and South Africa*, Oxford UP, 1933.

PLOWMAN, P, *Passenger Ships of Australia & New Zealand*, (2 Vols), Conway, 1981.

STEWART, IG, *The Ships That Serve New Zealand*, (Vol 1), Reed (Wellington), 1964.

3 Passenger Liners in General

BRAYNARD, F & MILLER, W, *Fifty Famous Liners* Vols 1, 2, 3. Patrick Stephens, 1982-87.

DE KERBRECH, R & WILLIAMS, D, *Damned By Destiny*, Teredo Books, 1981.

DUNN, L, *Passenger Liners*, Adlard Coles, 1961, 1965.

DUNN, L, *Famous Liners of The Past Belfast Built*, Adlard Coles, 1964.

GIBBS, CRV, *British Passenger Liners of the Five Oceans*, Putnam, 1963.

KLUDAS, A, *Great Passenger Ships of The World* (6 Vols), Patrick Stephens, 1976-86.

KLUDAS, A, *Deutsche Ozean Passagierschiffe (1850-1895)* (German Passenger Liners), Steiger-Verlag Moers, 1983.

MILLER, W, *German Ocean Liners of The 20th Century*, Patrick Stephens, 1989.

MILLER, W, *The Last Blue Water Liners*, Conway, 1986.

MILLER, W, *British Ocean Liners 1960-85*, Patrick Stephens, 1986.

MILLER, W, *The Cruise Ships*, Conway, 1988.

NEWELL, G, *Ocean Liners of The 20th Century*, Bonanza Books NY, 1963.

SHAUM, JH & FLAYHART, WH, *Majesty At Sea* (4-Funnellers), Patrick Stephens, 1981.

SMITH, EW, *Passenger Ships of The World, Past & Present*, G H Dean, Boston, 1963.

TAYLOR, A, *Great Liners*, Southern Newspapers, c1980.

WALL, R, *Ocean Liners*, New Burlington Books, 1977.

WATSON, MH, *US Passenger Liners Since 1945*, Patrick Stephens, 1988.

WATSON, MH, *Flagships of The Line* (3-Funnellers), Patrick Stephens, 1988.

WILSON, RM, *The Big Ships*, Cassell, 1956.

WORKER, CF, *The World's Passenger Ships*, Ian Allan, 1967.

4 Shipping Companies and Their Ships

ANDERSON, R, *White Star*, Stephenson, 1964.

APPLETON, TE, *Ravenscraig. Allan R M Line*, McClelland & Stewart, Toronto, 1974.

BLAKE, G, *B I Centenary 1856-1956* (British India), Collins, 1956.

CABLE, B, *A Hundred Year History of the P & O*, Nicholson & Watson, 1937.

COOPER, J, KLUDAS, A, PEIN, J, *The Hamburg-South America Line*, World Ship Society, 1989.

COURSE, AG, *Ships of the P & O*, Adlard Coles, 1954.

COWDEN, JE & DUFFY, J, *The Elder Dempster Fleet History*, Mallett & Bell Pubs, 1986.

DOWDEN, P, *Ships of the Royal Mail*, Adlard Coles, c1956.

DUNN, L, *Ships of the Union Castle Line*, Adlard Coles, 1954.

DE KERBRECH, R, *Shaw Savill & Albion*, Conway, 1986.

DE KERBRECH & WILLIAMS, D, *Cunard White Star Liners of the 1930s*, Conway, 1988.

EATON, J & HAAS, C, *Falling Star* (White Star), Patrick Stephens, 1989.

HAWS, D, *Merchant Fleets in Profile* — various volumes covering many companies, Patrick Stephens/TCL Pubs, 1978-90.

HOWARTH, D & S, *The Story of P & O*, Weidenfeld & Nicolson, 1986.

HEATON, P, *Lamport & Holt*, Starling Press, 1986.

ISHERWOOD, J, *Ships of the Orient Line*, Adlard Coles, c1954.

LE FLEMING, HM, *Ships of the Holland-America Line*, Marshbank, 1963.

LE FLEMING, HM, *Cunard White Star Liners of the 1930s*, I Allen, 1960.

MCCART, N, *20th Century Passenger Ships of P & O*, Patrick Stephens, 1985.

MCCART, N, *Passenger Ships of the Orient Line*, Patrick Stephens, 1987.

MCCART, N, *Atlantic Liners of the Cunard Line*, Patrick Stephens, 1990.

MITCHELL, WH, & SAWYER, LA, *The Cape Run* (U. Castle), Terence Dalton, 1984.

MORRIS, C, *Origins, Orient & Oriana*, Teredo Books, 1980.

MURRAY, M, *Union Castle Chronicle*, Longmans, 1953.

MUSK, G, *Canadian Pacific*, David & Charles, 1989.

OLDHAM, WJ, *The Ismay Line* (White Star), Chas Burchell, 1961.

RABSON, S, & O'DONOGHUE, K, *P & O, A Fleet History*, World Ship Society, 1988.

TAYLOR, J, *Ellermans − A Wealth of Shipping*, Wilton House Gentry, 1976.

VAN POPTA, W, *KNSM* (Dutch), De Alken Reeks Alkmaar, c1967.

WATERS, SD, *Clipper Ship to Motor Liner* (NZSC), New Zealand SC, 1939.

WITTHOFFT, HG, *Hapag-Lloyd*, Koehlers VG Herford, 1979.

Also numerous shipping company histories published by the World Ship Society (in addition to those mentioned above)

5 Books on Shipping in General

BOWEN, FC, *Ships For All*, Ward Lock, 1952.

BUCHANAN, L, *Ships of Steam*, McGraw Hill, 1956.

CHANDLER, G, *Liverpool Shipping*, Phoenix House, 1960.

HARDY, AC, *Merchant Ship Types*, Chapman & Hall, 1934.

HARDY, AC, *Ships at Work*, Newnes, 1939.

MUNRO - SMITH, R, *Merchant Ship Types*, Marine Media Management, 1975.

RANSOME - WALLIS, P, *Merchant Ship Panorama*, I Allen, 1980.

ROGERS COL HCB, *Troopships And Their Story*, Seely Service, 1963.

SAWYER LA, & MITCHELL, WH, *From America to 'United States'* (US Shipping) Parts 1-4, World Ship Society, 1979-86.

WINCHESTER, C, (ED), *Shipping Wonders of the World* (2 Vols), Fleetway House, c1937.

Annual Publications

Merchant Ships British Built 1953, Adlard Coles.

Merchant Ships World Built 1954-1970, Adlard Coles.

Ships Annuals, I. Allan various years.

Ocean Ships − Various authors & Editions, I. Allan.

6 War Histories of Shipping Companies, Individual Ships and Naval Publications

BUSHELL, TA, *Eight Bells* (R Mail W War 2), Trade & Travel Pubs, 1950.

HOOK, FA, *Merchant Adventurers 1914-18* (P & O, B I etc), Black, 1920.

HURD, A, *A Merchant Fleet At War* (Cunard), Cassell, 1920.

HURD, A, *The Clan Line in the Great War*, Cassell, 1924.

KERR, GF, *Business In Great Waters* (P & O), Faber & Faber, 1951.

LENTON, HT, & COLLEDGE, JJ, *Warships of W War 2*, I. Allan, 1973.

LESLIE, HW, *Royal Mail War Book*, Heinemann, 1920.

MILLER, W, & HUTCHINGS, D, *Transatlantic Liners at War*, David & Charles, 1985.

POOLMAN, K, *Armed Merchant Cruisers*, Leo Cooper, 1985.

ROSKILL, S, *The War At Sea*, Vols 1-3, HMSO, 1954-60.

SAUNDERS, H, ST, G, *Valiant Voyaging* (BI), Faber & Faber, 1948.

SILVERSTONE, P, *US Warships W War 2*, I. Allan, 1965.

WATERS, SD, *Ordeal By Sea* (NZSC), New Zealand S.C., 1949.

HMS Almanzora 1915-1919 by Ships Company

Janes Fighting Ships − Various Editions

Couhat's Combat Fleets of the World − Various Editions

Conway's All the World's Fighting Ships 5 Vols.

7 Books on Specific Ships

ARDMAN, H, *Normandie Her Life & Times*, F Watts, NY, 1985.

FOUCAT, B, ETC *Normandie Queen of the Seas*, Vendome Press, NY, 1985.

JORDAN, H, *Mauretania*, Hodder & Stoughton, 1936.

MALLET, AS, & BELL, AM, *The Pirrie − Kylsant Motorships 1915-1932*, Mallett & Bell Publications, 1984.

MERTENS, E, *Die Hapag Riesen Der 'Imperator − Classe*, Olms Presse Hildesheim, 1978.

MITCHELL, A, *Splendid Sisters*, Harrap, 1966.

POTTER, N, & FROST, J, *The 'Mary'*, Harrap, 1961.

POTTER, N, & FROST, J, *The 'Elizabeth'*, Harrap, 1965.

POTTER, N, & FROST, J, *Queen Elizabeth 2*, Harrap, 1969.

Also *Ocean Liners of the Past* − series of reprints from *The Shipbuilder* and *The Shipbuilder and Marine Engine Builder* published by Patrick Stephens. These include the following: *Queen Mary, Normandie, Empress of Britain, Olympic & Titanic, Lusitania & Mauretania, Aquitania, Canberra,* The second *Mauretania.* Published by *Engineering: Lusitania 1907, Mauretania 1907, Aquitania 1914.*

8 Autobiography-Biography

ARNOTT, CAPT RH, *Captain of the Queens*, Quadrant Books, 1984.

BAILLIE, CAPT DGO, *A Sea Affair (P & O)*, Hutchinson, 1957.

BISSET, SIR J, *Tramps & Ladies*, Angus & Robertson, 1960.

BISSET, SIR J, *Commodore*, Angus & Robertson, 1961.
BRITTEN, SIR E, *A Million Ocean Miles*, Hutchinson, 1936.
DUNCAN, S, & P, *The Sea My Steed*, (Capt Sorrell), R. Hale, 1960.
MACLEAN, CAPT D, *Queens Company*, Hutchinson, 1965.
MARR, COMM G, *The Queens and I*, Adlard Coles, 1973.
MCNEILL, CAPT SGS, *In Great Waters*, Faber & Faber, 1932.
MAKING, CAPT VL, *In Sail & Steam*, Sidgwick & Jackson, 1937.
ROSTRON, SIR AH, *Home From The Sea*, Cassell, 1931.

9 Marine Disasters

BARNABY, KC, *Some Ship Disasters And Their Causes*, Hodder & Stoughton, 1966.
BONSALL, TE, *Shipwrecks of The Twentieth Century*, Gallery Books, NY, 1988.
HADFIELD, RL, *Sea Toll of Our Time*, Witherby, 1930.
PADFIELD, P, *An Agony of Collisions*, Hodder & Stoughton, 1966.
SIMPSON, C, *Lusitania*, Penguin, 1983.
WATSON, MH, *Disasters At Sea*, Patrick Stephens, 1987.

10 Miscellaneous, Reference Books, Shipbuilding, Etc

BAKER, WA, *From Paddle Steamer To Nuclear Ship*, CA Watts, 1965.
DOUGAN, D, *The History of North East Shipbuilding*, Allen & Unwin, 1968.
HARRIS, N, (ED), *Portrait of a Shipbuilder (Vickers)*, Silver Link, 1989.
KEMP, P, *Oxford Companion to Ships and the Sea*, Oxford U P, 1979.
LANDSTROM, B, *The Ship*, Allen & Unwin, 1961.
VARIOUS AUTHORS, *The Lore of Ships*, Nordbok Gothenburg, 1975.
TALBOT BOOTH, EC, *Merchant Ships (various years)*, Sampson Low/Journal of Commerce

11 Titanic Books – These are very numerous – a short selection:

BALLARD DR RD *The Discovery of the Titanic*, Hodder & Stoughton, 1987.
BEESLEY, L, *The Loss of the Titanic* (survivor's story), Heinemann, 1912.
DAVIE, M, *Titanic. Full Story of a Tragedy*, Bodley Head, 1986.
EATON, P, and HAAS, CA, *The Truth About The Titanic* (survivor's story), Mitchell Kennerley, NY, 1991.
GRACIE, A, *The Truth about the Titanic*, 7 C's Press Conn. 1973
HARRISON, L, *A Titanic Myth* (The Californian Incident), Kimber, 1980.
LIGHTOLLER, CH, *Titanic & Other Ships* (Survivor's Story), Nicholson & Watson, 1935.

LORD, W, *A Night To Remember*, Longmans Green, 1956.
LORD, W, *The Night Lives On*, Viking, 1987.
MARCUS, G, *The Maiden Voyage*, Allen & Unwin, 1969.
PADFIELD, P, *The Titanic & The Californian*, Hodder & Stoughton, 1965.
WADE, WC, *Titanic End of a Dream*, Weidenfield & Nicholson, 1980.
Shipping Casualties – Report into loss of steamship Titanic, HMSO, 1912.

12 Magazines, Technical Journals, Proceedings of

Magazines: Marine News (Journal of the World Ship Society); Sea Breezes; Sea Classics; The Shipbuilder; The Shipbuilder and Marine Engine Builder; Shipbuilding and Shipping Record; Ships Monthly; The Motor Ship.
Newspapers: Lloyds List (daily); Southern Daily Echo (Southampton).
Proceedings: Institute of Naval Architects; Institution of Mechanical Engineers; US Naval Institute.

Index of Ships